THE SPOILS OF TIME

C. V. Wedgwood, one of the only two women to be made a member of the Order of Merit, began writing history when she was a child. Her first book was published in 1935 and she went on to specialise in the English, Scottish and European sixteenth centuries.

Also by C. V. Wedgwood

Strafford
The Thirty Years War
Oliver Cromwell
William The Silent
Velvet Studies
Richelieu and the French Monarchy
English Literature in the Seventeenth Century
The Last of the Radicals
Montrose
Poetry and Politics under the Stuarts
The King's War
The King's Peace
Truth and Opinion
The Trial of Charles I

THE SPOILS
OF TIME

*A History of the World from the
Earliest Times to the Sixteenth Century*

C.V. Wedgwood

PHOENIX
PRESS

5 UPPER SAINT MARTIN'S LANE
LONDON
WC2H 9EA

A PHOENIX PRESS PAPERBACK

First published in Great Britain
by Collins in 1984
This paperback edition published in 2000
by Phoenix Press,
a division of The Orion Publishing Group Ltd,
Orion House, 5 Upper St Martin's Lane,
London WC2H 9EA

A CIP catalogue record for this book
is available from the British Library.

Printed and bound in Great Britain
by Clays Ltd, St Ives plc

ISBN 1 84212 004 2

FOR
JAQUELINE

CONTENTS

NOTE FROM THE AUTHOR

The greater part of my working life has been devoted to the history of western Europe between 1550 and 1660. Late in the day, feeling a desire for wider knowledge, I turned to world history. Others have done the same with impressive knowledge and confidence. But the vast and confused record of world history – 'rich with the spoils of time' – was something that I had to study alone and in my own way.

This book is essentially a narrative, not a philosophy of history. It is about people, ordinary and extraordinary, of many different races, cultures and creeds, and the world in which they lived and died. It is a story which contains, perhaps, lessons for our time, but if so I leave them for readers to find for themselves.

C. V. W
1983

PREFACE

Of the many gifted and accomplished women historians of the twentieth century two, Eileen Power and Veronica Wedgwood, are outstanding for their contribution of original scholarship with an ability to transmit their perceptions to the common reader. Neither talked down to the reader or watered down the intricacy of what they had to say. Both, in a word, were born writers. And both had the feminine quality of acute observation, both were down to earth, as well as capable of high flights of imagination and sympathy. Both took the broadest view of their subject, not accepting Gibbon's summary 'the register of the crimes, follies and misfortunes of mankind', but insisting on the inclusion of the arts and sciences, above all on the inclusion of everyday life.

Eileen Power, indeed, was primarily a social and economic historian. Her *Medieval People* and *The English Wool Trade in the Middle Ages* breathed fresh life into a branch of history writing that might too well have been reckoned the province of desiccated calculating machines. But Veronica Wedgwood, though no less responsive to the diversity of human action and concern, centred her most important books on the traditional themes of politics and war. Boldly rejecting the fashionable theories of history that dominated the academic world of her time – what Sir Isaiah Berlin comprehended under the term 'meta history' – she put her money on the individual. Of course she was far too intelligent, too self-aware, not to recognise that all of us, even the most original, the most sceptical, are inevitably the children of our time, and that what goes for us goes for our forebears too. We may say that Montaigne or Shakespeare expressed ideas that seem to belong to a later age, as they undoubtedly did, but that does not mean that they would have been at home in the eighteenth century or the twentieth. Everyone is limited by the horizons of their epoch and everyone is shaped, sometimes deformed, by social and moral pressures, by the structure of society, which they may or may not accept but which nevertheless impinge on them, often in ways they cannot perceive.

In her essay *A Sense of the Past* Veronica insists that, try how we may, we cannot enter fully into the consciousness, the state of mind, of our ancestors. We know, and they did not, what happened next. We can try, we ought to try, to exclude this knowledge from our efforts at imaginative recreation. And it is this effort which, aided by a reading of the books they read, and by looking at their pictures, listening to their music, travelling, when we can find it, the landscape they knew, may perhaps help us to come closer to understanding them. At any rate it will soon show us how little we really know or ever can know of what the past felt like at the time and how much we should distrust the facile interpretations of history offered by the grand, sweeping theories. They may stimulate insights, prompt pertinent questions, but they do not supply answers.

The desire to understand, to imagine what it would be like to be someone else, however impossible of fulfilment, nevertheless lies at the heart of Veronica's work. Intimately, inextricably, entwined with it is the indispensability of narrative. 'If we can establish *what* happened and *how*, we shall have gone a long way to establish *why*' she wrote in one of her many defences of narrative history against analysis. Not that she despised analysis: indeed she was a brilliant exponent of the technique. But she believed that horse and cart should appear in the right order.

The present book, the last that she wrote, exemplifies two of her most striking, most unfashionable qualities, her boldness and her range. Under close examination it also displays her ability to communicate a great deal of information without overloading a passage or daunting the reader. Hers was certainly the power of art without the show. For a seventeenth century historian who had produced distinguished works on European themes but whose special field was the period of Charles I and the Civil War to cut loose and survey the world from China to Peru was dashing indeed. But dash, spirit, *élan*, was part of her nature, camou-flaged from the imperceptive by her courtesy and her generosity. Her first book, *Strafford*, had been an admiring, redefining, portrait of one of the hate-figures of history, Black Tom Tyrant, the architect of 'Thorough', that policy which generations of Whig and liberal historians had agreed to deplore. It is true that twenty-five years later, in the light of much further research, some of it her own, she revised and modified her opinion of him and wrote a fresh biography. But the instinct to challenge received opinion by re-examining contemporary evidence was always to remain characteristic of her work.

Her second book, *The Thirty Years War*, is the most conspicuous example of her range. Of all subjects in modern political history it is the most shapeless, like a stream of consciousness story without a plot that has a beginning, a middle and an end. Its sources are proportionate in extent and in variety of type and diversity of language. Veronica must have felt like the widow Partington confronting the Atlantic armed only with a mop. But what a mop it proved to be. Her education had included long sojourns in Switzerland in a household where no English was spoken, so that she was fluent in French, German and Italian. But a working knowledge of Swedish, Dutch and Spanish was also necessary.

Any present-day scholar, foolhardy enough to contemplate such an undertaking, would first equip himself with a tenured academic post, fortify it with a couple of research grants from the major foundations, and probably recruit several hungry Ph.D., students to comb the archives. Veronica set about this impossible task single-handed. She told me that it was the kind of thing one was only rash enough to take on in one's twenties. Yet the book is regularly reprinted in Germany and in England. Sixty years is a long span for a work of current scholarship. Of her other early books *William the Silent*, one of the most compelling historical biographies ever written, did much to confirm her growing international reputation.

Perhaps a word should have been said earlier about her background. She was born at Stocksfield, Northumberland, in July 1910. Her father was Managing Director of the London and North Eastern Railway, a member of that generation of Cambridge intellectuals who thought nothing of walking the fifty-odd miles to London and were, in general, unworldly agnostics. The arts and music (he was a first cousin of Ralph Vaughan Williams, who dedicated a symphony to him), not money making or power seeking were what mattered. Private education was followed by reading history at Oxford, where she was one of the earliest pupils of A. L. Rowse, with whom a long and fruitful friendship was only broken when she politely declined to accept his contentions about Shakespeare's Sonnets. It was there, too, that she began an even happier lifelong friendship with Jaqueline Hope-Wallace and her brother Philip, with both of whom she was later to keep house in London, to which was later added a cottage in Sussex. They shared, and enriched, that enjoyment of music, opera especially, and other arts which lies behind so much of her work, indeed sometimes, as in her essays and such works as *Seventeenth Century English Literature* claims the chief place.

She supported herself in all this by working as a historical reader and editor for the publisher Jonathan Cape and by assisting the often temperamental and sometimes eccentric Lady Rhondda in the production of her journal *Time and Tide*. Such work certainly contributed to her outstanding mastery of the English language. As P. D. James has recently pointed out in her *Time to be in Earnest*, there is nothing so useful to the writer as the constant practice of his craft. It was this that aroused the jealousy of scholars who knew themselves to be inferior in this regard. 'Her work is all style' snarled one of those who blocked her election to the British Academy. She must be the only Fellow of that institution not to have gained admittance until six years after she had received the far higher distinction of the O.M..

It is often assumed, from her surname, that Veronica was comfortably supported by the profits of the famous family firm. Such was by no means the case. Until comparatively late in life she lived on what she earned. This did not deter her from undertaking a heavy load of public duties. She was the first woman to be elected a Trustee of the National Gallery, serving for two terms, a total of twelve years, longer than any previous Trustee. Long a member of the Council of the PEN Club she served as President from 1951 to 1957. For twenty-six years she was on the Council of the Royal Historical Manuscripts Commission. She was President of the Society of Authors from 1972 to 1977. She was – but enough has been said to indicate the weight of her important public commitments.

Of her private ones, talking to schools, lecturing to local branches of the Historical Association, helping individuals to get their books published and encouraging unknown writers, there is an even longer reckoning. She was a very good woman – what a commentary on our age that such a description might seem to detract from the charm and brilliance of her personality. Yet one could not be conscious of the one without the other. She was also, in spite of the high-minded agnosticism of her upbringing, a devout, practising Christian.

All her books are, in their different ways, of high quality. *The King's Peace* and *The King's War* will illuminate that extraordinary passage in our history when the arguments about the English Revolution and the Rise or the Fall of the Gentry have been forgotten. Her brief biography of *Cromwell* and her poignant account of *The Trial of Charles I* will show how deeply she could sympathise with, how fairly she could present, the predicaments of men whose political ideas were not her own. It was a cruel stroke of fate that robbed her of her powers before she could crown the two volumes on Charles I and the Civil Wars with a third on Cromwell's Protectorate and the return of the Stuarts in 1660, but if ever a writer did justice to such time and talents as they were given, she did. And no one who saw the serenity with which she endured what she had to endure will forget the beauty of her character. She died in March 1997.

Richard Ollard
November 1999.

CHAPTER I

FROM THE BEGINNINGS TO CIRCA 1500 BC

I

ABOUT TWO MILLION YEARS AGO there evolved on this planet certain ape-like creatures with characteristics which distinguished them from apes. Their skulls and bones, discovered in the last sixty years in South Africa, Tanzania and Kenya, show that they belonged to three distinct groups. Some had large prominent teeth and heavy ridges over the brow, but relatively small brains. Archaeologists called them Australopithecines (Africanus or robustus), or southern apes, and classified them as *Hominids*.

The other group were smaller in stature, about four feet, but their brows were smooth and higher, their brains larger, and the objects found with or near them showed that they had been ingenious in making tools. Archaeologists were prepared to recognize them as distant relations, possibly even ancestors, and admitted them into the genus *Homo* under the name of *Homo Habilis*.

The bones of other primitive ancestors of man have come to light, over the years, in many parts of the world – in Java, in Peking, in Heidelberg: these were at first classified as *Pithecanthropus erectus* – Upright Ape-Man. The general consensus of archaeological opinion points to *Homo Habilis* as the forefather of mankind, although it was in all probability *Homo erectus* who invented the famous hand axe. This weapon, equally effective against wild beasts and human enemies, was a stone tool, laboriously chipped to a sharp point. The instrument, once discovered, was widely copied and spread to South Africa, the Near East, Asia, India, Europe, Britain and Scandinavia.

Peking man lived and died before the Second Ice Age, which

lasted for about 50,000 years, and was succeeded by the third inter-glacial period, an interlude of relative warmth, lasting for about 150,000 to 175,000 years. This was crucial for Europe and the Mediterranean basin, giving the remnant of human kind a long interlude in which to revive and multiply.

During this interval *Neanderthal* man appeared in central Europe, so named because the first skeleton was found in the *Neanderthal* valley in Germany. Traces of him were later found on the Mediterranean littoral, in the river valleys of central and South East Europe, in North Africa and the nearer regions of western Asia. He was a maker of bone tools, he clothed himself in skins carefully prepared, was familiar with the uses of fire, and formally buried the dead after eating their brains. More *Neanderthal* remains have been found than those of any other race but they seem to have died out, probably under the pressure of an irresistible immigration from the East. The *Cro Magnon* tribes advanced steadily from the Asian steppe, moving westwards in search of new pastures. They were divided into many different family groups and drove before them herds of bison and deer as well as horses. They were therefore strong on a diet of meat, active and full of ideas. They had in the course of their wanderings invented a spear thrower – for the long distance killing of their quarry – harpoons, barbed spears, almost certainly the bow, but also such domestic necessities as lamps fuelled with burning fat, bone needles with eyes, chisels, gravers and burins for making other tools.

Some of the earliest remains of man are found in the *Cro Magnon* caves in the Dordogne valley. These are probably about 30,000 years old. Their ancestors had begun to appear in the West about 10,000 years earlier. By the close of the Fourth Ice Age, about 20,000 years ago, they had swarmed over the whole Mediterranean basin as well as all the warmer and more fertile parts of Europe. The fact that they were advanced in the art of making tools, suggests an already established system; they must have had a well-developed language for they had flutes, and presumably danced and sang to them and told tribal stories glorifying their past.

Cro Magnon man was only one race of *Homo Sapiens*. In Africa men with dark skins were gradually populating the land south of the Sahara. Others of mongoloid type had adapted themselves to the bitter cold of north eastern Asia in the last Ice Age, and had learnt to cut up and sow together the skins of animals into close fitting bonnets, jackets and trousers. Thus equipped, they lived by hunting the reindeer, and came in course of time to follow the source of their food across the wastes of ice which, under favourable conditions, joined north eastern Asia to the empty American continent. Such conditions existed around 18,000 BC and again from 10,000–9000 BC.

So they crossed over and came in, little by little: these immigrants of the first influx seem, from their sparsely found remains, to have been of mongoloid stock. As time went on a fugitive remnant expelled by stronger tribes from the more fertile land and trekking ever further southward, must have reached the cheerless region of Tierra del Fuego about 8000 BC. Meanwhile the intermittent march across the melting ice-cap of the Bering Straits still trickled on; the last Asian wanderers may have crossed the straits as recently as 800 years ago.

30,000 years ago, while *Cro Magnon* man took over Europe and the Mediterranean basin, the Arctic and Antarctic ice drew so much water away from more temperate zones that the sea could have been more than 100 metres lower than it is today, so that many offshore islands were then joined to the mainland. Reindeer were plentiful in France, Denmark was joined to Sweden and *Homo Sapiens* reached the British Isles on foot.

In Asia the groups and tribes from the south and south east made their way across floating ice and rocks and shallows to parts of Japan, the Pacific Islands and the East Indies. The Sundra Shelf was then exposed, linking Java to the mainland. Some adventurers reached Australia, overland from New Guinea, before 25,000 BC; the edge-ground axes found among their remains appear to be of an earlier date than anywhere else in the world. Gradually a change of climate melted the glaciers, the sea rose again and the Aborigines in Australia and many of the Pacific Islands were cut off for thousands of years.

During these millennia of slow change—and rather more quickly as time went on – men and women in all their regional variations, learnt how to make themselves comfortable in caves, or to build themselves shelters; they improved their skill in trapping animals, catching fish, building boats, and controlling fire. They learnt also how to train at least one animal, the dog, to help in the hunting. The Natufians of the Zagros mountains, living in villages of about fifty huts, even had reaping knives, querns, and pestles and mortars for crushing cereals, and they may have herded gazelles. Meanwhile the grunts and growls and barking noises of man's first primitive communications had long since developed into a complex pattern of sound which expressed his needs more precisely. His vocal chords and tongue – altering in strength and subtlety of structure – had become the organs of intelligible speech.

About twenty thousand years ago, as the Fourth Ice Age gave way to the fourth interglacial period, *Homo Sapiens*, adventurous, persevering, resourceful and aggressive, with an ever increasing capacity for creating and for destroying and inspired by an insatiable curiosity and a powerful imagination, appeared destined to master the world. To him it was no manifest destiny. Life was very much in the present: a matter of securing warmth, food and safety from wild beasts. In the words of one of his more sophisticated descendants, his life was still 'nasty, brutish and short'.[1] There were compensations: he had a sense of awe and a sense of beauty; he had also the capacity to create an organic society, which meant that he could already envisage the needs of others and was capable at times of altruism and sacrifice.

For us who know very much more, though not all, of the story, the millennia of almost total darkness give way to the twilight of pre-history.

II

It is still only twilight, but shafts of brightness occasionally pierce the gloom. In the caves of Altamira in northern Spain, paintings of bison, deer, wild boar and bulls were accidentally discovered about a century ago. It was many years before cautious archaeologists accepted them as the work of Stone Age artists between 15,000 and 10,000 BC. In 1940 another superb group of cave paintings was found at Lascaux in the Dordogne. By that time twentieth-century critics knew better than to doubt the skill of their remote ancestors. Here again was the keen observation of form and movement, the subtlety of colour and line and the ingenious use of natural formations in the rock to suggest the modelling of the animals. These discoveries in western Europe were further enhanced when cave paintings of the same nature were found in the Urals.

Altamira and Lascaux are attributed to a gifted and comparatively widespread people called by archaeologists the Magdale-
nians. Stone Age men had little time for luxuries in their hard and
dangerous life. The pictures had a purpose, probably to ensure
successful hunting. But the artist's instinct for the beautiful, his eye
for essential detail, form and movement, and the controlled skill of
his hand were at the service of the magic formula: something besides
hunger for meat must also have been satisfied.

No one knows exactly when prehistoric men discovered fire, but
they were baking symbolic clay figures in their kilns by the Meso-
lithic Age, and there is evidence in some parts of Europe that they
were already burning coal. Travel of every kind was generally on
foot, but boats were built for river transport, and more cautiously
for use at sea as early as 8000 BC.

Man's efficiency in hunting increased with practice. The invention of the bow goes back at least 15,000 years, and the spear was
presumably earlier. Arrows and spears alike were tipped with
sharpened stones. These inventions, of incalculable importance to
those who made them, must have occurred at different times in
different places but, the world over, such inventions (like the
inventions of more sophisticated times) had drawbacks as well as
advantages. Hunters over-killed the game: the unwieldy mammoth
became extinct soon after the close of the last Ice Age, and in the
American continent the horse was wiped out.

In the Middle East the domestication of animals began about the
ninth millennium, with flocks of sheep in Iraq, goats in Iran, pigs in
Turkey about a thousand years later and, last of all, around 6000 BC
the domestication of the formidable wild cattle. Dogs had of
course established themselves in man's service from time immemorial.

Man could also support himself and his family on the fruits of
nature. As the game supply declined he turned first to plants, roots
and berries, then discovered that the food supply could be increased
by scratching the soil and planting seeds. Some modern historians
have, not unjustly, called this discovery by early man, the Neolithic
Revolution. Certainly man's belief that the workings of nature
could be improved, encouraged and exploited to minister to his
needs, is arguably the greatest discovery he ever made. The beginning seems to have been in Syria, and to have spread first to the
Caucasus, to Afghanistan, North West India, the Persian Gulf,

Arabia, Asia – not that any of these places were then known by name – reaching western Europe about 5000 BC.

The slow motion revolution was in the end world wide or nearly so, and its successes or failures governed the ordering of society and the fate of nations until the coming of the Industrial Revolution, amid the aftermath of which we live today.

As mankind multiplied and the world grew more complicated distinctions between man and man increased. There were rich and poor, Haves and Have-nots, long before the introduction of money. Every year that the harvest was lower than expectation, the leading men of the village had to distribute as fairly and efficiently as they could. Presumably they thought of ways to store the surplus in good years. (It can hardly be that Joseph in Egypt was the first to think of this solution.)

The great Arab historian, Ibn Khaldun, writing in the fourteenth century of our era, succinctly emphasized the effect of agriculture on civilization as he saw it; agriculture made men co-operative. For instance a group with a carpenter, toolmaker and herdsman for oxen, as well as ploughmen and tillers could produce surplus food, and on a surplus, civilization grows.[2]

The cultivation of crops had at first been subsidiary to hunting as a source of food. But in many regions, by about the sixth millennium, the position was reversed, and agriculture became more important. Hunting continued as a source of additional – or luxury – food. In more sophisticated societies it gradually came to be associated with a ruling aristocracy and the idea of sport. This social phenomenon has come down through the millennia from pre-history into re-corded history and survives into our own time. Kings of Egypt and Babylon would be depicted triumphantly destroying birds and beasts. In medieval Europe kings and nobles arrogated to themselves the right to maintain large tracts of uncultivated land for their personal hunting, whereby they kept themselves and their dependants supplied with meat, though porrage was good enough for the common people.

It was a paradoxical development because civilization – or power for that matter – was not built on hunting; it was built on agriculture. Agriculture required organization, co-ordination and division of labour. It made possible the storage of food against famine, the building up of reserves, the emergence of a more stable society. But, as far as individuals were concerned, it required more effort and more work than primitive man had devoted to hunting when beasts were still plentiful, or to pulling up edible roots for his breakfast. In some ways the life of the peasant (if it is permissible to use this word somewhat prematurely) became easier and less hungry than in the more primitive past. But he had far less leisure. In the old days when the whole tribe joined in the hunt, life had been more amusing – and dangerous; but that was in a forgotten time. Now the labourer had regular work to do while a privileged minority followed the hunt.[3]

The first impetus to agriculture came naturally enough in regions where wild cereals were plentiful – Anatolia, the south west flank of the Zagros mountains, the head of the Tigris and Euphrates valley, and Palestine. With patient ingenuity our forefathers encouraged barley and wheat to produce more grain to the ear and to retain it as it ripened, instead of scattering it at the first breeze. Gradually they succeeded. By about 7000 BC the food crop was more reliable. Villages had grown up, pigs were kept, wild sheep and wild goats were tamed for their wool and milk. Spinning and weaving were established as women's work. The men were beginning to understand how to make and fire pottery.

The excavation of two sites at Jericho in Palestine and at Catal Huyuk in Anatolia, reveal substantial cities of the early eighth and later seventh millennia that could not have existed without a self supporting agricultural economy, and a well-organized community. Jericho was supplied with spring water and surrounded by a massive stone wall with a tower thirty feet high. Among the debris of the ancient streets, bone and wooden instruments were found, set with sharpened flints: these were primitive sickles for reaping the corn and vegetable plots which surrounded the ancient city. There are also the remains of painting on the plastered walls of some houses.

Catal Huyuk is nearly two thousand years later than Jericho. The houses are of mud brick, some internally decorated with paintings. There are about thirty acres of them, with a possible population of 6000. The inhabitants grew wheat, barley, peas, pistachio nuts, almonds and crab apples. They hunted goats, deer and wild pig and drank hackberry beer. But they were also concerned in trade, exporting obsidian, textiles and pottery. Their religion appears to have been a fertility cult and they exposed their dead to vultures – forerunners of a custom which still survives in parts of India.

By the sixth millennium numerous village communities in south eastern Europe were growing beans, peas and lentils as well as cereals. Quite early too, on the southern slopes of the Alps and on the Mediterranean shores fruit was cultivated – the olive, the apple and the vine.

. By the sixth millennium the Neolithic Revolution had reached Thessaly, the Peloponnese, Crete, and Cyprus; emigrants from Dalmatia carried it to Italy, thence to the Iberian peninsula. About the year 5000 it reached India. Altogether it took about 3000 years for the revolution to spread from its source in Anatolia to the Mediterranean world, to North Africa, central Asia and India. Another millennium and a half would carry it through northern France to remote Britain.

In the plain of North China, the relatively advanced Yang-shao culture was well established in groups of agricultural settlements by the third millennium, with every indication that it had been in existence for many centuries. In other parts of the globe the cultivation of crops came late, or did not develop sufficiently to alter the character of society. In regions rich in wild life, whether in water or on land, or in regions where edible fruit and roots were plentiful, there was no need for intensive agriculture. The Tahitians and other Pacific islanders, well supplied with fish and fruit, changed little over the millennia. Though less bountifully blessed, the peoples who had reached Australia about 25,000 BC continued in their unchanged rhythms of hunting and collecting food, undisturbed and almost unchanged.

While agriculture in Egypt produced one of the great civilizations of the world, the story of Africa on the higher reaches of the Nile is still relatively unexplored. The Sahara was not then all desert; there is evidence of much vegetation, stone artifacts are found and pictures scratched in caves and on rocks of elephants, buffalo and giraffes, going back to about 10,000 BC.

Some groups notably the Pygmies of the Congo forests and the Bushmen of the Kalahari desert lead to this day lives nearly as primitive as their remote ancestors, hunting and collecting wild plants. The Pygmies, a secretive and happy people, appear to have no history and no records. The Bushmen, on the other hand, have a tradition of cave painting, though much shorter than that of their remote Palaeolithic cousins in France and Spain. Vigorous and lively, these paintings do not equal the animal paintings of Altamira and Lascaux; their purpose was different: they represent more men than animals and are not hunting-magic, but the primitive recording of history. Sometimes they depict combats between small, squat brown men and tall black men armed with lances. These latter are the Negro races who came, no one quite knows when or whence, and drove the Pygmies and the Bushmen back from the greater part of Africa. The invaders too lived by hunting, like the peoples they drove out; but their superior fighting skill and their tribal organization made them the victors.

The Bushmen and the Pygmies – more perhaps than other primitive people – have senses alive to the vibrations of nature, scent, sound, and the presence of hidden water, that civilized man has lost; they live in a tacit partnership with the earth, the air, the trees and grasses and elements. It is their only strength in a world where they have been, for generation after generation, driven back and contained.

In central and South America agriculture began rather later than in Europe and Asia, and development was slower and more difficult. There is evidence of the cultivation of crops in what are now the highlands of Mexico as early as the seventh millennium. Hunting still dominated the economy, but pumpkins, peppers, possibly beans and even the avocado pear, were grown. Maize was cultivated as early as 3000 BC, though not plentifully for another two thousand years, by which time cassava and the vine had also appeared.

In South America agriculture may have been practised by the peoples of the Pacific coast of Peru as early as the third millennium, but more probably not for another five or six hundred years; fish and other sea-food was their basic diet. By the second millennium, they were cultivating beans (the ancestors of the Lima beans of today), gourds, chile, potatoes and cotton. This latter they used for woven textiles and for fishing nets, but its provenance is a mystery. Was it a native plant, or did its seeds in some way cross the Pacific from Asia? Only about 1400 BC with the introduction of maize, which must in the course of centuries have spread from Mexico, did intensive cultivation begin here, and by about 1500 BC a Peruvian culture of some aesthetic distinction in the arts of pottery and weaving had come into being.

In North America, agriculture developed very much later. The rich wild life of the North American forests, rivers and lakes made agriculture of secondary importance to hunting and fishing; by 1500 BC there were permanent salmon fishing villages on the north west coast and big-game hunting on the central plains where the mammoth had been replaced by the bison. About 800 BC maize began to be cultivated in the Ohio valley and played its part in the legends and fertility rites of many of the North American tribes. Tobacco smoking was already widespread.

The lack of domestic animals gravely hampered the progress of civilization in the Americas. Horses had all been hunted and killed for food before their potential as servants of man was recognized. The formidable wild buffaloes of the northern continent could not be domesticated as draft animals, and in the southern continent only the lama in Peru was tamed and taught to carry burdens. In Peru also they kept and fed guinea pigs as an occasional delicacy for their feasts. They had knowledge of the wheel, possibly through some ocean castaway from China, but since they had no carts its purpose eluded them. They used it as a toy.

In Europe and Asia the ox, the wild ass and the water buffalo were early trained to draw primitive ploughs, and drag loads. The water buffalo, kin to the domestic cow, was kept for her milk. The pig, though chiefly a source of food, was also used in Egypt – and in China – to trample newly sown grain into the soil. Later, in India, brave and patient men trained the elephant for traction and for war.

Without horses or cattle, the people of the Americas depended on unaided manpower. They were short of the most useful metals and the only iron in the south was meteoric iron. They had gold and silver which they worked into ornaments by hammering under low heat. For knives and weapons they used obsidian – volcanic glass – which was sufficiently lethal. In the northern continent copper was plentiful in the region of the Great Lakes and as early as the seventh millennium the inhabitants had learnt how to hammer it, cold, into arrowheads and to trade it to their neighbours. But they knew nothing of metallurgy.

Much more advanced civilizations developed in central and South America, in Mexico, Yucatan, Guatamala and Peru with great empires, highly organized societies, cities, palaces, roads, bridges, and superb monuments like the Pyramid of the Sun at

Teotihuacan in Mexico, the foundations of which are probably coeval with the temple of Solomon: all created by the ingenuity, skill and sheer physical effort of these gifted peoples. In the sixteenth century of the Christian era their culture was ignorantly destroyed in less than fifty years by invaders from Europe who had behind them several thousand years of metallurgy – the Bronze and the Iron Ages – as well as horses and gunpowder. The humanitarian deplores the enslavement and degradation of the people; the archaeologist adds to this an enduring regret for the destruction of the most miraculously advanced Stone Age cultures which the world has seen.

III

When agriculture reached the region between the Tigris and the Euphrates, the Indus valley and the banks of the Nile, the complex process of civilization began in earnest. This was around 8000 BC, but which region developed first is still a matter of controversy. Probably the Indus civilization was the latest, but the primacy long accorded to Egypt was challenged when the Sumerian cities were excavated.

In Egypt, where the Nile flood occurred every autumn, cultivation was an easy matter. The Egyptians had only to wait for the waters to fall, sow their seed in the rich wet mud and wait for the harvest. An insufficient flood and a poor harvest sometimes occurred but not often. For centuries the Egyptians took no further pains than was necessary, and felt no need for any elaborate organization to improve their food supply.

The plain of the Euphrates presented more serious problems. The rivers, swollen by the melting snows in the mountains, poured down abundant waters in the spring which carried no fertile mud but created swamps and could be disastrous to early sown crops. The problem, from the first, was to guide and control the water so that destructive flood would not be followed by drought. The Sumerians, a hard-working, intelligent people embanked the river, and directed the surplus water into canals, ditches and reservoirs, which in turn had to be regularly cleaned and freshly dug to avoid clogging. Thus they increased the area of cultivable land, ensured the water supply for most of the year and managed to sow and reap two harvests annually. Some of their ploughs even had a labour-saving attachment which scattered the seed. Planning and co-operation over a large area of land and intensive, well-regulated work could alone achieve such results. Hence cities grew up, each one of which was an organizing centre where plans were worked out and orders issued to the surrounding country. In the midst stood the temple and government buildings, impressively set on a large raised platform reached by a flight of steps. Below, clustered streets of small mud-brick houses, over which awnings could be drawn against the sun, as in the *souks* today. The whole city was surrounded by a wall and beyond it lay scattered villages that brought in their surplus produce and looked to it for guidance.

Sumeria was thus a land of independent cities, each with its own king, government and god, a protective god akin to the forces of nature but with little taste for human sacrifice. The cities sometimes fought each other but rarely to the point of mutual destruction. The Sumerians were essentially a practical people, speaking the same language and having the same interests.

The houses were of sun-baked brick, buildings being ornamented with painted clay cones hammered into the walls. As for wood, they used the reeds of their widespread marshes, thickly plaited together. (There is great strength in reeds; the Egyptians who also lacked wood, used them to make boats. Thousands of miles and many centuries away, the Peruvians would make reed ropes strong enough to hang suspension bridges over the chasms of the Andes.) Later, as the Sumerians grew more prosperous, they traded their surplus corn for stone, timber, gems, aromatics, and tin (which they used to make copper) to India, Ethiopia, the Caspian and Mediterranean shores. As their agricultural knowledge increased they added to their crops groves of date palm, intensively cultivated, which gave them oil, sugar and basic food as well as useful fibres.

They were a pragmatic people, valuing material success, but also justice, learning and family loyalty. They had early perceived that a means of communication, other than speech, would be useful. First they evolved a primitive pictographic writing which they improved and simplified into a syllabic script. By about 2500 BC most of their cities had a 'tablet house' or writing school where clever boys – the future administrators – learnt how to write by impressing a wedge-shaped stylus on to a wet clay tablet. (In the eighteenth century an English traveller gave it the name of 'cuneiform', from 'cuneus' a wedge.)

According to Sumerian tradition, their earliest city was Eridu in the delta of the Euphrates, which they believed had been destroyed in a flood. As flood was their perpetual enemy the tradition is probably true. After the fall of Eridu, there arose the city of Uruk (the Erech of the Bible). It may have had as many as 50,000 inhabitants. They had wheel-turned pottery for common use, and stone vases (imported stone evidently) of the most delicate work-manship for the service of the temple and the palace. Uruk 'of the strong walls' had an encircling fortification five miles in circumfer-ence, traditionally built by their king Gilgamesh (c.2700), who was in life a successful ruler and in death a legend. Poems were com-posed in his honour and handed down partly in oral tradition and partly in writing. The written version which has reached us dates from a thousand years after the death of the hero, but is still the earliest surviving work of literature in the world.

Gilgamesh, Lord of Uruk, arrogant in his youthful strength, looked in vain for his equal among men until the gods matched him with Enkidu, a wild hunter from the forest, bred among the beasts. They wrestled together three days and nights, and out of their conflict a strong friendship was born. Together they sought adven-ture and subdued monsters. But a curse fell on Enkidu and he died, leaving Gilgamesh alone to lament him:

> O Enkidu my brother
> You were the axe at my side,
> My hands' strength, the sword in my belt,
> The shield before me,
> A glorious robe, my fairest ornament . . .[4]

Gilgamesh set out to seek his lost friend and, while still a living man, crossed the waters of death (like Aeneas in Virgil's epic two and a half millennia later, and Dante in the company of Virgil in the year 1300 of the Christian era). Gilgamesh spoke with his ancestors among the dead and heard the story of the flood, a story which disseminated by the Sumerians was later echoed in Hebrew scrip-tures and in the mythology of Greece. He returned from his far journey 'weary and worn out with labour' to die among his own people. Fragmentary and remote as it is, the *Epic of Gilgamesh* contains the perennial stuff of poetry: the confidence of youth, the joy of comradeship, the anguish of man before irrevocable separation and death.

Uruk was at that time the greatest city in Sumeria. Later it was surpassed by Ur which may have had more than 200,000 inhabitants, and where the jewelry and ornaments, the goldsmith's work, the bronze, glass and filigree ornaments recovered from tombs, are witness to their elaborate, elegant and cheerful existence. Small illustrative mosaics in blue and white show these squat, baldish, bearded, rather large-nosed people in flounced skirts banqueting to the accompaniment of music, sipping beer (made of barley) through tubes, riding in wheeled carts (by courtesy called chariots) drawn by wild asses. They had numerous domestic animals, cows, sheep, pigs and goats, from whose hair they wove carpets and hangings. They had discovered the uses of the wheel, both for carts and for pottery. Their diet was reasonably varied for they grew, besides the basic barley for bread and beer, emmer-wheat, millet, chick peas, lentils, vetch, onions, garlic, turnips, cress, leeks, mustard, cucumber, as well as the all-important date palm. They fished in the rivers, they snared birds, they hunted deer and boar and gazelle and they kept pigs.

The Sumerians, like all proud city builders, understood grandeur. With little wood or stone, they invented the column laboriously built up out of bricks in the likeness of the date palm. Every city was dominated by the temple, the palace and the government offices. Authority seems to have been divided between the priests and the king, but neither priests nor king claimed god-like powers. There must have been a powerful bureaucracy since administrative planning was all-important to survival. The excavated ruins and the evidence of innumerable clay tablets suggest a relatively large number of landowners and men of property: oligarchy, therefore, rather than autocracy or theocracy. There were some slaves, too, war captives or bankrupt citizens who had sold themselves to their creditors. But like other people who have believed in competition, hard work and enterprise, the Sumerians were concerned for fairness and equal opportunity. Thus, from the city of Lagash, about 2350 BC, we have a record of some significant protests against heavy taxation and the seizure of property for debt, against corruption among officials and extortion from the poor, in favour of a general amnesty for debt.

It would be rash to claim that the Sumerians evolved a just – still less a compassionate – society. But these jolly beer-drinking, energetic people whose rich young men competed in 'chariot' races in their little donkey carts, and whose rich ladies wore head-dresses of gold leaves in their black hair and collars of semi-precious stones on their dark bosoms, certainly believed in law and a measure of justice.

The many islands of the Mediterranean had their own gods who protected seafarers. The Mother Goddess was the greatest of these, and the most remarkable of her temples were those still standing in Malta. They date from the third millennium and are built of large blocks of dark stone carved with sacred symbols. A colossal statue of the Mother Goddess guards the door of one; in the shrine itself other statues reveal her recumbent, in sleep or giving birth. Always she is a massive figure, with thick arms and powerful thighs, a symbol of strength and fertility without a hint of the lascivious charm later to be associated with the female nude.

These Maltese temples were built about a century before the erection of the Egyptian pyramids or the coming of Egypt's great architect Imhotep. They are unique in their concentrated expression of power.

In the meantime the tempo of life had altered on the banks of the Nile. Some time in the fourth millennium, the Egyptians began to develop their practical and administrative gifts: they increased the land under cultivation by making canals from the Nile, used the fertile mud to better advantage and reaped two harvests annually. Two rival states emerged, Upper and Lower Egypt. These, about 3200 BC were united under a single king who wore henceforward the white and red crowns of Upper and Lower Egypt combined into a single lofty diadem. Greek historians later listed the Egyptian dynasties from the Pharoah Menes (Narner) and gave them numbers which, for convenience, we still use. Modern archaeologists distinguish an archaic period (c.3200–2700 BC) followed by the Old Kingdom (c.2700–2160 BC).

The king – the Pharaoh – who wore the double crown was not like the kings of the Sumerian city-states. He ruled, all powerful, over a large, obedient, united Egypt. He controlled the weather; his word was law. He was, in theory, begotten by the sun god, the principal figure in the Egyptian heaven, and he became one with the god when he died. He was surrounded and supported by priests and a small elite of officials. The first known capital was at 'white walled' Memphis. It was essentially a centre of worship and administration, without commerce, without a popular life of its own. After the union of the two kings Egypt developed fast. They had a calendar by 3000 BC.

The peasants lived in mud villages along the Nile, cultivating cereals, water melon, lettuce and other vegetables. In the slack seasons between sowing and harvest they laboured on public works. The central government sent out overseers to see that they repaired the dykes and canals. As early as the third millennium they had built a dam to regulate the flow of the formidable river. In effect the peasants became serfs, but received in return for their labour, some security against famine, some rudimentary justice, law and order, and protection against the raids of their predatory neighbours, Nubians and desert rovers. Besides, as the rites of temples grew more elaborate, and the palaces richer and more elegant, the need for pottery, textiles and ornaments increased and the gifted peasant had a chance of rising into the more privileged position of a skilled craftsman.

The fertile land brought forth wheat in abundance, barley and millet. The date palm was encouraged and cultivated, the fig tree and the grape vine. The Egyptians now grew flax and had early learnt how to make fine thread, which they wove into cloth on looms, by increasingly sophisticated methods. By 3500 BC they had discovered how to beat out the pith of the reeds which fringed the Nile, into flat, pale sheets called papyrus which could be used for writing. Their ink was made of black earth mixed with gum and their pens from reeds. Their hieroglyphic writing, a pictorial script, was in existence by the end of the millennium. It was less practical than cuneiform but writing on papyrus was quicker and more convenient than on cumbrous clay tablets. The script itself was hard to learn, and remained the specialized preserve of priests and high officials.

Unlike the people of Sumeria, the Egyptians had building stone in plenty. But their earliest buildings, the tombs of their first kings, were of brick solidly built like fortresses. About the middle of the third millennium, in the reign of King Zoser, the overseer of his works, Imhotep, the first great architectural genius whose name we know, built for his master a tomb of quarried stone, the famous stepped pyramid. A triumph of mathematical and engineering technique both for its impressive size and the precision and accuracy of its proportions, the pyramid of Zoser stands in a complex of stone-built temples, an astounding monument to the powerful conception of their designer. It is not surprising that Imhotep, long remembered and revered, was ultimately elevated to the rank of a god. Fit accompaniment to this great architecture in stone is the monumental sculpture of the epoch. The statue of King Zoser, mutilated by time and sacrilege, still conveys the awful loneliness of power.

Within a hundred years the pyramid of Zoser was surpassed in size and technique by the Great Pyramid of Cheops at Gizeh. Over two million blocks of stone went to the building of this colossal tomb; some of them weigh as much as fifteen tons, while the granite slabs which form the ceiling of the burial chamber weigh nearly fifty tons each. The Greek historian Herodotus, repeating what he was plausibly told nearly 2000 years later, said that the road alone by which the materials were transported to the site took ten years to build; the pyramid took another twenty, all by the labour of 100,000 men working in the slack season between harvest and sowing. The immense stone slabs were brought in barges, then apparently hauled on to ramps greased with wet gypsum, and so dragged by the sheer physical strength of thousands of men to their appointed places.

It was the successor of Cheops for whom that most enigmatic of monuments, the Sphinx, was made, a huge couchant lion, with a human head. Dug out of the sand four thousand years later by Napoleon's troops, it was freely adapted to the decorative art of the West.

These great monuments, still among the wonders of the world, represent only one aspect, and that the least human, of Egyptian civilization. Indeed the singular fascination of ancient Egypt lies in the mixture of a god-like dignity with a warm and cheerful humanity. Thus, the double statues of the Pharaohs – such as that of Menkaure and his wife (about 2200 BC) look, in spite of a formal pose, happy and confident young people, the queen with her arm affectionately round her husband's waist – a theme which not infrequently occurs in Egyptian sculpture.

The Egyptians believed that the Pharaoh would become an immortal god. They also believed in an after life for themselves, though it is not altogether clear how far this depended on the preservation of the body. Certainly in later centuries methods of preserving and embalming the human shell became ever more elaborate for those who could afford them. But there were also cheaper methods and, as they believed in a spiritual entity independent of the flesh – the Ka – there must have been some hope of an after life for everyone.

In any case throughout the third millennium the rich furnished their dead with the necessities and luxuries they had known on earth. The objects in the tombs have elegance and intimate charm – ornaments of beaten gold and copper, jewelry of semi-precious stones; painted pottery, graceful vases of crystal and alabaster, hollowed out to a fineness of texture which baffles all explanation. The mother of Cheops had her cosmetic boxes covered in gold leaf and inlaid with cornelian, a set of pretty chairs and her carrying litter all alike sheathed in fine gold.

A third great civilization came into being in the broad valley of the Indus. We know less of it because its destruction was more sudden and complete than anything that befell Sumeria or Egypt and no one has yet deciphered the fragments of pictographic writing which have been left behind. Its area seems to have been far larger than the other two – it stretched for close on 1000 miles from the Indus valley across north west India. The two greatest cities so far excavated, Harappa and Mohenjo-daro, were both in existence by the middle of the third millennium at the latest. They have citadels of a certain strength and grandeur, and large granaries and warehouses, but for the rest consist of streets built on a gridiron plan, the first known use of this practical design anywhere in the world. Some streets are flanked by substantial houses or blocks of flats built in fired brick. All seem to have had drainage, baths and rubbish shutes.

Since excavation reveals different strata with no appreciable change in building style, the inference is that the citizens were conservative, though practical and inventive. Their agriculture was well advanced; they grew millet, barley, wheat, sesame, peas, melons and dates. Also, they grew cotton, spun it into yarn and presumably wove it into cloth. They domesticated the water buffalo and – more courageously – the elephant. They kept pigs and cattle; at Harappa, they caught and kept jungle fowl for their eggs; thence this most familiar of all farmyard birds ultimately reached Egypt and in course of generations, all the West.

The people of the Indus were traders, too. The seals with which they fastened down their bales and jars have come to light in South India, Afghanistan, Iran, and on the further side of the Persian Gulf. They traded apparently in small things – pottery and beads. But they were adventurous on sea and land, for they crossed the Persian Gulf and penetrated the mountains of Afghanistan using asses and the one-humped camel or dromedary, an admirable beast of burden which they were the first to domesticate.

We know little of their art except from their seals which are of delicate workmanship. A few small bronzes have survived, one or two showing a lively sense of movement. We know effectively nothing of their society, politics or religion. A theocratic government has been suggested, and the single representation of a god which has survived bears a distinct resemblance to Shiva, the most popular of the Hindu gods today, who would thus be the oldest continuously worshipped god on earth.

IV

Scattered to the north and west of the Sumerian cities were pastoral tribes who spoke a language radically different from that of Sumer. The Semites (ancestors of the Assyrians, Babylonians, Phoenicians, Jews and Arabs) herded their flocks on the perimeter of the Sumerian world. But increasingly they settled in Sumerian towns and became administrators or merchants for both of which professions they had great aptitude.

Towards the end of the third millennium Sargon, a Semite official in the city of Kish, made himself king. From Kish he conquered Ur and Uruk, and within a few years was master of all the land 'from the Lower to the Upper Sea', that is from the Persian Gulf to the Mediterranean. Sargon the Great called himself king of Akkad; his empire, the first great empire in western Asia, controlled the gulf trade.

He was an administrator of sound ideals. In his time the cuneiform script was simplified and developed to suit the Semitic Akkadian language as well as Sumerian. Tablets have been found showing parallel words from both, perhaps the earliest dictionaries in the world. New arts, new luxuries, new fruits and flowers were introduced from the further boundaries of his empire, melons, figs, new varieties of the grape, leeks, cucumbers and, from Persia, the 'Queen of all flowers', the rose. Gold and silver were freely used, and lapis lazuli. Bronze casting reached a high point of skill and delicacy. One of the finest surviving pieces, the noble head of a king, may be a portrait of Sargon himself. His memory was for centuries preserved in legend. What we know of him for certain is little enough: he kept a standing army of over five thousand men, which is small for so large an empire, while the evidence of growing prosperity, peaceful trade, aesthetic and horticultural achievement leaves little doubt that he was a great ruler.

Recent excavations of Abla south of Aleppo reveal that another empire, comparable to that of Sargon, had its centre in what is now Syria. Here too the discovery of a library of clay tablets shows that there were schools of writing, an administrative class and diplomatic relations with other states, facilitated by the existence of tablets giving parallel vocabularies, which may pre-date those of the Akkadians.

The decline of Sargon's empire was followed by sporadic invasions of tribes from the Zagros mountains. Cities were captured, plundered and partly destroyed. The city of Lagash which managed to survive by paying tribute to the invaders became an oasis of peace, self-contained and self-supporting, in the midst of general disorder. Lagash was a city of perhaps 80,000 inhabitants, with a fine temple, ceremonial buildings, considerable trade and a school of sculptors who made effectively simple representations of their rulers in black diorite specially imported for the purpose. When these were discovered by French archaeologists at the close of the nineteenth century, their originality and power were a revelation to Europeans who had hitherto believed that, before the incomparable Greeks, only the Egyptians had produced works of art.

The epoch of invasion and disruption was followed by a revival of the ancient city of Ur, which controlled the river valley. With a new lease of life it became the greatest in Mesopotamia, more populous and prosperous than at any previous period. From time to time Semitic nomads settled in Ur as in other cities, and from time to time yielded again to their inborn tradition of pastoral wandering. The head of one such family, Abraham, is immortalized in Jewish tradition as the God-directed founder of their people. The nomads had family gods whom they carried with them; these were generally supposed to be less powerful than the gods who protected the great cities. But Abraham went out from Ur, trusting to the god of his own hearth and the promise he had made.

Abraham was like many more of his kindred who, while retaining their strong identity, lived among the Sumerians. In the reign and under the dynasty of the Semitic Sargon, the contacts of Sumerian and Semitic peoples must have been very close, so that Sumerian myths were absorbed into their traditions. The story of the flood in the *Epic* of Gilgamesh is clearly related to the flood in Genesis. The creation myths of the Sumerians also, the division of the land from the sea, the creation of man and of all living creatures, must have fertilized the ideas of the people who traced their line from Abraham. A chance of history, about 1400 years later, brought the Jews as captives to Babylon, where they met again the Sumerian myths, transmitted through the learned care of the Babylonians, and applied themselves in their exile to the revision and authentication of their own sacred writings.

Much about the time that Abraham traditionally went away from Ur, the king Ur-Nammu, a great builder and organizer, issued a code of laws (this was about the year 2100). There must have been many such codes in Sumeria, setting down the advisable practices by which society was maintained. The two best known are those of Ur-Nammu and of Hammurabi, an Amorite chief who, from Babylon, reunited all Sumeria as Sargon had done. His code of law, engraved on stone and now in the Louvre, was drawn up more than three centuries after that of Ur-Nammu, about 1790 BC. Both codes suggest a concern for justice and civic responsibility. They include measures for the care of widows and orphans, the respective rights and duties of husbands and wives, the control of alcohol, debt, the damages to be paid for injuring livestock, slaves, crops or other property, liability for military service and penalties for flouting the authority of the ruler. The code of Ur-Nammu recognizes only two classes, freemen and bondsmen. By the time of Hammurabi, another class had appeared, an aristocracy. Otherwise the two codes are very similar. Above all they mitigate the danger of feuds by making quarrels and reparations subject to the law; they are the codes of a practical people. Practical not only in law: the subjects of Hammurabi formulated mathematical rules, at first for business operations, but later for the study of the stars and the regulation of time.

Meanwhile, the nomads of the Asiatic steppe had domesticated the horse; as mounted warriors they terrorized their neighbours. Early in the second millennium tribes in the hills of northern Syria and on the fringes of Asia Minor were also fighting on horseback and had even begun to harness their horses to lightly-built carts, primitive war chariots. But some centuries had yet to pass before the barbarians with their horses and chariots brought down the civilization of the Sumerians and almost brought down the civilization of Egypt.

V

For 2000 years from the fourth millennium to the beginning of the second millennium Sumeria and Egypt developed independently of each other. Between them lay Syria and the peninsula of Sinai. They were in contact certainly, after Sargon the Great extended his power to the Mediterranean coast, but the Egyptians were not much given to trade, except up the Nile and occasionally as far as the Lebanon for timber of which they had none themselves. Sumerian trade was largely with the Indus valley or with the less civilized people on their borders who could in return supply the raw materials they needed. There was no common frontier and no clash of interests between Egypt and Sumeria; hence neither friendship, nor enmity, nor diplomacy.

For the greater part of the third millennium Egyptian society was stable, prosperous, remarkably comfortable for the Pharaoh, his priests and officials, and not unendurable for the peasant. Regular inundations usually ensured good harvests, and provision by storage was made against the lean years. Goats supplied them with milk, pigs and sheep with meat. Wine from grapes was for the rich only, but the ordinary people had palm and date wine, honey-dew and water melons. Honey was plentiful for sweetening. Flowers and herbs grew freely for the manufacture of scent and cosmetics. They had brought the spinning and weaving of flax to a fine art. For lack of suitable dyes, their linen cloth was colourless, but ingenious weaving gave it great variety of texture; it could be pleated and draped with consummate elegance and enriched by embroidery in gold thread.

Egypt had access, by way of Nubia, to almost unlimited gold from the desert sands. The main source for copper and turquoise was in Sinai. Silver was rare and little used. From Nubia they got ebony and timber. The Pharaoh asserted overlordship over Africa south of the Sahara, the region then called Kush (later the Sudan). Egyptian boats navigated the Nile as far as the present site of Malakal for ivory and slaves. Paintings on the tombs of Egyptian officials show men of Masai and Kikuyu type bearing tribute.

Unlike the cuneiform of the Sumerians, the hieroglyphic script of Egypt was not simplified for more practical use; writing remained the prerogative of priests, scribes and officials. The Egyptians attached a certain mystique to the written word, to the spells and prayers and formulae that they inscribed in tombs, on statues, on sacred amulets. It was possibly this, together with the picturesque and magical appearance of their writing to the uninitiated, which gave rise to the later and still surprisingly popular tradition of the 'wisdom of Egypt'. Egyptian society lacked flexibility. The professions, from the highest officers of state, priests, scribes, craftsmen, down to the peasants, were hereditary. This would lead in the end to stagnation and collapse – but in a still distant future.

Everything depended on the god-king. As in all despotisms, administration and justice were often venal and corrupt, though not usually to the point of undermining the government. The highest comforts and luxuries of life were the prerogative of the court, of priests, nobles and higher officers of state. A small middle class of minor officials, skilled craftsmen and hangers-on, presumably enjoyed the overspill from on high and were comfortably off. These clustered about the residence of the Pharaoh, still usually at Memphis, about the great temples of Amun at Thebes and of Osiris at Abydos. The Egyptian cities were wholly unlike the self-sufficient, busy hives of Sumeria or the Indus valley. They were essentially ceremonial centres; pilgrims and petitioners came to them, processions and ritual gatherings took place in them. That was all.

The mass of the people still lived in mud-built villages, with a headman, chosen from among them, to look after their interests and settle their quarrels. Some were tenants of the great temples, others of the Royal Treasury. A few owned their own land. Whole families, men, women and children worked together in the fields. Annually the tax collectors came to assess and take away the tribute of grain – usually a third of the crop. Annually the men went away to do their stint of labour on public works, between August and October when the fields were under water. Their life had compensations, the local gossip and local feasts of small self-contained communities, and their work was alleviated by a warm climate, a fertile soil, relative security against famine and war and, for many of them, a native pride in the splendour of the temples and the majesty of the pyramids which they and their forefathers had helped to build. The government did not rely wholly on their forced labour; successful wars by the Pharaoh against frontier raiders brought in prisoners of war whose slave labour may have lightened the load of the Egyptian peasants.

Towards the end of the third millennium, however, a long sequence of poor floods and failed harvests brought famine. The quality of tomb furniture declined and tomb robbery began to occur. There was unrest among the peasants and revolt among the nobility, while the frontier people of Nubia and the desert took advantage of Egypt's weakness to redouble their plundering raids.

This period of disintegration marks for historians the end of the Old Kingdom of Egypt. The troubles lasted about a hundred and fifty years before the authority of the Pharaoh was re-established and civil order restored under the eleventh and twelfth dynasties, who inaugurated the so-called Middle Kingdom ($c.2100-1786$ BC). Once again under the twelfth dynasty Egyptian civilization touched a high point of prosperity and confidence. A new humanity developed in their art, and a few surviving fragments indicate the existence of literature.

Daily life is easy to imagine because the Egyptians recorded it vividly in the tombs of their kings and nobles for the pleasure and consolation of their dead. Usually they provided an attractive meal, arranged on elegant dishes often cut out of schist or crystal to resemble leaves. Games too might be included to pass the time, a form of drafts was popular. The tombs were decorated with representations of the living world; some were painted on the walls, others were little wooden models. Since the tombs were always those of the rich, there were naturally pictures of banquets with dancing girls and musicians, pictures of fowling and fishing parties and of hunting expeditions against lions, boars and the hippopotamus (an early Pharaoh had been killed hunting this dangerous beast). There were also representations of ordinary things – peasants sowing and harvesting, labourers at work on buildings, bakers, weavers and butchers at their accustomed tasks, craftsmen in their workshops, boatmen on the Nile – and all these painted or modelled with an evident pleasure in the business of living.

Thebes in Upper Egypt (now Luxor) was the Pharaoh's main residence, close by the temple which was the chief seat of the worship of Egypt's greatest god, Amun-Re, the sun. Osiris, a fertility god whose cult had developed over the last five hundred years until he was now second only to Amun, had his sacred city at Abydos. A multitude of minor gods, depicted with the heads of animals, were probably the object of local popular cults and were tolerated by Pharaoh and his priests on the convenient theory that they were lesser manifestations of Amun. The ordinary people did not enter the temples except to do their work as craftsmen.

The kings of the twelfth dynasty began by reasserting their control over the Nubians, a necessary measure for the protection of their people and to ensure the supply of gold. Next they extended the authority of Egypt beyond Sinai into Syria. They needed Sinai for the copper mines which Egypt had long exploited; they probably had an eye to the cedars of Lebanon when they decided to have outposts in Syria. But they were troubled also by the rumours of raiding and unrest from the pastoral tribes of those regions. This extension of Egypt's sphere of influence, temporarily successful, was later to prove disastrous.

The pastoral tribes of northern Syria learnt about horses from the nomads of the Asian Steppe. Having acquired horses and the skill to control them, in the eighteenth century BC they retaliated on Egypt. Hordes of invaders, with horses and chariots, swept through Sinai and down on Egypt. For something over a century Egyptian civilization was disrupted. An alien Syrian dynasty, rather absurdly called by later historians the 'Shepherd Kings', set itself up but never seems to have controlled all the country. Thebes continued independent, though with much reduced authority.

Defeated, humiliated, but not destroyed, the Egyptians learnt to alter their way of fighting; they too acquired horses and evolved their own type of war-chariot, carrying two men, a driver and a warrior armed with a mighty bow. By about 1550 BC they effectively challenged the intruders. The dominance of the Pharaoh was re-established over all Egypt and internal peace restored under the rulers of the famous eighteenth dynasty (c.1570–1304 BC). This was the beginning of what is for convenience called the New Kingdom of Egypt.

VI

While Egypt survived and rose again, the civilization of the Sumerian cities disintegrated, though much of their experience was absorbèd and preserved by their conquerors. They had been long vexed by invaders from the Zagros mountains and Asia Minor. Disturbances among the nomads of the Asiatic steppe created a chain reaction, and the more primitive peoples on the outskirts of the Sumerian world were all on the move by the end of the third millennium. The ultimate winners were the squat, energetic Hittites who appeared in Asia Minor about 2300 BC. They had little aesthetic sense but great organizing gifts and an ability (not unlike that of the Japanese at a much later date) for imitating and adapting whatever impressed them in the achievements of other peoples.

The Hittites came from north western Asia Minor, and however far they conquered they faithfully retained – but of course enlarged and beautified – their mountain capital of Hattusas (now Boghaz Köy) although it was far from the centre of their power. They had probably learnt their skill with horses from the Mitanni, a branch of the Hurrian tribes who raided Asia Minor before establishing a kingdom from the Upper Euphrates to northern Syria, which lasted for about two centuries. The Hittites studied and imitated their achievements; the archives of Hattusas contain four tablets of instruction in the training of horses by a Mitanni expert. They quickly learnt to ride and soon possessed highly effective war chariots built to carry three men, one to drive, one to attack and one to defend. It had, like that of Egypt, spoked wheels.

The Sumerians depended in war on well-disciplined infantry. They, too, by the beginning of the second millennium, had tried to harness the might of horses but they were no match for the expert Hittites. Moreover, the Hittites had another more formidable secret: they understood the technique of hardening iron by repeatedly hammering it under great heat. Other peoples, from Sumeria to Egypt, had weapons of copper and bronze; but iron was more effective and the Hittites had access to it.

The Hittites gave the *coup de grace* to Sumerian civilization. First they overran and controlled all Asia Minor. Then they boldly raided into Mesopotamia, and mastered the whole of the fruitful plain between the rivers. About 1500, while in Egypt the eighteenth dynasty increased its power, the Hittites conquered Babylon. Now they held all that Sargon and Hammurabi had ever held, and Asia Minor as well.

The frontiers of the Hittite and the Egyptian empires – or it might be truer to say their spheres of influence – were now contiguous. The first two Pharaohs of the eighteenth dynasty, determined that Egypt should never again suffer invasion from the east, had by force of arms brought the kings, princes and tribes of Syria to acknowledge their suzerainty. They also established their authority as far as the fourth cataract of the Nile, compelled the Nubians to pay regular tribute, and extended their power into the Sudan.

The frontiers between Egypt and the Hittites were too vague for there to be immediate confrontation, but the size and contiguity of the two great empires held a menace which the civilized world had not yet experienced.

The power of Egypt suffered a setback with the accession of a minor, Tuthmosis III (c.1490–1436). His masterful stepmother, Queen Hatshepsut, maintained herself as regent for more than twenty years. She encouraged commerce; she enhanced the splendour of her court; and she built for herself under the sheer cliffs of Deir el Bahri the stateliest tomb in Egypt. But she lost control of Syria.

Tuthmosis III, when he at last came to power, proved to be the most successful of his dynasty, reckoned by the extent of his conquests and the ostentation of his government. He re-established his authority in Syria and Palestine and made an alliance with the Hittite king which ensured a long period of peace. Egypt was now fabulously rich, having direct control of the Nubian gold mines; it is alleged that the mines yielded up to 40,000 kilograms of gold a year, as well as emeralds. Tuthmosis further enlarged the temple at Karnak and among other monuments and buildings recorded his victories on great obelisks, three of which many centuries later were carried away to Constantinople, London and New York where his hieroglyphic glories are incomprehensibly proclaimed to those that pass by.

The network of diplomacy that he had set up with the Hittite empire and the tributary states of western Asia was continued and extended by his successors, reaching its height under Amenophis III. Egypt was now more cosmopolitan than it had ever been. Diplomatic alliances filled the Pharaoh's palace with plain Hittite princesses from Syria and Palestine and beautiful brides from the powerful kingdom of Mitanni on the Upper Euphrates; all brought with them ornaments, jewelry and ideas new to Egypt. Luxuries of every kind were imported – horses and cattle, silver, lapis lazuli, furs and feathers, rare woods of every kind and especially the cedars of Lebanon.

Amenophis III was succeeded by his son Amenophis IV (1379–1362), one of the most controversial figures in the history of Egypt. He is shown in his statues with a prognathous jaw, narrow shoulders, a protuberant belly and a face unduly narrow. He identified himself with the sun god, but not with the traditional Amun-Re at Thebes. He called his god the Aten – the disc or radiance of the sun; a more spiritual conception than that of Amun. Also he asserted that there was no other god. There can be no doubt that his conviction was sincere, even fanatical and that he may have been – as he thought he was – both genius and mystic. But the cult of the Aten could have been planned in his father's time to break the power and wealth of the priesthood of Amun who had begun to overshadow the throne. At first Amenophis IV merely neglected Thebes together with the cult of Osiris and all the lesser deities. But gradually his fanaticism grew: he moved his capital to a city planned and built in honour of the Aten with a new temple 200 yards in length. He changed his name to Akhenaten (meaning 'it is well with Aten'). He seized the wealth of the priests of Amun, dismantled the temple at Thebes, and finally had his father's name chiselled out of all inscriptions because it contained the hated syllables of Amun's name.

All this caused much confusion among his subjects and made him powerful enemies. Furthermore he seems to have neglected diplomacy and defence so that Egypt lost influence in Syria and the tributary states revolted or fell away. His defenders do not necessarily accept this view, preferring to see him as a truly pacific prince who has been traduced.

He encouraged sculptors and artists probably with the help of his wife Nefertiti, a most lovely creature thought to have been a Mitanni princess. The art of his reign shows an astonishing change from the conventional style of Egypt. The greatest masterpiece is the coolly exquisite head supposedly of Nefertiti which has become world famous since its discovery early in the present century. This, with hundreds of other treasures – as well as 300 documents, actually clay tablets, the remains of his diplomatic correspondence

– came to light when the city he had built was dug out from beneath the modern village of Tel-el-Amarna. The wall paintings of this period contain beautifully observed details of birds and animals and landscape painted in a free and flowing manner. They seem to reflect the spirit expressed in the hymn to the Aten attributed to the king himself:

> O living Aten, Beginning of Life!
> When thou risest in the eastern horizon
> Then fillest every land with thy beauty . . .
> The trees and the plants flourish,
> The birds flutter in the marshes,
> Their wings uplifted in adoration to thee;
> All the sheep dance upon their feet,
> All winged things fly,
> They live when thou hast shone upon them.[5]

In some of the reliefs of Akhenaten, his wife and daughters have strange proportions and curiously elongated figures, in spite of the naturalism of their attitudes; the royal pair are depicted dandling their children in what would be an attractive and intimate group but for the evidently deliberate deformation of the figures. Amarna art – as it has come to be called – remains, like its patron, enigmatic and paradoxical. Nevertheless there were great artists among them who made some of the most beautiful things ever created by man.

Was this religious revolution the work of a powerful thinker who tried to impose monotheism on Egypt? Or was it not monotheism but monolatry or even megalomania? Akhenaten, in spite of his insistence on the worship of a single god, never denied that he was himself a god. The idea of a single god, whose power was visible to everyone, could have been political, with no more spiritual purpose than to enhance the unity of Egypt and her tributary states by binding all together in a single faith. The questions are many and all unanswered.

Akhenaten's successor, Tutankhaten, his son-in-law, and possibly also his son, was only nine years old. His wife was a few years older, but both were too young to resist the inevitable priestly reaction. The young Pharaoh restored the worship of Amun-Re (and of all the lesser local gods), changed his name to Tutankhamun, returned to live at Thebes, and gave back all the property taken from the priests. Before he died at the age of about eighteen, Akhenaten's revolution had been wiped out.

But the delicate and intimate work of the Amarna artists continued during his brief reign, and when, in 1922, his tomb was found and opened it contained highly wrought jewelry and sophisticated furniture in a characteristically slender and elongated style, and also some tender and disarmingly natural representations of the young king and his queen – the two elements of the Amarna style in a final perfection.

After the eighteenth dynasty the civilization of Egypt began its slow decline. There was a resurgence of glory with Rameses II (c.1298–1232 BC), a great boaster and builder who completed the magnificent Hypostyle hall at Karnak (begun by Seti I) and built the temples at Abu Simbel. He claimed a victory over the invading Hittites at Kadesh. The battle in fact was drawn and the combatants accepted the even balance of power, which was consolidated by treaty (perhaps the earliest recorded treaty in history) and strengthened from time to time by the marriage of a Hittite princess.

Among the minor events of this declining epoch, probably towards the middle of the thirteenth century, a pastoral tribe which had sought refuge in Egypt during a year of famine (as wandering tribes not infrequently did) and had subsequently settled there, became restive under their lot. This was not surprising and the biblical story which represents the Jews at the forced labour of brick-making sounds authentic; there was much building and much forced labour in Egypt. A leader appeared among them, who was neither warrior nor priest, but a man inspired by the voice of God – *his* god, his people's god, the god who had called Abraham from Ur, who had promised them victory over their enemies and a land of their own, and who wrote the law on tablets of stone for Moses on Mount Sinai. The journey across the peninsula to the Promised Land was long and arduous; by tradition it took forty years, and after that several generations of fighting, before this pastoral people were masters of their new home, made settled villages and towns, tilled the soil and planted olives and vines.

The Israelites are rarely mentioned in Egyptian records; neither their departure nor Pharaoh's pursuit of them, nor the alleged destruction of his chariots in the passage of the Red Sea are recorded. Egyptian civilization, too firmly bound by tradition and by unchanging forms of government, sank slowly into stagnation. The tomb paintings, after the Amarna interlude, reverted to the older manner but were less lively, and dealt less with the pleasures of living and more with the fate of the dead in the nether regions, scrupulously following a guide to conduct after death which every rich Egyptian took to his grave, the *Book of the Dead*.

Meanwhile the borders and the coasts were troubled by the raids of Libyan nomads and the attacks of the 'sea people', great bands of roving adventurers from the Aegean. 'The isles were in tumult', wrote a historian in the time of Rameses III (*c.*1182–1151). The Hittite empire broke up under this new attack and the invaders poured into Egypt. Rameses III held and defeated them but he was the last great Pharaoh. After him came a long period of disorder, invasion, poor harvests, collapsing administration and peasant distress, with tomb robbery almost a professional occupation.

Some of the invading 'sea people' settled in Anatolia and created the kingdom known in classical history as Phrygia; some of them reached and occupied part of the Iranian plateau. But in Mesopotamia the Assyrians built up a growing power as the Hittite empire disintegrated. Their reputation for ruthless violence was enhanced by their king Tiglathpileser I (*c.*1116–1078) who became master of Mesopotamia, established his capital at Babylon, compelled all neighbouring states to pay tribute, and moved subject populations in thousands from one part of his empire to another to suit his whim.

VII

The 'sea people' as they were called by the land peoples who feared them, were not a united body but groups and waves of adventurers, sometimes raiders, more often immigrants seeking land to settle in. Some, but by no means all, were barbarians. In the second millennium two civilizations flourished in the eastern Mediterranean: in the island of Crete and in southern Greece.

The people of Crete were bold seafarers, using short, broad-beamed ships rising at the stem and stern, propelled by oars and sail. Their seamanship and enterprise made Crete the central mart of the eastern Mediterranean. They were in continual contact with Egypt, Asia Minor, Mycaenae and the merchant cities of the Syrian coast, Byblos and Ugarit. They transported wood from the Lebanon, copper from Cyprus, lead and tin from Anatolia, lapis lazuli from

Persia to the Egyptian market, and cleared the Mediterranean of the pirates based on the Cyclades.

Their relations were closest and most fruitful with the Mycenaeans of mainland Greece. The fortified city of Mycenae in the north eastern Peloponnese had come into existence at the end of the third millennium (about the same time as Stonehenge in England). By about 1400 BC it was encircled by Cyclopean walls, had storage tanks cut into the solid rock, and was entered by a noble but primitive Lion Gate. All was designed for strength and defence. Within the walls was a stone circle of graves, the royal burial place. Rather later the Mycenaeans interred their kings by digging out gigantic beehive hollows in the neighbouring hillside and supporting them with stone internal walls, to make vast burial vaults. Within a few miles of Mycenae two other cities, Argos and Tiryns, were allies or tributaries. Little remains today of the citadel of Argos, but the dark walls of Tiryns, built of huge blocks of rough-hewn stone, still lower across the plain. The narrow passages and storage chambers cut in the thickness of the walls seem like precursors by more than two thousand years of the strong, secretive castles of medieval Europe. Each citadel had its royal residence, with the *megaron*, or central hall, richly painted, and smaller rooms opening from it. The Mycenaeans used, and also copied, the pottery of Crete and eagerly acquired all that Cretan traders brought, but they were essentially a military people.

The *megaron* of the royal palace might be very handsome, and their rulers wear rich ornaments and drink from golden vessels, but the palace was still a fortress, unlike the spacious residences of the great in Egypt or Crete. They needed fortresses because the danger of raids from their wilder neighbours, or from the sea, was never absent, and increased, rather than diminished, with their own enviable prosperity.

Population grew with the spread of agriculture, but in Greece and the islands there was no quick renewal of fertility as there was in the lands of the great overflowing rivers. The soil became thinner and poorer with over-cultivation and over-grazing. This meant increasing pressure on the land, land-snatching, fighting between villages and piratical attacks on the islands or on the islanders on the mainland.

Crete lived under a different kind of menace, the threat of natural cataclysm. Cretan civilization met with a violent check from the earthquake which about 1750 BC devastated the island and the great palace of Knossos on the north coast. The Cretans recovered; Knossos rose again; trade was resumed especially with the Cyclades and Greece. The Egyptian influence which had marked their earliest prosperity gave way to a style more wholly their own. Their pottery became delicate and imaginative, sometimes decorated with designs of flowers and sea creatures, the many-tentacled octopus being a special favourite.

A second earthquake about two hundred years after the first, again devastated the island, and again the adaptable Cretans recovered. The fifteenth century BC saw a great and final flowering during the latter part of which there is evidence of Mycenaean influence. Knossos may have had as many as 100,000 inhabitants; then there were the villas of the countryside, the lesser towns along the coast, the great subsidiary palaces. The rebuilt palace at Knossos had superbly frescoed walls; brightly sensual pictures tending now to an almost frivolous exaggeration of slim waists, large eyes, and graceful gestures; the flowers and sea creatures on their elegant jars were increasingly fantasticated.

At this period the bull-fighting, vividly depicted in Cretan painting, was practised, half as sport, half as a religious rite. It is tempting to see some allegory, or even some historical tradition behind the legend of Theseus, and the tribute of Greek youths and maidens sent to feed the monstrous Minotaur in the Cretan labyrinth. But our knowledge is too doubtful to read the riddle.

Some time about or shortly before 1400 BC central and eastern Crete was apparently invaded by mainland Greeks, possibly Mycenaeans, who made Knossos their headquarters. Some fifty or sixty years later it was suddenly and totally destroyed. Fire? earthquake? tidal waves from the volcanic eruption of Santorini? In the present state of our knowledge we cannot tell for sure. But the luxurious, creative civilization that had grown from seafaring and commerce vanished. The more adventurous survivors probably swelled the marauding bands of 'sea people' and an impoverished culture of fishermen and farmers was all that remained in Crete except for the legend which survived, until in the twentieth century the astounding ruins were brought to light by Sir Arthur Evans, who gave the name of 'Minoan' to the long lost culture now recognized as one of the great civilizations of the Mediterranean.

Mycenae now dominated the trade of the eastern Mediterranean, a domination which became increasingly piratical. There was also rivalry and fighting with the seaports on the coast of Syria and Asia Minor. On one pretext or another about the year 1200 BC the Mycenaeans may have burnt the city of Troy which occupied a highly favourable position near the narrow straits into the Black Sea. Numerous cities had been built on this site; some had been destroyed by earthquake, some by enemies. The city which the Mycenaeans are said to have destroyed is labelled 'Troy VIIa' by archaeologists. It was not by any means the finest city in the series and no contemporary source records that it was besieged at that time. But its supposed fate became the stuff of legends and ballads; it was celebrated in epic verse about the end of the tenth century, written down for the first time at Athens four hundred years later and attributed to the mythical Homer. Thence it fertilized the imagination of Rome and Byzantium, the Gothic Middle Ages, the European Renaissance, the Neo-Classical and the Romantic movements. The Romans claimed descent from a Trojan fugitive; so, until the dawn of more critical history, did the British. The face of Homer, invented by the sculptors of fifth-century Greece, is familiar over all the West to this day.

The greatness of Mycenae did not last long. At about the same time as the troubles and temporary victory of Rameses III in Egypt, other roving bands of 'sea people' laid waste the Mycenaean world. Tiryns was abandoned and many smaller settlements destroyed, but in spite of devastation and poverty evident from the archaeological record, the old way of life lingered on. Warfare and destruction do not seem to have arisen from any planned invasion, rather from the continual 'tumult of the isles' and of mainland Greece. But some time in the eleventh century the last traces of Mycenaean life disappear. A new and far greater civilization would ultimately emerge but for many generations there was darkness in Greece.

Egypt stagnated; the Hittite empire had crumbled; Crete was a memory; even the Assyrians were divided and weak. But through the troubles and disorders of the eastern Mediterranean the cities along the coast of Syria and Palestine maintained their single-minded interest in commerce. The earliest of these cities, Ugarit and Byblos, had come into being in the third millennium, and seem to have been founded by emigrants from the shores of the Persian Gulf, known to history as the Phoenicians. They chose sites with good harbours and fortified the modest amount of cultivable ground that they needed on the landward side. They had no imperial ambitions but formed a loose confederation founded on mutual interest.

These cities built their prosperity on trading with Egypt for the cedarwood of Lebanon. Later, their commercial enterprise was overshadowed by that of Crete. At this stage the Phoenicians were cautious mariners, sailing by daylight and hugging the coast all the way round to North Africa. The bolder seafaring of the Cretans gave them an example which they developed after the destruction of Knossos. In spite of the piracy of the 'sea people' and the Mycenaeans, the Phoenicians, with increasing experience and cunning, gained control of the Mediterranean trade, and occasionally sailed as far as Cornwall for tin.

Ugarit and Byblos gave place to the famous cities of Tyre and Sidon, further to the south, with several lesser cities in the same confederation. They were not merely carriers; almost every city had its own speciality. Tyre made the famous and indispensable purple dye, from crushed shellfish, the murex. Other cities made aromatic gums, incense and perfume. Soon also their craftsmen became expert at imitating the ivory carving and goldsmith's work of Egypt, and sold their imitations by land as well as sea, over all the Middle East. They had a reputation too for fine embroidery, and were quick to develop any craft or manufacture for which there was a market. The Egyptians at their height had exacted tribute from them; the Cretans had surpassed them; the Mycenaeans had rivalled them, but they persisted and from the twelfth to the ninth centuries flourished exceedingly.

The Phoenicians about 1200 BC developed a simplified form of the cuneiform script that they had learnt from the Sumerians by way of the Hittites. Hitherto all writing had been pictographic, or syllabic, or a mixture of both. The Phoenicians seem to have been the first to realize that a much smaller number of characters each representing a *sound*, and not a syllable, could be used in an almost infinite number of combinations to produce any word the writer wanted – and any new word that might be invented. The script initiated at Ugarit was more fully developed at Byblos and by about 1100 BC was transmitted to the Greeks. Europeans owe the evolution of their alphabet to the ingenious Phoenicians.

While the Phoenician cities flourished on the coast, the numerous small tribal states of the interior, released temporarily from Egyptian tutelage on one side and the threatening power of Assyria on the other, began to settle down, establish their own areas of dominance, regularize their government usually under kings, and enter into primitive diplomatic relations with each other, interspersed with angry little wars. It was in the eleventh to tenth centuries that the Jews under their warrior kings, Saul and David, defeated the Philistines (Phoenicians) and established their hold on the territory they believed had been promised to them by their god. Under David, a dynamic leader who was warrior, diplomatist, administrator (and traditionally poet and musician as well), they made their capital at the hilltop city of Jerusalem. It was gloriously rebuilt with a magnificent temple by David's son, Solomon, who profited by the division of the surrounding peoples to extend his kingdom to the borders of Egypt. He alone of Jewish kings was on equal footing with the Pharaoh, whose daughter was one of his wives. But his power did not outlast his life and his successors sank again to the level of petty local kings.

During the three thousand years or so that had seen the rise and fall of the Sumerians, the Hittites, the luxurious civilization of Crete, the heroic and restless world of Mycenae, and the long-lasting, now slowly dying civilization of Egypt, great developments had happened elsewhere. It is time to turn from the Middle East which had suffered, and would suffer, so much destruction and change, to the civilization which was steadily expanding in the northern plain of China, and which was to have a traceable continuity down to our own time.

CHAPTER II

———•———

CIRCA 1500–500 BC

I

CHINESE CIVILIZATION has probably the longest continuous development of any in the world. There have been upheavals, invasions, alien conquests, natural cataclysms, periods of high achievement, centuries of stagnation. But until recently there have been no interruptions so violent and disruptive as those which scar the history of other civilizations – Egypt, India, Persia, Greece or Rome.

Ancient China was geographically isolated by the ocean on the east and south east, by the Tibetan plateau and high mountain ranges on the south and south west, by deserts and steppes on the west. But the north west lay open to the predatory inroads of the nomadic tribes who ranged from eastern Europe across the expanse of Asia. They were called by many names, Scythians in Hungary, Hsiung-nu on the Chinese borders. Although they harassed and preyed on the peasants, demanded tribute from the rich and sometimes overran and conquered whole provinces, the Chinese seem never to have lost confidence in the greatness and immortality of their country – a confidence which time and experience would justify. The Hsiung-nu were the enemy, but they were also the channel by which the Chinese knew about the vast expanse of Asia and the existence of other countries far beyond.

For centuries, the historical past of China was obscured by legend. A god-like father figure, the Yellow Emperor, had laid down the rules of astronomy, agriculture and government. His wife had taught the people how to make silk. His immediate successors had established law and the art of writing. Chinese tradition named three royal dynasties: first the Hsia, alleged to have ruled from the twenty-second to the nineteenth century BC, in Honan and southern Hopei; then, the Shang, who had indeed ruled for about four centuries; finally the Chou, from the eleventh to the eighth century.

Archaeology in the last seventy years, gathering confidence and speed in the last thirty, has converted legend into knowledge. It began with the interpretation of the so-called 'dragons' bones', which the peasants of northern Honan sometimes found in their fields and sold to local apothecaries to grind down for medicine. In 1899, a scholar recognized the scratches on the bones as archaic Chinese characters: they were in fact 'oracle bones' with questions written on them. If they were cracked by exposure to great heat, the shape of the cracks could be interpreted as the answers to the questions. The method, called scapulomancy, is less repellent than the Roman habit of studying the entrails of animals and quite as reliable.

The names of early Shang rulers, written on some of the bones, showed that they were not figures of legend. Investigation of an area where the bones were very plentiful, led to the discovery and excavation of Anyang, a city which flourished from the fourteenth to the eleventh century BC and is traditionally regarded as the fifth capital of the Shang dynasty.

Other buried cities have since come to light. A capital older than Anyang, excavated at Chengchow, was found to cover a square mile of ground, defended by walls over sixty feet thick at the base. An increasing number of rediscovered sites – cities, burial grounds and graves of the mighty – have firmly established the Shang dynasty in historic time. No trace of their alleged forerunners, the Hsia, has been convincingly established, and the Yellow Emperor was probably invented much later by the Taoists.

But the origins of Chinese civilization go far back beyond the Shang, and archaeology is gradually establishing their outline. A Neolithic site excavated by a Swedish team in 1921 at Yang-Shaots'un in northern Honan revealed a peasant agriculture which was already mature by the fourth millennium. The villagers used stone tools, possessed dogs and pigs and – later – a few goats, sheep, cattle and poultry, though their diet was largely vegetarian. They wove hempen cloth on looms and made pots by coiling strips of clay into a rounded shape. These they painted with abstract designs which already show the vigorous grace typical of Chinese brushwork.

In due course the Chinese had their own version of the potter's wheel and developed a glossy black ware of great elegance. But their way of life was essentially agricultural. They dug the soil with wooden hoes, mattocks and spades shod with sharpened stone or shells. Their principal crops were millet, beans, and a little wheat. By the third millennium it appears that they were already cultivating tea.

All this was in the North China plain where the Yellow River flows. The soil is a rich, light, calcareous deposit, extremely fertile, but interspersed with marshland, threatened by floods which destroyed the crops and by dangerous beasts – tigers, elephants and rhinoceros – and of course human enemies, the wandering nomadic tribes from the interior.

A strong authority was needed to organize defence against raids and floods. A warrior class inevitably arose; they built fortifications, recruited troops from the peasants, and were themselves united, by consent or compulsion, under strong leaders – the emergent rulers of the Shang dynasty.

It was during the Shang epoch, in the latter half of the second millennium BC, when the Middle Kingdom was still powerful in Egypt, that the Chinese formulated their art of writing. Conceivably they could have been influenced by some indirect contact from Egypt, or Sumeria. But this seems improbable. Chinese characters resemble neither Sumerian cuneiform nor Egyptian hieroglyphics. All three, it is true, use symbols denoting words or syllables: none is alphabetic. But there the similarity ends.

By the time of the Shang the mathematical Chinese had calculated the length of the year, divided it into twelve months of thirty days each, and planned an extra intercalary month at necessary intervals. They studied the stars and watched the skies for omens, took particular care to record lunar eclipses, and divided the day into fixed periods of time. The intelligence of their best thinkers was disciplined and acute.

Their cities were small and, in the shortage of stone, were built of earth, even to their palaces and fortifications. The houses of the great had thatched roofs supported on carved and painted wooden pillars, sometimes set in stone sockets; sometimes also they were raised above mud, dirt and flood-water on substantial platforms. The peasants in the country and the poor in the towns lived in earthen huts with a central aperture in the roof to let out smoke. Sometimes they eliminated walls by digging a hole in the ground, plastering over the bare earth and putting thatch over the top. The few large buildings of Anyang dominated a huddled conglomeration of hovels within the protecting circuit of the walls.

In theory, the Shang ruled all the land from the foot of the Shansi plateau to the mountains of Shantung and the valley of the Huai. But the local chiefs who commanded their own peasant troops and looked after the safety of their own regions, were more important than any distant emperor to the peasants whose daily toil supported Chinese society. The emperor's functions in this early time seem to have been chiefly religious: he performed rites which were intended to assure good weather for the harvest.

The supreme god, Ti, controlled the weather and, as a natural corollary in an agricultural civilization, all human affairs as well. There were lesser gods – of the earth, the sun, the moon and the clouds. But the worship of dead ancestors was equally important; it was practised in all ranks of society, with splendour by the rich, with humble offerings by the poor. Ancestors, who had cultivated the land for generations, were a natural object of devotion to their descendants; the fertility of the soil and the prosperity of the family depended on them. This attached the people to their land, for if they moved elsewhere, who would perform the necessary rites for their dead? In the same way reverence for the hereditary dynasty was bound up with the welfare of the land.

Excavated graves are a main source of information about life under the Shang. Princes and rulers took their slaves and personal servants with them into death. Sometimes the position of skulls and skeletons indicates a mass sacrifice of prisoners; sometimes the attendant dead lie like willing victims. Skeletons of horses have also been found, indicating the horse sacrifices that the Chinese had probably learnt from their nomad neighbours. As society became more stable these human sacrifices slowly gave way to the practice of burying life-size statues of the distinguished dead, and pottery models of servants and concubines, houses and possessions.

Shang graves often contain stone and ivory carvings of animals in strong simplified forms, nephrite ornaments of fine workmanship and decorated pottery. About 1500 BC great bronze vessels and bells appear. Designed for temple ceremonies and sacrifices, they were elaborately constructed, with richly textured surfaces and some were based on the formalized shapes of animals. Very different from the bronzes of the West, they were technically the most advanced in the world. Yet of earlier and more primitive bronzes from which they could have developed there seems to be no trace.

The art of bronze casting could have reached China from the Middle East, by way of the nomads, who often carried off crafts-men-prisoners to work for them. Certainly the Chinese developed contacts with the nomads which were not always hostile and their animal carvings often suggest nomad influence. But Chinese art in bronze has a grandeur and character which puts it beyond all comparison.

Shang China was an insecure society. The mass of the population lived by primitive agriculture exposed to the hazards of climate and – on the long irregular frontier – to the attacks of the nomads. The countless tribes of central Asia wandered over the steppe from the Caspian Sea to the mountains of Shantung, pasturing the horses which were their livelihood and their pride. The men, in tunics, trousers and felt boots, rode ahead; their women and children came jolting after them in waggons. Their villages were movable tents made of animal skins. The tribes fought each other for pastures, and their perpetual unrest caused a chain reaction across the whole continent which erupted at the perimeter into explosive invasions not only of China, but of Mesopotamia, Asia Minor, Russia and the fringes of the Mediterranean world. The Chinese were recurrent victims but in the intervals of peace they traded with the nomads for horses and the skins of animals. They also learnt from them how to use the short-bow, which the nomads fired from the saddle but the Chinese used as an infantry weapon.

Though trade with the nomads was not extensive, it demanded organization and a knowledge of distant routes. Modern excava-tions at Anyang or elsewhere indicate a wide variety – salt, tin, lead and turquoise among the imports.

About the twelfth century BC the Shang were overthrown by the Chou, a warlike Asiatic tribe whose strength lay in their swift, lightly-built four-horse chariots, and their deadly skill with a primi-tive cross-bow. Invading the plain of North China, they conquered the subjects of the Shang, while adapting themselves to the customs and civilization of the conquered – a pattern which would be repeated by many subsequent invaders.

In later tradition the Chou would appear as the founders of Chinese administration and imperial authority. Evidence for this is doubtful, to say the least, although they seem to have encouraged agriculture. For rather more than two centuries their principal chief claimed sovereignty over more territory than the Shang had ever held, but much of it consisted of independent regions whose chieftains gave no more than formal recognition to their titular sovereign. Then, about 770 BC the nomads attacked in force, the Chou emperor moved his capital east to Loyang, and for the next five hundred years – the Chou were a remarkably long-lived dynasty – his successors exercised such authority as they had over increasingly independent chieftains who paid lip service only to the imperial idea.

But the last centuries of the dynasty were nonetheless one of the great epochs of Chinese art, especially in lacquer, bronze and nephrite. Chinese jade, as nephrite is more often and less correctly called, was said to be 'crystallized fragments of moonlight' in Chinese legend. It certainly has no resemblance to the familiar green 'jadeite' of Burma so popular in the West since the eighteenth century. Nephrite is a hard crystalline stone, varying in colour from white through the whole spectrum to black. It needed infinite patience and skill to drill, cut and polish it into a decorative plaque, a bowl, or hair ornament, the likeness of an animal, or the hilt of a dagger. It was dangerous to obtain as it came from the heart of the nomads' country, Khotan in central Asia. Its rarity and subtle beauty gave it symbolic significance as the emblem of purity and strength.

The tradition that the Chou were the true founders of Imperial China is not therefore without meaning. Their direct rule was limited, but they carried what they had learnt of Shang culture southwards to the Yangtze valley, enlarging and enriching the area of civilization. After their decline, independent chiefs strove to surpass each other – not merely in war, but also in prosperity, taste and skill. By exploiting and encouraging their peasants, they stimulated agriculture, manufacture, commerce, technology and even the arts. Chinese historians retrospectively simplified the process, by ascribing the advances of this epoch specifically to the dynasty.

But the major technical advance came through the development and rapid diffusion of iron casting. The Chinese were nearly a millennium later than the West in using cast iron but from the fifth century onwards they developed it for ploughshares, sickles, scythes, hoes, and runners for their wooden sledges; for axes, saws, wheels, chisels, knives, awls, needles, drills, and weapons.

This was not, of course, an industrial revolution; technology was still primitive, and the organization of society hieratic and feudal. The peasant depended on his overlord for the protection of his crops against marauders; and the overlord depended on the peasant for his labour. The relationship did not change. But the use of iron gave a new impetus to agriculture, craftsmanship, manufacture and commerce from which both the overlord and the peasant stood to gain.

With the advance towards the Yangtze the area of civilization extended about 1000 miles from north to south and from east to west and was highly populated. It became, therefore, essential to improve communications. Towards the end of the eighth century (c.720) the 'Great Ditch' (Hung Kou) was dug from the Yellow River south eastwards to join a tributary of the Huai. A hundred years later a reservoir in the province of Anhwei supplied a thousand square miles of country with water. About 487 BC the ruler of the fertile state of Wu on the lower waters of the Yangtze dug a canal which joined the river Huai to the Yangtze. These canals were not for transport only: hundreds of ditches along their course drew off water for the fields of the peasants and Wu became a principal granary of China. A further advance was made when the torrential waters from the melting snows of the Tibetan plateau were successfully distributed through a network of channels to irrigate the plain of Chengtu.

Meanwhile the Chinese laid the foundations of maritime trade by exporting iron and iron tools to South East Asia and the islands, also surplus grain and textiles, especially silk. The original cultivation of the silk worm goes back into pre-history. Already in the time of the Shang the Chinese had evolved techniques of weaving unknown in the West before the Middle Ages.

Industry, however, played only a small part in the early history of China. The country was overwhelmingly agricultural, and the great majority of the people were unprivileged peasants. Effective government was in the hands of the local nobility, whose rule – though not always cruel – was always despotic. The theoretical allegiance which they owed to the emperor, though sanctioned and supported by religion, was often ignored. Some of them were highly educated, patrons of learning and the arts; others were almost solely involved in local rivalries, feuds and petty warfare.

The five centuries of Chou decline are divided in classical

Chinese history into the 'Spring and Autumn' period when over a hundred petty states existed, and the period of the 'Warring States' when the multitude of small states had been reduced by conquest and amalgamation to seven, which fought each other intermittently until one, the state of Ch'in, conquered all the others. Competing princes strove to increase their resources by improving agriculture and encouraging trade. By the sixth century metal coinage was in circulation – small spade-shaped pieces usually of copper, occasionally of gold. About 300 BC glass-making was introduced from the West.

It is therefore permissible to associate the closing years of the Chou with some advance in culture and prosperity, while the dynasty faded sadly away at Loyang.

A few at least of the peasant population must have benefited as better irrigation and more plentiful crops decreased the danger of famine, but did not otherwise lessen their heavy burden. From spring to harvest they toiled in their fields and, in the winter, hibernated in their hovels, man and beast together, through the dead season or as long as their stores lasted. Generation after generation they were bound to the land by the lack of any alternative way of life and by their ritual duties to their ancestors' graves.

The local overlord lived close to, but apart from, the villagers. His house was supported on wooden columns, with a courtyard before it, and orchard, kitchen garden and mulberry trees planted close by. He had his war chariot and horses, his armed retainers, his band of artisans for building, for general repairs, for making armour or horse-furnishings, silk and other necessities. His slaves (mostly prisoners of war) performed the menial tasks. He exacted his tribute from the peasants' annual crop and gave them protection in time of war. Once the peasants had paid their dues they were supposedly free to play their individual parts in a self-governing village community – a freedom narrowly circumscribed by the conditions in which they lived.

The servitude of the Chinese peasants was, if not mitigated, rendered more tolerable by certain festivals and beliefs. The names 'Spring and Autumn' period – bestowed by later historians on the centuries of the Chou decline – commemorate the celebration of two great festivals in the rural year. In the spring the peasants emerged from their cabins, danced, sang and celebrated marriages, while their overlord formally cut the first sod of the earth. In the autumn, the overlord, in peasant dress, presided over harvest thanksgiving and all partook together of a great feast before withdrawing to their homes for the somnolent winter. The soil, blessed and sanctified, lay untouched until spring. These festivals lasted in some parts of China until the twentieth century and shed a ritual significance over the social order. The same phenomenon can be found in other forms in other parts of the world; the May-Day junketings of the medieval West are an obvious example.

But there was something more in China. Philosophers in the time of the later Chou developed the conception of *Yin-Yang*. They believed that all nature was governed by two principals – Yang the active principal of light, and Yin its opposite number, the passive principal of darkness. Everything in the natural world was governed by these two principals; they were the complementary forces, male and female, that explained all aspects of life in their continual and innumerable relationships. The idea was high philosophy among Chinese sages; but came through to the people as a popular belief in good and evil forces, light and dark, benevolent and malevolent spirits and, as a natural by-product, it lowered the status of women. It was nonetheless a kind of philosophy that made life endurable because fore-ordained by mysterious powers greater than man.

II

The half millennium which saw the foundation of Chinese civilization saw also the resurgence of Egypt under the first Pharaohs of the eighteenth dynasty and the destruction and slow recovery of the civilizations of North India.

The Indus civilization, already in decline, disintegrated altogether after 1500 BC under the pressure of Aryan invaders. Succeeding waves of this prolific race poured through the passes of the Hindu Kush in search of better land. They were a pastoral people by origin, but had learnt the use of iron, had a primitive plough and understood how to grow crops. Shepherds, smiths, agriculturalists, they were also warriors and horsemen. Their horses alone gave them decisive advantage over the natives of North India who – like the Mexicans facing the Spanish invaders 3000 years later – had never seen such animals before. Poems of the Aryans, preserved by oral transmission, describe the irresistible power of these noble steeds and the rapidity of the conquest, though in fact the subjection of North India was the work of several generations. Coming through the mountain passes in separate tribal bands they took time to found their village settlements and establish mastery over weaker native groups. The cities of the Indus civilization (see Chapter I) were abandoned and forgotten, until archaeologists in the twentieth century dug out their massive remains.

For the most part the people fled before the invaders, making new settlements which would in time be captured, or infiltrated and dominated by the Aryans. Tradition ascribes the foundation of Varanasi (Benares) to fugitives from the Aryans. There is no evidence to prove or to disprove this; the earliest known reference to the great city on the Ganges occurs about the seventh century BC, several hundred years after the onset of the Aryan invasions. But the city seems early to have developed an active commerce, trading up river to the interior, and overseas to the coasts and islands of South East Asia – as, in their time, the ancient people of Mohenjo Daro and Harappa had traded with the Middle East, Egypt and the Mediterranean.

Here too, at Varanasi, from very early times pious pilgrims came to bathe in the sacred river which the great god Shiva had checked in its destructive course from the Himalayan snows by catching the waters in his abundant locks and wringing them through his hair. Shiva, the oldest god in India, survived the Aryans, the Persians, the Macedonians, the Moslems, survived Arab, Afghan and Turk, Portuguese, Dutch, French and British: survived into the twentieth century.

The Aryans were organized in tribes and families, forming a patriarchal society in which the hearth was sacred. Warriors were important, but priests even more so. They seem to have had, before they reached India, something like a priestly and a warrior caste, later to be called the Brahmans and the Ksatriya. Below them were the cultivators, the Vaisya. The conquered race – called at first the Dasas – were outside the system, but over the centuries became incorporated into it, by assimilation and doubtless also by intermarriage. Although this was not encouraged by the conquerors there must have been some intermingling between the lowest Aryan caste – the Vaisya, the farmers – and the subject race. But the Vaisya tended to rise in the world, to become traders and landowners, so that another caste, the Shudra appeared – the non-Aryans, who worked as labourers and minor craftsmen. Below that still there would gradually develop the great outcaste majority, casual workers, beggars, street cleaners.

In spite of its evident injustice the system had advantages. It created solidarity and a certain pride within each caste – even the lowest. Since caste was regarded as a divine institution imposing hierarchy and order on society, it became a force which – however unjust – gave the Indian population a coherent and comprehensible social structure which survived many centuries and many invasions.

The Aryan aristocracy, Brahmans and Ksatriya (priests and warriors), left manual labour and vulgar commerce to their own commoners and to the subject race. This was to the advantage of the Vaisya, originally the caste of farmers, who acquired commercial tastes by mingling with the older race. By the eighth century BC Vaisya merchants were trading pottery and textiles to the peoples bordering the Persian Gulf; money was in circulation; banking, usury and trade guilds had appeared.

The tribal organization of the Aryans led naturally to the development of many small states. This caused rivalry and minor wars, but also stimulated local responsibility and self-government. In the hills of the north west the government of these small states was often a primitive democracy, carried on by means of public discussion with the chief as chairman or 'raja'. In the plains, monarchy was quicker to develop, and the king soon came to be credited with god-like attributes. Republics and monarchies alike left the villagers to govern themselves. They chose their own headman and settled their own problems by discussion. Great distances and difficult communications perpetuated this tradition; the concept of village self-government on a small scale is indigenous to India and of long survival.

If the Indus people had a literature, we know nothing of it. Indian literature began with the Aryans. They brought with them traditional poems of praise and propitiation to the capricious gods of nature. Sung or recited by priests and worshippers, they were passed on by word of mouth, in almost unchanging form over the centuries in a great oral collection known as the *Rig Veda* – roughly translatable as the 'Praise of Knowledge'.

Their priests practised elaborate rituals and the sacrifice of animals, after which worshippers became ecstatic on *soma*, a potion extracted from an unidentified plant, closely associated with Indra, the weather god who controlled lightning and thunder. Their worship later attained a more spiritual quality, inspired perhaps by the potent magic of the Indian climate, the spatial grandeur of the Indian landscape and the dazzling depth of the Indian sky. The opening lines of the invocation to Savitri, god of light, the so-called *gayatri mantra*, have been chanted as a prayer in India for the last 3000 years:

> Let us think on the lovely splendour
> Of the God Savitri,
> That he may inspire our minds . . .[1]

These words became holy to all Hindus, spoken with reverence by Indians of Aryan or non-Aryan descent, moved by the same impulse to worship.

The Aryan belief in many gods was gradually elevated into the praise of a single disembodied unseen power which had many manifestations. 'He is One, though men call him by many names . . .', so ran the words handed down in the *Rig Veda* when the Aryans had been settled in India for upwards of four centuries. The *Hymn to Creation*, in which words of praise are intermingled with a hint of philosophic doubt, is of about the same epoch:

> But after all, who knows and who can say
> Whence it all came and how creation happened?
> The gods themselves are later than creation,
> So who knows truly whence it has arisen?[2]

The introduction of iron into India at an uncertain date facilitated the clearing and tilling of land. This in turn increased leisure, at least in some degree, and thus stimulated religious and metaphysical speculation. The wise man, the *guru*, now first appeared. Unlike the sages of China, the *gurus* were not concerned with political or philosophical argument, and only indirectly with the inculcation of morals. They were concerned with the discovery of ultimate truth through mystical experience. They sought out solitary places, in the forests or among barren rocks, where they meditated, taught and gathered disciples. They founded the tradition of wise ascetic hermits which still persists in India, and their teaching, though it aimed ideally at liberating man from preoccupation with material things did much to co-ordinate the varied and often conflicting aspects of Hindu culture.

More continuously influential on the ideas and attitudes of

educated people was the greatest of Indian epic poems, the *Mahabharata*, which was probably handed down in varying forms for several generations before oral tradition, about the end of the fifth century BC, crystallized it in the version which survives. It was not preserved in writing until several hundred years later.

The *Mahabharata* is an illuminating example of the mingling of material and spiritual values in the Hindu tradition, a confusion common to many religions. It is a story of rivalry between princes, of love, revenge, loyalty and valour, based on some minor war which caught the imagination of Indian poets as the – mythical – siege of Troy caught the imagination of the Greeks. In the *Mahabharata* – the longest epic poem in the world – there is a good and a bad party, and a stronger moral dilemma than in the *Iliad*.

At some time rather late in the period of its oral transmission, a moral dialogue was inserted into it, the so-called *Bhagavadgita* or *Song of the Lord*. On the eve of a critical battle the hero-prince falters as he looks across at the young warriors of the opposite side: can it be right to kill? His charioteer, the god Vishnu in disguise, resolves his doubts in an eloquent exposition of right and wrong, moral duty and social obligation. The *Bhagavadgita*, which became one of the most important of Hindu scriptures, taught that the renunciation of self was the only way to inward peace:

> Desire, anger, greed: this is the
> triple gate of Hell . . .

The good man must have compassion, tolerance, charity and a sense of social responsibility based on caste: he must perform the duties to which he is born. The warrior prince must fight the necessary battle however unwillingly, but he need not mourn the slain, for the soul cannot die:

> Never is it born nor dies; never did it come to
> be nor will it ever come to be again: unborn,
> eternal, everlasting . . . primeval. It is not slain
> when the body is slain.

> If a man knows it is indestructible, eternal,
> unborn, never to pass away, how and whom can
> he cause to be slain or slay?[3]

The disguised god, Vishnu, speaks these words, which sum up the classical doctrine of *Karma* – rebirth – which became central to Hindu belief. It was associated also with the idea of a universal spirit, present not only in man but in every living thing. Thus while thoughtful worshippers contemplated 'Brahman' – the eternal, universal soul – the majority of the people preferred livelier myths and a multitude of local gods. Hinduism, for it is convenient to give it this name although it was not so called for many centuries, thus became one of the most comprehensive religions in the world.

Order and hierarchy of a kind was evolved for the principal gods. The formidable Indra, the weather god, declined in power as time passed. Brahma, the Creator (not to be confused with Brahman, the universal soul) should have been the highest, but he was not as popular among simpler people as the more comprehensible and accessible gods. Over the centuries Vishnu and Shiva, somewhat vaguely defined as the Creator and the Destroyer, came to be involved in the greatest variety of rites, functions and local cults. Vishnu was most beloved in two of his human incarnations. In folk legend he was the young prince Krishna who made love to the milkmaids. In one of India's most beautiful epic poems, the *Ramayana*, he was Rama the brave ruler and constant lover who rescued his wife Sita, herself the ideal of Indian womanhood, from an abducting tyrant, with the help of Hanuman the king of the monkeys.

But six-armed Shiva had the greatest number of temples in the end; a grand and terrible figure symbolic of the violence and fruitfulness of nature, he was worshipped often in the form of the *lingam*, the stylized phallus. His consort, Parvati, was like him a symbol both of mercy and destruction. In her most fearful form she was Durgha or Kali, the bringer of death; her cult, which involved ritual murder, was especially prevalent in times of distress and disorder. More genial and immensely popular to this day was Ganesha, the elephant-headed god, son of Shiva and Parvati. He was probably once a symbol of the destructive forces of nature, but popular tradition transformed him into a god of prudence and good luck, depicted with blithely waving trunk and plump human body, sometimes holding a bowl of sweets, his favourite diet.

Gods multiplied over all India, local cults rose, flourished and fell. The Hindu Pantheon was infinitely hospitable; it accepted gods of many kinds in many guises, worshipped in many different ways. All are one and mankind is one with them.

III

While the civilization of North India slowly assimilated the Aryan invaders, the Assyrians – with some fortuitous help from the 'sea people' – had absorbed the Hittite empire and thereby gained access to the trade routes of western Asia. They exploited the iron ore once controlled by the Hittites and evolved the battering ram, an engine of war which outlasted their time for many centuries.

The first capital was at Babylon, seat of a civilization much older than their own, but they came to prefer Nineveh, the city they themselves founded on the Tigris. They were however only intermittently dominant over a period of five hundred years, during which periods of energy and additional conquest alternated with periods of indecision, dynastic quarrels, withdrawal and return.

The harsh rule of Tiglathpileser I (1116–1078) led to an Aramaic invasion which kept out the Assyrian dynasty for well over a hundred years. Towards the end of the ninth century they fought their way back to re-establish their harsh unpopular rule. In the seventh century they defeated the Egyptians, took Memphis and ultimately Thebes. Their king exercised absolute power as chief priest and supreme judge. His statue was set up beside that of the tribal god Ashur, while huge human-headed winged lions of granite stood on guard as fitting symbols of his power.

Assyrian armies were highly trained and well equipped. Their war chariots were designed to be quickly dismantled and reassembled for transport across rivers or difficult ground. Such operations could be carried out in the face of an enemy under cover of a screen of arrows from their bowmen. They understood how to build pontoon bridges, and they equipped their infantry with inflatable skins on which to swim the rivers. But their strength lay above all in their numbers.

The persistent revolts of their tributary people sufficiently indicate their cruelty, yet they had redeeming characteristics. They valued good craftsmen, especially artists in sculptured stone, sought them out among the conquered peoples and carried them off to practise and propagate their skill in Assyria. The imperial palace walls were decorated with vigorous reliefs, showing the triumph of their kings, in war and on hunting expeditions.

They brought water into their cities by aqueducts and improved irrigation by cutting canals, which much increased the material prosperity of the country. Naturally they relied on the slave labour of expendable captives for these public works.

One of their most formidable kings (and almost the last) Ashurbanipal (c.668–626) systematically organized the creation of a reference library, sending out scribes to collect all such works as handed down the traditions and rituals necessary for the preservation of the king and the state, together with a selection of technical and educational works. Here, on clay tablets, in the long buried ruins of Nineveh's library, archaeologists discovered much of what we know about Sumeria and Babylon as well as the Babylonian version of the story of the Flood as recorded in the *Epic of Gilgamesh*.

Nineveh, enriched by the tribute of subject peoples, was very glorious. Its palaces were fragrant with incense and adorned with the purple-dyed cloth of the Phoenicians. Beams from the cedars of Lebanon supported the ceilings. In this sumptuous setting moved the impressive great ones whose towering head-dresses and stiffly curled beards we know from the stone reliefs on their palace walls.

The power of the Assyrians was threatened by the mountain people of the north, the Medes, whom they never wholly subdued, and by some lesser, wilder tribes. It was threatened too, from the heart of their empire, by the conquered people of Babylon. Medes and Babylonians at length rose in alliance, the Assyrian empire tottered under the feeble successors of Ashurbanipal, Nineveh was besieged, taken and sacked: Assyrian rule was at an end. The new ascendancy of Babylon lasted little more than seventy years (c.612–539) but had significant results.

Early in the sixth century Nebuchadnezzar the Great, king of Babylon (605–561), decided to make an end of the small, persistently surviving kingdom of Judah. (The Assyrians had already overwhelmed the kingdom of Israel.) He besieged and took Jerusalem but the indomitable Jews revolted and were not finally overcome until a second capture of the city, eleven years later. This time Nebuchadnezzar destroyed the city, burnt the temple and carried off the noblest, richest and ablest of the citizens to exile by the waters of Babylon.

Babylon was an ancient city, founded by the Sumerians; its people were curious, lively and hard-working. Their religion was not authoritative and nationalist like that of the Assyrians. It was comprehensive and generally tolerant. There were difficulties, as the

Jews were exclusive and accepted no god but their own. A tolerant government can be forced into intolerance when confronted by a people who do not themselves tolerate other gods. (The Romans had the same trouble with the Christians.) Some tension between Babylonians and Jews there evidently was, but there was also a natural sympathy between two peoples both by nature self-reliant and ambitious. In the outcome the Jewish exiles enriched the culture of Babylon and the Babylonian exile enriched and deepened the Jewish way of life.

The Jews were an unusual people in three respects: their conception of God, their peculiar sense of history, and their moral code. Their god was invisible and no representation of him was permitted. (The pervading deity of the Hindus was invisible, but the need of Hindu worshippers was satisfied by any number of images of any number of lesser gods. So, in later times, the Christians would believe in the invisible God of the Jews, but nonetheless paint and carve their own idea of a bearded father figure, not to mention countless saints as well.) The Jews, like the Moslems after them, were austerely resolved to make no images of a being unimaginably great: this in the world of Assyria, Babylon and Egypt was remarkable.

Most human beings, from all time, have made images of their gods. It is a natural urge. When the Jews came out of Egypt to the Promised Land, they found the local tribes worshipping fertility gods with many interesting rites and images. Not unnaturally they wanted to do the same, but were sternly and, in the end, effectively prevented from doing so.

The second characteristic of their faith was that they recognized in history the operation of God's will on earth. Unlike most other peoples, they were less concerned in writing their history to glorify themselves or their rulers and more concerned to tell the truth, or the truth as they saw it. Their defeats and misfortunes, inflicted on them by God for their sins, were as significant as their successes, and were faithfully set down. Their enemies were not always shown to be in the wrong; rather they were the instruments of God's chastisement. Their historical writing is neither unprejudiced nor scientific, but it is purposeful and conscientious and their chroniclers, unlike the usual flatterers of kings, tried hard to write accurately because history was to them sacred, and knowledge of it a key to the mind of God.

The law of the Jews differed from other codes of law, not merely because it was God-given (other codes made that claim) but because it was permeated throughout by a sense of religious obligation. Their laws established a code of rights and duties, crimes and punishments, the observation of which was essentially a part of their religion. Transgressions of every sort, from muzzling an ox to murder, were transgressions against God's law not to be settled merely by compromise or the payment of damages. An unseen but omnipresent God was the judge of all they did, and their daily life and conduct was permeated by their fear of arousing his just wrath. Other rituals and forms of magic practised by their neighbours were wholly forbidden. Jewish rabbis had no magical power, no occult knowledge hidden from the people. Their kings had no heavenly mandate to protect them from retribution when they offended. All were subject to God's law as manifested in the unrolling of their history. Other peoples have worshipped angry gods who had to be propitiated with sacrifices both animal and human; these were incalculable and irrational gods. The Jewish God was not angry without cause: he had a stern moral code, clear and comprehensible. If they deviated and were punished they had only themselves to blame. But if they obeyed God through all their vicissitudes they would (and did) survive.

In the dangerous centuries of the Assyrian menace certain men called prophets had appeared among them. They were neither magicians nor soothsayers nor priests; drawn from all walks of life, from humble shepherds to palace officials, they claimed to speak to the people words inspired by God. The prophets of this period – Amos, Hosea, Isaiah, Jeremiah – began to speak of God as a universal power; he was no longer the God of Israel alone but the God of all nations, speaking to Israel as to a chosen (though erring) people. These prophets foretold the wrath of God not merely, as their predecessors had done, for idolatry and neglect of outward observances, but for hypocrisy and spiritual pride, for social and moral sins – injustice, exploitation, lack of charity. But those who fed the hungry, succoured the poor, protected the defenceless, would never themselves lack bread or shelter. Nothing in their religion at this time suggested a life after death. Their righteousness and its reward would be of this world.

Before the Babylonian captivity the Jews already possessed the Books of Moses which contained the law and the sayings of the earlier prophets – the writings which would become known as the Law (Torah) and the Prophets. In Babylon, with its long-standing traditions of scholarship and good libraries, they experienced a great revival of faith. The visionary prophecies of Ezekiel date from this time, and the second part of Isaiah – called the Deutero-Isaiah Chaps 40–66. (The Book of Daniel is of a later period and was attached to the Babylonian exile for prestige reasons.) In exile they studied their ancient writings, thought deeply of their traditions and experiences, discussed these things with Babylonian sages and began to compare texts and set their sacred books in order. The work was only completed after their liberation and the rebuilding of Jerusalem, but a colony of their most learned men – a kind of unofficial university – continued in Babylon, for almost a thousand years longer, revered and consulted as a principal source of Jewish learning.

IV

In Greece, towards the end of the second millennium a new civilization emerged. It was once thought that Dorian invaders from the north destroyed Homeric Greece. More recent archaeological and linguistic research suggests that internal revolt stimulated by such calamities as flood, famine and plague as well as the resentment of the unprivileged, brought down the rule of kings and warriors. Their ruined strongholds – Mycaenae, Argos, Tiryns – became the slum tenements of a rebellious, impoverished people fighting for the essentials of life, until with the passage of time a new ruling class appeared.

Sparta, founded about the ninth century BC, was an oligarchy, governed in time of peace by a senate of fifty members, and in time of war by two kings, elected for life, but exercising power only in war. Very early the Spartans overwhelmed the neighbouring Messenians, an agricultural people, who became in all but name their slaves. The neighbouring peoples of Argos and Arcadia, who were also subdued, fared only slightly better. The Spartan youth, bred under a harsh discipline, were indoctrinated with a conviction of their superiority to all outsiders. They boasted that their city had no walls; its citizens were its defence.

Meanwhile the Greeks of Attica sought freedom and adventure at sea. They made settlements on the Ionian Isles, while other Greek seafarers colonized the Cyclades and the coast of Asia Minor. By the eighth century Greeks from Euboea had established trading links with Italy and a permanent settlement on Ischia. Adventure, seafaring and commerce went together.

The art of writing, submerged in the Dark Age, was rediscovered. Poetry came back without the help of writing, for poetry was sung. It began about the ninth century with the *Iliad*, the *Homeric Hymns* in honour of the gods and – a little later – the *Odyssey*. Stories, ballads and epics, some new, some recovered from a buried past, were sung over all Greece and in the Greek settlements of Asia Minor and Italy.

The eighth century saw the beginnings of the city-state, the *polis*, which would be the central institution of Greek society. Theories of government, morality and justice were keenly debated. There was a new impetus to compete in the arts, in music, in poetry, in athletic skills.

At Delphi, where the lower slopes of Parnassus dipped steeply to the sea, and the great eagles swept wing-wide over the ravine, a noble shrine was dedicated to Apollo. Here his oracle, speaking through the lips of a priestess, enigmatically answered the questions of pilgrims from every part of Greece.

Other cults revived, or survived, elsewhere. Not far from Athens, at Eleusis, the Eleusinian mysteries were annually celebrated in honour of the goddess Demeter. The formidable Dionysus, god of fertility, reached Greece from the outer region of Thrace. The frenzied women who surged about him – the Maenads – tore kids in pieces, and wound serpents in their hair. Yet he was a god much beloved of women, the downtrodden sex; he responded to that yearning for the irrational and uncontrolled which persists in all societies.

Zeus, the father of the gods was celebrated at the Games held in his honour in the valley of Olympia; these began early in the eighth century, took place every four years and continued until they were abolished by the emperor Theodosius in AD 394 as being a pagan orgy, unfit for the Christian world. The Games were not, in the modern sense, a sporting event. They were contests carried out with religious intent and intensity. The victors were crowned and glorified, the vanquished despised and humiliated. Visiting foreigners –

the Egyptians and the Jews for instance – thought the contests barbarous.

But the Games at Olympia and the oracle of Delphi were the binding forces of the Greeks. They needed such forces. Their country was surrounded and infiltrated by the sea, the coast was rock bound, the fertile land divided by high, barren mountain ranges. Their rivers were angry torrents for a few months in the year and beds of dry boulders for the rest. Their civilization, which would become one of the greatest in the world, was fragmented between small, jealous, rival states. But a spirit of reverence, or rivalry, or curiosity, drew them from all regions to make offerings at Delphi, and the pride of each city in its strong young men drew them to compete at Olympia.

Theirs was not, like Egypt, with its regular flooding of the Nile, an easy land to cultivate. It was more difficult than Mesopotamia, where two great rivers and organized irrigation had solved the water problem. No such general organization was possible in Greece. Each farmer must clear and cultivate his rocky acres as best he could, and make his own provision against drought and storm. The peasants were self-reliant and independent. In their villages as later in their cities, they tended to oppose authority that had no mandate from the citizens. It was not in their nature to be docile.

They grew wheat and barley, olives and vines, but toil was hard and the pressure of a growing population on the land was heavy. Within reach of the coast, fish was a staple diet and plentiful. Further inland the thin soil was easily exhausted, the sparse vegetation over-grazed. Their surplus young men would be sent out (not always willingly) to find a living elsewhere. Greek colonization was not an adventure but a necessity.

A farmer on the slopes of Mount Helicon, about 700 BC, made a new kind of poetry out of his labours. Hesiod, in the poem called *Works and Days*, describes his hard life with its rare days of rest, many anxieties, and rewarding moments of joy. He follows the rhythm of the year from autumn sowing to summer's plenty:

Take heed, what time thou hearest, high in the clouds, the crane
Calling her yearly call, for plough time come again,
Crying that the rains of winter once more are nearing now,
Bitter her voice to his hearing that hath no team to plough.

But when the artichoke flowers – when with quick quivering wings
Through the heavy heat of summer the shrill cicada sings . . .
Then in a great rock's shadow, with milk-bread, let me lie,
With biblian wine, and milk from goats just going dry,
And flesh of an uncalved heifer, fed in a forest glade . . .
With a bellyful within me, sipping at my ease
The fire-red wine, and turning to face the western breeze.[4]

New temples rose in honour of the gods. New cities sprang up, their young men full of confidence and energy. Cities commanding the coast like Corinth and Megara, turned their aggressive energy to commerce overseas. Megara founded among other colonies, Byzantium on the Bosphorus. The Corinthians built a slipway four miles long across the isthmus which divided the Aegean from the Ionian sea, so that goods and vessels could be dragged across. (More than two thousand years later, in 1893, the Corinth canal was opened.)

Soon Greek colonies appeared on all the Mediterranean coasts. Cumae, founded from Chalcis, was the first in Italy. It was soon followed by Tarentum, a Spartan colony, though later famed for most un-Spartan luxury. Colonies throve in Sicily – at Syracuse, Gela, Messina, Akragas. Other colonies on the Black Sea had access to the rich harvests of the Lower Danube and South Russia, whence they acquired much needed grain to sell in Greece.

The North African coast was another tempting site. As the Phoenicians already dominated the western Mediterranean from Carthage, the Greeks looked towards the decayed kingdom of Egypt, now a tributary of the Assyrian empire. The seat of government was at Sais in the Delta where Neko I reigned as the first king of the Saite or XXVIth dynasty, by gracious permission of the Syrian emperor Ashurbanipal. His son and successor Psammetichus I (663–609) liberated himself from Assyrian power and planned to restore the ancient culture of Egypt. The so-called Saite revival was a gallant and not altogether unsuccessful effort to recreate the architecture, the art and the literature of the Old Kingdom. His son, Neko II (609–594), planned to restore the territories of the ancient empire of Egypt. In this he failed, but at least he successfully defended his existing frontier, and gained a certain military glory from defeating King Josiah of Judah at the battle of Megiddo. We owe to Herodotus the two most interesting facts about Neko II: he planned to link the Nile to the Red Sea by a canal – in this he failed – and he sent a Phoenician expedition to circumnavigate Africa. They sailed down the Red Sea and eventually returned through the Pillars of Hercules, having made a number of interesting observations, though few believed their story that for some part of their journey they had seen the sun shining in the north.

Some years after Neko's death the Greeks established a colony in Cyrenaica and utterly defeated the reigning Pharaoh when he tried to expel them. But his successor, the bluff and genial Amasis (568–526) saw profit in the intruders, made them welcome, encouraged his people to trade with them, himself acquired a Greek wife to take an honoured place in his harem, and sent offerings to the temple of Apollo at Delphi. He had his reward while living in the renewed prosperity of Egypt, and after death was immortalized in the friendly pages of Herodotus.

Greek enterprise was by now causing serious alarm to the maritime Phoenicians, who had long regarded themselves as masters of the Mediterranean. The Greeks, with the multiplication of their colonies, were capturing all the markets. They exported wine, oil and perfumes, bronzes and pottery, and brought home metal from the mines of the Appenines, salt fish, leather and pelts from the Black Sea, and supplies of grain wherever they could get them. Yet they rarely ventured far from the coasts of the Mediterranean, still less into the dangerous unknown ocean at the world's end. Their trade with the north – for they knew and prized the amber of the Baltic – went overland: the northern barbarians brought their goods down by the river routes to Greek trading stations on the Black Sea.

Though less bold than the Phoenicians, the Greeks were good seamen. They learnt to navigate the dangerous currents of the Hellespont and already by the seventh century were building ships for the Black Sea trade, broad and low in the water, which would not easily capsize.

The Phoenicians meanwhile strengthened their flourishing colony at Carthage, established bases on Malta and Minorca, founded Gades (Cadiz) in southern Spain and held their own in the western Mediterranean. But the Greeks were ahead of them in gaining a hold on the rich fisheries and fine harbour of Massilia. The Greeks in their literature stigmatised the Phoenicians as crafty, grasping and unscrupulous. Doubtless the Phoenicians said the same of the Greeks, but they were to be the losers in the end, and their words have perished. Such are the accidental injustices of recorded history.

About this time the Greeks began to make advances in astronomy, influenced by the Babylonians with whom they had contact through Asia Minor. Thales (c.636–546) who made observations of the stars by which, on a clear night, mariners could steer with tolerable accuracy, came from Miletus in Asia Minor; so did his near contemporary Anaximander who is credited with drawing the first map of the inhabited world. In the next century Pythagoras (c.531 –497) discovered the numerical ratios between notes in music, applied mathematics to nature and conceived of a numerical interpretation of the physical world.

Meanwhile Greek craftsmen made important practical advances. By the sixth century the potter's wheel was already widely known – in Egypt and Sumeria, as in China. The Greeks took it from their neighbours, but the subtle and complex technique of their black figured vases was their own invention. Here technical ingenuity went hand in hand with an incomparable sense of form: craftsmen and artists combining to produce works of art which were also important articles of commerce.

The Greeks abounded in practical inventions – the bellows, the lathe and, in seamanship, the anchor. An unknown Greek farmer invented the oil press which at once simplified and increased the production of olive oil, a basic necessity of life.

Quite early Greek craftsmen discovered that accurate and exacting work was better done by a man seated on a bench and working at a table than by one squatting on the ground. This improvement in technique was in course of time taken over from the Greeks by the peoples of western and northern Europe. It was rejected by the older, more conservative civilizations of Egypt, the Middle East and India.

Among the Greeks, arts, crafts, sciences and literature advanced together. But at first most of the pioneers came from Asia Minor and the neighbouring islands. The island of Lesbos contributed poets; here Sappho and Alcaeus flourished. He was the first lyric poet of Greece; most of his poems have been lost and he is remembered chiefly through the gentle genius of the Roman poet, Horace, who knew his work and used his rhythm: the Alcaic stanza. Sappho, the first woman poet of the West, has been more fortunate. Enough of her work has survived to reveal her as a writer in whom an intense concentration of sensibility finds expression in strong simple words, defying effective translation:

Moon's set, and Pleiads;
Midnight goes by;
The hours pass onward;
Lonely I lie.

or

All things thou bringest, Hesper, that the bright Dawn did part –
Sheep and goat to the fold, and the child to the mother's heart.[5]

In Asia Minor, behind the line of Greek colonies on the coast, a new kingdom had arisen, the kingdom of Lydia friendly to the Greeks and shedding its influence on them in music ('soft Lydian airs') and sport and possibly in philosophic thought. The Lydians were rich, too, from the gold and silver sands of the river Pactolus, gold and silver which merged in the friction of the water into the alloy called electrum. A king of Lydia (it was probably Gyges in the seventh century) proclaimed that an ingot of electrum of a specific weight, bearing his authenticating stamp, was negotiable money – the first in the West.

The idea spread fast, and soon the clumsy ingots gave place to silver coins, easier to handle and more beautiful. The mainland Greeks, who worked their own silver mines at Lauriun, preferred silver to electrum. Even Croesus, the last king of Lydia, abandoned the ingots of electrum and minted gold and silver coins instead. By the middle of the sixth century nearly all Greek city states were minting their own coinage – usually silver or bronze. The Spartans held aloof: they claimed to live on their own self-sufficient agriculture cultivated by the helots, and to despise the corruption of money and trade. This was a pose. The cleverest of them were quick to learn every trick and subterfuge by which they could get their hands on other people's coinage.

The Greeks were by no means united among themselves. Although all alike made offerings and pilgrimages to Delphi, and although hostilities were always suspended for the Olympic Games, the city states fought each other vigorously for possession of fertile land. These early wars gave them experience of organized operations by sea and land. Because the Greeks were as practical and ingenious about fighting as about any other craft, they evolved efficient warships and, on land, the close infantry formation known as the phalanx: developments which, at a later date, preserved the independence of Greece. But the wars, which in time gave place to a balance of armed, suspicious neutrality, left a dangerous legacy.

No nation in the ancient world repudiated the conception of slavery, and the enslavement of prisoners of war was its crudest form. The Greeks of the eighth century for the most part worked with their own hands; Greek cities (with the exception of Sparta) did not in their early days base their system on forced labour. Yet by the end of the sixth century most of them had become dependent on slaves.

There was more than one kind of slavery. The more fortunate slaves were employed as household servants, even in such trusted positions as stewards and teachers; in humbler families, they shared domestic tasks and family life with their masters. But there were others (by far the majority) who worked under compulsion on the land, on public works or – worst of all – in the mines. Domestic slaves were part of the household, the *oikos*, the basic social unit of Greece – the word from which we get our loaded nineteenth-century word 'economy', which in Greece meant the ordering of a household. Slaves in the *oikos* had a home, had customary rights, and may well have been better-off than the overworked, underpaid, easily dismissed skivvies in the free societies of the last century.

No Greek at that time, no Roman later, and few indeed in the world before the eighteenth century of our own era, thought slavery wrong: regrettable sometimes, if masters were needlessly cruel, but not morally wrong. So there grew up in Greece, among independent self-reliant citizens who valued freedom above all, a large population who did the heaviest and most unpleasant tasks – street-cleaning, building, mining, quarrying – who had no freedom and were always ripe for treason and revolt. The Spartan ruling class, bred from childhood to be a master-race, dealt ferociously with helot revolts. Conditions were generally better in the more complex, sensitive, and intelligent world of Athens, or among the subtle, rich Corinthians. Yet every Greek city-state depended on slavery, and the great and gifted nation which gave to the West the concept of government by agreement and the people's will was itself a confederation of slave-owning states.

Round the Mediterranean shores, a kind of stability had by now been achieved between Greeks and Phoenicians. The situation was more complex on the Italian mainland, where, in the south, Greek colonies had multiplied: Cumae the earliest, then Tarentum – the sole colony founded by Sparta – later Paestum and Heraclea. But the Greeks were not the only founders of cities in Italy; soon they confronted rivals. These were the masterful and gifted Etruscans, who were long settled in Italy but not native born. Before they came the inhabitants seem to have been simple pastoral folk content with huts of mud and wattle and far behind the natives of north western Europe in building skill. The Etruscans appeared in Italy about 1000 BC. They were accomplished smiths who could work iron as well as bronze. By the time the Greeks began to settle in the south, the Etruscans intermingling with and dominating the natives had already spread from the Arno to the Tiber through fertile country with mountains rich in mineral ores.

Like the Greeks, they were divided into city-states, often hostile to each other. Like the Greeks they were a sea-going people having outposts on Corsica and Elba. Their mineral wealth was the source of their prosperity, they had copper, lead and tin, and above all iron: modern economic historians estimate that they exported an average of 10,000 to 12,000 tons yearly for about four centuries. They traded the precious ore to Greece, Carthage, Egypt and the Middle East. They received in return gold, silver, ivory and the prized vases of Greece. The gold, silver and ivory they kept mostly for themselves but they exported some of the Greek vases, no doubt at a great profit, to the tribal chieftains of southern Gaul, who thus early showed the aesthetic discrimination we have come to associate with France.

The Etruscans understood luxurious living. They were skilled craftsmen in precious metals and in bronze, expert also in jewelry. Their most famous work in bronze is the lean, muscular Capitoline Wolf, a marvel of simplified form, which became – by an odd chance of history – the symbol of their enemy and destroyer, Rome. But they were distinguished also for lesser luxury arts, fine textiles and elegant leather shoes. Like the Egyptians they believed in keeping their dead happy and few peoples created more convivial tombs. Married couples recline in effigy, side by side on their sarcophagus, bedizened with jewelry and happily smiling as though at a banquet. The surrounding walls of the tomb are often painted with pictures of dancers, flute-players, and grotesque demon masks. Later, when Etruscan power was threatened, their tombs became more gloomy, as they do also in Egypt where the later tombs emphasize the fears of the nether world rather than the pleasures of this one.

So much for the rich, but Etruscan wealth was built on a large population of peasant labourers and captive slaves. Their enemies, the Romans, later gave them a bad name for greed and cruelty which may well have been exaggerated, but it is certain, at least, that they enjoyed gladiatorial combats, and bequeathed the bloodthirsty idea to the Romans.

The Etruscans did not care for rivals either on sea or land. They founded a colony at Capua to keep a check on the Greeks at Cumae; they raided the Greek coastal colonies, and extended their masterful dominion over a petty confederation of pastoral villages on hills overlooking the Tiber, the future city of Rome. Later this Etruscan occupation was to be dramatized in Roman history as the rule of the Tarquins. It could well have been unpleasant while it lasted but at least the Etruscans brought more advanced techniques with them. They paved the forum, began to build a road, the Via Sacra, laid the foundations of the temple of Jupiter on the Capitol, improved the crops by irrigation and gave Rome its first effective drainage by building the *Cloaca Maxima* which is still in use.

They pressed hard against the Greeks but were defeated by land near Cumae and by sea off Syracuse. Thereafter they ceased to be a danger, withdrew from their Roman outpost (*c.*509 BC) but maintained their declining power for another century in the region which they had first settled and made their own. The Romans, tentatively at first, then more resolutely, began to enlarge their boundaries when they and the Etruscans alike were assailed from the north by the incursions of a formidable fighting people, the Gauls. Rome was almost captured but rallied from the disaster. The Etruscans were fatally weakened.

While the Italian peninsula was the scene of Greek–Etruscan rivalry and the early expansion of Rome, another formidable power had arisen in the Middle East. About 549 BC Cyrus the chief of a Median clan, made himself master of the mountain kingdom of the Medes. Gifted with outstanding powers of leadership he planned to unite the known world. He, or his trusted lieutenants, overthrew or brought under control an empire that extended from the Punjab to the eastern shores of the Mediterranean. He conquered first the rich kingdom of Lydia, then seized on the Greek colonies of Asia Minor, but he did not yet attack the Greek mainland or the islands for he had no fleet.

Next he brought the Phoenician coastal cities and all Palestine under his sway, then conquered Babylon and its empire (c.538). The Jews averred that Belshazzar, the vain-glorious deputy left in command at Babylon, had blasphemously drunk from a holy vessel stolen from their temple, and had then seen in terror the fingers of a hand appear and foretell his doom in the writing on the wall. They had cause to see the hand of God in the overthrow of Babylon; for Cyrus, a conqueror of generosity and vision, encouraged them to return to Jerusalem and rebuild the temple of Solomon.

Cyrus now ruled over the largest empire in the West. He planned to conquer Egypt but was forestalled by death while quelling rebellious tribes near the Caspian sea. He was buried near to his favourite palace, Pasargadae in the heart of Persia, where his tomb still stands foursquare and solitary on the vast plateau, the great arch of the sky above and far off on the horizon the Zagros mountains. His son, Cambyses, with the help of his Phoenician tributaries, built a fleet, attacked Egypt by sea and land and added it to the Persian empire which now stretched from the Nile to the Indus and the Jaxartes. A huge, well-disciplined army and a network of communications enabled the Great King to command supplies from every province and a navy largely manned by Phoenicians.

What hope of resistance had the Greek Islands or the vulnerable mainland? When Lydia, Babylon and Egypt had fallen, could Greece survive?

V

Five of the great founders of religious systems and ethical codes lived·in the seventh and sixth centuries BC. Zoroaster in Persia, Buddha and Mahavira in India, Confucius and Lao Tsu in China. The Jews also experienced a renaissance of their faith.

Zarathustra – or Zoroaster as the Greeks called him – lived probably in the seventh century, but the traditions of his life are so confused that some have attempted to place him as early as the tenth, or even the fifteenth century BC. His teaching was adopted and spread throughout the Persian empire from the time of Cyrus onwards, and became the official religion of the state about 500 BC. The teaching of Zoroaster was enshrined in writings called the *Zend Avesta*; much has been irrecoverably lost, and the earliest surviving manuscripts date from the fourth century AD. Inevitably therefore our knowledge is incomplete. But it is certain at least that his teaching gave moral force and spiritual meaning to the age-old fire-worship and nature-worship of the Persians, which in the hands of their priests, the Magi, had degenerated into a corrupt superstition. He recognized in their traditional god Ahura Mazda or Ormuzd, the eternal god, the First and the Last, the creator of light and the world: the embodiment of the Good and the Right, of an eternal and unchanging morality.

Ahura Mazda, the one true god, gave free-will to his creation, whether men or spirits. A powerful spirit, Ahriman, used his free-will to choose evil and to mislead lesser spirits and many men. Zoroaster explained the existence of Evil, in a world created by a god who was wholly good, by defining Evil as negative, a refusal to accept the Good. Man, he taught, is a compound of body, conscience and will; he is free to reject good and accept evil but in doing so he loses his chance of immortality.

Some of the more pleasing elements of ancient Persian fire-worship were incorporated in the teaching of Zoroaster, or retained by his later followers. Thus the realm of light (the domain of Ahura Mazda) is defended by an army of 486,000 stars against Ahriman, who will – at the end of the world – be overthrown. Again, the Fravashi, invisible winged guardians of men, found their way into Zoroastrian belief. These winged spirits, mid-way between gods and men, were common also to the Assyrians and Babylonians and passed on some of their characteristics to the angels – God's messengers – of Jewish belief, and so to the Christian West.

Zoroaster condemned outright all the cruder forms of idolatry, all fertility rites, and the multiplicity of lesser gods. He taught an ethical code which emphasized justice and compassion, since all created things are alike children of god. His doctrine of free-will, however confused by the idea of parallel powers of Good and Evil, imposed on men the necessity of making a choice between right and wrong and of accepting the consequences of their actions; it encouraged a sense of responsibility and the cultivation of the judgement. The priesthood – the Magi – continued to officiate at their fire-temples but acquired a new reputation for wisdom, and seem to have maintained a higher standard of learning and conduct than other pagan priesthoods. Zoroastrianism continued as the official religion of Persia for nearly twelve hundred years, until it was swept away by Muslim conquerors in the eighth century of our era. A few small groups of believers persisted in Persia, but the greater number fled to India, there to preserve the elements of Zoroaster's religion under the name of Parsees.

While the teaching of Zoroaster took hold in the Persian empire, the Jews were encouraged by Cyrus and his successors to return to Jerusalem. A minority of them courageously did so. After the rebuilding of the temple and the city – a process which stretched over at least a century – came a new and firmer discipline, a new way of life. It is convenient, if not absolutely certain owing to the confusion of records, to attribute the rebuilding of the city to Nehemiah (c.445 BC) and the reforms to Ezra (c.438), a leader of uncompromising views with great powers of organization. Ezra insisted on the annulment of all marriages with foreign women. He knew, too well, from past history that wives taken from heathen peoples brought with them the worship of false gods and passed them on to their children. Only the utmost rigidity on this point would prevent further corruption.

Until the time of the Babylonian exile the temple of Jerusalem had been the only place of common worship. Ezra instituted synagogues in towns and villages, where the people could meet regularly and listen to the reading and explanation of the Scriptures by the more thoughtful or pious of their community, men who would later come to be called 'Rabbi' or master. The Rabbis were not, in the religious sense, priests. The priests served the temple only; with the Jewish revival they increased in number (though not necessarily in learning or virtue) and became an important part of the establishment of the capital. Local religious worship was a form of communal discussion and debate. Only at the national level, in Jerusalem, was the atmosphere authoritarian.

Under the influence of the learning acquired in the libraries of Babylon, Jewish scholars were by this time sifting and setting in order the legends, histories, prophesies, songs and sayings which had accumulated over a thousand years. The Psalms, the visions and the warnings of the prophets were carefully collected. From the sixth century onwards these writings were studied, expounded and learnt by heart. There was nothing secret or occult about this study.

All who could read recognized obedience to God as their first duty, and followed the precepts laid down for them. The Jewish scholars who remained in Babylon continued their studies until they established an authoritative text. This tradition of textual and verbal knowledge was later handed on to the two religions which derived from Judaism: Christianity and Islam. They too became 'the people of the book' – the New Testament and the Koran.

Reading and learning the Scriptures, keeping the festivals appointed in memory of past sufferings and mercies, going on pilgrimage to Jerusalem for the Passover: these things gave the Jews a solidarity and coherence out of all proportion to their material strength. These things enabled them, in years to come, to survive as a people through disasters compared to which the Babylonian exile was a holiday excursion. The darkest times lay still ahead: the fifth century found them at peace, an autonomous province of the Persian empire.

The Jews saw God as universal and omnipotent, concerned in every detail of human action. The supreme spirit conceived of by the followers of the Buddha in India existed beyond time and space, in eternity, and was in no way concerned with the petty process of human history. There was, in a manner of speaking, no god at all in the teaching of the Buddha. His revelation has been described in modern terms as a psychological discovery rather than a moral guide, and his purpose was to free the eternal soul from the temporal body.

He was born Gautama, a prince, or rather a tribal chieftain, from the highlands of north eastern India in about 560 BC. His personal life and his teachings (like those of Zoroaster) are encrusted with legend. The earliest surviving writings about him date from 500 years after his death – somewhat closer than the thousand year gap between Zoroaster's teaching and our surviving records of it. Yet the doubtfulness of our knowledge is immaterial: what the Buddha is *believed* by his followers to have taught is more important than what he may, or may not, have taught himself.

As a young man he was profoundly disturbed by a sudden confrontation with the horrors of age, disease and death. This caused him to flee by night from his father's palace, his wife and new-born son, and to become a wandering beggar in search of peace and the answer to the mystery of human decay.

After years of privation, enlightenment came. In the deer park of Sarnath, near to Varanasi (Benares) in the shade of a beautiful tree, he preached to his disciples the sermon called the Wheel of the Law. It embodied the Four Noble Truths which are the heart of Buddhist teaching: the world is full of suffering, all suffering is caused by desire, renounce desire and you will attain salvation. Salvation is to be reached by the Eightfold Path: right belief, right feeling, right speech, right action, right living, right effort, right memory and right meditation.

Henceforward he was called the Buddha, or 'the Enlightened One'. His enlightenment was inward-looking, concerned neither with the physical world nor with material benevolence; he had made a psychological discovery – that self-knowledge, self-discipline and self-abnegation can annihilate all personal desire and lead to absolute serenity. The ultimate goal was that man should lose himself in the infinite and be released from the cycle of reincarnation which constantly re-imprisoned the soul in the flesh. He would then have attained Nirvana – the perfected state of bliss.

Such hope and belief might seem remote from the poor peasants of India among whom the wandering Buddha lived. But in a scorching climate the idea of peace and an end to struggle has greater attractions than in the cold atmosphere of the West, where people must be active to keep warm. The ascetic serenity of Buddha and his monks appealed to the poor and oppressed among whom they freely moved and whom they tended in sickness.

Buddha rejected caste, though he himself had been born a high-caste warrior. He rejected also the many empty rituals and animal sacrifices of the Hindus. But he and his disciples respected the ascetic hermits and the humble popular shrines which proliferated in India. Buddhism was, from the beginning, a form of mysticism which brought comfort to the poor as well as the rich.

This religion which taught withdrawal from the world and release from personal desires, was very soon modified, like every other religion, to suit its believers. The Buddha was deified: he became one of the many incarnations of Vishnu. Being a god, he could multiply himself indefinitely, and hence the paintings and sculptures of 'the thousand Buddhas' which cheered the hearts of worshippers who feared that one Buddha would not suffice to help all who came to him.

Next, auxiliary helpers were called in: the Boddhisatvas were holy men who voluntarily postponed their own state of selfless bliss to stay in touch with all who needed them in the temporal world.

Buddha had at times instructed his disciples by examples taken from Indian fables. After his death, a myriad popular fables – known as the *Jataka* – were sanctified by the simple method of making Buddha himself the hero, in one or other of his previous incarnations. Since the human soul can be reincarnated in any living creature, this permitted animal fables, in which the Indians delighted, to become tales of the Buddha – the Buddha as a deer, as a hare, as an elephant . . .

The teaching of Buddha was submerged in a flood of loving popular worship. Later, and several times, it was reasserted in a purer form, and became in many different guises one of the most widespread religions of the world. It spread beyond the borders of India, to the mountains of Nepal and Tibet, to China, Japan and the islands of the South East. But in India itself over the centuries it was almost totally submerged in Hinduism.

During the life of the Buddha, and also in North India, another teacher appeared with somewhat similar ideas. Vardhamana Mahavira believed that the human soul was naturally bright and luminous but darkened by *Karma*, the corruptions of human temperament. The aim of man was to get rid of this tarnish by the virtue of his life, though a great number of incarnations might be needed before the shining soul could at last be taken into bliss. This process has been described as 'a theory of cosmic justice' because only a series of rebirths can in the end establish a just account of a man's real world. Believers, who were called Jains, ate no meat, would kill no living creature, even to the smallest insect, and avoided all violence: this at least was the ideal at which they aimed. *Ahimsa*, or absolute non-violence, was their cardinal doctrine. Those who gave up the world to become Jain monks practised standing or sitting motionless for hours, wore no clothing, and frequently starved themselves to death. The Jains however believed that study as well as contemplation was a way towards perfection, and they did not reject caste. Thus they attracted a following among intellectuals and in the merchant communities of India, since merchants are generally pacific people, and literate. Jain monks, as they gradually deviated from the suicidal asceticism of the founder, became scholars and poets and played a valuable part in preserving, and increasing, the literature of India. Though Jainism never extended beyond the borders of India to become a world force like Buddhism, it has remained alive and vigorous to the present time.

Very different from Buddha and Mahavira was their great Chinese contemporary, Kung Fu Tse (*c.*551–479), known to the West as Confucius, a latinized adaptation of his name, first used by the Jesuit missionary Matteo Ricci in the sixteenth century. There was nothing other-worldly in his teaching. It was a code of social conduct, not a passport to the hereafter but rather 'the ethics of a dignified aristocracy'.[6] Born in the state of Lu (in modern Shantung) he survived to old age in a period of great unrest and disorder. But it was also a time rich in art, invention and philosophical speculation, for this period of the Warring States is also known as the age of the 'Hundred Schools' because of the number of philosophers who were then teaching. Aware of his unusual abilities, Confucius hoped in vain that one of the numerous petty rulers among whom China was divided, would employ him as adviser. It did not happen. His biographer (writing, however, about 400 years later) represents him as saying, 'I have not sought fame during my life, but would like to feel that my work would keep my memory green. But alas! my doctrines have never been tested by use, since none of the rulers have been intelligent enough to employ me'. The sage had a posthumous revenge several centuries later when the Han emperors who had pacified and reunited China, made his teachings compulsory reading for all aspirants to state employment: a pre-eminence which (with occasional lapses) they retained until the Maoist Revolution.

Confucius reflects the practical outlook, the respect for elders and for historic tradition which are – or were – characteristic of the Chinese. He believed, a common enough belief in many countries of ancient civilization, that everything had been very much better in the past: in this case the period of the Hsia emperors and of those godlike rulers, the traditional founders of the civilization of China. The Hsia and their predecessors were legends, but to Confucius and his contemporaries – and indeed up to the nineteenth century – their achievements had the authority of history to the educated Chinese.

Confucius has been well described by a modern writer: 'a man evidently of extraordinary force of character, ability and goodness of heart, who, after making himself thoroughly acquainted with the great oral and written tradition of his country, lectured upon it unceasingly in an earnest endeavour to preserve it from neglect'.[7] But he added to this, in the questions and answers that he exchanged with his few devoted disciples, rules for the conduct of private and public life.

The modern western reader may feel that Confucius insists too much on the performance of ceremonial rites and the minutiae of polite manners, but in a period of disorder and change, tradition and ceremony can be of real significance in preserving society. The survival of Chinese culture, through a long and troubled history, owed much to the continuity of these things.

Confucius believed that the educated man – he had no interest in the uneducated – should aim at an ideal of conduct which sounds very much like the western concept of stoicism. He should feel neither fear nor anxiety, be always calm and at ease. But he should also revere Heaven's laws, great men and the wisdom of sages.

The basic doctrines of Confucius are sensible and humane. Loyalty, truth, modesty and respect for tradition are essential. Support and help should be given to the old, love and cherishing care to the young. There should be moderation in all things, excess neither in joy nor grief. Asked by a disciple to sum up his teaching in a word, he said: 'Reciprocity. What you do not wish for yourself do not do to others'. The virtues to be cultivated were humility, magnanimity, sincerity, diligence and courtesy. All his teaching shows a respect for human dignity and a strong vein of common sense. On hearing a wise man praised because he never acted without thinking three times, Confucius said: 'Twice is quite enough'.

His precepts were pre-eminently sensible, but some pupils wanted more: 'Our master's views concerning culture and the outward insignia of goodness, we are permitted to hear but about man's nature and the ways of heaven he will not tell us anything at all'. In other words Confucius would not speculate on mysteries beyond his understanding. The rites and ceremonies established in the past could take care of that. He concentrated on what he most valued in human conduct: the calm self-control of an honourable man.

The genius of the Chinese inclines more to the practical than the speculative. But the period of the Warring States produced at least one school of thought that, like Buddhism, advocated withdrawal from the world. This was Tao-ism. Its teaching is attributed to Lao Tsu, allegedly a contemporary of Confucius, to whom he and his pupils were totally opposed. They could see no virtue in the cultivation of self-control and self-improvement in an irredeemable society. A satirical story describes how Confucius went to Lao Tsu for advice and was told: 'Rid yourself of your arrogance and your lustfulness, your ingratiating manners and your excessive ambition. That is all I have to say to you'.

No such interview ever took place but it illustrates the antagonism of the anti-social Tao-ist outlook to the essentially social Confucian code. The earliest existing biography of Lao Tsu was not written until four centuries later, and it seems more than probable that he was an invented character. But writings exist, collected under his name, which teach the philosophy of Tao-ism. It is closely linked to the worship of nature, identified with Heaven: Heaven which, while appearing to do nothing, does everything. 'Tao' means 'the Way', and 'the Way' seems to be simply the acceptance of life as it is.

> In the pursuit of learning one knows more every day;
> in the pursuit of the Way one does less every day;
> One does less and less until one does nothing at all,
> and when one does nothing at all there is nothing that is undone.

As for rules of government, the people should be kept well-fed, uneducated, and incapable of initiating action.

'There is no disaster greater than not being content', recalled Buddha's advice to conquer desire. But it is not linked in Tao-ism to any apparent hope of purifying the soul. What appears to be advocated is no more than withdrawal from a world where 'the Court is corrupt, the fields are overgrown with weeds, the granaries are empty, yet there are those dressed in finery with swords at their sides, full of food and drink . . .' Confucianism and Tao-ism long existed together, and both had great influence – Tao-ism more especially in later times when it was infused with a more spiritual message by Buddhist missionaries from India.

The widespread belief in *Yin-Yang*, which increasingly permeated Chinese life in the period of the Warring States, also reflected a resigned acceptance. All things in the natural world, it was said, depended on the interaction of a negative element (Yin) and a positive element (Yang). These forces obey their own laws and establish their own harmony. Man, nature and all things in creation are subject to them. It was the age-old doctrine of submission and reconciliation to the rhythms of the universe and may well have helped men and women to endure the dangers and disturbances of the epoch of the Warring States.

Philosophic speculation however continued to flourish, often imbued with a noble idealism greatly at variance with the harshness of the times. Mo-Ti (c.470–391) urged his disciples to seek and obey the will of Heaven; if men would but cultivate mutual love all wars would cease. The philosopher Meng K'o, called Mencius in the West, taught that men were innately good and needed only the right education and circumstances – which good rulers should be able to provide – to live in harmony and peace. (It is very noticeable that Chinese philosophers place great trust in the benevolence of the ruler; this was not often justified.)

The philosophy that triumphed, if it can be dignified by such a name, was the so-called Legalist teaching of which the terrible Shang Yang, the minister who governed the state of Ch'in from 359 to 338 BC, was the principal exponent. Stability was the ideal – not in itself a bad one. But it was to be gained by the suppression of all free opinion, and the destruction of all books which dealt with ideas, and enforced with fearful punishments. Such was the political philosophy which became for a time all powerful in the state of Ch'in, and which made Ch'in by conquest the dominant power in China.

On the shores of the Mediterranean, in a society almost equally restless, philosophies of a different kind had developed – philosophies which fertilized political thought and social conduct in the West for many centuries. Their centre was in Greece and more especially in Athens. But first the Greeks had to defeat the Great King of Persia.

CHAPTER III

———————•———————

CIRCA 500—300 BC

I

THE PERSIAN EMPIRE in the sixth century BC was possibly the largest and probably the·best organized in the world. Cyrus the Great had conquered Mesopotamia, Asia Minor and the eastern littoral of the Mediterranean; his son conquered Egypt. Gandhara in North West India was added by his kinsman and ultimate successor, Darius I, who also conquered Thrace and Macedonia, but failed to quell the barbaric Scythians north of the Black Sea. Mainland Greece with most of the islands remained precariously independent.

Darius I who now ruled from the Nile to the Indus planned to consolidate his power by conquering Greece: a logical intention for a ruler who already controlled Asia Minor, and almost all the eastern Mediterranean through the Phoenician ports and the delta of the Nile. As conquerors the Persians, in comparison with the Assyrians, were not cruel, or at least not after they had conquered. They wisely confined their effective rule to the plains and the cultivated agricultural land, and interfered very little with the nomadic mountain tribes, though they encouraged their adventurous young men to join the cavalry of the imperial army.

By origin a pastoral people, the Persians desired peace and prosperity within their dominions and having little expertise in government left administration largely to their Babylonian subjects who had both experience and skill. Courts of appeal ensured a reasonable standard of official integrity. Government was simplified and trade encouraged by the adoption of a single official language for the whole empire: this was Aramaic, which had long been the *lingua franca* of merchants in the Middle East. An alphabetic script, related to Phoenician usage, was substituted for the old syllabic cuneiform.

Writing was for commerce and for law: the Persian nobility was above such practical matters – they learnt to ride, to shoot and (in theory at least) to speak the truth. Their priests, the Magi, were Medes; their scribes were Babylonian or Elamite. Their commerce was in the competent hands of the Phoenicians, while immigrant Greeks served them as doctors, interpreters and sometimes as artists.

Dynastic quarrels, punctuated by murders, made life at court uneasy for members of the royal family and their favourites, but ordinary people reaped their crops and marketed their merchandise with little disturbance. Trade increased and caravans travelled safely along the well-marked roads from the East to the Persian Gulf. The orderliness of common life was an agreeable contrast to the hazards of the imperial court.

The empire was divided into autonomous provinces governed by satraps, the military commander and principal secretary of each satrapy being appointed by the king. A system of conscripted labour, in rotation and for a set period, ensured the construction and maintenance of the canals and roads which guaranteed communications and water supply. Conscripts were also employed to maintain the palaces and public monuments which glorified the Great King.

The roads which linked the empire were constructed, when possible, in the plains and lowlands, avoiding the difficult mountain regions. Travellers were expected to carry passports or permits stating their right to rations for man and beast at the statutory halting places. The postal service for imperial and official use was marvellously efficient and quick. Herodotus has left a vivid description:

> There is nothing in the world which travels faster than these Persian couriers; the whole idea is a Persian invention and works like this: riders are stationed along the road, equal in number to the number of days the journey takes – a man and a horse for each day. Nothing stops these couriers from covering their allotted stage in the quickest possible time – neither snow, rain, heat nor darkness. The first, at the end of his stage passes his despatch to the second, the second to the third . . . as in the Greek torch race.[1]

The capital of Cyrus had been at Pasargadae; later it was moved to Susa, in southern Iran, the old capital of the Elamites who had flourished in the third millennium and been overwhelmed by the

Assyrians. The king's summer residence was usually at Ecbatana (now Hamadan) the ancient capital of Media, encircled by mountains. It was from the Medes that the Persians derived some of the ceremonial luxury of their court, though they learnt also from Egypt and Assyria.

Darius I (c. 521—486) laid the foundations of the famous palace at Persepolis. Its ruins still proclaim the grandeur of the Achaemenid empire. The majestic columns of the hall where the Great King once gave audience, the huge stone reliefs of Darius, his son and their royal guards – the 'Immortals' – and the procession of tribute bearers, on a suitably smaller scale, marching step by step on the walls of the great staircase: this was public architecture on the grand scale. The vast bull-headed columns, once encased in polished Indian teak, supported coffered ceilings of cedarwood from Lebanon. Gold ornaments adorned the statues and enriched the ceilings. Carpets covered the walls; heavy curtains, gorgeous hangings and a profusion of burnished lamps created an oppressive effect of splendour. Persian art of this epoch is not subtle; it lacks delicacy and variety, but it is matchless in dignity. Builders and craftsmen were brought from every province, as a deliberate policy to enhance the sense of unity in the empire. This too could have been oppressive; there are few individual variations in the sculptured figures which present a series of harmoniously stylized types, impressive by force of repetition.

Conscripted craftsmen must also have been responsible for the rock-carvings commemorating the Achaemenid kings, cut into the limestone crags near Persepolis, and elsewhere. Darius I had himself depicted in relief five hundred feet up on the towering crags of Behistun, with the story of his achievements cut in cuneiform script and in three languages – Old Persian, Babylonian and Elamite. In 1835 an Englishman, Henry Rawlinson, with the help of a Kurdish boy suspended on a rope, managed to copy them all and by careful comparison made a memorable breakthrough in the decipherment of cuneiform.

In lighter moments, Darius and his courtiers played polo, which was already traditional. Order, discipline, wealth, a well-trained army, huge reserves of manpower, and the sea-faring experience of their Phoenician subjects: with all these to support them the Persians appeared invincible. They failed to conquer the Scythians because the Scythians were still a nomadic people, without walled cities, and could therefore resist by retreating, driving their herds before them and harassing the invaders by sudden forays. The Persians recognized that it was pointless to fight a people who could not be brought to pitched battle. Conquering the Greeks would be easier and more profitable.

The Greek cities were by nature competitive rather than co-operative. Apart from their rivalries with each other, many of them were troubled by discontent among their own citizens. The rigid constitution of Sparta, by which the military élite alone became full citizens, was designed to prevent such troubles and to ensure unity of purpose in all decisions. Though irritated by sporadic revolts of the oppressed helots, the Spartans were seldom afflicted by rebellious aspirations among their own citizens.

They contemplated with a sense of superiority the recurrent troubles of Athens, Corinth and other cities where the older landed aristocracy had difficulty in sustaining their power against pressure from below. Furthermore though other cities had brave soldiers, Sparta was the only state which had, at all times, in its ruling citizen body an organized military force ready for action. Thus, as the danger from Persia drew nearer, the Spartans led the way in forming a league of cities to meet it. The policy was sound, but the Spartans were not popular with their fellow Greeks.

The Greek cities were rooted in agriculture; their leading citizens traded in wine and oil or had interests in manufacture and mines but were in the first place landowners. Every city depended in part on its own vines and olives, grain and flocks, but most of the larger cities also imported food. The land from which each city drew its sustenance was unevenly divided. In Athens the *Eupatridae*, the 'well-descended', usually owned large estates. But many Athenians were small farmers, gaining a bare livelihood and burdened by debt. Although they were free men they were excluded by poverty from the privileges of citizenship. In most cities, too, craftsmen, mariners and small traders – free, poor men, immigrants from other regions, without land of their own – were not eligible as citizens. Women, as a matter of course, had no voice in politics – and this was so even for the women of Sparta who, as girls, had done their physical training along with the boys.

In the later seventh and sixth centuries there arose, in one city after another, the so-called 'tyrants', popular leaders who took up the cause of the excluded groups and imposed a more realistic order than the older aristocratic rule. They were the new men for the new situation and have been justly described as 'the essential interlude between aristocracy and democracy'. Some were remarkably successful. Corinth, under the rule of successive tyrants for seventy years, was by the beginning of the sixth century, the most prosperous city in Greece.

Athens at that time was in grave trouble, through the bitter animosity of the people against the nobles who alone wielded political power. A glut of coined money, mistakenly thrown into the economy, raised prices and interest rates and caused the bankruptcy or enslavement of many poor citizens. The situation was saved by Solon, a man whose career had already shown him to be of strong character and good judgement. He was chosen *archon* (chief magistrate) in 594, and given absolute power to remedy a desperate situation. He began by cancelling all debts, thereby enabling poorer citizens and especially the farmers to make a fresh start. He abolished the practice by which men could raise loans by selling themselves into slavery in default of payment. He gave Athenian citizenship to immigrant craftsmen, thus bringing new trades and new labour into the city. Above all he altered the structure of government, so that the *Eupatridae* no longer had the monopoly of power. In future a council of four hundred freely elected every year, was to prepare the programme of legislation which went forward to a general assembly of the citizens. He did not abolish the property qualification for election to the governing body, but he made it low enough to take in most free citizens.

These arrangements, though they caused some dismay to the *Eupatridae*, worked tolerably well for over thirty years. During that time Athens drew ahead of Corinth and became the acknowledged centre of Greek pottery manufacture and export. But Solon's measures mitigated only for a time the recurrent distress of the farmers. One reason for their burden of debt was the lack of a stable currency, and hence of the means to save money against bad times. Peisistratus, a popular leader – three times tyrant of Athens between 560 and 527 BC – had interests in the silver mines of Thrace, and, nearer to Athens, in the rapidly developing mines of Laurium. He successfully undertook to provide a reliable silver coinage which made Athens the richest city in Greece, and enabled farmers to sell their surplus and build up reserves.

Soon, however, the Persians overran Thrace, the resources of Laurium proved inadequate and Athens was again in difficulties. Cleisthenes (c. 510 BC) divided the citizens into ten tribes based on domicile, abolishing an older classification by family descent which excluded the most recent immigrants. He enlarged Solon's annually elected advisory council (usually called the *boulè*) to 500, and allowed no citizen to be elected to it more than twice; in this way he hoped to increase the number of citizens familiar with public affairs. Herodotus called this 'taking the people into partnership'.

But the system gave too much opportunity to ambitious men with persuasive tongues and provided too little safeguard against the effects of popular emotion. It could only function well in a small city-state and Athens was probably already too large. But for a time it worked, and gave to the Athenians a civic pride and a passion for political argument greater than that of any other people in Greece.

By now the Persians had occupied Thrace, added Macedonia to their dominions, and were in control of Asia Minor and most of the Ionian Islands. Physical force rather than intellectual energy would be needed to repel them when they chose to invade Greece.

In these conditions the Spartans, as the leading military power, set out to unite the Greeks. Profiting by the disorders of the smaller city-states, they systematically liberated them from their native tyrants, and took them into the alliance which they named the Peloponnesian League. It was a sound idea, or would have been if the Spartans had been more conciliatory and less domineering. Few of their allies liked them, and the unconcealed rivalry between Sparta and Athens was a critical weakness of the league.

Thus when the Greeks of Asia Minor and the Ionian Islands rebelled against Persian rule, Sparta refused help but Athens gave it – very mistakenly according to Herodotus, who was wise after the event. Athenian intervention kindled the wrath of the Persians without saving the Ionians, who were defeated after five years' vain resistance. The Great King of Persia reorganized his forces against the mainland and, in the late summer of the year 490 BC, disembarked his army in Attica on the plain of Marathon about twenty-five miles from Athens.

The Athenian infantry, the highly trained, heavily armed hoplites marched out against them. A contingent from Plataea joined them, but the Spartans, whose help they expected, had religious scruples and could not come before full moon. This delay lost them their part in the victory.

The Persian forces far outnumbered the Athenians, but made too little allowance for the skill and daring of their general, Miltiades, whom they had encountered before. They were also wholly unprepared for the speed and weight of the hoplite attack. Yet they put up a powerful resistance and almost broke the Greek centre. But the Greeks overran and scattered the wings of the Persian army, and closed in to overwhelm the centre. The Spartans reached Marathon to find the battle over, the Athenians and Plataeans triumphant, 6000 Persians dead on the plain and the rest embarked on their ships and escaping by sea.

This was only a prelude. The Persian empire, with almost unlimited resources and manpower, would strike again. But Marathon destroyed the legend of Persian invincibility. Herodotus describes the infantry at Marathon as 'the first Greeks, so far as I know, to charge at a run, and the first who dared to look without flinching at Persian dress and the men who wore it; for until that day, no Greek could hear even the word "Persian" without terror'.[2] Marathon raised morale as nothing else could have done, and gave the Greeks an interlude in which to build up their defences. The Spartans, again taking the lead in organization, brought together a league of thirty cities, and the Athenians built a fleet to defend the coast.

In 480, Xerxes, the son of Darius, advanced with an army which Herodotus reckoned at five million – an unlikely figure but one which indicates the terror that it caused. The Persians were supported by a fleet of which three hundred Phoenician triremes was probably the most formidable part. They crossed the Hellespont on a pontoon bridge while, to save a long and exposed sea passage, Xerxes had a canal driven through the isthmus of Mount Athos.

Three hundred Spartans, vainly attempting to hold the key pass of Thermopylae, were outflanked by treachery and died fighting to the last man. The Persians came on by land and sea. The Athenians left their beloved city to the mercy of the invaders who landed and burnt the Acropolis – then, by guile, lured the Persian fleet into the narrows between the island of Salamis and the mainland, where Greek ships cut off their escape. The heavily loaded Persian vessels and Phoenician triremes with their three banks of oars were at a disadvantage against the smaller, swifter Greek vessels. With no room to manoeuvre, they rammed each other in trying to escape and were almost all destroyed. Xerxes, in sullen rage, escaped with the remnant leaving his army to prosecute the war by land. Next year under Spartan leadership, the Greeks utterly defeated the Persian army at Plataea.

In the afterglow of victory the Greek genius reached maturity. Not for nearly two thousand years would the western world again produce such a concentration of thinkers, teachers, poets, artists and craftsmen as those who sprang up in Greece and were drawn to Athens in the fifth century. Italy of the Renaissance is the only parallel. No such brilliance issued out of, or took root in, Sparta, yet without Spartan leadership and organization in the war there would have been no victory at Plataea, no long relief from the Persian danger and neither time nor opportunity for the incomparable glory of Athens. The union of Sparta and Athens achieved victory and the essential conditions for a golden age; their enmity brought it to a premature and unnecessary end.

As the immediate danger from Persia receded, the Athenians resented the Spartan claim to pre-eminence and abandoned their allegiance to the Peloponnesian League. Confident in their fleet, they sought instead to draw the Ionian Islands and cities into their protection, to create a maritime power strong enough to challenge both the Persians and their Phoenician tributaries.

Initially successful, this Delian League (as it was called from its headquarters on the island of Delos) failed because the Athenians alienated their allies by dictatorial treatment, and were faced by rebellion and desertion when they most needed help in their ultimate war against Sparta. But this came later.

In the middle years of the fifth century, the Athenians found a great leader in Pericles, who believed in sea power as the principal defence and strength of Athens. He also believed in the intelligence of his fellow citizens and their right to greater participation in the government. Thus he developed the powers of the popular assembly and of the local courts of justice whose members were chosen from a wide cross-section of the people. He supported the policy of increased sea power and the Delian League, founded numerous small Athenian settlements at strategic points to act as permanent garrisons, and completed the building of the Long Walls which extended from Athens to the Piraeus, ensured access to the sea in case of a siege by land, and enclosed enough land to receive and feed refugees from the surrounding country in time of invasion.

Although he was re-elected fifteen times by popular vote to the office of *strategos* (literally, general – but in effect much more than that) he had not the obvious attributes of a popular leader: eloquent certainly and impressive, but reserved and almost cold in manner. The comic poets called him 'the Olympian' and an air of aloof distinction is the immediate impression given by surviving representations of his noble and fastidious face.

But under him, Athenian democracy worked. Speech was free; no coercion or persecution was used against his opponents. Citizens gave their votes and raised their voices freely and frequently on public affairs. He did not blunt the edge of his natural authority by frequent intervention, but kept his powerful eloquence for crucial occasions when the people looked to him for guidance.

His contemporary, Thucydides, unsuccessful general and great historian, who had begun in aristocratic opposition to Pericles, ended by recognizing his unique qualities:

> Pericles, because of his position, his intelligence and his known integrity, could respect the liberty of the people and at the same time hold them in check. It was he who led them rather than they who led him, and since he never sought power from any wrong motive, he was under no necessity of flattering them: in fact he was so highly respected that he was able to speak angrily to them and to contradict them. When he saw that they were going too far in a mood of over-confidence, he would bring them back to a sense of their dangers; and when they were discouraged for no good reason he would restore their confidence. So, in what was nominally a democracy, power was really in the hands of the first citizen.[3]

Five hundred years after the death of Pericles, when Greece had long been a province of the Roman empire, Plutarch singled out as his greatest achievement the temples and public buildings with which he had enriched Athens. He saw in them 'the sole testimony that the tales of the ancient power and glory of Greece are no mere fables . . . the buildings arose, as imposing in their sheer size as they were inimitable in the grace of their outlines, since the artists strove to excel themselves in the beauty of their workmanship. And yet the most wonderful thing about them was the speed with which they were completed. Each of them, men supposed, would take many generations to build, but in fact the entire project was carried through in the high summer of one man's administration . . . Each one possessed a beauty which seemed vulnerable the moment it was born and at the same time a youthful vigour which makes them appear to this day as if they were newly built'.[4]

The nineteen centuries which have passed over Athens since Plutarch stood on the Acropolis have left fallen columns and shattered walls where Plutarch saw temples, gates and porches. Yet it was possible until recently, as one ascended through the great gateway of the Propylaeum, and as the sun touched the columns of the Parthenon, to feel with Plutarch that 'a bloom of eternal freshness hovers over these works as if some ageless vitality had been breathed into them'. Modern pollution may have put an end to that vision.

Pericles stands among the few great men of history whose aesthetic and intellectual gifts were equal to his political insight. He gathered about him, as his personal friends, philosophers, poets and artists; learnt from the philosopher Anaxagoras to believe in a higher intelligence which governs the universe; conversed with Sophocles, and found in Pheidias the inspired architect and sculptor to design and supervise his building programme.

Under Pericles the civic life of Athens, at once popular and ceremonial, achieved unique beauty. The Acropolis was the most splendid in Greece; the city was enriched with arcaded walks, gymnasia, noble trophies and fine statues. Everywhere artists and craftsmen were at work, not merely for private patrons but for the public pleasure. The Greek theatre reached its highest achievement: the aged Aeschylus was still writing when Pericles came to power; Sophocles was at his height; the younger and more controversial Euripides was approaching maturity. Soon after the death of Pericles, Aristophanes would use his brilliant wit and bitter satirical gift to raise laughter in the shadow of defeat and death. The theatre at Athens was not for mere amusement: it was a living part of civic and political life: for this reason Pericles created a special fund to enable poorer citizens to attend. The remnants of this unparalleled dramatic poetry remain with us, shattered and fragmented like the temples of the Acropolis. About three hundred plays survived into Roman times: less than fifty have reached our own.

The theatre was the centre of Athenian life and a mirror of

opinion. But ideas were formed, promulgated and discussed in the open meeting places of the city. Philosophers and sages, the 'Sophists', came from all over Greece and the young men of Athens collected around them to listen, learn and argue. Some were pretentious, conventional or fraudulent: others had original ideas to offer – theories and observations on life and thought and the relation of man to the world about him. All created an atmosphere of argument and inquiry. Among them Socrates, a native Athenian, ugly, poorly dressed and deceptively simple in his approach, attracted the most brilliant of the young listeners.

A thinker of powerful originality, he rejected the traditional Greek attitude to philosophy as an examination of the natural world and turned to the analysis of ethics, pursuing a relentlessly logical quest for the meaning of justice and truth. He was a demolisher of loose-thinking, a champion of logic and clarity in the use of words and the definition of meaning, exhilarating to listeners who heard him step by step entangle an opponent by a ruthless process of question and answer; less exhilarating for the opponent, caught in the mesh of logic like a bird in a net.

All this time jealousy between Athens and Sparta smouldered, with intermittent clashes and periods of uncertain peace. But their opposing policies – the sea empire of Athens and the land power of Sparta and the Peloponnesian League – created a tension that could only end in war. It began in 431 BC with Sparta technically the aggressor. Pericles accepted the challenge: he relied on the capacity of Athens to hold out against any attack by land as long as the sea route was open and the mines of Laurium with their essential silver could be relied on to maintain Athenian wealth.

Within the Long Walls which ensured the access of Athens to the sea there was room and food enough to sustain the fugitives who took shelter there from the Spartan invasion. But plague broke out among them, the infection spread to the city and wiped out a third of the Athenian population. Panic spread. Pericles was voted out of office, then almost immediately recalled, but his spirit was breaking. He had lost both his sons; at the funeral rites of the younger he was seen for the only time in his life to break down in tears. He died himself within the year. Had he lived he might have found means to end the war. As it was the resilience and obstinacy of the Athenians prolonged the fighting for twenty-five more years, with alternations of success and disaster, no consistent plan, and an increasing ruthlessness which alienated their friends. In an unprovoked attack on the island of Melos, they killed or carried off into slavery almost the entire population. An expedition against Syracuse, intended to deprive the cities of the Peloponnesian League of their Sicilian corn supplies, ended in catastrophe; the Athenian fleet was destroyed and the survivors of the army died as captives in the stone quarries of Syracuse (415–13).

As the situation deteriorated, the slaves who worked the mines and toiled on the land deserted in great numbers. Coinage and food were equally scarce and government was shaken by the intrigues of ambitious men. In the end, the Spartans, with substantial help from Persian gold, destroyed the last Athenian fleet. Athens capitulated (405 BC).

Distress, disorder and defeat had changed the intellectual climate. The examination of traditional prejudices in the light of reason, and the substitution of logical analysis for passionate statement now seemed to most Athenians irrelevant and even harmful. Superstition and occult religious practices multiplied. Popular opinion put down the defeat to neglect of tradition. Aristophanes, in The Clouds (423 BC), made savage mock of the Sophists and of Socrates above all, to the delight of most of the spectators. It was unfortunate and undeniable that among the most famous pupils of Socrates were Alcibiades and Critias. Alcibiades was an able soldier intermittently given to treachery; Critias became the foremost of the so-called Thirty Tyrants who later ruled the defeated Athenians under Spartan protection and executed fifteen hundred of his fellow citizens.

With the courage induced by despair, the Athenians rose, threw off the Spartan yoke, and began slowly to rebuild their shattered democracy (403). The new rulers pronounced an amnesty, but four years later a private citizen lodged an accusation against Socrates for corrupting the youth of Athens. A private accusation and a public hearing before a jury of five hundred citizens was normal Athenian procedure. Judgement was by a majority vote. The majority condemned Socrates, and posterity has condemned them. Plato, the greatest of his disciples, in the Apology composed some years later, put into the mouth of his dead master words of incomparable dignity, irony and force. They reflect the spirit of Socratic teaching, but probably bear little resemblance to what he actually said at his trial. The surviving recollections of a more prosaic, but no less devoted disciple, Xenophon, are different, and there is some evidence that Socrates spoke little and feebly in his own defence. He was, after all, used to addressing a small group of philosophically-minded young men, not a large audience of hostile citizens. He was condemned to death but could easily have saved himself by a timely escape; this he refused to do. As a conscientious citizen, who had in his youth served as a hoplite in the army, he chose, in the words of Xenophon, 'to die through his loyalty to the laws rather than to live by violating them'. When the day of execution came, he drank the hemlock without rancour and without regret.

He left nothing in writing. He lives for us in the records of his pupils, compiled after his death – the subtly wrought *Dialogues* of Plato and the more prosaic *Memorabilia* of Xenophon. As in all such posthumous records the master is seen through the mind of the pupil: the logic, the pertinacious technique of questioning, the value set on truth and justice is in both. But the Socrates of Xenophon is down-to-earth, humorous and commonsensical while the Socrates of Plato is subtle, ironic, profound, exposing the absurdities of received ideas and relentlessly dissecting the accepted conventions. Plato undoubtedly added something of his own original and richly furnished mind. Xenophon may have been the more accurate reporter. At least, the essentials emerge. Socrates made logic and ethics the significant elements of Greek philosophy and by so doing created a way of thought which has recurrently dominated the best minds of the West.

Athens continued to be famous for the teaching of its philosophers. The Academy, founded by Plato, was for long the principal school of philosophy, though rivalled soon after his death by the school of his pupil Aristotle, in the Lyceum. Later, in the third century, the amiable Epicurus established his school very suitably in his garden. The opposing school of Zeno met in a porch, the Stoa, on the north side of the Agora, whence his followers were called Stoics. For centuries young men came from far and near to dispute and study in the groves and porticoes of Athens. It remained the intellectual capital of the western world long after all political greatness had gone.

II

Aristotle had a more practical turn of mind than Plato, an insatiable appetite for knowledge and a genius for classifying it. The breadth of his interests and the usefulness of his classifications gave him great posthumous influence, especially in medieval Europe. In his own time his reputation as teacher and polymath brought him a valuable appointment in a royal household when Philip of Macedon sent for him to educate his son Alexander.

This half barbaric king from a region which the Athenians regarded as uncivilized, had made himself in the course of twenty years, by a mixture of craft, diplomacy and warfare, the arbiter of Greece. He had united the quarrelsome tribes of his own kingdom and created a strong, well-organized army. He had wrested the silver mines of Thrace from the Persians, and had systematically established his authority over the cities of Greece. Sparta, exhausted by war, with a dwindling population, yielded without a struggle. Athens joined with Thebes to resist him but he defeated their combined forces at Chaeronea (338 BC).

After forcibly uniting Greece, Philip of Macedon planned to invade Persia but was assassinated before his plans matured (336 BC). The young Alexander was vociferously acclaimed by the army, and once on the throne with their support executed those of the opposing faction who were foolish enough to be caught.

He was in his twentieth year when he succeeded to his father's ambitions with even more than his father's ability. At sixteen he had acted as regent in Philip's absence and repelled a Thracian attack; at eighteen he had commanded the left wing at Chaeronea.

He combined an exceptional intellect with a gift for long-term organization and quick decision in warfare. Aristotle had given him an interest in many fields of study and had encouraged his latent gifts for music and literature – his favourite reading was the *Iliad* and his favourite poet Pindar but, under the veneer of Greek civilization Alexander was a Macedonian chieftain, crafty, fearless, vindictive, with warfare and the taming of horses in his blood. He was imbued too with the myths and legends of his family – descended through his father from the demi-god Hercules, and from Achilles through his passionate mother, herself a devotee of occult religions. He had the indomitable courage of a natural leader, and a ready charm by which he bound men to him. He was also a man of genius.

His father had created and trained a superb army. Good cavalry was easily raised in Macedon, and Philip had learnt from the Scythians a wedge-shaped formation which was remarkably effective in attack. Once the enemy line was pierced, the infantry – bowmen and slingers – completed the havoc. Philip was able to keep his soldiers in permanent training because he sent all prisoners of war to work on the land, thus releasing able-bodied Macedonians for the army.

Alexander had little difficulty in persuading the Greek cities to support him in the war on Persia already planned by his father. But a false rumour of his death caused the Thebans to withdraw, whereupon Alexander razed the city to the ground, slaughtered – it is said – 6000 citizens and enslaved the rest, sparing only such as could prove their descent from the poet Pindar, whose house he also left standing.

His army – Macedonian, Scythian, and only partly Greek – now consisted of 30,000 foot and 5000 cavalry. He took with him historians to record the campaign and surveyors to examine and report on the lands he conquered. He also arranged to send his old teacher Aristotle, now lecturing in Athens, choice specimens of rare plants and animals for his natural history museum.

The opportunity was favourable for attacking Persia. A great part of their army and most of their ships were engaged by a revolt in Egypt. Also the pattern of intrigue and murder at the Persian court had become more complex than usual owing to the machinations of a eunuch who was systematically poisoning his way through the royal family in order to secure his own position. The emperor Darius III, who (after several mysterious deaths) had succeeded a rather distant cousin, first used and then executed the eunuch, but his throne was still by no means secure.

The Persian army, so formidable under Darius the Great, had declined in efficiency over the last century. Alexander defeated them first in Asia Minor, then in Persia on the plain of Issus, where he captured valuable prisoners – the mother, wife and daughters of Darius, whom he treated with scrupulous chivalry.

With well-calculated strategy, he reduced the cities of the Phoenician coast – Tyre held out the longest. His own ships were now in possession of the essential bases and Persian sea power was destroyed. Darius recognized defeat and offered to cede all his dominions west of the Euphrates in exchange for the release of his mother, wife and children. Alexander saw no reason to be content with part of the Persian empire when he could have it all. He refused, but turned next towards Egypt where he was hailed as a liberator and the heir of the Pharaohs.

Here he founded Alexandria as a valuable naval base, but also as a centre of Greek culture. As a trading port it soon replaced Tyre which he had sacked in the previous year. But this, the first city that he called by his own name, was to have much greater fame, to be the home of what for many centuries would be the greatest library in the West, a centre for scholars of many nations and religions, and a light shining in the darkness.

Before leaving Egypt he visited the temple of Amun in the Libyan desert, where he went alone into the sanctuary and was hailed as king and god. This was the customary salutation to Pharaohs, but Alexander may have been unaware of this, and have left the sanctuary perhaps, with the conviction that he was himself a god, descended through Hercules from Zeus-Amun.

Meanwhile Darius had brought together an army from the eastern satrapies, from Afghanistan and from India, a formidable array with 200 chariots of war, about 20,000 cavalry and a contingent of Indian elephants to add to its terrors. Alexander, gravely outnumbered and wholly undismayed, won by the sheer genius of his tactics (331 BC). The battle, variously called Arbela or Gaugamela, should never have been fought. Darius might have starved Alexander's army by a scorched earth policy and compelled him to waste time and men on besieging Persian garrisons. The direct confrontation was fatal; Darius risked all he had on a single throw and lost. He fled into Media while Susa, Babylon and Persepolis surrendered.

At Persepolis Alexander celebrated a feast which became memorable for the destruction of the superb palace of Xerxes. It could have happened by accident, but was more probably a deliberate act, symbolizing the end of the war and the Greek triumph over Persia. The rich treasure of Darius was broken open and distributed among the army.

Alexander now pursued Darius to Ecbatana whence the unhappy king escaped with as much gold as could be carried, women, children and a broken, demoralized army. He was found soon after, alone, deserted and dying, murdered by a disloyal satrap. Alexander gave him royal burial, then tracked down, captured and executed his murderer.

Alexander had now been four years absent from Greece. But still he would not turn back. He had a vision of a great empire where Greeks and Persians, Egyptians, Phoenicians, Arabs and Indians should live together in harmony, and over whom he would rule as the Great King. Before advancing into Persia's Indian province he spent nearly three years securing his eastern flank, from the Caspian to the foothills of the Hindu Kush, subduing the nomadic tribes of the mountains, conquering Bactria and Sogdiana, where he married the king's daughter Roxana. He began now to adopt Persian customs and on occasion Persian dress, as the oriental conception of a king as god gained influence over him. In warfare he risked his life and suffered hardships with his men, and so retained their loyalty. But he became suspicious and incalculable with his friends. Stress, fatigue, possibly the pain of old wounds made him drink more heavily. He adopted the fashion of a Persian king and insisted that all should prostrate themselves in his presence. He stabbed one devoted friend in a drunken brawl and had another assassinated on suspicion of conspiracy.

But he led his army successfully through the dangerous passes of Afghanistan, defeated and made an ally of the Indian king whom the Greeks called Porus, and advanced into the Punjab. He was now beyond the confines of the Persian empire, but he still looked further. He was told that a river larger than the Indus, the huge and sacred Ganges, flowed out into the eastern ocean at the end of the world. On its banks were cities which belonged to the kingdom of Magadha. Its ruler, so the Greeks were informed, could muster 200,000 infantry, 20,000 cavalry, 2000 chariots of war and 3000 elephants. Such an account naturally stimulated Alexander's desire for conquest but his troops muttered, verging on mutiny. They had been campaigning for eight years and were far from home, in a strange country with an enervating climate where they suffered from fever and died of snake-bite.

Accordingly Alexander turned towards the sea by way of the Shelum and the Indus valley, fighting off the Indian forces which intercepted him. Here he built a fleet to transport the heavier equipment back to Persia, instructing his admiral to follow the coast and carefully observe and record it. Alexander himself made the journey overland, through the mountains and stony deserts of Baluchistan, sharing with his men the hazards of a long, appalling march on which many died.

Ten years after leaving Greece, he wintered in the old Persian capital of Susa. Here he announced a policy of fusion between the peoples of his empire; Macedonians, Greeks and Persians must marry and create families. He had himself shown the way when he married Roxana. Now he married two more wives, both Persian princesses, while eighty of his principal officers married daughters of the Persian nobility. The troops were urged to marry the concubines whom they had miscellaneously acquired, and bribed by dowries which Alexander paid to the brides. According to one account no less than ten thousand marriages took place.

Far off in Macedon there was critical murmuring at Alexander's absence, and in Persia there had been unrest, revolt and some treachery. But Alexander's mind was filled nonetheless with schemes for a united empire of the East and West, as well as more practical plans for better irrigation of the Euphrates plain, and the exploration of new sea routes between India, Persia and Egypt. Then in June 323 he fell ill of a virulent fever and died in Babylon in the thirty-third year of his age.

No provision had been made for a successor or a regency. Roxana was pregnant but within a few years both she and her son had been murdered.

Sooner or later Alexander's principal lieutenants were bound to make themselves kings over the regions where they held command, if only to maintain some order and authority. Of the dynasties thus created the Ptolemies in Egypt (303 BC–30 AD) and the Seleucids in Syria and Persia (312 BC–65 AD) lasted longest.

Alexander left an inheritance of which the subsequent history of the Ptolemies or the Seleucids is only a fraction. In his career of conquest he had moved the centre of civilization eastward and initiated a tide of Greek colonization in the Near and Middle East. If Aramaic remained the common language of the people, Greek became the language of educated men, and Greek culture dominated Persia, Egypt, and the Near East for generations. In overthrowing the Persian empire Alexander had opened up new ways of thought and new influences. That part of the world would never again be so united, or, probably, so efficiently governed as it had been under the dynasty of Cyrus. But Greek influence breathed a new and long-lasting vitality into the art and thought of the whole region.

Had Alexander lived he might have turned his powerful genius to establishing Greek control more firmly in the Mediterranean from his new city of Alexandria. Phoenicia had been subdued but Carthage was still independent and powerful, and the Carthaginians had for the last century contested the possession of Sicily with the Greeks. In Greece itself, with Alexander gone, the various states fell back into their customary disunion, and the north lay open to new invaders.

These were the Celtic Gauls, a race of handsome, gifted barbarians who had first invaded Italy, overthrown the Etruscans and in 300, captured and sacked Rome. Later they turned their aggressive energies to the Danube valley and about 279 BC appeared in northern Greece. Their farthest thrust reached the mountain sanctuary of Delphi, but they were defeated with heavy loss as they retreated through Thessaly.

In Italy, after the inroads of the Gauls, Rome mastered the Etruscan cities piecemeal, though hampered by the internal strife of their own Patricians and Plebeians; a similar problem had afflicted the Greek cities a hundred years before. Few would have predicted, at the close of the fourth century, that Rome would come to dominate all the Mediterranean coasts, Carthage, Egypt and Greece, Asia Minor, Syria and Palestine.

That would take time. The immediate beneficiary of Alexander's wars and his early death was the state of Magadha in North India.

III

In his expedition to India Alexander conquered only the north western state of Gandhara, which had long formed part of the Persian empire. He had been unable to lead his army further to challenge the principal kingdom of Magadha on the Ganges. Magadha was rich through its own river traffic and the coastal trade to South India; rich in agricultural land, in forests which provided timber for building and elephants for the army; and rich in deposits of iron, both for export and for the making of weapons. But its greatest strength was the broad and holy river.

Magadha had been founded by the conqueror Bimbisara at about the time that Cyrus the Great founded the Persian empire.

Like the descendants of Cyrus, the descendants of Bimbisara were addicted to parricide; but like the descendants of Cyrus they chose capable ministers, had an effective administration and built good roads. They made use of the natural Indian unit, the village community, as the basis of their system. Round the cultivated land of each village lay the jungle; the king's permission had to be gained for new clearances. The taxes, paid in kind, were regarded as legitimate tribute for the use of the land.

The peasants, the *shudra* caste, did not own the land that they worked: although bound to it by custom and oppressed by the burden of taxes, they were not slaves. The distinction between labouring peasant and slave is slight enough in terms of material welfare, but it is significant. When agriculture became dependent on imported slave labour (as it was beginning to do in Greece, and as – later – it did in Rome) peasant proprietors were edged out by large landowners employing slaves and a social change took place that cankered a whole society.

In Magadha the oppressed but technically free *shudra* peasants looked down on a group of people even lower than themselves, which (in our unworthy human condition) is often a source of comfort. This lower group consisted of the original inhabitants – tribes without agriculture, who lived by hunting and food-gathering, and whose only marketable craft was weaving mats and baskets of rushes. Outside the caste system, they were gradually absorbed into the most despised and menial occupations. Later, they made grades and distinctions among themselves, a hierarchy of poverty in which no one believed himself to be the lowest of all.

The state of Magadha flourished until about the time of Alexander. By then, a new dynasty, the upstart Nanda, had taken over, greatly enlarged the army and improved agriculture by new irrigation. They had not been called upon to confront Alexander, but were faced by another conqueror very soon after his death.

During Alexander's Indian expedition a young warrior, whom the Greeks called Sandrocottus, made something of an impression in Alexander's camp. He was the military adventurer known to Indian history as Chandragupta Maurya, the founder of the Mauryan dynasty and empire. With Alexander dead, he embarked on his own career of conquest. First he united the Punjab, then overthrew the Nanda and made himself king of Magadha (*c.*321 BC), then overran some of the smaller states on his southern flank. Feeling himself secure, he turned to the north west and challenged the Greek ruler of Gandhara, Seleucus Nicator.

The most gifted of Alexander's successors, Seleucus was more anxious to consolidate his rule over Persia, Syria, the Middle East and Asia Minor than to retain Gandhara. He ceded it to Chandragupta in return for a present of five hundred well-trained elephants which greatly assisted him in his wars (c.304). It is possible that he gave a daughter in marriage as well; at any rate the diplomatic alliance thus formed lasted for three generations. Megasthenes, resident Greek ambassador at Chandragupta's court, recorded much (not always quite accurately) of Indian life: the fine physique of the men, slender and tall, frugal in their habits, fond of curry; the fakirs who fasted and stood motionless for days; the immense river; the 'trees on which wool grows', from which a light cloth was woven; tame monkeys; parrots which could speak; ferocious tigers; then – as imagination took over – he added unicorns with soft yellow manes, winged serpents which could swallow a stag whole, and gold-digging ants the size of foxes, although these he had not positively seen.[5]

The most powerful ruler in North India, Chandragupta imposed on his subjects administrative methods he had learnt in the kingdom of Magadha. These were rationalized and extended by his right-hand man, the Brahman Kautalya. At once intellectual and practical, Kautalya saw that prosperity must be firmly based on sound agriculture. If food production rose above subsistence level, it would be possible to build up reserves of grain against famine, supplies for the growing towns and also, of course, more revenue from the land tax.

The first essential was a reliable water supply, planned, built and serviced by the government which levied a water tax to defray the costs. Canals for irrigation, dykes, reservoirs and dams thus came into being. The clearance of jungle and waste-land was enforced by drastic methods. Great numbers of peasants – conquered peoples – were moved into uncultivated areas, provided with essential tools and left to clear and sow the land. Surplus crops, when there was a surplus, were taken by the government. In time these unwilling colonists were joined by more willing immigrants and gradually pioneer villages matured into settled communities.

Kautalya is credited with the completion of the first manual of politics in Indian history, the *Arthashastra*. Although the earliest surviving text dates from a later period it probably embodies the tradition and practice of Mauryan government. While the 'social engineering' which insured the food supply was harsh, the method of assessing and collecting taxes was reasonably fair, and was supported by emphasis on justice, order, and the adequate payment of officials to prevent extortionate practices. Protective measures were also laid down for the treatment of women and slaves.

Having conquered, united and governed a great kingdom for many years, the founder of the Mauryan dynasty became a convert to the ascetic teaching of the Jains, abdicated in favour of his son, and quietly fasted to death (c.296 BC). Such at least is the tradition: it could well be true for the Indian temperament tends towards extremes of active energy and passive endurance. Some of the same characteristics would reappear in Chandragupta's grandson Asoka.

Chandragupta's immediate successor, Bindusara, extended Mauryan rule as far as Mysore and by the time of his death dominated almost the whole of India either by conquest or by alliance. Like his father, he maintained friendly diplomatic relations with the Greco-Persian kingdoms, and his son, Asoka, whom he made viceroy in the north west, was in close contact with Hellenic and Persian influences. Asoka (c.268–231 BC) inherited a fighting tradition and early in his reign rounded off his father's dominions by conquering the kingdom of Kalinga. Following the usual practice he deported most of the peasant survivors and massacred those in arms. Suddenly appalled at what he had done, he experienced a change of heart, was converted to Buddhism and renounced all further wars of conquest. So far the legend goes, emphasizing the total and sudden change, the rejection of violence once and for all. It cannot have been quite so dramatic; heart and mind must already have been prepared for it.

During the rest of his long reign he applied the principles of Buddhism to government, and sent missionary monks not only to all parts of India and to Ceylon (which was successfully converted) but to his fellow monarchs in Egypt, Syria and Macedon. The ashes of the Buddha were reverently divided, so that the many *stupas* set up throughout India to cover his relics might each have their share.

It was Asoka's noble ambition that his government should embody the principle of *Dharma*. The Sanskrit word had no precise equivalent in English – 'righteousness' is perhaps the nearest. Social, political and economic life were to be ruled by this idea. He made his intention known by having his edicts cut in cliffs and rocks, wherever his subjects congregated – a practice he may have learnt from Persia. If no rock surfaces were available he set up tall inscribed pillars. His edicts were practical and didactic. In one he declared that trees were to be planted along the roads of India, wells dug at regular intervals and rest-houses built, thus to provide shade, refreshment and rest for man and beast 'in order that my people may conform to *Dharma*'. He meant that they should be able thankfully to share the comforts and necessities of life with each other and with their animals. In another edict he advocated consideration towards slaves and servants, obedience to parents, generosity to friends and respect for other men's opinions.

His intention was tolerant, but he discouraged argument. The Buddhists and the Jains were only the two most significant religions of many in India. Free discussion of such matters which was (very much later) to become in the West the essential mark of a tolerant society, would almost certainly have led in Asoka's India (as indeed it often does in the West) to expressions of anger, arrogance and contempt which offended against *Dharma*. Harmony was best preserved by courtesy and discretion.

In the administration of his empire, Asoka took over the system first developed in Magadha and perfected by Kautalya. The local unit was the village council with its headman. Villages were grouped into districts, districts into provinces. The provincial governor was the ultimate link in the chain between the emperor and his people and if the system worked as it was designed to do, communication should have been possible from the highest to the lowest. Asoka appointed inspectors to tour the country at regular intervals, to check the working of the system, to report or redress grievances and see that the taxes were fairly assessed. These officials were well paid, as a safeguard against corruption.

Asoka also employed agents, or more simply spies, who lived among the people and kept him informed of their opinions. In the absence of modern methods of communication it is hard to see how Asoka could have kept in touch with his people's wants, hopes and fears in any other way.

His government aimed at harmony and prosperity, and seems at least temporarily to have achieved it. The special structure of the caste system, already established by custom and religious sanction, was on the whole acceptable to his people. It had the merit of checking the growth of slavery. While the lowest caste, the *shudras*, laboured on the land, and the more unpleasant menial offices were assigned to the landless dispossessed there was little need of slavery, except in the households of the relatively well-off where the slaves were a part of the family. The brutalized gangs who worked in the mines of Greece and Etruria and the hot, unsheltered cornfields of Sicily were unknown. The abuse of women slaves, too, was checked by a law which gave freedom to the slave who had a son by her master, and made the child free from birth. Slaves could also buy back their freedom. Slavery was not, like caste, an immutable status.

The prosperity of the Mauryan empire was however based on the river traffic of the Ganges, on agriculture and a reasonably efficient land tax. Trade had been encouraged by Chandragupta and stimulated by the laws of Kautalya. Asoka thus inherited a sound economy, while the peace of India, which he maintained for over thirty years, provided ideal conditions for expansion. Trade and industry developed fast. Already the *vaisya* (merchant) caste was splitting up into a number of groups based on different crafts and occupations which had some of the characteristics of guilds.

The north western invasions first of the Persians, then of the Greeks, had opened up new markets, and commerce was further stimulated by the religion of the Jains, who, possibly because so many of their earlier converts had been of the *vaisya* caste, put their renunciation of killing to practical use, by becoming traders and moneylenders and developing the art of banking.

A road was built from the Mauryan capital at Pataliputra (Patna) following the Ganges then branching, near the modern Allahabad, east to the coast and north east to Taxila, the chief city of Gandhara. At Taxila caravans converged from Persia and the Middle East to exchange merchandise with caravans from India. Another route went overland to the west coast, and thence by sea to the ports of the Persian Gulf and the Red Sea. Exploratory Indian ships found their way through the straits of Malacca to the Chinese coast and brought back silk which at first they sold in India, though later it was transported to the luxury markets of the Mediterranean.

Some trade also developed with Burma, combined with the activity of Buddhist missionaries sent by Asoka. They were well received, built a monastery, established friendly relations with the Burmese, and appear to have conducted a mixture of cultural and commercial exchange with their hosts for several generations.

The internal trade of India brought in quicker returns. By Asoka's time there was already a flourishing manufacture of cotton textiles sold mostly within India itself. Pottery was also in demand. A potter who organized five hundred workshops and had his own fleet of boats for transport on the Ganges was probably exceptional, but the case is indicative of the extent of the industry.

Asoka had diplomatic relations with at least five of Alexander's successors – the rulers of Syria, Egypt, Macedon, Greece and Epirus – and may have exchanged ambassadors with Rome. He is traditionally believed to have extended his sovereignty over Kashmir and to have founded the city of Srinagar. He certainly had power in the foothills of Nepal, and perhaps gave one of his daughters in marriage to a chief from the highlands.

His relations were closer with South India, though the region of his direct control did not go beyond Mysore. But he was in friendly contact with the principal kingdoms of the south, where there is an old established belief that the *Brahmi* script, in which Tamil (the earliest literary language of the south) was first written down, was introduced about this time from the north. It is clear from one of his carved edicts that Asoka despatched Buddhist missionaries to Ceylon. Legend has it that he sent one of his sons and that the young man was successful in converting the king. Asoka then sent a slip of the tree at Sarnath under which the Buddha had received his great enlightenment. Planted in Ceylon at Anurhadapura it grew into the famous Bo Tree which still flourishes.

Asoka reigned for thirty-seven years. After his death, in 232 BC, the Mauryan empire fell into decline. It has been argued that his preoccupation with Buddhism caused him to neglect social and fiscal problems, but the evidence is too scanty for generalizations. Inadequate government revenues and the consequent bribery, corruption and administrative decline seem the most probable cause of the disintegration of India's first great empire. Provinces split off, became autonomous, or broke up still further into splinter kingdoms and petty chieftaincies.

The memory of a united India and of a great ruler remained, though centuries of division and recurrent invasion wiped out most of the evidence. Only in the twentieth century, when the rock-hewn edicts and inscribed columns were identified and deciphered was the memory of Asoka restored. In 1947 the group of upright lions which crown the noble column at Sarnath were chosen as the emblem of independent India, thus associating its future with the memory and the ideals of a great ruler.

IV

An unreliable Tibetan tradition credits Asoka with visiting an Indo-Chinese settlement in Khotan in central Asia on the further side of the Tibetan highlands. A few enterprising Indian merchants may have traded as far as China, but contact was slight. The civilization of China continued to unfold in isolation. In Asoka's time China was reaching the end of that epoch of division known as the 'Warring States': an epoch which was nonetheless productive of technical improvements, of philosophic speculation, and in certain states, notably the kingdoms of Wei and Ch'u, was fruitful in literature, painting and the arts.

Between the fertile state of Ch'u, in the beautiful valley of the Yangtse and the dangerous wastes of central Asia, lay the mountainous kingdom of Ch'in, the least cultured and most warlike of the Chinese states. Its rulers believed in the ideas of Shang Yang (see Chapter II, V), the political philosopher who taught that all successful government was founded on agriculture and war, and that, as the common people dislike both labour and fighting, they could be ruled only by compulsion backed by drastic penalties. The application of this policy made the state of Ch'in the most formidable in China. About the year 256 BC the ruler of Ch'in deposed the feeble shadow emperor, the last of the Chou. In the next thirty years the disciplined armies of Ch'in overwhelmed all other states, and in 221 BC the king of Ch'in became emperor of the whole country, known from that time by the name of the conquering state, the name later adopted in the West as 'China'.

He took the name of Shih Huang Ti. Huang Ti, the Yellow Emperor, was the legendary founder of the Chinese state: 'Shih' means 'first', because he claimed to be the Yellow Emperor re-born. But he was no benevolent father figure. His enemies said that he had 'the chest of a bird of prey, the voice of a jackal, the heart of a tiger . . . Cracking his long whip, he drove the universe before him . . . his might shook the four seas . . . the hundred lords of Yüeh bowed their heads, hung halters from their necks and pleaded for their lives

... he burned the writings of the hundred schools in order to make the people ignorant ...'[6] He reigned as emperor for only eleven years. With a mixture of enlightenment and obscurantism, vision and brutality that has rarely been equalled, he moulded the Chinese empire into a form which did not wholly disappear for two thousand years. Not until Mao Tse-tung were the Chinese people to experience any comparable revolution.

His energy and ruthlessness were alike legendary: it was said that he dictated a hundred and twenty memoranda to his officials in a single day: he constructed a strategic road from his capital to the frontier, cutting straight through the hills and filling in the valleys ...

In sober fact, he rationalized the hierarchy of the imperial officials, subdivided the provinces into manageable units, increased the number of civil servants and ensured standards of efficiency by good pay, rewards for merit and unspeakable punishments for dereliction of duty. He destroyed, or tried to destroy, regional loyalties by dispossessing thousands of landowners. They and their families were deported to cultivate the wastes on the border, while their land was divided among the peasants at home. To break the influence of such local nobility as he permitted to remain, he compelled them to attend his court regularly, and at great expense – a method used nearly two thousand years later by the Tokugawa dynasty in Japan and by Louis XIV of France.

Early in his reign Shih Huang Ti put an end to the incursions of the nomad raiders. From time immemorial the Chinese had believed in defensive walls; they had built many on the northern and north western frontiers. Shih Huang Ti repaired, strengthened and linked these together into a barrier fourteen hundred miles long, broad enough to carry a road, with watch towers two bow-shots apart for all its length. Smoke signals by day and beacons by night gave warning of invaders. For this colossal work he used the forced labour of conscripted peasants, war-captives, beggars, criminals and slaves. The building of the Great Wall is believed to have cost a million lives.

It cost still more lives to maintain. Every watch tower had to be manned and conscripts who reached the Wall seldom saw their homes again. Their women, left behind in half deserted villages, not only tilled the soil but had to spin the yarn for making tents, a form of taxation that imposed an intolerable burden.

The Great Wall was only the most spectacular of Shih Huang Ti's achievements. He organized a network of roads over all China, and tried to control the Yellow River by a system of dams and weirs. For this too he used conscripted labour. The peasants, who had benefited when he deported their landowners and gave them land of their own, were in all other respects subjected to heavier burdens than before. But his tyranny created a united, well-organized empire. He standardized weights and measures, laid down the precise breadth of the new roads, the size of carts, and the breadth of wagon axles. He employed scholars to disentangle the confusion of scripts which had grown up in different states over the last centuries. There should be one, and only one, accepted way of writing the Chinese language: this was to be of vital importance in future administration. China abounded in dialects so different from each other that there was no *spoken* dialect comprehensible to all. But the ideographic Chinese script which, unlike an alphabetic script, is related to the *meaning* and not to the *sound* of words, is comprehensible to the literate everywhere. The great mass of the population was of course illiterate.

Writing was for essential communication only. Other uses of writing and reading were suspect. The private possession and circulation of books was forbidden: one copy of each classic was to be preserved in the imperial library, to be read only for research and then with a special permit. All the rest were confiscated and burnt. The penalty for withholding, reading, or merely discussing a book was forced labour or even death for the entire family of the culprit. About 460 people were in fact executed. In the circumstances it is not surprising that this monster 'Burning of the Books' achieved its crushing aim. Shih Huang Ti also commanded the destruction of all regional records to break down the local loyalties which they enshrined.

A megalomaniac, and much afraid of death, Shih Huang Ti made repeated unsuccessful attempts to discover an elixir of life. His many palaces were linked by secret covered ways, for safe retreat in danger. No courtier was allowed to come armed into his presence – a rule which might have cost him his life when a bold assassin broke in and drew a dagger; of all the unarmed courtiers, only the royal physician hit out at the assailant with his medicine bag. The murderer was incompetent and Shih Huang Ti after some undignified catch-as-catch-can round a pillar managed to draw his own sword. As for the courtiers, so the historian Ssu Ma Ch'ien tells us, they 'were utterly dumbfounded and milled about in disorder'.[7]

In the end, he died a natural death before he was fifty and was buried with six thousand life-size pottery soldiers to protect him (210 BC). He believed that his dynasty would endure for 'ten thousand generations'. It survived him less than five years.

After an interlude of civil war between his generals, victory went to Liu Pang, the founder of the Han dynasty, whose regnal name was Kao Tsu. He came of peasant origin, from the province of Han, had been driven to banditry in bad times and finally emerged as a successful soldier. He was fond of saying that he had made himself emperor with nothing but a linen tunic and a three-foot sword and to the end of his days he liked to wear his peasant bamboo hat. His sly old peasant wife had the honours of an empress, and, like other empresses before and after, tolerated his concubines but intrigued for her own children.

Kao Tsu took over the administration of Shih Huang Ti, the roads, the irrigation, the public works that had been planned, and of course the Great Wall. The Great Wall was still incomplete and probably undermanned. Early in his reign Kao Tsu intrepidly marched out against the nomads, was cut off and captured. He bought his way out by offering a Chinese princess to a Barbarian chief, and an annual tribute. One of the articles of tribute was silk, and the Chinese noted with contempt that the nomads wore it for hunting, fighting and other rough work, tore it to shreds and then complained that it did not wear well.

The date of the Han empire is reckoned from the reign of Kao Tsu in 202 BC to AD 220, a span of over four hundred years, and its earlier centuries are one of the greatest epochs of Chinese civilization. (It is tempting to compare these dates with those of the greatness of Rome for about the same span of time.) The founder of the dynasty was not among its greatest rulers; but he must be credited with humanizing the policies of Shih Huang Ti while preserving the administrative structure. He called himself a Confucian, and was essentially tolerant. Not intellectual enough to think intellectuals dangerous, he relaxed the prohibition on reading and discussion: let these educated men jabber away if they wanted to – they would do no harm. At the other end of the scale he gave the people freedom to worship as many local gods as they liked, and even to maintain their shrines and practise their rites in his capital city, Chang-an. After Shih Huang Ti, Kao Tsu was popular; though coarse, capricious and sometimes cruel he was easy of access, enjoyed a joke, and was full of earthy commonsense. He was also fond of his family and grateful to his supporters; he raised a hundred and forty-three of his friends to the nobility, and put far too many of his kindred in high offices of state. The result was half a century of murder, intrigue and renewed civil war after his death.

The great epoch of the Han came with the emperor Wu Ti who reigned for fifty-three years, from 141 to 87 BC, and was perhaps as significant for Chinese and East Asian history as the emperor Augustus for the Roman West. But he was not an innovator; his work was to stabilize methods of government and consolidate political and moral traditions which were more widely influential than those of Rome and retained their vitality for much longer.

Wu Ti saw the exceptional fitness of Confucian teaching for the servants of the state, and made a thorough knowledge of his work essential for passing the entry examination into the civil service, which was established in 124 BC. Administrative authority was thus confined to a necessarily small but highly educated class. Naturally the system did not always work: a certain amount of bribery must have seeped in, and under less conscientious emperors and less exacting examiners, civil service standards inevitably dropped. But the standards were maintained under Wu Ti, and bad periods under later emperors almost always led to new reforms.

Though he was convinced of the importance of Confucian doctrine in civil government, Wu Ti himself was attracted in his private life to the nature mysticism of the Taoists. He felt keenly the need for a religious concept that would unite the nation and sanctify the authority of the emperor. He instituted two annual ceremonies, one dedicated to the Supreme Being on the sacred mountain of T'ai Shang in Shantung, whose topmost peak was supposed to reach the heavens; the other in honour of the earth spirit. This latter was in part a concession to the many local gods worshipped by the peasants, in part a symbol of his own position as a link between earth and heaven for the welfare of his people.

Wu Ti did not conform to the traditional Chinese belief in the wisdom of the old. On the contrary, he sought out younger advisers. He encouraged learning by founding the Imperial Academy, an establishment for the higher education of the young which can claim to be the first formal university in the world. He also set on foot a project for compiling an encyclopaedia of knowledge which did not materialize in his time, but was completed by later generations. In his time began also the Chinese study of the theory of numbers, the first maps, the introduction of the sundial and the observation of sun spots.

Among the glories of his reign was the compilation of the *Shih chi*, a work on Chinese history by the scholar Ssu Ma Ch'ien which is a masterpiece of historiography. Ssu Ma Ch'ien had great understanding and a comprehensive interest in human affairs. He covers political history, the geographical background, the significance of rivers and canals, social and cultural history (showing a deep knowledge of music), the problems of currency and credit, economic structure and change, and the biographies of great men. He was an indefatigable enquirer and a dedicated historian. In middle life he had the misfortune to be suspected, wrongly, of some disloyal action towards the emperor. Offered the choice between death and castration, he decided, after agonizing thought, that it was better to suffer the greatest degradation that could be inflicted on a Chinese gentleman than to leave his work unfinished.

In the long reign of Wu Ti the culture of the Han reached its zenith. Jade carving had never been more delicate; the rich prized it for seals, pendants, intricate clasps and buckles, which to the educated Chinese combined aesthetic delight with the sensual pleasure of touch. The vivid art of lacquer reached great perfection. Boxes, bowls, trays, tables, handles were in continual demand; in Szechwan, the centre of the industry, many busy workshops supplied the luxury market. Painting on silk achieved a rare perfection, while the invention of paper, at some time in the first century BC, offered a new kind of surface to the artist's brush. There were also great wall paintings in the houses of the rich. The emperor's palaces were gorgeous with inlaid and painted woodwork, and were surrounded by parks elaborately landscaped with streams, lakes and waterfalls and stocked with rare birds and beasts.

As all Chinese buildings were of wood very few have survived but the custom of burying painted pottery models of them in tombs enables us to imagine something of their elegance, while humbler models, showing farms and farm buildings, give an idea of how the more prosperous peasants lived.

But most peasants were not prosperous and all times were not good in the long reign of Wu Ti. It was his intention to give peace and prosperity to his people. Yet he thought nothing of demolishing farms and moving villages to make way for his hunting parks. The prince, his brother, and princess whose funeral suits of jade made so great a stir when they were found in 1968, provided a striking example of the materialism and superstition which still flourished among educated Chinese. Works of art of great beauty were buried with the royal pair, but the funeral suits which cost so much in care and craftsmanship are curiosities which give no aesthetic pleasure and conspicuously failed in their object of eternally preserving the dead.

Against Wu Ti's clearances for his hunting parks, must be set his successful schemes for reclaiming waste and marsh land, for embanking and controlling the Yellow River, and for further irrigation linked to the canal system of transport. All this increased the productivity of the land and helped the peasant. When famine struck the north, intensified by a new outburst of nomadic raids, he moved great numbers of the stricken population and resettled them in the south. This cannot have been done without much individual loss and suffering, but in the long-term it was a constructive measure which saved many from starvation and increased the general food supply.

More important for the welfare of his subjects were his resolute and ultimately successful plans for stopping the incursions of the Hsiung-nu. He extended the Great Wall westward to cover the pass called the Jade Gate in Kansu. In the meantime he developed, or got his generals to develop, new tactics for repelling the invaders if they by-passed the Wall. Hitherto the Chinese fought either on foot or in chariots: the chariot was now abandoned in favour of light cavalry, mounted on horses from the steppe, like those of the nomads. These were able to skirmish and harass the invaders with something like their own tactics. But the main defence, when it was completed, was the Wall itself, fully manned by conscripted peasants, many of them using a newly invented cross-bow with trigger release for its arrows. The Hsiung-nu for several generations thereafter abandoned their raids on China and looked for other victims.

Before the completion of the Wall, it occurred to Wu Ti that he might seek allies against the invaders. Another nomad people known as the Yueh-chi, once a group of border tribes on the south western frontier, had been driven out of their pastures by the

Hsiung-nu and were believed to have withdrawn westward into the hinterland of Asia. If they could be contacted, they might join with the Chinese and harass the Hsiung-nu in the rear.

A brave man, half ambassador and half explorer, Chang Chi'en, was sent to find them. He returned thirteen years later, by which time the Wall was completed, the Hsiung-nu had withdrawn and there was less need for an alliance. But his astounding voyage had more important results.

He had left China by the Jade Gate and skirted the desert of Taklamakan where he was captured by the nomads and held up for several years. Nonetheless, he pushed on, to meet with a strange and pleasing surprise. The Yueh-chih in their long trek westward had reached the mountain kingdom of Bactria. This region, conquered by Alexander the Great, had become after his death part of the Syrio-Persian dominion of Seleucus Nicator – the same monarch who bartered his Indian province, Gandhara, to Chandragupta Maurya for 500 elephants. In the course of time Bactria split off from the Seleucid empire under a rebellious governor, and became an independent kingdom in which Greek and Indian influences coalesced. The most interesting of its kings, Menander (whom the Indians called Melinda) was a convert to Buddhism and is important in Buddhist literature for an account of his conversion embodied in a work known as the *Dialogue of Melinda*. Not long after his death, the fugitive but still formidable Yueh-chih invaded the Indo-Greek kingdom of Bactria, looking for somewhere to settle. They took over, but they were not destroyers, and their rule acquired much of the Indo-Greek character.

This was the country in which Chang Chi'en found himself after his long pilgrimage; a civilized country, with fine buildings and sculpture, and a literate governing class. He returned alive and safe to China, with no great hopes of an alliance but with other treasures: the grape vine, alfalfa grass, and news of a superb breed of horses. This immediately excited the emperor, and the so-called 'heavenly horses', the horses of Bactria, were introduced into China to be the pride and glory of the imperial stud, and (for the delectation of posterity) to inspire some of the loveliest Han bronzes and jades.

In Bactria Chang Chi'en heard of great countries further west – Syria, Egypt, Carthage, Greece. He probably saw Chinese silk already in use in Bactria, and learnt that it was imported from India.

There were clearly possibilities of a direct trade here, to Bactria, or further west.

Where the Yueh-chi had gone, and where Chang Chi'en had followed, a trade route could be developed by creating a caravan track, setting up camping stations, and organizing military patrols. The emperor Wu Ti, marshalling the organizing power of his empire, sent an army reckoned at 30,000, partly to establish the Chinese claim to safe passage but more to get the 'heavenly horses'. The demonstration was successful but at a heavy cost in human life. In the next century the famous Silk Road from China to the West came into being – by Kashgar, then branching south to Bactria and India, west to Persia, Syria and the Mediterranean. Silk was the principal export along this route, the lustrous textile of which the manufacture remained for many generations a Chinese secret. But there was other merchandise – embroidery, ivory carvings, and many small, easily portable works of art in bronze and jade; in later centuries tea and porcelain would be added. In return for the grapevine and alfalfa grass, China also gave to Europe the apricot and the peach.

The journey of Chang Chi'en had wider repercussions. Why should not the Chinese carry their wisdom and their manufactures across the sea as well as the land? Chinese ships ventured further from their coasts; they reached Korea and effectively colonized a great part of it. They reached Japan, but found it too backward and barren to tempt them. But soon they were competing with Indian traders in the southern seas.

The Silk Road remained, however, the most important result of Chang Chi'en's journey. Along this road some idea of the remote, immense and powerful Chinese empire reached the Mediterranean; the Mediterranean where another great empire was growing to maturity.

CHAPTER IV

CIRCA 300 BC—70 AD

I

AFTER THE SACK OF ROME by the Gauls (see p. 109) the city was rebuilt and better fortified. It was already thickly populated, though little more than an unplanned conglomeration of crooked unpaved streets. The great temple of Saturn on the slope of the Capitoline hill was perhaps the only building of any grandeur. The new encircling wall was seven miles in circumference. As the original settlements were on the hilltops, the central market place, the forum, was in the valley, through which also ran the main drain, the Cloaca Maxima. The first attempt to improve the water supply, a covered conduit ten miles long, was not built until 312 BC.

The Romans were less intellectually curious than the Greeks but they were energetic, persevering and acquisitive. They were also resolute fighters and outstanding organizers, as they had proved as early as the third century, when the growing population of their city made it necessary to plan the supply and distribution of corn at a fair price and on a very large scale.

Though the Gauls never threatened Rome so closely again, they remained a recurrent menace for more than a hundred years. Their raiding parties were ubiquitous, reaching even as far as Sicily. Only towards the end of the third century BC, after the Roman victory at Telamon, were they finally confined between the Alps and the Appenines.

Success as a warrior was the recognized road to power of Roman aristocrats, and the unification of Italy under Roman rule became their goal. This meant the reduction of the Greek colonies in the south. These appealed for help to Pyrrhus, the king of Epirus, a bold adventurer who mistakenly believed that he was another Alexander. He did in fact defeat the Romans twice, but with losses so heavy that he could not continue the war. Leaving his allies to their fate he returned to Greece and was killed soon after in a street fight. The term 'Pyrrhic victory', applied to a battle that costs too much to win, is his only monument. The Romans continued their policy of expansion and by the end of the third century were masters of Italy.

Where possible they reconciled the defeated by friendly treatment but checked resistance with a firm hand. They gave Roman citizenship to the most amenable of the subject colonies; others paid tribute and sent a quota of troops to the Roman army but were allowed to govern themselves; the most recalcitrant were under the direct control of Rome. In all the newly-won territory they planted colonies of their own, at first at strategic points but later wherever there was good land to cultivate. Their growing empire was linked by well-built roads to which they applied their practical mathematical skills. The Via Appia from Rome to Capua was the first, begun late in the fourth century and lengthened with the extension of Roman power, as far as Brindisi. Next came the Via Flaminia linking Rome to Rimini and the Adriatic coast; intended primarily for military use, it also helped civilian communication and trade, which was further stimulated by the minting of silver and bronze coins of an agreed weight.

The Carthaginians, hitherto masters of the western Mediterranean, took alarm at the extension of Roman power into South Italy. Once they had offered a patronizing friendship to the pastoral city on the Tiber: the earliest authentic Roman record is a treaty with Carthage of the sixth century BC. Their later enmity was not the outcome of commercial calculation but of rivalry and fear. Carthage had settlements in Malta, Sardinia, Minorca, on the south coast of Spain and in western Sicily. But when they occupied Messina, just across the straits from Italy, the Romans fought back. This was the beginning of the First Punic War which lasted for twenty-three years (264–241) and ended when the Romans, who had rapidly developed their naval skill, destroyed the Carthaginian fleet.

The Carthaginians paid an indemnity and evacuated Sicily. They were not yet beaten but were hampered by the inevitable delay in rebuilding their fleet. Moreover their own population was insufficient for their army, so that they had to rely on mercenaries, who rose against them in revolt when their pay ran short. The Romans profited by their discomfiture to occupy Sardinia and parts of the

Illyrian coast. But the Carthaginians meanwhile were building up their power in Spain.

Before the Romans could take full stock of this development the Carthaginian general, Hannibal, left Spain with a formidable army including a contingent of elephants, and marched through southern France towards the Alps, the great northern bastion of Italy. It is uncertain which pass he chose for his famous crossing of the Alps into the Po valley, where many of the Gauls joined him. Two Roman armies confronted him on the Po and both were defeated. A third army which intercepted him after he crossed the Appenines, was defeated on the shore of lake Trasimene. A much larger force was now despatched from Rome only to be routed at Cannae, with a loss the Romans estimated at 50,000 men (216 BC). The cities of southern Italy and Sicily now rose in revolt against Rome.

But the Roman navy blockaded Syracuse, which yielded to them after a siege of three years. (The event is now best remembered because Archimedes, the greatest mathematician of antiquity, was mistakenly killed, since he was too deep in his calculations to answer the challenge of a Roman soldier.)

Rome meanwhile, deserted by the cities of South Italy, rejected the terms offered by Hannibal. In spite of his victories his position was insecure. He had no control of the sea, no effective support from Carthage, and the Romans were steadily re-conquering Sicily. They were also wooing the Greek states for support, but they failed to win over the king of Macedon.

Hannibal now conquered Tarentum, but this gave the Romans the opportunity to besiege Capua. Once Hannibal relieved it, but the siege was re-formed and the Romans this time refused to abandon it, though Hannibal marched almost to the gates of Rome in an effort to draw them off. Rome was well defended; it was Capua that surrendered.

Meanwhile the Roman commander in Spain, Scipio (later to be surnamed Africanus) drove out the Carthaginian force which had been left there, then turned to Greece and defeated the ruler of Macedon, the ally of Carthage. His next objective would be Carthage itself. Hannibal had no choice but to return to Africa. The crucial battle was fought at Zama where Scipio defeated Hannibal (202). The Carthaginians bit the dust. The Romans took everything except the city of Carthage itself.

The Second Punic War had lasted seventeen years. Southern Italy, devastated by both sides, lost half its population more by famine than war. Its once flourishing agriculture took centuries to recover. The Romans now controlled Sicily, Corsica, Sardinia and all of Spain except the far west. In the next half century they steadily gained ascendancy over Greece by calculated involvement in the wars and rivalries of the different states. It was at the battle of Pydna (168 BC) that the famous Greek phalanx – unconquerable for nearly two centuries – faced the Roman legion and was destroyed in less than an hour. The victors took over Macedon, and sent the best of the Macedonian captives, male and female, to be sold as slaves in Rome. When Antiochus IV of the Seleucid dynasty, sought to invade Egypt the Romans made it clear that Egypt was under their protection. Antiochus had to content himself with bullying the Jews of Palestine. Corinth, which rashly defied the Romans, was razed to the ground and in the same year (146 BC) Carthage, which had attempted to rebel, met the same fate. It had taken the Romans little more than half a century to destroy all their most powerful enemies.

The island of Rhodes had for many generations been the principal port of the eastern Mediterranean. But the Romans set up the island of Delos as a free port, thus ruining the commerce of Rhodes. The fading dynasty of the Ptolemies in Egypt retained their independence, but the Mediterranean had become a Roman lake.

Expanding power changed the character of Rome and transformed the economy of Italy. A teeming population, dependent on imported grain, now crowded the city. Three aqueducts supplied water; two carried it underground but the third, the Aqua Marcia, carried it over uneven country in a channel supported by arches, a pioneer example of Roman engineering, looking forward to those stupendous aqueducts which still dominate the town of Segovia in Spain and the Rhone valley at the Pont du Gard in France.

But Rome lacked the arcades and theatres that distinguished even the smaller cities of Greece; temples and shrines were built of brick and the forum had as yet few buildings of any grandeur. A project for a public theatre was vetoed by the senate on moral grounds in 154 BC. Romans of the old school clung to an ideal of manliness and austerity, which contact with the Hellenic world and trade with the Near East had already undermined. Rare spices, elaborate food, rich jewelry and silver ornaments grew fashionable, together with such eastern luxuries as bed curtains and dancing girls. There were useful novelties too: the Romans of this period invented a lantern with windows of transparent horn.

Such things were trivial compared with the changes wrought in urban and rural society by success in war. Prisoners had long provided the main supply of slaves. In earlier conflicts with neighbouring peoples, captives had come into the slave market intermittently in scores, occasionally in hundreds. They were easily absorbed into domestic occupations or, the less fortunate, into public works and the mines. They had little effect on the peasant farming which was the basic economy of Italy. The Punic Wars changed this. A vast new influx of slaves provided the labour not only for mines and public works, but for the land. The harvests of Sicily and Sardinia, so vital to Rome, could not be garnered without slave labour; slave gangs worked the silver mines of the Sierra Morena in Spain and elsewhere.

Meanwhile Roman landowners, enriched by the spoils of war, bought out peasant farmers to enlarge their own ancestral holdings. The process was all the easier because peasants, whose able-bodied sons had been conscripted, were often unable to carry on alone. Most of the large proprietors aimed chiefly to support their households in comfort. They organized their estates to produce all the necessities and many of the luxuries of life – corn and oil, vines and fruit, meat and poultry, fleeces and flax that could be turned into cloth in the estate workshops; wood from their plantations, sometimes building stone from their own quarry. Such self-supporting properties employed domestic and agricultural slaves in great numbers not only for household and field work, but often also as managers, overseers, accountants, schoolmasters and secretaries.

A few commercially-minded landowners aimed to make a profit, as well as a good life, out of their estates by supplying the markets of Rome and the larger cities with wine, oil, honey, rare fruits and such table delicacies as peacocks, pheasants and doves. The marketing was usually in the hands of middlemen, since aristocratic Romans left trade to aliens – Greeks, Syrians and Jews – or to the growing class of freedmen, or even to slaves who conducted business by arrangement with their masters and had their share of the takings.

Slavery was thus vital to the Roman economy and lifestyle as it had long been to that of the Greeks. If the supply of war captives ran short, other sources were tapped. Tribal warfare among the barbarians on the fringe of the Greco-Roman world enabled dealers to buy prisoners from victorious chieftains. Piracy in the Mediterranean was another source. This traffic had its centre on Delos where it was said that as many as ten thousand human chattels might be disposed of in a day.

Peasant farmers, defeated by the new methods, abandoned the land to swell the numbers of the urban poor. This meant, inevitably, that their sons who had once filled the Roman armies, were no longer available. But free craftsmen in the towns found work hard to get because of the many entrepreneurs who preferred to employ well trained slaves in their workshops. This fundamental change in Roman society was one cause of the upheavals which destroyed the Roman Republic, though the long history of internal dissension within the city itself tended inevitably to the same end.

The origin of the division into patricians and plebeians goes back to a time beyond reliable record. The patricians, the ruling class, were presumably the descendants of the original pastoralists native to Rome, and the plebeians descendants of later immigrants. Intermarriage between the two was forbidden and the plebeians were excluded from all offices of state or participation in government.

The plebeians soon found a weapon of coercion. They invented the 'secession' – in modern English, a strike. They simply stopped work and withdrew outside the walls of the city. By this means they secured first, two tribunes of their own election to protect their rights, then equality with patricians in courts of justice, the right of intermarriage with the upper class, eligibility to the various magistracies, offices of state, and the senate, the right to hold their own consultative assembly, and, by the end of the fourth century, the ruling that one of the two annually elected consuls (the chief magistrates of Rome) should be a plebeian. Finally, in 287 BC, after the longest of all their 'secessions', they gained power to legislate. A resolution passed by a majority in the assembly of the *plebs* (a *plebiscite*) was to have the force of law.

So much for the theory: the practice was somewhat different. The plebeian power of legislation was not generally exercised and came to be regarded as theoretical. Moreover the once sharp division between patrician and plebeian was blurred by changing economic conditions. There had from time immemorial been a system by which a poor man, or social inferior, could become a 'client' of a patrician. This was a very strong relationship, often hereditary. The client could be called upon to support his patron, in arms if necessary; the patron had to assist his client to obtain justice, and generally to protect his interests. Almost all plebeians of any respectability were linked by clientage to some patrician family. The client system persisted at least as long as the relatively few great patrician families existed; this gave the patricians prestige and power not wholly based on their material wealth. But over the centuries many plebeian families became as wealthy and powerful as the patricians; they had no clients, but they no doubt had grateful dependants, and they could gain popular support by taking up the cause of the poorer plebeians when it suited them.

There was no real division of interest between rich patrician and rich plebeian. There were, of course, alliances and factions and differences of opinion and policy in the ruling class of which both patricians and plebeians formed a part. There were also the perennial problems of the debtors, the landless and the urban poor for which in times of crisis one or other of the ruling factions might propose solutions.

The situation was further confused by the emergence of a third group, the *equites*, literally horsemen, or knights. These had originally supplied the cavalry of the Roman army. They were by origin the descendants of small landowners rich enough to provide their sons with horses. The *equites* were rarely great landowners, but had enough land to ensure their financial independence: the value of 400,000 sesterces was the basic sum. They refused to compromise their independence by clientage and, as they were neither patricians nor plebeians, they had no official standing in politics. It is therefore misleading to equate them with the modern middle class. A minority of them engaged in commercial or business activities. They contracted to manage mines, to oversee road building and public works, to organize the collection of taxes, customs and harbour dues. Some became moneylenders, though moneylending was sometimes also taken up by patricians. The *equites* were a large and indispensable group but they were not eligible for the senate.

The newly acquired territories had to be governed. Roman governors and their staff, sent to take up positions of power remote from central control, had plentiful opportunities for enriching themselves. These ranged from deducting their legitimate expenses from the proceeds of reasonable taxation, to milking a province for all that it was worth – by corruption, blackmail and charging extortionate interest on loans made to provincial cities in difficulties. Governors varied considerably in the uses they made of their opportunities, and it is only fair to add that corruption was rife in almost all their new territories long before they came. Local tax-collectors and other officials had well established 'rights' of their own on which they insisted and which even the best intentioned Roman governor could not check. It could doubtless be argued in a number of cases that the provinces corrupted the Romans, not the other way about. The get-rich-quick governor was a disaster to Rome as well as to the governed. By the second century BC, wealth was becoming the key to power and very many of the governing class, outwardly prosperous and extravagant, were trapped in a labyrinth of speculation and debt. Their predicament was made no easier by their use of actual coinage – loans were made in chests of silver and interest paid in the same way, subject to all the hazards of loss and robbery by sea or land.

The dreadful prelude to the disintegration of the Republic was the slave revolt in Sicily in 135 BC which was not finally brought under control for three years. This disrupted the grain supply of Rome, caused bitter distress among the poor, famine and riots.

In the midst of these troubles Tiberius Gracchus was elected one of the tribunes of the people. He had been brought up by his widowed mother, a daughter of Scipio Africanus, in an austere, intellectual and self-righteous atmosphere, with high ideals. He had served in the Numantian war and knew from experience and observation that it was essential to get a yeoman population back on to the land to supply reliable recruits for the army.

He planned as tribune to resettle the people on the land by dividing and confiscating land illegally held by wealthy citizens and limiting the amount that rich citizens might appropriate. He was not without support in his plan, from one of the consuls, from the leader of the senate and, surprisingly, from the consul's brother, the richest man in Rome. The opponents of the plan were more numerous than its supporters but lacked efficient leadership. The fellow tribune of Tiberius, one Marcus Octavius, was a waverer who seems to have anticipated a serious crisis if Tiberius persisted.

Tiberius, not to be moved from his purpose, inspired a resolution in the assembly of the *plebs* for the confiscation and re-distribution of land illegally held. Marcus Octavius vetoed the bill. Tiberius expelled him from his office (illegally), proceeded with the confiscation and resettlement of the land and even persuaded the senate to vote money for the purpose. The childless king of Pergamum in Asia Minor who had long been an ally of Rome had recently bequeathed his immensely rich kingdom to the Romans. From this source thousands of smallholders were safely established on the land.

But Tiberius miscalculated the venomous hatred that he had aroused. His year of office over, he stood for re-election. This almost unprecedented action alienated many of his supporters, and enraged his enemies. He was assassinated in the middle of the election and three hundred of his adherents were later hunted down and killed.

Rome's long tradition of respect for law was broken. The sequence of mob incitement, fear, retaliation and murder was the pattern of things to come. Ten years later Gaius Gracchus, younger brother of Tiberius, was elected a tribune. An abler man than his brother, he courted simultaneously the *equites* and the oppressed poor. He authorized a general distribution of corn to the people at a cheap subsidized price – the Lex Frumentaria – and continued his brother's policy of re-settlement, creating new colonies of peasant farmers in South Italy and Africa. He won over the *equites* by a programme of public works on roads and harbours which gave them managerial scope and secured them profitable contracts, tax farming in Pergamum and elsewhere. By making them eligible as jurors for the trial of extortion cases he aimed to put a check on the greed of senatorial governors.

The success of his first year's achievement, the breadth, generosity and wisdom of his measures, seemed to assure his future. Re-elected tribune, he proclaimed his intention of giving citizenship to *all* Italians. Citizenship had previously been the prerogative of Rome and the Romans. The result was disastrous. The Roman poor were angry that a privilege of which they had been proud should now be common to all. *Equites* and senators were deeply offended. Gaius found it necessary to be attended by a bodyguard. The senate raised the cry of 'The Republic in Danger', issued the so-called Last Decree proclaiming him to be a public enemy and sent troops to arrest him. He fled the city but knew he had lost the game, and in the Stoic fashion which his famous grandfather would have approved, ordered one of his slaves to kill him (121 BC). Like his brother he had underestimated the ruthlessness of his enemies, who celebrated their triumph by slaughtering his followers – according to some accounts three thousand died.

Meanwhile both senators and *equites* at their different levels plundered the kingdom of Pergamum, which had been renamed the Roman province of Asia. It was a land rich in agriculture and famous for stock-breeding, while its harbours had a flourishing trade with the East. It has also a tradition in sculpture derived from the Greeks – some of its best pieces would naturally find their way to Rome. The so-called 'Dying Gladiator' in the Capitoline Museum today is one of the finest examples. Pergamum had been a loyal and valuable ally for several generations. But the Romans took little more than fifty years of plunder and corruption to suck it dry.

The patricians now began to call themselves the *Optimates*, the best: their opponents took the name of *Populares*. The measures of the Gracchi, resettling the people on the land and distributing cheap corn, were later successfully imitated. Their sincerity in trying to solve the problem of urban poverty can hardly be doubted but both of them showed a masterful over-confidence and too strong a taste for personal power. They bore at least some responsibility for the violence which they provoked and which henceforward became a characteristic of Roman politics.

Fourteen years later Marius, an able soldier of little education and no ideals, was elected consul chiefly to deal with the revolt of Jugurtha in Africa. Successful in this, he was elected consul for three years running (104–102) to deal with barbarian incursions in North Italy. Having to raise troops fast, he by-passed the traditional manner of conscription and called for volunteers in Rome, promising rewards of land when the fighting ended. Thousands of the poor – the *proletarii*, rich only in children – hastened to enlist. Marius welded and trained them into a powerful army, devotedly loyal to him. His second-in-command Sulla (an impoverished patrician of whose military skill Marius was bitterly jealous) recognized immediately, as Marius did not, the full significance of what had happened: a new political weapon had been forged, a *client* army loyal only to its general.

Victorious over the barbarians, Marius was received with

vociferous acclaim in Rome and by some machinations with a couple of demagogues again got himself elected consul. Though he was the hero of the Popular party, in opposition to the *Optimates*, the intimidation and gang warfare practised by some of his supporters discredited him, and his reputation sank further when Sulla distinguished himself in putting down the revolt of the Italian cities whose people were demanding Roman citizenship. The revolt – the Social War as it came to be called – did in fact lead to the recognition of their right to citizenship.

When Mithridates, king of Pontus in Asia Minor, shortly after rose in revolt, he was joined by the enraged and oppressed people of Pergamum, who set upon and massacred their Italian exploiters. Sulla was appointed to deal with this new war. The *Populares* called for Marius. Street fighting broke out, the consul fled, and Marius assumed command. Sulla returned at the head of his troops, *his* client army now, and overthrew the Roman gangsters. Marius escaped to Africa, Sulla restored order in Rome before leaving for Asia Minor. Within months Marius was back in Rome at the head of his own veterans. One consul committed suicide, the other was killed. Marius proceeded to the systematic elimination of all who had failed to support him, but fortunately died soon after, or few patricians would have survived (86 BC).

Four years later Sulla, loaded with the spoils of victory, including the library of Aristotle, but with the sack of Athens to his discredit, fought his way back into Rome. Proclaimed dictator by the surviving *Optimates* he set to work to exterminate the *Populares* (or anyone else he distrusted) and to reward his friends out of their confiscated property. Much of it, however, he used more constructively to resettle his veterans on the land. He retained some vestiges of patrician education and virtue, restored (in theory at least) the supremacy of the senate, and improved the administration of justice by increasing the number of law courts. He even abdicated power a few months before he died (78).

Marius and Sulla were followed in the struggle for power by three rivals of less repellent character, one of whom was a man of genius.

Pompey, Crassus and Julius Caesar worked within the conventions of their corrupt epoch. Crassus, who had seen war-service with Sulla, grew rich as a property-developer, slave trader and moneylender. He exploited the many fires which broke out in Rome by buying up cheap (presumably through agents on the spot) the burning houses and any others in the path of the fire. He then rebuilt and sold at a profit. Pompey had gained the favour of Sulla as an outstanding soldier and received from him the title of Magnus – the Great. Julius Caesar, on the other hand, who was a nephew by marriage of Marius, narrowly escaped death in the Sullan proscription, and subsequently built up a reputation as a popular leader by lavish entertainment of the populace on borrowed money. He had a far more powerful intellect than the other two, great political acumen and a prose style of persuasive simplicity and strength.

The Roman aristocracy, to which all three belonged, enjoyed no security, but great comfort and a rich culture. The epicure Lucullus was the most famous of many who, in the capital city and in their country villas, discussed philosophy, studied Greek authors in texts efficiently copied by workshops of scribes, and exquisitely cultivated the intellectual and sensual pleasures of life. It was Lucullus who imported the first cherry trees from Asia Minor to Rome – in course of time to spread to all Europe.

Roman literature, a slow starter, was now developing fast. Lucretius (99–54) composed, in six books, his powerful philosophical poem *On the Nature of Things* – one of the greatest, and least translatable, poems of the western world. The poetry of young Catullus (87–57), wit, libertine, and unhappy lover, partly deriving from Greek models, brought a new intimate and colloquial mood into Latin verse, but conveyed anguish and embitterment as powerfully as lyric love.

Below this thin crust of civilization, society was disintegrating. Fear of slave revolt was ever present, the Roman poor were bought off by doles of cheap corn and free entertainment. It was one of the most immoral and murderous politicians of this epoch, Publius Clodius, who changed the supply of cheap corn to the poor into a *free* distribution which was never afterwards withdrawn. Political power lay with those who could pay the largest gang of toughs. Senators were beaten in the public street, assassinated, lynched, driven to suicide. In the law courts justice was bought and sold, and intimidation practised when bribery failed. On occasion rival gangs shouted each other down, then fell to blows before the seat of justice itself. Even men who cultivated the old Roman virtues of fortitude and temperance involved themselves in speculative moneylending. Brutus 'the noblest Roman of them all' shocked Cicero by advancing money to a Cypriot city at 48%. Cicero thought 12½% was enough.

Not long after Sulla's death, southern Italy was convulsed by another slave revolt. It began in Capua, led by the Thracian gladiator Spartacus, an outstanding leader who gathered about him an army of deserters, fellow gladiators, runaway slaves and renegades of all kinds – a host estimated at 90,000 men. For a time they made their stronghold on Vesuvius, then thought to be extinct. Masters of southern Italy, they marched north, at first defeating all who came against them, until Crassus confronted them at the head of disciplined troops. They fell back; outmanoeuvred, they were cut off in the mountainous region of Lucania and defeated. The survivors were crucified. But Crassus was deprived of military fame by Pompey, who arrived in time to mop up the last remnants and win most of the praise.

After this victory in the year 70, the two rivals were joint consuls, but Pompey went on in the next ten years to win further laurels; he cleared pirates off the sea, and made the Mediterranean safe for trade, inflicted final defeat on the rebel king Mithridates in Asia Minor, annexed Crete, Syria and Judaea. Returning to Rome in the year 60, he was granted a Triumph: his third. Crassus, on his money bags, raged with envy: but took steps to get Caesar on his side by paying his debts.

During these years, Julius Caesar had divided his time between soldiering in Spain and cultivating popular favour in Rome, an expensive task. Elected one of the consuls for 59 BC, he displayed uncanny diplomatic skill in persuading both Pompey and Crassus, who were scarcely on speaking terms, to support him. He bound Pompey to the alliance by promising that allotments of land should be made to his veterans and giving him his only child, Julia, in marriage. Pompey had the prestige, Crassus the money, Caesar the ideas.

Strong in these powerful allies, Caesar was able to do safely what Tiberius Gracchus had done with fatal consequences. He disregarded his fellow consul (a conservative who consistently opposed him) and presented his legislative plans to the assembly of the *plebs* rather than the senate. Among his measures were agrarian laws which gave more land to army veterans and the people. Equally important was his punitive law against officials who enriched themselves by corrupt practices. These laws indicated the

measure of his statesmanship. Playing for his own hand and knowing that his legislation made him powerful enemies, he compelled
the senate to confer on him the pro-consulship of Cisalpine and
Transalpine Gaul – northern Italy and southern France. His consulship over, he left for his provinces and did not return for nine
years. He intended to build up a military reputation greater than
that of Pompey and reserves of wealth (through the sale of booty
and captives) which would pay his debts and give him the financial
strength he lacked. Thus when he was next elected consul, he would
wield dictatorial powers. By successfully overruling his fellow
consul and the senate he had already shown during his year of office
that the constitution of the Republic was dead.

In the next nine years he brought Transalpine Gaul into submission and compelled the invading German tribes to fall back beyond
the Rhine. The names and deeds of their greatest leaders – Ariovis-
tus, the Germanic chief who invaded Gaul and was driven back over
the Rhine, and Vercingetorix, the Gaulish chieftain who once
defeated Caesar, before he was himself defeated and sent prisoner to
Rome – are recorded in his own account of the wars. They passed
thence – with some necessary changes of emphasis – into the
histories of Germany and France as national heroes.

The Gauls were rich in flocks of sheep and fine horses, and are
one of the several peoples credited with the invention of stirrups.
Their courage in fighting was beyond question and their surviving
metal work in brooches, clasps, necklaces and polished mirrors is
proof of their aesthetic gifts. As part of the Roman empire they
evolved, in the south at least, a Gallo-Roman culture, rich in poetry
and the arts, lively, enterprising, resilient in the face of disaster; a
heritage which still survives.

Two unnecessary and mismanaged expeditions against the island of Britain added nothing to Caesar's reputation but received
disproportionate attention in later times because the first certain
and recorded date in the history of the island – 55 BC – can be
deduced from his *Commentaries*. (The Roman conquest of Britain
was postponed for a hundred years, and achieved at last under that
homely and kindly figure, the emperor Claudius – who broke all
precedent by sparing the lives of the principal captives whom he
brought to Rome.)

During his absence Caesar kept in touch with the politics of
Rome by means of informers. As his wealth and military fame

increased, so did Pompey's mistrust. Caesar, from his consulship onwards, aimed to be the leader of the Popular party. Pompey had wavered in his career between *Optimates* and *Populares*, but the death of his young wife, Caesar's daughter, broke the last bond between him and his rival. In a bid to increase his popularity he gave Rome its first permanent theatre, in stone, with seats for 10,000.

As for Crassus, he fell a victim to his thirst for military glory, set forth to destroy the power of the Parthians on the empire's eastern frontier, plundered the temple at Jerusalem on his way, and lost two-thirds of his army and his own life in a shattering defeat at Carrhae (53 BC). The remnant of his army was extricated by the skill and courage of a younger man, Caius Cassius, who is better known to history in another context.

Pompey and Caesar were left in the ring. The senate, supporting Pompey, voted Caesar out of his command in Gaul and threatened, if he returned, to prosecute him for breaking the law during his first consulship. The *Optimates* struck impressive attitudes and spoke of saving the Republic. The two consuls presented Pompey with a sword 'to fight Caesar on Rome's behalf', then left the city with a great number of other senators, Pompey, sword and all, to fight Caesar from a distance. Strategically this was defensible; psychologically it was disastrous. Caesar took no notice of the senate's threats, but crossed the river Rubicon, the boundary of his province, and, at the head of his army, marched on Rome which he entered unopposed, amid popular jubilation (49 BC). He spoke of 'arming ourselves with compassion and generosity as our weapons'. He started no proscriptions. Having made sure of Italy, he reduced the rest of the empire to obedience. Pompey was defeated in Greece and murdered in Egypt, not by Caesar's wish. Egypt was brought into close alliance when Caesar put his young mistress Cleopatra, the last of the Ptolemies, on the throne. Returning victorious to Rome, he enlarged the senate to 900 and packed it with his supporters. They declared him dictator for ten years.

He began at once to restore and rebuild the Roman state. He stopped gang fighting and terrorism in the streets. He tightened the laws against extortion and the bribing of jurymen, reformed abuses in the distribution of free corn, ruled that, on large estates, one-third of the labourers were to be free men, extended Roman citizenship to Sicily and North Italy, began the reconstruction of the two great cities the Romans had destroyed – Corinth and Carthage – and encouraged emigrants to go to them; he settled his veterans on the soil, some in Italy, some in Spain and Transalpine Gaul, where he founded colonies at Narbonne, Arles and Fréjus.

He tried to curb the gross extravagance of rich Romans by laws on food and dress, planned public libraries, new law courts, a new temple, a new forum, and cheered the people with splendid games and shows of wild beasts, in which appeared, for the first time in Europe, the shy, long-necked, spotted 'cameleopard' – the giraffe from Africa.

With the help of Egyptian astronomers, he also reformed the Roman calendar which was two months out of step with the natural seasons. To straighten the record, one year (46 BC by our dating) was lengthened to 445 days and the new calendar was introduced in January of the following year. It had 365 days with an extra day every fourth year and has lasted in the West, with some later adjustment, until our own time.

But his policy of clemency to his opponents failed to win them over. He lacked the easy gifts of popularity – with all his brilliance, he was without persuasive charm. He had said that the Republic was dead, and this was plain for all to see. But there were those who would not admit it. The venerable Cicero, to whom Caesar was friendly, was outwardly correct but inwardly hostile though he was not at his age to be drawn into conspiracy. Instead he devoted himself to perfecting those literary essays which were destined to become the staple of classical education throughout Europe from the Renaissance to the nineteenth century, and still exercise their influence today.

It was in February 44 that the subservient senate extended Caesar's dictatorship for life. A group of die-hards among the *Optimates* saw in this the extinction of the Republic which they still hoped to restore and resolved to kill Caesar before it was too late. Foremost among them were Brutus and Cassius.

They struck him down in the senate house on the Ides of March in the year 44 BC, and precipitated, as he could have warned them, seventeen more years of fighting, proscriptions, massacres, suicides, and destruction.

The ultimate winner was Caesar's great nephew and heir, Octavian, who reached Rome immediately after the murder. He was eighteen at the time and neither impressive nor attractive but he soon showed himself to be a cool political operator, dividing his enemies, using and discarding his allies. He joined in the bloody proscription which followed Caesar's death and agreed to the inclusion of Cicero's name; although Cicero had been friendly to him, he had with fatal indiscretion talked of 'disposing of the young man' after he had served his turn.

The next essential move was to eliminate Brutus and Cassius who had left Rome to take up the governorship of, respectively, Macedonia and Syria. Between them they controlled a considerable army, but were defeated on two consecutive days at Philippi by the forces of Octavian and Mark Antony. Both killed themselves.

Mark Antony became a potential danger to Octavian when – after taking Octavian's sister as his wife – he became Cleopatra's lover in Egypt. So Egypt was duly conquered and turned into a province of the Roman empire – Antony and Cleopatra dying within a few days of each other, by suicide. Alexandria remained the capital. Octavian had the two great obelisks of Tuthmosis III transported there from Heliopolis. Hence a Moslem writer of the twelfth century called them 'Cleopatra's needles', the name by which one of them, now on the embankment of the Thames, is still known.

Octavian was now fully in command of the Roman empire. All the power was his and once he was certain of it, he used it well. He was elected consul for a sequence of thirteen years, made commander-in-chief for life (though he is not known to have led his troops in battle), and surnamed Augustus, meaning revered and majestical. He re-cast the state under his supreme authority. He did not say that the Republic was dead but claimed that he was 'restoring' it. He kept the senate as an honourable debating society; he retained the old names of the civil magistrates and did not, as Caesar had done, appoint them himself; instead, he issued lists of names from which they were elected. Later in his reign, in 2 BC, he created the Pretorian Guard – the imperial bodyguard, nine cohorts of 1000 men each, horse and foot. The Guard which in its first century protected the emperor was in later times to become the emperor's master, killing, deposing and proclaiming emperors on its own authority.

Wars and proscriptions had reduced the numbers and undermined the power of the governing class in Rome from whom the ambitious politicians of both parties had largely been drawn.

Augustus was therefore free to establish a new and more stable balance of classes and interests. Provincials like himself infiltrated and filled the places of the declining Roman aristocracy. He sought also to recreate the Italian peasantry by demobilizing more than half the army and settling the veterans on the land.

He also stopped the plunder of the subject provinces by politicians on the make. With peace restored he enforced laws against extortion and bribery, by keeping appointments in his own hands and encouraging petitions to check malpractices. Egypt and North Africa now became more important than Sicily and Sardinia as the granary of Rome. Roman legions reconditioned the irrigation based on the Nile and brought more land under cultivation. The regular dole of corn for the Roman poor was thus assured. Traders and sailors of Alexandria blessed Augustus for their expanding trade and the safety of the seas, for he had exterminated the pirates. Italian merchants, and not Italians only, gave thanks for a ruler who restored peace, encouraged trade and had built a network of military roads during his wars which made transport easy. The people of Pergamum blessed him for reforming a corrupt, predatory government and restoring their old prosperity.

Trade between the provinces of the empire, and beyond, flourished. The soldiers of Pompey first saw Chinese silk in the Syrian campaign. The doomed army of Crassus is said to have been dazzled by the bright reflection of the sun from the silken banners of the Parthians. (The Parthians commanded the direct silk route to China.) In the time of Augustus, silk, as a luxury fabric for the rich, came to Rome – sometimes by way of India, more often by the caravan road across Asia to the Black Sea. Thus, remotely, the Romans heard of another empire in the Far East, and Chinese traders knew of a growing market in the West and a large, wealthy but, in their view, inferior empire. Eastern luxuries from nearer at hand, from India and the Middle East, freely flowed into Rome: spices, textiles, jewels, parrots, apes and peacocks for the amusement of the wealthy. An Indian mission to Rome in about 25 BC brought with them tigers, pheasants, snakes, tortoises, a Buddhist monk and an armless boy who manipulated his bow and arrow with his toes.

Of all the subject peoples, the Greeks were treated most favourably. The Romans were in awe of their pre-eminence in the arts, philosophy, poetry and scientific knowledge. We owe much to the reverence which inspired them to copy not only Greek texts, but also Greek statues. Many of the books were destroyed later by illiterate barbarians, but statues are not so easily destroyed, and scores of the noblest works of Greece are known to us through Roman copies.

The empire of Augustus has been compared to 'a great reservoir into which the currents of ancient civilization flowed, and out of which rose all the streams of later history in the western world'. He was celebrated by poets and men of learning for the blessed restoration of civil peace in which they could cultivate their talents, helped by the state libraries he had set up in the principal temples and by the patronage of wealthy citizens who now spent their money on the arts instead of on bribery and private armies.

The character of the Roman aristocracy had changed in the last fifty years. Civil war and proscriptions had taken their toll, while the clamour of some of the provincial cities to be granted Roman citizenship had of course created a new kind of citizen. Many provincial *equites*, as times at last grew peaceful, must have been drawn to Rome and have stayed there. This would have created substantial support for the government of Augustus, and have blurred the rigid distinctions of society certainly in the middle ranks, and to some degree also among patricians and senators. The Rome over which Augustus ruled was as much Italian in character as Roman. This development was probably encouraged by Augustus who, after the defeat of Caesar's murderers and the expedition to Egypt, did much to recreate the glory of Roman culture and Roman architecture.

Two of the greatest patrons of the arts were close friends of Augustus – Agrippa who built the Pantheon in Rome and made a geographical survey of the whole empire, and Maecenas, an Etruscan by descent, the patron of Virgil, Horace and Propertius. Virgil, whose fame during life rested on the *Eclogues* and the *Georgics*, had scarcely completed his epic *Aeneid* when he died, directing that the poem should be burnt, as being not yet perfected. Augustus himself intervened to preserve it.

Augustus rebuilt Rome in a style more worthy of so great a city: he created a new forum and filled its colonnades with statues of Roman heroes as examples to the people. He restored more than eighty temples, embanked the Tiber, and added three new aqueducts to supply the city, distributing the water through five hundred fountains and innumerable lesser pipes, taps and basins. (The fire service which he instituted was not, however, effective; the great fire of Nero's reign (AD 64) raged for six days and led to yet more extensive and well-planned rebuilding.) The Palatine hill became the fashionable quarter, and here Augustus lived, unostentatiously, in a modest palace. The wall paintings of his wife Livia's rooms have survived, green and flowing decorations, sky, trees, fruits, garlands and birds.

Augustus had never been physically strong and no one would have predicted that he would live to be seventy-six, and reign for over forty years. Consequently he planned carefully for the continuance of the empire, for he had no son and was doubtful of the merits of his ultimate heir (his stepson Tiberius). He built up a team of advisers, and by good appointments created an administrative meritocracy which was in some degree self-perpetuating. He drew the servants of the state largely from the *equites*, but saw also that freedmen – intelligent slaves whose masters had rewarded them by liberation – were good material for the lower echelons. The administration of the empire, as he left it, was strong enough to withstand the irresponsible follies of a Nero or a Caligula. They might afflict the capital, but rarely disturbed the even tenor of provincial life.

The last years of his reign were darkened by a military catastrophe. The Germanic tribes beyond the Rhine had found a remarkable leader Arminius – to use his latinized name: it was probably something more like Herrman. He had served in the Roman armies, spoke their language and understood their method of warfare. In AD 9 he rose against the Romans. Augustus appointed Varus, governor of Syria and presumably an experienced soldier, to command the legions sent against him. Arminius who had the advantage of knowing the character of the country, defeated Varus with the irreparable loss of three legions. Varus committed suicide. The crushing defeat cast a shadow on the last years of Augustus. It was said that on sleepless nights he could be heard moaning: 'Varus, Varus, give me back my legions!'

Judged by his achievement Augustus is among the greatest of western statesmen; he brought lasting benefits to the Mediterranean world and left lasting gains to civilization. He did for western Europe what Shih Huang Ti had done for China. Both achievements were remarkable in themselves and valuable to posterity. It is qualified praise to say that Augustus had finer moral qualities than Shih Huang Ti whose far-sighted planning was combined with egoism and cruelty to the point of madness. Augustus was coldly sane: in his youth he had played the perilous game of Roman politics with indifference to the claims of gratitude, friendship or mercy. His restoration of order and prosperity was preceded by the ruthless removal of all opponents. He desired and loved power but exercised it with a high sense of responsibility. He did not rule in accordance with any rigid political philosophy but aimed at the best government that could in practice be attained. He was not a likeable man and never played for popularity. His legislation to restrain luxurious dress and loose-living and to restore the supposed morality of more primitive days was neither successful nor popular: the misconduct of his promiscuous daughter Julia was much more typical of Roman *mores*. A hard man who cared only for work and for his conception of duty, he inspired his ministers with his own sense of purpose, was capable of friendship for a few, and seems to have loved his wife Livia, whose character was as devious and austere as his own.

II

Many peoples have believed that they or their rulers enjoyed a special relationship with the gods. By the time of Augustus educated men in the Mediterranean world had grown cynical about such beliefs although it was politic for the state to support them. In Rome the emperor was also Pontifex Maximus, the high priest: he performed public rituals in the efficacy of which he can scarcely have believed, and was on his death accorded divine honours by the equally irreligious senate. These things presumably enhanced his prestige with the superstitious multitude, possibly even with some of the barbarian peoples in the empire.

Religions which are built into the fabric of the state usually decay with it, as the religions of Babylon and Carthage and Egypt had decayed. Among country folk, lesser local gods were more important – spirits who were thought, if propitiated, to bring rain, to avert famine, to help women in childbirth: entrenched superstitions which embodied the triumph of hope over experience, an indestructible human characteristic.

Among the state, or national, religions the faith of the Jews in their god repeatedly survived disaster. He had brought them – some of them at least – out of Egyptian bondage into the Promised Land. The Promised Land had its brief epochs of glory, more especially under David and Solomon, but it was small, vulnerable and – geographically – a buffer state, the prey of aggressive neighbours.

Invaded by Assyrians, conquered by Babylonians, snatched at between the Greco-Syrian empire of the Seleucids and Egypt of the Ptolemies, paying tribute almost always to one threatening neighbour or another – the Jews still trusted in the God of Abraham. They still lived by a code of conduct which set them apart from their neighbours, they still saw the hand of God in their tribulations, still trusted that he in his own time would restore and redeem them.

In the middle years of the second century BC, Antiochus IV of the Seleucid dynasty, ruling in Syria, seized on Jerusalem, took over the temple and – to demonstrate the idea that all gods are the same god – set up the worship of Zeus and Baal beside that of Jehovah. Outraged, the Jews found a leader in Judas Maccabeus, son of a priest and the eldest and greatest of a family of soldiers known to history as the Hasmonean dynasty. They liberated Jerusalem and, for a time, re-established the independence of their country.

Later generations proved unworthy of their predecessors and broke out into jealous quarrels. The Romans, meanwhile, extended their power eastward, and in 63 BC Pompey the Great (as he liked to be called) occupied Jerusalem and made Palestine into part of the Roman province of Syria.

Some years after this an able and attractive young man named Herod, of Arab descent, made his way to Rome and found favour among the great. On his return to Palestine he married Mariamne, the last of the Hasmonean dynasty, and was recognized as king of Judea, independent of Rome.

Herod the Great as he came to be called, was never popular though he protected the Jewish religion, restored the temple – in the Hellenistic manner – built market places and theatres to please the people, organized relief in years of famine, and above all, maintained the independence of his kingdom.

He had learnt in Rome that Greek was the fashionable speech for men of education. The fashion, encouraged by the flow of Greek visitors and merchants into Judea, spread from the court to the wealthier sections of society. It increased the distance between the ruling class and the mass of the people, who had no Greek, little Hebrew, and spoke Aramaic.

In the last years of his life Herod went out of his mind. Tortured by arterio-sclerosis, in constant pain, he became insane with jealousy. He killed his once-loved wife Mariamne, her two sons, his own eldest son . . . No one at court, no one in a place of power was safe. The reign of terror ended only with his death.

The disputes which arose after his death enabled the Romans to impose a military occupation and a governor of their own. This was a time of deep embitterment and division among the Jews. The priests who served the temple in Jerusalem supported the secular authority of Rome, while administering the established rites and upholding the Mosaic law in its initial austerity. They were Sadducees, an hereditary caste who rejected belief in an after-life, were secure in their present power, exclusive and corrupt. Annas, high priest in the early years of the Roman ascendancy, was ejected from office but retained his influence by placing in turn five sons and one son-in-law – Caiaphas – in the high priest's chair.

In sharp distinction to the Sadducees were the Pharisees whose influence spread among the educated. Defenders of Jewish tradition against foreign influences, they were careful interpreters of the Scriptures and observers of the law. They differed from the Sadducees in their national pride and in their belief that the Mosaic law had been modified, enlarged and given greater spiritual force by the prophets. Men of good lives and often of great learning, they were sometimes over-conscious of their righteousness.

Other sects abounded. The white-robed, ascetic Essenes, 'the holy remnant of Israel', as they called themselves, lived in communal settlements where they combined cultivation of land and the study of medicinal herbs with copying out the Scriptures. They believed that the Day of Judgement and the End of the World were near at hand. They were a secretive, dedicated group, little known to history before the discovery in 1947 of the so-called Dead Sea Scrolls, in which they had set down their beliefs.

An underground movement of a much cruder kind consisted of the Zealots, who harassed the Roman government and sporadically broke into armed revolt. They had a great following in the province of Galilee and were most active in regions where they could take cover easily and exact help – willing or unwilling – from the inhabitants. Their supporters included a few men of substance and Pharisees, some idealists, many brave and devoted fighters, but more brigands, robbers and criminals on the run. The Romans quelled them ferociously, punishing revolt by mass crucifixions, but the Zealots were ineradicable.

The hopes of the Jews were often sustained by new doctrines, or cryptic passages in the prophets. The Pharisees had introduced belief in the soul's immortality and life after death, an idea which brought comfort to thousands who had no hope of reward in this world. Some of the Essenes, and other ascetic sects, foretold a second David, a Messiah, an Anointed One, who would bring spiritual freedom and establish the Kingdom of God on earth.

In this unquiet time, among a people torn with political dissension and hungry for spiritual sustenance, a carpenter's son grew up in the Galilean village of Nazareth. Although the greater part of the western world came to accept the supposed year of his birth as the beginning of the Christian era, there is no historical evidence as to precisely when Jesus was born. The year 4 BC seems to be the date which is most widely accepted.[1]

He was a man of the people. His language was Aramaic. His knowledge of Greek and Roman culture, which had greatly influenced the wealthier and more worldly inhabitants of his country, was slight. He knew about the burdens of taxation, the price of corn, the daily troubles and rarer joys of the manual workers among whom he lived.

When Jesus was about thirty, a gaunt, ascetic preacher appeared on the banks of the Jordan. John was one of those holy men, spiritual descendants of the ancient prophets, who from time to time during this troubled epoch, called on the people to repent and to purify themselves by baptism for a new life and the coming of the Messiah. Jesus of Nazareth joined the crowds who heard him and received baptism from his hands. Not long after, John was seized and put to death by the decadent successor of Herod the Great who ruled in Galilee by favour of Rome.

By that time Jesus himself had begun to teach and preach in Galilee. The appeal of his eloquence, the directness of his teaching and the compelling quality of his personality soon drew great crowds. He spoke in the downright language of the people and illustrated his teaching with parables, drawn from their daily life:

from the tasks of the farmer, shepherd or fisherman, from the experiences of hired labourers at harvest-time, of women darning ragged clothes or searching for a lost piece of housekeeping money.

Some of his ideas resembled the teaching of the Essenes and other holy men, John among them: for he preached the coming of God's Kingdom on earth. In rebellious, excitable Galilee, too many thought that God's Kingdom meant material liberation from Rome. ('We thought it had been he which should have redeemed Israel', lamented one of his chosen disciples after his execution.)

Jesus preached above all a fervent and trusting love of God. God was the father of all mankind, not merely in the sense of authority, reward and punishment (which others had believed before) but in the sense of an infinite love, needing only a response of love from his children towards him and towards each other.

As a devout Jew, he knew the Scriptures and respected the law, but was prepared to depart from it when it conflicted with his gospel of divine love. He shocked the Pharisees by sometimes breaking the Sabbath, and by mingling with 'publicans and sinners'. Publicans were the despised but often rich Jews who collected the Roman taxes; sinners were the social outcasts who were naturally drawn to Jesus by the doctrine of forgiveness and love.

Soon his adherents claimed that he wrought miracles, that the blind saw, cripples walked, lunatics became sane, the dead returned to life. Miracle workers are often considered dangerous by authority; how much more so when the miracles were combined with a prophetic vision of a coming Kingdom of God, among a people ripe for revolt.

Though Jesus insisted on the spiritual nature of the Kingdom of God, the people associated this all too easily with political liberation. It is possible that he left Galilee, and the crowds which followed him there, to check the growth of this error. In the latter months of his mission, he taught in villages and towns nearer to Jerusalem. How long his mission lasted is doubtful: three years, by tradition, but some scholars think it was less. Certainly by the time he went up, with his small band of chosen disciples, to keep the Passover in Jerusalem, he had not been absent from Galilee long enough for his followers to forget him. The Holy City, as always at that time of year, was crowded with pilgrims, among them many Galileans, who gave him a vociferous welcome, waving palm branches and calling him 'Son of David'. The demonstration marked him out, in the eyes of the temple priesthood, as a potential trouble-maker to be silenced as soon as possible. In view of the sieges, revolts and massacres which Jerusalem had endured in the last century, their fears of further trouble are understandable.

Jesus knew his danger. By day he intensified his teaching in the temple precincts undisturbed because, while crowds were listening to him, his arrest might have caused a riot. By night he camped with thousands of other pilgrims outside the city on the Mount of Olives, and here after dark on the third evening he was arrested. Caiaphas, the high priest conducted the trial. Asked if he claimed to be the Messiah, Jesus gave a cryptic reply which was construed as blasphemous. It could also be construed as treason against Rome which gave Caiaphas the cue to hand the prisoner over to Pontius Pilate, the governor of the province.

Pilate was an unimaginative man who repeatedly made blunders that outraged the religious susceptibilities of the Jews. The prisoner seemed harmless to him, but he came from the notoriously disaffected province of Galilee and had apparently claimed to be King of the Jews, which was of course sedition. All the same if he was a holy man and popular, it might be advisable to release him, a customary grace at a time of public holiday. This Pilate offered to do but the crowd, possibly disillusioned by the ease with which Jesus had submitted to his capture, clamoured instead for the release of a popular Zealot-brigand named Barabbas. Jesus of Nazareth was crucified.

It could have ended there, with yet another Jewish idealist destroyed by faction and the Roman power. But the disciples who had scattered in terror and dismay, now gathered courage. They claimed strange things: that the tomb in which Jesus had been laid was found empty; that he had been seen, newly risen from the dead, at first by a few, then by many; that he had come among them, for a month or more after his death, had spoken to them, broken bread with them, and at the end been lifted bodily into Heaven.

The disciples did not speak in allegorical terms; they did not speak of a vision or a ghost. They were convinced of the material resurrection of their Lord. They believed him now to be the Christ, *the anointed one*, the Messiah foretold by the prophets. His resurrection had proved the ultimate triumph of life over death and the sovereignty of God, whose Son they now knew him to be. Through this belief the Christian Church was born.

His followers in Jerusalem began at once to make converts. The most impulsive and fluent of them, Peter, a fisherman from the lake of Galilee, was the principal spokesman. There was at first no thought of breaking with the Jewish faith, rather of fulfilling the prophesies of the Scriptures; God's Kingdom, they thought, was close at hand, and they called on the people to purify themselves by baptism in the name of Jesus in preparation for that great day. The number of converts grew.

The temple priests feared the political consequences of the new teaching and the Pharisees its disruptive effect on Judaism. Many converts came from the communities of Greek-speaking Jews, visitors or immigrants from the Jewish colonies in the Greek cities of Asia Minor: co-religionists who were not always popular with the native born. One of these, the young enthusiast Stephen, was stoned for blasphemy, and became the proto-martyr of the faith. His death was the signal for a persecution which scattered the disciples to different cities and spread the new religion beyond the bounds of Judaea.

Among those who watched the martyrdom of Stephen was a formidable young Pharisee named Saul. A native of the Greek city of Tarsus, he was well-educated, had studied with Gamaliel, one of the most distinguished rabbis of Jerusalem, and was resolved to crush this ignorant and pestilential new sect. But on his way to suppress it in other cities, he had a dazzling vision of Christ the Messiah, on the road to Damascus; stunned and for some days blinded by the shock, he was himself converted.

Henceforward, under the name of Paul, he was the most zealous of the apostles, daring every danger by sea and land and glorying in his suffering: 'Thrice was I beaten with rods, once was I stoned, thrice I suffered shipwreck . . . in journeyings often, in perils of waters, in perils of robbers, in perils by my own countrymen, in perils by the heathen, in perils in the city, in the wilderness . . . in watchings often, in hunger and thirst, in fastings often, in cold and nakedness . . .'

Paul was much more than a 'freedom fighter' confronting authority and courting martyrdom. He was a thinker of high intellectual power, capable of presenting the new faith comprehensibly to the Gentiles. He founded Christian groups at such great cities as Corinth and Antioch – in which city the term 'Christian' was first used – and in many lesser towns of Asia Minor, Greece, North

Africa, Macedonia and Italy. Soon there was a Christian community in the heart of the empire, in Rome. Paul corresponded with most
of these communities in Greek. He was emancipating Christianity
from Judaism and preparing it to conquer the classical world.

The missionaries who were sent out to spread the Gospel, visited
first the Jewish colonies which existed in every commercial city of
the empire. (*Pax Romana*, the imperial creation of Augustus, served
the Christians well: travel and communications were relatively easy
within the bounds of the Roman empire.) Some of the Jewish
communities accepted the new teaching, but the orthodox were
usually hostile, and it soon became clear that the Christian message
made its strongest appeal to spiritually-minded pagans, disillusioned and unsatisfied by the rites of their own temples.

Legends of a god who died and rose again had long been familiar
among the peoples south and east of the Mediterranean. The story
of Christ's death and resurrection was close enough to the ancient
legends of their countries, and to their own fears and desires to give
a new magnetism to the moral teaching of the Christian missionaries. But it was the idea of God's love for all men, and the promise of
eternal bliss for the penitent and for true believers, that appealed
most to the poor, the unhappy, to women and slaves. It brought to
thousands who heard it hope, comfort and self-respect. The original
belief that the Second Coming and the Kingdom of God was at hand
faded with the passing years; Christians, no longer set on their
apocalyptic hopes, became less provocative of authority, less
noticeable altogether. They proselytized steadily, unobtrusively,
underground.

How exact is the surviving record of the words spoken by Jesus? He
wrote nothing himself and all that he said, as reported in the
Gospels, can be read in a few hours. From Paul onward there would
be elucidations, .elaborations, commentaries, analyses to fill
volumes and libraries. But a few pages suffice for the basic text.

Our evidence for what Jesus said is not strictly contemporary. In
point of time the evidence of Paul comes first: Paul who never saw
Jesus, but claimed to be among those who had directly received the
message because of the vision on the road to Damascus. He *believed*
he had seen Jesus. What he knew of him must have come from
disciples who had known him. It is from Paul, who was not there,
that we have the first reference to the incident that became central to

Christian worship: that Last Supper in Jerusalem when he broke bread and offered wine saying, 'This is my body: this is my blood . . .'. Paul, writing to the Christians at Corinth about AD 57 first refers to this, in a way that shows the sacramental meal of bread and wine to be already an established rite.

The Gospel of St Mark seems to have been composed between AD 45 and 60, that of Matthew between 40 and 60, that of Luke between 50 and soon after 60, that of John between about 40 and 65 or a little later.[2] The evidence is therefore not contemporary evidence, but is derived from the evidence of contemporaries. Ear and eye witnesses may have partly forgotten, or unconsciously elaborated what they remembered to suit the beliefs of a religion already in its second generation.

Yet the records we have of Jesus are closer in time to his life than the records of any of the other great founders of religions. The earliest known sayings of the Buddha are divided from his life by nearly three centuries. The surviving texts of Confucius were compiled four hundred years after his death. Authorities differ as to the date of Zoroaster by as much as four centuries: documentation is virtually non-existent. Muhammad, like Christ, left nothing in writing, and the earliest surviving biography was written by a disciple born seventy-five years after the Prophet died. The Gospels, in the words of Dr C. H. Dodd, are 'unreliable as documentary history' but have a validity based on social memory.

The comparative strength and fullness of the story of Jesus, as told in the Gospels, derives from the Jewish tradition of history: history had always been to them the evidence of God's will on earth, therefore to be set down with careful attention to material details – how much more so when the story to be told was that of God himself on earth.

Such textual questions did not trouble the first Christians or their converts. They had other problems. In Jerusalem the close kindred of Jesus, who had not conspicuously supported him during his life, were prominent in the Christian community. But they regarded his teaching as something exclusive to the Jews. If Gentiles wished to join in, they must first conform to Jewish laws and practices. This view was abandoned by both Peter and Paul so that a schism occurred, the first of many in the Christian faith.

Elsewhere, in Antioch, in Corinth, in Rome, converts who did not belong to the Jewish colonies there were naturally unwilling to accept circumcision and the whole Mosaic law along with the moral teaching of Jesus. Baptism 'in His name' was enough, and the right to join in the mystical sacrament of bread and wine which sealed their belief in salvation hereafter.

Buddhism had offered to its adherents the forgetfulness of self, the annihilation of desire, and a final blessed oblivion as the petulant self dissolves into the world soul. Hinduism (and Tao-ism in its later forms) offered something which the Egyptian, the Greek and the Roman gods failed in the end to give: a sense of unity with the forces of nature. These were personified by the multitudinous gods of the Hindus and poeticized by the cult of calm acceptance among the Tao-ists. Both annihilated or assuaged the compulsive egoism of human beings. Yet egoism is the life-force, the source of all unhappiness, the source of all effort. In the West it is sometimes called individualism, which sounds better.

The teaching of Jesus penetrated to the core of this human characteristic. He insisted that the love of God was directed individually to each human being. He did not teach annihilation of self but the imaginative projection of the self into the lives of others. 'Do unto others . . .' You know what you yourself need and want: use the knowledge to understand the needs of others. The salvation that he taught was an individual salvation, to be achieved not through self forgetfulness but through self-discipline, self-sacrifice and the love of others.

The doctrine appealed to the active Greco-Roman world where the virtues of self-reliance, self-denial in the interests of state or nation or family, and personal honour had long been valued. Christianity therefore moved westward more surely than it moved eastward, although tradition credits one disciple, Thomas, with carrying the faith to India. He could have done so, along the trade routes. Certainly, thirteen hundred years later, western travellers to South India found a recognizable form of Christianity associated with the name of Thomas in the neighbourhood of Madras. But the mainstream flowed westward.

At first, although there was local opposition, little notice was taken of the Christians by the imperial government. The change came under Nero, after the great fire of Rome in AD 64. Rumour attributed the disaster to Nero himself, who had not been in Rome at the time. To divert suspicion he is said to have accused the Christians. Several hundred innocent victims were executed, among them – traditionally – Peter and Paul.

This persecution was the first indication of Christian vulnerability and endurance. Their refusal to recognize any god but their own was, to Roman thinking both intolerant and irreverent to other people's gods. But the crux was that they refused to burn incense to the deified emperor. This practice, which had been initiated by the emperor Augustus, was more an act of state than an act of faith, though it took the form of an implied acceptance of the emperor's divinity. (Only mad emperors actually thought themselves divine.) It was more comparable, in its meaning and function, to the oath of allegiance of medieval times. But the Christians could not see it that way. As far as possible they avoided confrontation with the state, worshipped privately in each other's houses or, in time of danger, in cellars and catacombs. When put to the test, most of them courageously refused to burn incense to a mortal man and suffered accordingly. Even so sane a man as the emperor Marcus Aurelius, whose own religion was philosophy, regarded the Christians as political dissidents and therefore a danger to the state.

The secrecy which was forced upon Christians inevitably aroused suspicion. They were thought to engage in obscene and occult practices. The historian Tacitus, described them as 'enemies of the human race', because they put their god above loyalty to the family or the state. The emperor Trajan asked his friend the younger Pliny, then governor of Bithynia, to investigate their behaviour. Kind-hearted Pliny was relieved to be able to report that they were relatively harmless: they met to chant verses in honour of Christ 'as to a god', took an oath to abstain from theft, robbery and adultery, and partook together of a harmless meal. Their belief was 'nothing but a degenerate sort of cult carried to extravagant lengths'. Of course if they refused to honour the statue of the emperor or the images of the gods, they must be punished: that was another matter.[3]

There was much self-sacrifice, sincere effort and devoted teaching in the young Christian Church. But secrecy and oppression inevitably modified the lucent message of Christ. When the Christians emerged into power and daylight three centuries later they had already learnt to persecute their own heretics, and many of the priests, who had heroically sustained their faith in time of persecution, had acquired the necessary habits of authority and the inevitable taste for power.

The largest and most prosperous Jewish colony in the Roman world grew up in Alexandria. Here, in an atmosphere wholly different from that of Jerusalem, Babylon or Rome, a largely Greek-speaking Jewish community was receptive to the influence of Hellenic thought. As early as the third century BC Alexandrian scholars translated the sacred Scriptures into Greek for the benefit of their compatriots, many of whom no longer spoke Hebrew. The *Septuagint*, as this translation is called because of a tradition that seventy scholars worked on it, was highly suspect to the Jews of Babylon and Jerusalem, but was used by Greek-speaking Jews and in due course by Christians and Moslems.

While the short life of Jesus of Nazareth ran its course in Judea, a great teacher arose in Alexandria. Philo Judaeus, or Philo of Alexandria, was born about 15 BC and lived until at least AD 40. A devoted Platonist and a devout Jew, he was a great reconciler of ideas. He took from Zeno and the Stoics the conception of Logos – the Word, the all-pervading wisdom of God – a conception which was transmitted to Christian thought through the Gospel of St John.

Such ideas were acceptable to the Jewish intellectuals of Alexandria where Philo's loyalty to his own religion was never in doubt. He had for instance, with the utmost courage, led a deputation to Rome in AD 40 when the mad, murderous Caligula was on the throne, to protest against the setting up of the emperor's statue in the temple at Jerusalem. But the more orthodox teachers in Judaea and Babylon were suspicious of his ideas which in the end had more influence on Christian – and even Muslim – thought than on Jewish theology.

The Alexandrian community itself, a few years after his death, broke into revolt in sympathy with the rebellion raised by the Zealots in Judaea in AD 67, and never fully recovered from the destruction which followed.

A few days before his death, Jesus had predicted the fall of Jerusalem. The prediction could have been an allegory but in the disturbed state of Judaea such a prophecy did no more than express a fear which had long hung over the nation. Disaster came in AD 70. The governors appointed by Rome were uniformly bad. In the year 67 the Zealots precipitated a general revolt and were successful until the coming of Vespasian, an experienced veteran who laid siege to Jerusalem.

Recalled to Rome and elected emperor, he left his son Titus to reduce the city. In spite of overcrowding (Jerusalem was filled with fugitives and pilgrims), famine, thirst and disease, the defenders held out for 139 days before the city was finally taken by assault. Titus razed the city walls, sacked the temple, and carried the twelve-branched candlestick back to Rome to be displayed in his Triumph. It can be seen to this day depicted in a now much battered relief on his triumphal arch in the Roman forum.

The Zealots defied Rome for three more years from the Masada, a towering fortress of natural rock. When all hope was gone and their supplies exhausted they killed themselves with their wives and children, preferring death to slavery. (Two frightened women, probably slaves, appear to have hidden themselves and survived to tell the tale to the victors.)

It looked like the end of the nation, but it was not. The destruction of the temple and the annihilation of its privileged priesthood made way for a spiritual rebirth. A group of Pharisees, led by Johanan ben Zakkai, a famous teacher, interpreted the ancient Scriptures to meet the new situation. The Diaspora had by this time extended to most of the Roman empire: they had only to impress upon the scattered communities of Jews that the preservation of their law and their faith was now their bond of union. The still prosperous community in Babylon brought its own long tradition of learning to support and strengthen the dispossessed. So evolved the Talmud, the great compilation of law and history which preserved the continuity and national consciousness of the Jews.

Sixty years after the fall of Jerusalem, a bold guerilla leader, Simeon Bar Kokhba, led a last revolt against Rome and was for a time successful enough to set up a viable state, to issue coinage and to be hailed as Prince of Israel by some, and as the Messiah by others. But he had no chance against the colossal might of Rome and found his death in the hour of his defeat. The wreckage of Jerusalem was replaced by a Roman settlement from which Jews were excluded, and the Latin name of Palestine was imposed on their country (AD 135).

CHAPTER V

CIRCA 50 AD—500

I

THE TWO GREAT EMPIRES of China and Rome, even at their height, knew very little of each other. The Greek geographer and traveller Pausanias surmised that China lay somewhere to the south of the Red Sea and was inhabited by Ethiopians; Ptolemy, on the other hand, drew it with a sea coast on the west and attached to Africa.

Small groups of merchants from Europe are said to have reached Tonkin once in the second century AD and again about sixty years later. Though Roman coins occasionally appeared in central Asia, most trading contacts were indirect through Indian, Arab, Greek, Syrian and Jewish middlemen. There is evidence of one strange incident when a body of Roman soldiers, possibly fugitives or escaped prisoners from the defeated army of Crassus, fought as mercenaries for the Chinese and subsequently were allowed to found their own city within the Chinese empire.[1]

While Augustus restored order to the Roman world, the Han dynasty was temporarily overthrown by a usurper. Wang Mang was an ascetic reformer with far-reaching ideas who had long been a trusted servant of the Han. But when the senior line of the dynasty came to an end with the death of two princes not yet of age, Wang Mang seized the throne. He planned to expropriate the nobility and re-distribute the land, allotting a hundred acres to each family, whether peasant or noble. The price of essential food was also to be controlled and slavery was to be abolished – not that there was much slavery in China compared to the Mediterranean world. His reforms, hampered by renewed incursions of nomadic tribes, were ultimately defeated by the Yellow River which changed course twice, destroying villages and crops and turning thousands of peasants into hungry fugitives. Landowners and merchants were

already outraged by his policies and the troops restive. The catastrophe of the Yellow River lost him the support of the peasants. A
rumour that he had reached the throne by making away with at least
one of the two young princes was widely believed. An angry mob
stormed the palace and Wang Mang was not seen alive again. He
had reigned for fifteen years (AD 8–23).

The restored Han dynasty enjoyed another century of power. In
the reign of the emperor Ming Ti (AD 58–75) border incursions
were decisively checked and the Silk Road, which had been made
impassable by marauding tribesmen, was re-opened. Oases in the
Gobi desert and camping places in the Tarim basin were fortified
and the tribes brought under control. This was the work of a
remarkable soldier-statesman, Pan Ch'ao, who extended Chinese
authority as far as the Pamirs, brought Khotan, the source of the
finest jade, under imperial suzerainty and even imposed tribute on
the tribes of north west India.

The boundaries of the Chinese empire stretched southwards
into the province of Kwantung, towards Tonkin and the perpetually
disputed country now called Vietnam. The Chinese viewed with
indifference a string of islands a couple of hundred miles out in the
Pacific Ocean. The Japanese had hardly yet emerged from a state of
tribal warfare while their northern islands were still inhabited by a
primitive tattooed people, the hairy Ainu. Yet their ruler, probably
in the reign of Ming Ti, sent envoys to the Chinese court with
greetings 'from the Emperor of the Sunrise country to the Emperor
of the Sunset country'. The Chinese were more amused than
offended by such pretensions of equality from outer barbarians.

Nothing further came at this time of the proposed contact
between the Chinese and the eager, active people who longed to
know and imitate them. The gap was still too wide. China, at the
zenith of the later Han, was intellectually as advanced as any
country in the world, in some ways the most advanced. The
university at Loyang had thirty thousand students. The libraries of
the emperor, of the university, and of educated families were
well-stocked with works of literature and manuals on the natural
sciences. Scholars had compiled a standard dictionary containing
over ten thousand characters, and the Chinese invention of paper,
early in the second century AD, greatly facilitated the production of
books. In mathematics and astronomy they were fully equal to the
Greeks had they cared to make the comparison.

After the reign of Ming Ti the ascendancy of women and eunuchs gradually enfeebled the dynasty. Corruption spread downwards into the administration. Civil servants were chosen and promoted by family influence and bribery; the Confucian examinations were neglected. Peasants exploited by landowners, taxed by the government and victimized by corrupt officials fled to the mountains and joined the bandits. The most dangerous of these were led by a group called the Yellow Turbans. They claimed to be Taoists, though their ruthless ferocity seems very far removed from the true character of Taoist belief. The imperial troops, such as they were, could make no stand against them. The palace at Loyang went up in flames with all its accumulated treasures, books, textiles and works of art. In AD 221 the last of the Han emperors abdicated and the great dynasty which was great no longer came to an end.

Three and a half centuries elapsed between the disintegration of the Han empire and the reunion of China under the Sui (581) followed by the T'ang (618). Chinese historians divide this long epoch of disorder between the Three Kingdoms (221–65) and the Six Dynasties (265–581). The names are imprecise and nearly meaningless. One way and another, about thirty dynasties rose, competed and fell in different parts of China. 'The land was divided like a melon, or shared like beans', wrote the poet Pao Chao.[2]

The north fell a prey to raids, and finally conquest, by the nomadic tribes of the interior. Loyang was again sacked and its citizens massacred. Chinese noblemen, unable to defend their lands, collected their movable wealth and emigrated with their households and their tenants to the fertile Lower Yangtse, or the remoter safety of Szechwan. After sixteen different tribes had disputed possession of the north, a Turkic people, the Toba Wei, gained the upper hand in the fifth century and settled down to imitate, not unsuccessfully, the administration, customs and dress of the Chinese whose language they also officially adopted. In time they rebuilt Loyang and made it their capital.

The south, though disturbed by dynastic upheavals, was more prosperous and more populous; its agriculture benefited by the influx of northern immigrants. So did standards of living and education. These troubled centuries were a period of vital transition during which the south became the true centre of Chinese culture.

The rulers of the Chin dynasty at Nanking, who were distantly related to the Han, styled themselves emperors, though they had no authority outside their own kingdom. Their court was violent, envious and corrupt but superficially elegant and cultivated. They collected books and works of art; in their time, anthologies of poetry were made, and the classics freely transcribed. The ruling class, though not conspicuously good at ruling, developed interesting theories of aesthetic criticism. The more sensitive minds took refuge in the arts. The poet Lu Chi, who died soon after, a victim of political intrigue, wrote a luminous analysis of the joys and sorrows of writing (c. AD 300). He knew (what writer does not?) those moments 'when the Six Senses are stranded, when the heart seems lost and the spirit stagnant', and those other moments when 'writing is itself a joy . . . it is a sound wrung out of Profound Silence; in a sheet of paper is contained the infinite and, evolved from an inch-sized heart, an endless panorama'.[3]

The poet, T'ao Ch'ien (365–427) had the misfortune to be trapped for thirteen years in the 'Dusty Net' of the civil service, but he got away in the end:

> The flocks of birds
>   Are glad to have their refuge,
> I no less than they
>   Love my little house.
> Ploughing is done
>   And also I have sown –
> The time has come
>   To return and read my books.[4]

Others retreated in groups, like the Seven Sages of the Bamboo Grove, to lead a simple but comfortable life devoted to philosophic thought. The best advice for bad times is given in the words of Pao Chao:

> Retain your noble aims:
> Enjoy your food and your friends,
> For they alone can repel
> Your worries and fears.[5]

As long, of course, as you have food and friends . . .

Painters, like poets, found both escape and fulfilment in their art by cultivating an almost mystical union with nature. Something like comparative criticism also developed. Hsieh Ho prefaced a rather laborious account of famous Chinese painters by setting out Six Principles which became the foundation of Chinese art criticism, among them attunement to nature, faithful observation and harmony of colour. A more sympathetic character was the wandering painter Tsung Ping. He wished to be a Taoist mystic, but found it too much of an effort. So he wandered with his wife humbly and blissfully over the hills, and later tried to capture their spirit with his brush.

Few treasures of this epoch have survived the accidents of time. One emperor, when forced to abdicate, deliberately burnt his library of 200,000 books and all the works of art he had collected. Government was corrupt, taxation heavy; hungry peasants took to robbery and bandits terrorized the countryside. Educated and uneducated alike yearned for spiritual comfort – religion, philosophy or magic. The code of Confucius no longer met the needs of weaker spirits.

A few Buddhist monks from India had made their way inconspicuously into China in the last century of the Han. As times grew harder their teaching took root. More wandering monks made the long mountainous journey from India, using a branch of the Silk Road. Converts multiplied. Buddhist shrines appeared on or near the Silk Road. From the fourth to the fourteenth century shrines and monasteries grew up. Caves were excavated and their walls painted with scenes from the life of the Buddha, or with innumerable representations of the Buddha himself. Abandoned much later, when transport went more safely by sea and the Silk Road fell into decay, sand silted over them. It was not until the present century that the pioneer excavations of Sir Aurel Stein revealed the first of the Thousand Buddha Caves, and opened up long buried treasures to more recent explorers.

But in the fourth century AD, the goal of the Buddhist missionaries was China itself. In North China their message was welcomed by the Toba Wei, the Mongol tribe who had recently settled there. In spite of their admiration for Chinese institutions, the code of Confucius was too cold for them. Soon there were more than forty Buddhist monasteries round the old capital of Loyang.

Tao-ism in its uncorrupted state – China's own philosophy of withdrawal – developed and changed with the times. The ironic purity of its original teaching became overlaid with nature mysticism and linked to magic rituals. The older contemplative Tao-ism merged with Buddhism, but as the number of converts grew, spiritual intensity diminished; believers found what they needed merely in the incense-laden glow of temples, in ritual phrases and the turning of the prayer wheel.

Yet the experimental and scientific curiosity of the Chinese was by no means dormant. The rapid development of cultivation and the growth of population in the Yangtse valley stimulated trade with India and South East Asia. Tea was introduced from Burma. Oranges were cultivated and lichees. Observant gardeners discovered how to control fertilization by the use of insects. In the north the Mongols introduced new methods of welding and tempering sword blades.

Other practical inventions appeared: the watermill, the wheelbarrow, mica for lanterns and window panes. The horse-collar was not yet perfected, but a harness was devised which transferred the weight of the load from the horse's neck to its powerful shoulders.

P'ei Hsin, a geographer at the court of the Chin, produced a map of China with a grid system, about 30 miles to the inch: a practical invention centuries in advance of the rest of the world though the map to which it was applied was largely imaginary. Mathematicians, studying the structure of the circle, worked out the value of π more accurately than had yet been done even by the mathematical Greeks.

The Japanese from their mountainous islands rightly looked with awe towards the superior civilization of China, but they were not above taking advantage of its political division. Several times already in the past they had tried to gain a foothold in Korea where three kingdoms paid tribute to China. The largest of their own kingdoms, Yamato, mounted an attack on Korea (the Japanese were resolute fighters by sea and land) and about the year 369 they established a bridgehead at the southernmost tip, whence they intervened in wars between the Korean kingdoms and received as reward, along with more material advantages, the *Analects of Confucius* and the Chinese dictionary (the *Ten Thousand Character Classic*) complete with a party of scholars who could interpret them. The Japanese got the point at once; they learnt to read and write, and gradually to adapt the Chinese script to their own very different idiom. By the end of the fourth century they had flourishing colonies and considerable influence in Korea.

They continued, nonetheless, to send respectful embassies to the court of whatever prince was currently styled emperor of China.

Their awe of Chinese learning was unabated. When a Korean king sent them a casket of Buddhist scriptures and a golden statue of the Buddha they were at first mystified by the expression of the Buddha – 'of a severe dignity such as we have never seen before'.[6] Was this new god to be worshipped or not? The knowledge that it came originally from China swayed the balance, and they worshipped it.

But they held on to their outpost in Korea until the Koreans themselves drove them out. The pattern of Sino-Japanese relations started thus early and was perhaps inevitable: they loved and hated, respected and envied and were as eager to learn as they were quick to take advantage.

II

When the Mongol tribes of north east Asia were deflected from their easy prey in China by the strengthening of the Great Wall and the extension of Chinese military control into Central Asia by the Han dynasty and the great Pan Ch'ao, they had to look elsewhere for pasture and plunder. This set up a chain reaction which, in the course of time unsettled the population south of the Aral sea and on the borders of Persia and Afghanistan. A people whom the Indians call the Shakas, probably a Scythian tribe, came through the mountains of Afghanistan and made themselves masters of Gandhara, the Indian province of Alexander's empire. This was about 80 BC. About sixty years later a second and more formidable wave of invaders, who are known to Indian history as the Kushana, conquered all the north from Kabul to the Ganges. They came from Bactria and brought with them a complex heritage, being descendants of the Yueh-chi (see Chapter III.IV). Their culture was a mixture of Asiatic, Hellenic and Persian, but this hardly affected the mass of their Indian subjects. They changed little in the settled agricultural life of the peasants, whose immediate concerns were dealt with by their own council of village elders under their own headman.

The Kushana dominance in North India lasted for about two hundred years. They became generous patrons of Sanskrit scholarship, and of the Buddhist faith. Their hybrid style of sculpture, which combined the more human Greco-Roman with the formalized style of Persia, strongly influenced the Indian sculpture associated with the schools of Gandhara and, later, Mathura.

The greatest of the Kushana kings, Kanishka, is said to have called a council of sages together to reform the confusions which had overlaid the teaching of the Buddha in the seven centuries since his death. Since there is no certainty as to when Kanishka reigned (any time between AD 78 and 96) and no certainty as to the date of the council, it may have had nothing to do with him. But a council did take place under Kushana protection, the fourth recorded council since the death of the Buddha, who had by this time become almost indistinguishable from a god. As a result of its deliberations, believers broke up into two distinct groups. The orthodox minority held firmly to the recorded sayings of the Buddha himself as their guide: for them, the only way to perfection lay in striving to follow the Eightfold Path. The less austere majority believed that they could also pray for help to the many Bodhisattvas, those holy followers of Buddha who had achieved perfection but out of compassion had remained in touch with struggling humanity. (The parallel with the Christian cult of saints is inescapable.) This kind of Buddhism was called *Mahayana*, or Great Vehicle, since it was evidently a more capacious conveyance to salvation than the purer creed. Indeed the believers in *Mahayana* denigrated the orthodox doctrine under the name of *Hinayana*, the Little or Narrow Vehicle.

The purer form of Buddhism persisted in Ceylon, Burma, and South East Asia. *Mahayana* continued for some time longer in India, but was diluted as Bodhisattvas assumed more and more the nature of popular gods in the Hindu Pantheon, so that the Buddhist faith was almost wholly re-absorbed into Hinduism. In the meantime it had spread to Tibet and Nepal, where a variety of other gods, rites and magical practices were added to it, including the prayer wheel, and the association of sexual with mystical union which characterizes Tantric Buddhism.

In more thoughtful philosophic forms it made progress in China, Korea and Japan. The missionary advance across the Himalayas to the Far East had its origin in the discussions of the fourth council. These gave impetus to monks whose teaching took hold in China in the difficult times after the fall of the Han. But the Kushana were overwhelmed in the third century by a resurgent Persian dynasty, the Sassanids, who conquered Afghanistan and made a vassal state of their Indian kingdom.

Central and southern India were not afflicted like the north with recurrent invasions, but the great number of small rival states caused frequent wars. Occasionally a strong dynasty established peace for a time over a large area. Such were the Satavahana or Andhra dynasty who ruled in the Deccan for three centuries (*c.*100 BC–AD 225).

Further south, where, in spite of Aryan infiltration, the original Dravidians still predominated, three peoples long strove for power, the Chera and Kerala on the Malabar coast and the Pandyas in the extreme south. Their warfare was fruitful at least in songs and legends in Tamil, the richest of the surviving Dravidian languages.

It was, however, at a later date after AD 300 that the two great Tamil classics were composed – *Chilappatikāram* (The Jewelled Anklet) and its sequel *Manimēkalai*. The first tells the sad story of an unfaithful husband and his devoted wife. The second follows the fate of the unfaithful husband's daughter by his mistress. The virtue chiefly celebrated is the devotion of good women, although kings, gods and the supernatural also play their part. But the greatest charm of these poems today is the background picture of domestic, agricultural and mercantile life in the Tamil kingdoms.

Wars between rival kings using soldiers drawn from an hereditary warrior caste were localized, and destructive only of the luckless minority in the direct path of the combatants. These politically confusing centuries were thus, for so vast a land as India, a time of rising prosperity during which commerce steadily expanded.

A substantial merchant class and thriving industries grew up. Indian textiles, especially the gossamer-fine cotton fabrics of the Ganges valley, were in demand in the Mediterranean world and especially in Rome. Domestic weaving could not supply the market; large workshops and commercial manufacture developed. The mining and processing of iron, copper and salt were also organized industries. So was the cultivation of musk and saffron in the foothills of the Himalayas. Asoka's roads, still in reasonable repair, accelerated the exchange of goods between Indian cities, and her merchants reached China and the islands by sea, bringing back silk and spices for the Indian market, or for re-export, by way of the Red Sea to Egypt and the Mediterranean.

Internal trade throve, the prosperity of merchants increased and the luxury market grew at home as well as abroad. Mediterranean wines, Italian and Greek glass, linen cloth and purple dye were imported. At Massawa on the Red Sea coast Arab middlemen sold cheap cotton cloth to the Africans, iron for their spear tips and copper for their bracelets and other ornaments. They took back, for the Indian market, ivory, tortoiseshell, gold and a few black slaves. Eastward, they traded to Cambodia and China, but Rome was a principal luxury market. The chief demand was for fine Indian cotton, textiles, silk, either imported from China or made in India, jewels, spices and exotic pets – peacocks, parrots and apes. Some Roman settlements grew up in South India, where merchants ordered and collected for shipment the goods most in demand. Pliny complained that 50 million sesterces were annually drained away to India. His figure is probably too high; there was after all a small return traffic in Roman pottery, beads, wine, glass and occasional works of art. But certainly the balance was in favour of India.

The caste system was helpful to commerce and craftsmanship. Manual workers on whom the textiles, the pottery, the carving and the metalwork of India depended, were closed caste groups with hereditary skills and trade secrets, a sense of solidarity and a vocational, almost religious, pride in their work. This built up a tradition of fine craftsmanship which became a permanent element in Indian culture. Furthermore, the beliefs of the Buddhists, and in the south of the Jains, stimulated mercantile enterprise. Buddhists and Jains abhorred violence and merchants could claim spiritual justification for adopting their peaceful vocation. The contradiction between a religion which taught contempt for worldly wealth, and a way of life which promoted it, could always be excused in terms of reincarnation. Perfection required many rebirths and thousands of years. For the time being it was enough to repudiate violence.

Merchants, manufacturers and craftsmen paid their tribute to spiritual things by supporting hermits, and paying for the building, painting and carving of temples and sacred caves. So, from the second century onwards the long series of caves at Ajanta were hollowed out and harmoniously painted with scenes from the Buddha's life. So over many centuries was built the noblest of Buddhist shrines, the *stupa* of Sanchi, near Bhopal, surrounded by a stone balustrade and gateways of miraculously intricate sculpture. These beautiful things, and the offerings and worship that went with them, were not what the founders of Buddhism or Jainism would have wanted; but they were what a great number of ordinary human beings want, have always wanted, may always want: the outward and visible signs of some other-worldly power, part spiritual, part magical, that transcends, uplifts and consoles.

About the year AD 405 a Chinese Buddhist scholar, Fa-Hsien, visited North India to see the holy places where the Buddha had preached and to collect original Buddhist writings in Sanskrit and Pali. (Chinese scholars were nothing if not thorough.) Coming from a troubled and divided China he was amazed at the peace, order and prosperity of the country and impressed by the civilized splendour of the court. Northern India had been fortunate. After the Persian attack which destroyed the Kushana dominance, there had been no invasion for more than two centuries. All India north of the Deccan was united under the authority of the Gupta dynasty: a long lived family, four reigns covered a hundred and thirty years. The greatest of their kings, Chandragupta II (c.375–415), was on the throne at the time of the Chinese visit. A later legend, enshrined in a play, represents Chandragupta as an adventurous character, taking great risks for love and honour. All that can be said for certain is that he combined the several excellences of a warrior, a diplomatist and a patron of the arts. He checked raids from hostile tribes on the north west frontier, held the kings and chiefs of the Deccan in alliance by well-planned dynastic marriages, and filled his court at Ujjain with poets, philosophers and artists.

The roads of Asoka were now served by innumerable Buddhist monasteries where travellers could rest and refresh themselves. Some of these were also schools or centres of more advanced learning. Some specialized in the study of mathematics, astronomy or medicine. The Indian genius is less immediately practical than the Chinese, more given to abstract speculation, tending to the mystical and visionary. But they were good mathematicians: they invented decimal numerals and the use of zero. The Romans in other things so practical were content with one of the most cumbrous numerical systems ever invented. Even the Chinese were slow to discover the great convenience of using the scale of ten. It reached the West very much later, through Arab intermediaries, so that our figures have ever since been generally and incorrectly known as 'Arabic'. (Even so, many people – including the Indians – used the scale of ten in mathematics for centuries before they had the sense to apply it also to their coins, weights and measures.)

Chandragupta II did not proclaim his intention of benevolence and Buddhist principles as Asoka had done. He was himself a

Hindu, but it is clear from Fa Hsien's account that he ruled with genuine benevolence, which extended beyond the mercantile community to the villages and the peasants. Fa-Hsien saw much of North India and measured its prosperity by the low standards of his own time but it seemed to him, compared with the state of China as he knew it, a happy country.

This could have had something to do with the different attitude of the Chinese and the Indians to government. In both countries the supreme ruler (whatever he called himself, emperor, raja, king) was an autocrat. But in India each village had its own local headman and council, as responsible to his fellow villagers as to the central government, and by tradition the spokesman of village grievances to higher authority. The central administration was less efficiently organized than in China: no examination system, no deep-seated, hereditary sense of duty to the state. But then, in China, the relationship of officials to the subject populations was different. Government officials were expected to dress as became their high office and to travel in carriages. They had to maintain their distance as 'leaders of the people' and delegates of the high imperial authority, even when that authority was in ruins. The village headman in China was far inferior to the official who embodied the emperor's will, his right to express grievances was largely theoretical and his power to organize the village community was circumscribed by the many imperial edicts on conscription for the army or for public works which afflicted peasant communities. The Chinese system was efficient at its best, but in bad times it was corrupt, tyrannous and incompetent.

The Indian system was no less subject to corruption, but it was more humane. The village council often met and had the elements of democracy. The officials of the government reflected the attitude of the government: under a benevolent ruler it did not pay to browbeat the poor because complaints and petitions would reach the king, and the official would be answerable.

Hence the happy impression recorded by Fa-Hsien. He may have been too easily impressed but he cannot have been wholly wrong in thinking that the peasant, however poor, was at this time better off in India than in China.

He noticed also a system of free hospitals all over the country. Charitable Christians in the West were also, by this time, beginning to found hospitals for the poor and sick. But India seems to have been first with the conception of a hospital service as the responsibility of government.

The Hindu faith of the Gupta kings was widely tolerant, based on ancient traditions and a mythology which mingled the Dravidian with the Aryan gods. Primitive legends and a multitude of local gods satisfied the superstitious, while the more sophisticated could work out their own symbolic spiritual interpretations. Buddha himself had not turned against the Hindu faith of his ancestors but had imbued it with a greater meaning. In the time of the Gupta, the older religion gradually absorbed Buddhism once more into itself.

The Gupta period saw a fruitful revival of the glorious past. That great epic, the *Mahabharata*, was revised to the glory of a unified India under god-like emperors. Buddha and Vishnu were alike presented by sculptors as figures of ideal majesty. With Persian and Hellenic influences now fully assimilated, Indian sculpture reached its highest achievement in figures like the recumbent Vishnu in the ruined temple at Deogarh, and the incomparable Buddhas of the Sarnath school. The finest of these are Greek in the proportion and noble elegance of the body, but the formalized position, the symbolic gesture, the carved stone halo which perfectly frames the Buddha's head and shoulders – these are the expression of the Indian genius, equally satisfying to the religious and the aesthetic sense.

The Gupta period was also rich in literature. Besides the revival of ancient classics, new poets and dramatists were writing. Chandragupta II was the patron of many artists, scholars and poets. The greatest of these 'jewels of the Crown' may have been Kalidasa, prolific poet and playwright, sometimes called the Indian Shakespeare. 'May have been' because there is some doubt about the precise period of his life except that he belongs to the classic Gupta period of Sanskrit literature. His most famous work, the verse-play *Shakuntala*, which was translated into English in 1789, inspired Goethe to write a poem in its praise, and influenced the romantic movement in western Europe. It is a legendary love-story, full of coincidences, mistaken identities and adventures, but Kalidasa fills it with compassionate insight into the human condition – as Homer filled with human meaning a primitive heroic tale, as Shakespeare transformed trivial novelle and improbable fairy tales.

The records of politics, social life, commerce, literature and the arts during these centuries, though very incomplete, are full enough to reveal the evolution of a rich, varied and enterprising civilization. Little is recorded, whether in India or anywhere else, about the lives of the peasants whose back-breaking toil scarcely altered its character over the centuries. They are seen imperfectly in legal codes, in traditional folk-tales, in the margin of literature.

III

The Roman empire at its height reached from the foothills of the Scottish highlands to North Africa and from the Atlantic coast of Spain to Syria, Cappadocia and the Black Sea. Its contacts through trade and occasional diplomacy reached India and China, and an embassy from the island kingdom of Ceylon is said to have been received by the emperor Claudius.[7]

By the middle of the first century AD the structure was rotting at the centre. Claudius conquered the valuable province of Britain rich in metals and timber. He was succeeded by his stepson Nero (54–68) who, after a deceptively promising start, became wholly concerned with his own fame and glory, more especially as a singer, poet and actor. A first conspiracy against him was discovered and conspirators who were not executed were compelled to commit suicide. Among them was Nero's old tutor Seneca and the poet Lucan. The great fire which ,soon after devastated Rome was thought by some to be Nero's own doing. He rebuilt the city with great magnificence but this did not dispel the rumours against him. Another conspiracy, involving a revolt in Gaul, found Nero deserted and friendless. He fled to a house outside Rome, hesitated until the soldiers sent to kill him were already fast approaching, then committed suicide. There is a legend that his last words were, 'What a genius dies in me!'

Three emperors came and went in the next eighteen months. The first, elected by the Pretorian Guard – a dangerous precedent – was Galba, already over 70, a competent soldier who might have been a good ruler had he been a younger man. In the laconic phrase of Tacitus: *Omnium consensu capax imperii nisi imperasset* – 'By common consent worthy to be emperor had he never reigned'. After less than eight months he was murdered by Otho. A friend of Nero, until Nero stole his wife, Otho had calculated on being chosen as Galba's heir. When Galba made a different choice, Otho had him assassinated by the Pretorian Guard. His own rule lasted from January to April of the year 60.

At the time of Otho's election the legions on the Rhine had also decided on a new emperor. Their choice fell on Vitellius, who is remembered chiefly as a glutton, though he was not without intelligence and loyalty. He had been appointed to his command on the Rhine by Galba, and felt it therefore his duty to challenge Galba's murderer. He invaded Italy where his legions faced and defeated Otho near Cremona. Otho committed suicide.

Vitellius, who was immediately recognized by the senate as the new emperor, made his way to Rome but had not long to enjoy his imperial grandeur.

News came that the troops in Alexandria had proclaimed Vespasian emperor. Vespasian was not of Roman still less of imperial stock. Born in Spain, the son of a tax collector, he had become a soldier young, had been recognized by Claudius as fit for high command, and had been largely responsible for the conquest of Britain. In the year 68 he had been sent to put down a Jewish revolt and was besieging Jerusalem while Vitellius marched on Rome. Leaving his eldest son Titus, whom he trusted completely, to continue the siege, he moved to Alexandria, and was there hailed as emperor by the troops. The example of Alexandria was followed by all the legions in the east.

Vespasian was deliberate, not to be hurried. He sent two trusted subordinates to take possession of Rome. The army despatched by Vitellius to meet them was defeated near Cremona as the army of Otho had been in the previous year. The victors marched on Rome and met at first some strong but disorganized resistance. But this soon broke down. Vitellius, hardly an inspiring leader, was caught and murdered. Vespasian was recognized as emperor by the accommodating senate.

Vespasian himself made his way to Rome with imperturbable deliberation, investigating the frontier fortifications and annexing the Upper Rhine and the Upper Danube to make the line of defence shorter and stronger, while trusting his subordinates to establish his position in Rome. He entered the city ten months after the senate had acclaimed him as emperor.

Titus in the meantime had taken Jerusalem and returned to join his father in Rome, rich in spoils. Father and son celebrated a joint Triumph, before getting down to the serious business of government. The heavy expenditure caused by the continuous wars of the last years had exhausted all resources. But it was possible with some stringent economies to raise the money to keep the eastern frontiers effectively guarded.

Vespasian, himself a provincial, always had the interest of the provinces at heart. He enlarged the senate by introducing more senators from Italy and other provinces. He understood administration and made appointments on merit in spite of muttering from scions of ancient families. He believed also in education and appointed and endowed men of learning as teachers. He was, after the painful sequence from Nero to Vitellius, entirely sane, experienced both in war and in administration, and indefatigable in his pursuit of sound government. He was sixty when he became emperor and died ten years later making Titus his heir.

Titus combined much of his father's ability with an easy charm which his father had never possessed. There was one social difficulty. While in Judea he had fallen in love with the Jewish princess Berenice. She was not popular in Rome and he had to part with her. (Racine's play on this subject is one of the greatest of French classics, true in spirit to the tragic dilemma on which it is based.)

But Titus reigned only for two years. In the first year, all Italy was shaken by the appalling eruption of Vesuvius, which had been dormant since beyond the memory of man. The total destruction of Pompeii and its surrounding villages – a crowded and fashionable resort filled with the country villas of wealthy Romans – was a major catastrophe.

Titus was succeeded by his brother Domitian – an enigmatic figure, who began his reign with every appearance of a good ruler, but was progressively soured by his lack of success in frontier wars. Vespasian had sent to Britain an admirable governor, Agricola. Domitian recalled him for no reason except jealousy. His jealousy grew ever worse; it could have been that he had some illness of the brain. In the last seven years of his life he saw conspiracy everywhere and put all suspects to death. The situation became unendurable and he was duly murdered.

But this did not lead to a sequence of palace murders such as had darkened the days of Nero and his three successors. The new emperor approved by the senate, Nerva, was a just and peace-loving man. He suppressed the informers who had swarmed round Domitian and declared that no senator would be executed in his time. His short reign (96–98) was an interval in which sanity was restored. Before he died he adopted as his successor, Trajan, who, like Vespasian, came from Spain, and was an experienced soldier.

In a reign of nineteen years Trajan extended the empire by successful wars. He made Dacia (Roumania) into a Roman province; subsequently defeated the Parthians and renamed their land the province of Mesopotamia. He was also a competent administrator with the welfare of his subjects at heart. Within the empire he improved the roads, founded public libraries, built baths, and endowed Rome with an additional forum which bears his name. He also started the *alimenta* – a regular distribution of food for poor children. On his death he was succeeded by another Spaniard, Hadrian, whom he had brought into his own family as a boy of ten, when his father died.

Hadrian (117–138) was the greatest in a sequence of five able emperors from Nerva to Marcus Aurelius, a span of eighty-four years (96–180). An intellectual of subtle tastes, comprehensive interests and outstanding ability, a good soldier and a good administrator, Hadrian travelled into every province of the empire, investigating conditions, redressing grievances and strengthening the defences. He tightened military discipline on the German frontier, and in Britain ordered the building of the famous wall from the Tyne to the Solway, with forts and watch towers, to keep out raiders from Scotland. As a feat of military engineering it was less ambitious than the Great Wall of China, but designed with greater consideration for the morale and welfare of the troops.

In spite of maintaining a strict discipline, Roman commanders were well aware of the necessity of keeping their men in good health, of having enough surgeons and doctors to attend the wounded and the sick, of establishing their camps where fresh water was available and providing sanitation and, if necessary, heating against hard weather, also room for exercise and recreation. The remedies applied by the doctors were mostly herbal involving careful study of the qualities and characteristics of a great number of herbs, and a sufficient supply of them; some were no doubt effective. Such medical care was not of course confined to the stations on the Roman wall; it was provided as far as possible thoughout the Roman army.

Hadrian was alive to the barbarian menace. Rome had lived with it since the days of the Republic and the Gaulish invasions;

revolts and incursions repeatedly broke the Pax Romana. Tribes beyond the frontiers were a constant danger, and although the people of Gaul and Spain, the Britons and Belgae had been (for the most part) Romanized, the German tribes beyond the Rhine needed perpetual vigilance, while those beyond the Elbe and the Danube were continually on the move.

In his last years Trajan had conquered Mesopotamia and Armenia to strengthen the imperial frontier. But Hadrian thought it safer to consolidate than to extend Roman power. He abandoned some of Trajan's conquests as needing too many troops to secure them, and concentrated on holding Asia Minor, the Mediterranean littoral and the south bank of the Danube. He stationed the major part of the Roman army in garrisons. Mobile operations were increasingly entrusted to cavalry recruited from barbarian allies.

He was a great builder. He enriched Nimes with a new temple, known to later generations as *La Maison Carrée*. He enlarged Agrippa's Pantheon in Rome, adding to the majestic columns of the portal a superb rotunda, the first great dome in the West. At Athens, which he loved, he completed the temple to Olympian Zeus below the Acropolis, restored the theatre of Dionysus, built a library and public baths. Only at Jerusalem he over-reached himself, when he tried to bring the Jews into harmony with the empire by replacing Solomon's temple with a shrine to Jupiter. This provoked a last revolt, which ended in the expulsion and dispersal of the Jews.

Twice in the course of his reign of twenty-one years Hadrian undertook to visit his whole empire, two journeys lasting six years each, on the first of which he visited the Roman wall in Britain. In general his policies were well judged and his legislation welcome. He appointed circuit judges to speed up the processes of law, he regularized the salaries and grades of civil servants, he encouraged learning and the arts, he even did something to improve the condition of slaves.

He spent his last years at the peaceful villa he had built for himself at Tibur (now Tivoli), enjoying the conversation of philosophers and friends. A philosopher himself, a musician and something of a poet, he is said to have composed at the end of his days a gently ironic farewell to the soul:

> Animula vagula blandula
> Hospes comesque corporis . . .

Little wandering gentle soul, guest and
companion of the body . . .[8]

The successor whom he had chosen and adopted, Antoninus
Pius, ruled peacefully for twenty-three years (138–161), a reign
devoted to the maintenance of social order and marked by a few
cautiously humane reforms.

The invaders against whom Hadrian had guarded broke
through again in the time of the philosopher emperor, Marcus
Aurelius (161–180) who had to fight the Parthians in Syria and,
later, repel the attacks of the Marcomanni, most savage of the
Germanic tribes, on the Danubian frontier. He led his armies
conscientiously and on the whole with success, consoling himself at
quiet moments by writing his *Meditations*, a manual of stoic
endurance which has given strength and comfort to thousands over
the centuries. He died on the Danubian campaign, far from civilization and comfort, at a bleak military outpost that the Romans called
Windobona; the same place which later became the magical city of
Vienna.

From the reign of Marcus Aurelius until the dissolution of Roman
rule in the West the empire was never free from trouble; always in
one or another province there was tribal rebellion or peasant revolt
and on one or another of the long frontiers invaders broke through.
Marcus Aurelius planned to establish a neutral zone north of the
Danube by settling friendly tribes there to keep out other barbarians. But would the tribes remain friendly? The shortage of manpower and of recruits for the army left the emperor no alternative.

A more lethal enemy invaded the empire before Marcus Aurelius died. Troops returning from the Parthian campaign brought
with them a plague which ravaged Italy and the provinces for
almost a decade and became endemic. The population had long
been declining in spite of all efforts to stimulate its growth – such as
the charitable grants to poor children, the *alimenta*, which Trajan
had organized to encourage larger families. One cause in central
Italy may have been the decay of the Campagna; once regarded as
the market garden of Rome it had become a malarious swamp. It
seems possible also that the very efficiency of the water supplies to
Rome and other cities may have increased the prevalence of water-
borne diseases.

There is no need to associate the diminishing population and the waning of Roman strength with moral decadence, as was once the fashion. The soldiers and administrators of the empire in its later years, stimulated from time to time by remarkably able emperors – such men as Septimius Severus, Aurelian, Diocletian, Constantine and Theodosius – postponed the ultimate collapse for at least two hundred years. There was nothing decadent in that achievement.

By the end of the second century administrative and military expenses were too heavy for the declining population to bear. From the time of Domitian onwards, increased taxation to support larger armies oppressed the provinces. The emperor Caracalla, in 212, threw open Roman citizenship with its privileges and responsibilities to all inhabitants of the empire except slaves. What had once been a coveted privilege now served to compel thousands of humbler citizens to pay higher taxes. Even so the financial problem was unsolved. Armies continued to grow, chiefly for defence, and taxes to rise. By the beginning of the third century the wealth of the empire was dwindling as fast as the population.

The drain of Roman gold to India and the Far East in exchange for spices, silk and other luxuries caused old-fashioned Romans to shake their heads in disapproval, but the trade gathered momentum. The need for ready money led to the multiplication of local mints, by no means all authorized. Copper coins dipped in a thin wash of silver were freely circulated. Gold went out of circulation altogether, vanishing into the vaults of intelligent speculators.

In the last analysis, the economy of the empire was based on agriculture. There was some manufacture but little of it for export. Pottery, always a localized industry, flourished in different regions. The famous red-glaze ware of Arezzo was widely distributed over the provinces in the early days of the empire. Various branded wares – *terra sigillata* – came from potteries in Gaul, Britain and the Rhineland. The oddly-named Samian ware came from Gaul. Mosaics of popular subjects were also sold to provincial buyers in transportable sections. The empire had at one time presented a sufficiently large market, but by the third century it had reached and passed its fullest expansion. Demand slackened and disappeared as money grew ever more scarce.

Roman agriculture was also declining. The cultivation of great estates by slaves, whether for luxurious living or commercial profit, had come to an end. The supply of slaves had diminished since

Roman conquests ceased. But a more constructive cause for the change was the practice of settling veterans on the land, which Tiberius Gracchus had attempted and Marius had restored in the last century of the Republic. The peasant farmer had again become essential to Roman agriculture. Large estates existed, but the owners kept under their direct control only what they needed for a comfortable family life; the rest was farmed by tenants; it was little more than subsistence farming. And over all Italy, as the population steadily fell, unwanted land reverted to waste.

Rome, with a quarter of a million inhabitants, drew its corn supply from North Africa – which was one reason why the city could not afford to lose control of the Mediterranean.

These shadows were already discernible in the Antonine period – that golden afternoon of Roman rule before the long sunset. The literature, art and thought of the time was interesting, rather than great, a falling-off from earlier centuries.

The first century had seen Seneca, moralist and dramatist, more highly thought of by our seventeenth-century ancestors than he is today, also his nephew Lucan who told the story of Caesar's war with Pompey in his epic *Pharsalia*, and – like Seneca – killed himself in the reign of Nero.

More sympathetic than either, was the elder Pliny who compiled an encyclopaedia of natural history. (He originated both terms, using the words 'enkyklios paideia' in his preface and calling his book *Historia Naturalis*.) In this work he collected all that his predecessors, Greek or Roman, had imagined or observed about the world, its flora and fauna. His authority was not questioned until the Renaissance, and his book, right or wrong, is still a delight. The gallant old gentleman perished at the age of fifty-six suffocated by the fumes of Vesuvius when organizing relief for the victims of Pompeii.

The slave-born philosopher Epictetus, educated in Rome but active most of his life in Greece, taught self-discipline, the cultivation of the mind, and indifference to worldly prosperity; he had had a hard life himself and rightly claimed to have found an answer to human troubles in this simplified Stoic philosophy. His later influence on European morality extended from the Renaissance to the Victorian age.

Juvenal, most ferocious of Roman satirists, wrote his best work in the reign of Hadrian, revealing the nastier side of Roman society in language that easily embraces the rhetorical, the colloquial and the pornographic.

The most sympathetic writer of the period, at least to the historian, is the Greek, Plutarch (*c.*50–120), who believed that the fusion of Greek ideas with Roman political ability, would be the foundation of good government. His famous *Lives* serve in part to illustrate this conviction, but the care with which he compiled his facts and the humanity of his interpretation make his biographies perhaps the fullest and most sympathetic composite picture that we have of the lost world of classical antiquity.

Galen and Ptolemy, names familiar in the natural sciences for the next twelve hundred years, also lived in the second century. Galen, who came from Pergamum, studied anatomy as physician to a troop of gladiators, made some experiments with animals, later became fashionable in Rome and left a body of work behind him which, in garbled form, influenced western medicine at least until the sixteenth century. Some of his observations were useful, and his belief in the value of experiments was sound, but his theory that the body is composed of Four Humours, illness being caused by disequilibrium between them, was a rich source of error. Another physician, famous in his day, was Aulus Celsus, whose *De Medicina* in eight books is available in an English translation.

Less is known of Ptolemy except that he lived and worked at Alexandria, by that time (in spite of the historic prestige of Athens) the intellectual capital of the empire. Mathematician, geographer and astronomer, his most useful work was to collect, enlarge and correct the work of the Greek astronomer Hipparchus (161–126 BC). Ptolemy mapped the heavens, placing over a thousand stars in his *Syntaxis* (called the *Almagest* in the Middle Ages) and proved to his satisfaction that the earth was the centre of the universe, a view which prevailed until Copernicus in the sixteenth century showed it to be wrong. The *Almagest* was of real use in navigation nonetheless. His work on geography, though more inaccurate and misleading, was used by later geographers and consulted by Columbus.

Second only to Hadrian as a restorer of famous buildings was Herodes Atticus, a landowner of immense wealth whose family came from Marathon. He built the largest odeon in Athens for musical performances, and restored the stadium; he embellished the fountain of Peirene and rebuilt the theatre at Corinth, endowed

Delphi with a new stadium and Olympia with a reservoir, and rescued countless other ruins in Greece: a benefactor who well deserves to be remembered. The Greek traveller Pausanias also deserved well of his contemporaries and of posterity; his manual on the wonders of Greece, an excellent guidebook in its own time, has been invaluable to archaeologists in ours.

Architectural confidence outlasted the great period of Rome. The splendid arch of Septimius Severus, the gigantic ruins of the baths of Caracalla and Diocletian, the colossal apses of the basilica of Maxentius show that the imaginative scope and technical skill of Roman builders survived political decay. In decorative sculpture the Romans did not excel; they were essentially illustrators and story-tellers and the reliefs on the arch of Titus at one end of the forum, and of Severus at the other, still more the bronzes that encircle Trajan's column are historical documents rather than works of art. Everyone and everything has somehow to be represented, regardless of space, design and the problems of perspective.

In one form of sculpture the Romans excelled: this was the portrait bust. From the last century of the Republic to the decline of the western empire they cultivated portraiture. Taste and technique altered: dry and austere under the Republic, softened by neo-Hellenic influences under the empire, assuming an almost baroque elegance by the time of Marcus Aurelius. At their height, in the first century AD, the anonymous Roman portrait sculptors were among the finest the world has ever known.

IV

The Parthians, the restless mounted bowmen from the Caspian, who broke up the Seleucid empire in Persia and several times defeated the Romans, were at different periods between 100 BC and AD 200 masters of Armenia, Asia Minor, Mesopotamia and the greater part of the old Persian empire.

Indifferent, or perhaps impervious to the art of government, they were overlords of Persia rather than rulers, and only their strongest kings exerted effective sovereignty over the native aris-tocracy. The long-established Persian administration under provincial satraps functioned reasonably well whoever was on the throne.

Hadrian's predecessor, Trajan, conquered most of the Parthian empire (AD 115–6) but Hadrian relinquished it, as too difficult to hold. A century later, in a revolt supported and inspired by the Zoroastrian priesthood, a Persian nobleman overthrew the Parthian king and founded the Sassanian dynasty, the first truly Persian dynasty since the defeat of Darius III by Alexander the Great. The Sassanid empire lasted over four hundred years (226–640) thanks to the support of a powerful priesthood, and a sequence of warrior kings strong enough to hold the nobility in check. The form of government continued much as before but for the introduction of a principal minister of state entirely dependent on the king who could be responsible for unpopular policies and dismissed (or executed) if things went wrong, leaving the prestige of the crown intact. This office was later perpetuated by the Islamic conquerors under the name of Grand Vizier.

The first clash with Rome occurred when an inexperienced young emperor, Gordian III, invaded Persian territory as a preventive measure and was there murdered by his troops in favour of an emperor more to their liking. The new emperor, Philip the Arab, sued for peace and withdrew. Returning to Rome, he celebrated with great pomp the thousandth anniversary of the city's foundation. Such celebrations of the past are apt to occur when a people loses its faith in the future. Within months, Philip was eliminated by a rival emperor, Decius, who was himself defeated and killed soon after by Gothic invaders on the Danube frontier.

Ten years later the emperor Valerian, a respectable veteran commander, made another attempt to keep the Persians out. He too was abandoned by his troops and captured by the king of Persia, Shapur I, who subsequently overran Armenia, sacked Antioch, invaded Syria, reached the Mediterranean coast and began to build a fleet. No one knows for certain what became of Valerian. With the Persians on the Mediterranean and the most powerful of all the German tribes, the Goths, over the Danube – and even raiding Athens with impunity – the Roman empire may have seemed lost beyond recovery.

Gallienus, son of the unfortunate Valerian, whom he did nothing to rescue, reorganized the army, moving the headquarters to Milan and greatly strengthening the cavalry. It was his cavalry that utterly defeated the Goths at Naissus (now Nis in Jugoslavia) as they returned from one of their plundering raids; they left 50,000 dead. Gallienus aiming now to be emperor, was murdered by the supporters of a rival, the emperor Aurelian – known as *Manu ad ferram* (Hand on hilt).

He was indeed a man of speed and ferocity, a great disciplinarian and an outstanding cavalry general. He drove out the Goths and fought two successful battles against the German tribes now pouring through the Brenner pass. He overthrew a gaggle of lesser generals who had set up as emperors in Britain, Spain and Gaul, then celebrated a Triumph in Rome, displaying among the captives Zenobia, queen of Palmyra, who for several years had successfully asserted her independence of Rome and controlled a vital trade route into Asia.

Aurelian next built a massive new wall round Rome, the city having long outgrown its ancient defences. He also introduced a new religious cult, that of *Sol Invictus*, the unconquerable sun, designed to raise the morale of the troops. He sought to improve the coinage by using a thicker coating of silver on the ubiquitous copper coins. He planned to settle with the Persians, but he too was murdered by mutinous troops as he crossed into Asia Minor (275).

The Romans had better luck than they deserved. A decade of confusion was followed by the election of Diocletian. Born obscurely in Dalmatia, he had risen from the ranks, the first Roman emperor of servile origin. In a reign of twenty-one years this indefatigable soldier, organizer and improviser dragged the empire to its feet. He drove the Persians out of Syria and Asia Minor, suppressed a revolt in Egypt, re-established Roman control of the Mediterranean, repelled the barbarian tribes on the Rhine and Danube, stationed permanent garrisons with strong contingents of cavalry at all vulnerable points on the frontiers. He re-organized the army, greatly increased the strength of the cavalry and introduced skilled bowmen to stiffen the infantry. The new cavalry and the bowmen were mostly recruited from barbarian allies, born horsemen and practised archers; besides there was no alternative. As the population dwindled, the army grew less 'Roman' with every generation, even with every decade. By the fourth century, barbarians were freely recruited. Legionaries stationed in the remoter parts of empire married the local women; garrisons became self-perpetuating as sons grew up to take their fathers' places.

For strategic reasons Diocletian created three additional capitals. Rome was geographically ill-placed and the fossilized senate was out of touch. The new capitals were Treves in the Rhineland,

Sirmium on the Sava (about fifty miles from modern Belgrade) and the headquarters of the Danube legions, and Nicomedia in Asia Minor. He also appointed a trusted comrade-in-arms as co-emperor with himself and two assistant emperors (called Caesars), one to assist each emperor. The first task of his co-emperor, Maximian, was to put down a widespread peasant revolt which had brought civil government almost to a standstill in southern Gaul and a great part of Spain. (Peasant revolts on a smaller scale were by this time as common as strikes in modern Europe.)

Turning his attention to finance, he simplified taxation by instituting a single tax on land, controlled the mints, reformed the currency, tried to restore the standard of silver coinage, re-introduced gold and fixed prices. It was a valiant effort that lasted only a few years: the tax on land proved unworkable; the supply of precious metal from the mines ran low; neither the fixed prices nor the (temporarily) better currency revived a stagnant economy.

His administrative reforms were more successful. He regularized the hierarchy of judges and civil servants, subdivided the over-large provinces into regions, increased the number of officials and divided the civil from the military authority. At a lower level, he reorganized sewage disposal and the postal system. All this made for quicker solution of local problems, or should have done so had there been enough men to do the work. But in government as in agriculture the men were lacking. Diocletian tried to solve the problem by making all essential professions, from civil servants to bakers and farmers, hereditary by compulsion. This was useless when there was no son to inherit; and over all the empire such 'tied' workers often deserted their toil for vagabondage or (near the frontiers) joined the barbarians.

Diocletian was no theorist; he solved what problems could be solved by rough and ready means. Nonetheless his success in war, his reforms in the army and some of his administrative changes postponed the dissolution of the empire for another century. His strong character, his indefatigable work, and his concentration on reform and readjustment were in themselves enough to change the atmosphere of delay and resignation which had weakened the general will and prevented necessary reforms during the past century.

In the nineteenth year of his reign, he celebrated with his co-emperor a joint Triumph in Rome, and endowed the demoted capital with the last of its luxurious baths, so huge that four churches and the National Museum are all now accommodated in the ruins.

The distresses of the Roman world drove men and women towards occult and mystical religions. Mythras, a sun god from Persia, whose rites were celebrated underground and involved the sacrifice of a bull, was especially popular in the army. Aurelian's introduction of *Sol Invictus* on his coins (continued by succeeding emperors) could have been a gesture towards the followers of Mythras. Secrecy was an integral part of the worship of Mythras, a religion which, incidentally, excluded women.

The secrecy which surrounded the Christian religion arose from fear of persecution, but during the third century both the fear and the persecution had declined. Christians who openly denounced pagan gods, or ostentatiously refused to burn incense to them on public occasions were asking for trouble. But those who acted with reasonable discretion were generally immune. Christians were still, like the Mythraists, the followers of a minority religion. But the number of converts was growing and some of them held offices of state and a few of them were soldiers.

It has been observed that the conquest of classical civilization by Christianity is one of the wonders of history. After all, the Christians exercised no compulsion, had no support from the ruling classes, and used persuasion alone. But the organization of Christian communities in such great cities as Alexandria, Rome, and Nicomedia was impressive, and in time of trouble the overworked civil authorities had been known to enlist the help of Christian bishops and priests to keep order or alleviate distress.

From time to time, for no very clear reason, new persecutions broke out. One had occurred about the year 250. Suddenly at the latter end of his reign, Diocletian issued an edict for the destruction of all Christian writings and places of worship, with death to those who resisted. All Christians who failed to recant were deprived of Roman citizenship and their clergy were required to prove that they had abandoned their faith by sacrificing to the gods. The cause of this outburst is obscure. It seems possible that Diocletian, who had previously taken little notice of the sect, suddenly became aware of its continued growth and saw it as forming a 'state within the state', and constituting a danger to government.

The persecution outlasted his reign and continued with intermittent ferocity for ten years (303–313). Legend has greatly mag-
nified the number of martyrs; many Christians temporarily con-
formed; others evaded notice. The Scriptures were sometimes
hidden with the connivance of friendly authorities. After all, in this
sphere as in others, the imperial bureaucracy was short-staffed.
Even so, many Christians were executed and many more sent in
chain gangs to the mines. The attack was more widespread and
longer lasting than any the Christians had previously endured.

After twenty years of unremitting toil Diocletian abdicated and
compelled his unwilling co-emperor to do the same. Their respective caesars succeeded as emperors. The abler of the two, Constan-
tius Chlorus, was in Britain at the time and died a year later at the
northern town of Eboracum (York), (306). His son Constantine
was instantly acclaimed as emperor by the troops, a claim strongly
contested by the surviving emperor and the two new caesars.

Constantine was patient, unscrupulous and clever. First, after
leaving Britain in good order, he established himself in Gaul; then
(not without provocation) invaded Italy, defeated and killed his
rival, Maxentius, and entered Rome (312). Here he profited by his
victory to abolish the Pretorian Guard, which had been the bane of
the empire for the past two hundred years.

Having settled the frontiers between himself and the emperor
ruling in the east – one Licinius – he issued, with his co-operation,
the Edict of Milan which put a stop to the persecution of Christians
in the west (313). Licinius, who persisted in persecuting Christians
in the east, was murdered ten years later. Thereafter Constantine
ruled as sole emperor until his death in 337.

He claimed that he had been told in a dream to put the Christian
symbol on his banner before his critical victory outside Rome.
Naturally therefore he respected the power of the Christian God.
His mother, also a convert, devoted herself after the manner of
women to the more spiritual, not to say magical, strength of the
Christian faith. With imperial prestige to support her, she set out for
Jerusalem, discovered the site of the Crucifixion and found three
crosses at the bottom of a well. The cross of Christ was regarded as
authenticated when a sick man lay on it and was healed. While his
mother added to the legends and miracles of Christianity, Constantine was impressed by Christian tenacity in the face of persecution,
and recognized the power with which a well-organized Church

might underpin the civil administration of the empire. The first essential was to unite and organize the faithful. For this reason he convened a council at Nicaea to eliminate the dangers of theological dispute, by which he meant the Arian heresy which threatened to split the Church and make it politically useless to him.

The priest Arius had challenged the identification of Christ with God, arguing that he was not an integral part of the divine essence but a separate being of like nature created by God. At the council, over which Constantine presided, unity and orthodoxy triumphed – but not for long. The Arian heresy, which became increasingly entangled in politics, was not finally stifled for another fifty years. By that time a number of Gothic tribes had been converted by Arian missionaries, adding further confusion to the state of Christianity in the empire.

In spite of this, Constantine's judgement in bringing the Christian priesthood into close association with the government proved to be sound. For the rest, both in military and civil affairs he developed the policies of Diocletian. In the east, however, he moved the capital from Nicomedia to the ancient Greek city of Byzantium, commanding the entrance to the Black Sea. Renamed, enlarged, endowed with a gigantic underground reservoir, with palaces, churches and a huge stadium, his city of Constantinople remained an imperial capital for over a thousand years. As the centre of a fruitful culture, at once Hellenic and Christian, and based on the Roman conception of civil law, its influence radiated over the Greek mainland and the eastern Mediterranean, over Asia Minor and the Danubian basin, and far into Russia. Rome, on which Constantine bestowed the last and least distinguished of its triumphal arches, stagnated in slow decay.

Less noticed was the decline of Pergamum, for centuries the centre of trade routes from east to west, and the home of artists and sculptors. The trade routes and the traders henceforward met in Constantinople and Pergamum slowly died.

Constantine's conversion to Christianity arose almost certainly from conviction rather than calculation; conviction admittedly of a superstitious kind. The Christian god had given him the victory in his most critical battle outside Rome, and was therefore more powerful than Mythras, *Sol Invictus*, Jupiter or any of the others. Neither his political nor his personal conduct was in the least influenced by his conversion. He was baptized only on his deathbed, a common arrangement at the time among pagan converts, anxious to have their sins washed away at the last possible moment. He showed his respect for his saviour by substituting other – and no more merciful – forms of execution for crucifixion, because it was unseemly that common criminals should die as Christ had died. In future they would be burnt alive.

Constantine had the usual characteristics of the tough, successful soldiers of his time, but he was morally not inferior and mentally far superior to the men he overthrew, the unworthy successors of Diocletian, whose policy in every respect save one, he confirmed, developed and completed.

V

Roman success against the Persians in the time of Diocletian owed as much to the misfortunes of Persia as to the revival of Rome. A sequence of unlucky or short-lived kings weakened the Persian state which was further disrupted by religious disturbances. The prophet Mani, whose influence long outlasted his capture and execution (c.273), taught that all matter is essentially evil and only the spirit is good. This Manichaean heresy spread later to Christian North Africa, then went underground to reappear sporadically in medieval Europe, with the Bogomils in the Byzantine empire, the Albigenses and the Cathari in France and Italy.

In the minority of Shapur II (who, on his father's premature death was symbolically crowned as king while still in his mother's womb) Persia was devastated by Arab invasions. At seventeen he led a punitive attack which ended the danger from that quarter. During his long reign, Shapur the Great (309–379) gave his people supremacy abroad and a long period of peace at home.

Persian attacks on the Roman frontier were naturally resumed. The emperor Julian (361–63) forced the passage of the Tigris and inflicted a serious defeat on them, only to be fatally wounded a few weeks later. His successor relinquished Armenia as the price of peace and, with that improved frontier, Shapur for a time rested content.

Julian, last male survivor of the house of Constantine, had first proved himself as a soldier by repelling the barbarian Franks on the Lower Rhine. Embittered by the intrigues and murders in his

supposedly Christian family and well-grounded in classical philosophy, he reverted to paganism and, had he reigned longer than a bare
two years, might have checked the conversion of the empire. His
policy did not command much popular support, but neither did it
provoke great opposition. The Christians were still a minority and
Mythraism was still popular in the army. It is only a dramatic fable
that he died with the words 'Vicisti Galilei!' on his lips. ('Thou hast
conquered, Galilean!')

His successor, Jovian, elected by Julian's army, made peace with
Shapur, withdrew from Persia and dropped the persecution of
Christians. It is doubtful whether Mythraism could, in the long run,
have been a serious rival: it excluded women and had not the
widespread organization that held Christianity together. In any case
Julian had no intention of giving imperial support to any *specific*
pagan cult. He revered the School of Athens and hoped for a return
to serious philosophy among educated men, leaving superstitious
cults of whatever kind to the multitude. In this he was out of key
with his age: a great deal of mystical nonsense was talked, thought
and believed in the fourth century, but faith, not philosophic doubt,
was dominant.

The empire's eastern frontier was temporarily stabilized. The
Danube frontier was the danger zone. The Goths established on the
north bank were hard-pressed by the Huns, the most destructive
tribe which had yet emerged from Asia. The Goths, who had been
Christians (of the Arian variety) for the last thirty years, appealed
with unusual humility to be received into the empire. After laying
down their arms, they crossed the Danube as refugees and friends.
But their arrival provoked the ill-feeling of the natives and, within a
year or two, they attacked their hosts. The emperor Valens, who
intervened, was overwhelmingly defeated near Adrianople and
never seen again. Meantime the Goths ravaged the Balkans (378).

Theodosius, an experienced soldier from Spain who was elected
emperor immediately after the catastrophe, saved – or at least
stabilized – the situation. By military skill, diplomacy and patience,
he divided the Gothic chieftains against each other, enlisted some of
them in the Roman army and settled others as colonists, called
foederati – confederate allies. His policy saved the eastern empire by
attracting the tribes most amenable to settlement, and deflecting the
more aggressive to the west.

In civil government Theodosius relied on the Christian Church to unite the empire, proclaimed the doctrine of the Trinity according to the Nicene creed, forbade all discussion of religion and prohibited pagan worship. He even abolished the Olympic Games as a dangerous relic of paganism. But he could not dominate the ministers of the Church as Constantine had done. Constantine had used them: Theodosius needed them. Having offended the archbishop of Milan, he had to assuage his wrath by doing penance because he could not afford to alienate him. Increasingly the maintenance of order devolved on the Church.

On the death of Theodosius in 395, the empire was divided between his two inadequate sons. The eastern empire, based on Byzantium, was reasonably secure. But the Goths were soon overrunning Italy. In 410 they took Rome, sacked it with enthusiasm (piously sparing the churches) then departed with their booty, which included the emperor's sister (Galla Placidia) whom they gave as wife to one of their chieftains. The emperor himself – whose name is of no consequence – had taken refuge in Ravenna.

The fall of Rome, the Eternal City, was inevitable, but the memory of Roman greatness had not faded, and the barbarian conquest caused an outcry in the Mediterranean world. This should not have happened: this would not have happened – the pagan whisperings grew louder – if the old gods had been respected.

Some of the Goths – the so-called Visigoths – were persuaded to invade Spain rather than Italy, to fight the Vandals who had got there first. The Vandals harried their way southward, left their name to the province of (V)Andalusia, whence about 80,000 of them, under pressure from the Goths, crossed into Africa. Here they overran the north coast as far as Carthage and cut off the grain supply on which Rome depended. Spain, meanwhile, was divided between Visigothic chieftains usually at war with each other. Roman administration and the use of Latin in some sort survived, but the decay of this, once one of the most civilized provinces of the empire, was hastened by the ill-feeling between the Christians of Spain from their bishops downwards, and the heretic Arian Goths, a situation not resolved for more than a century.

A new menace appeared when the Huns, whose headquarters was on the Danube, began to make annual raids into the west under their leader Attila. They came for plunder and slaves, not for conquest. Aghast, the contemporary historian Ammianus wrote, 'This race of untamed men without hearth or law, aflame with an inhuman desire for plundering others property, make their violent way amid the rapine and slaughter of their neighbours'. Checked in Gaul by an imperial army with Gothic allies, Attila turned aside to invade Italy, sacked Padua, Verona and Milan and advanced towards Rome. The cowering emperor turned to the bishop of Rome, Leo I, who had been recognized as primate, Pope of all Christendom, and appointed him to lead an embassy to Attila. Leo set out boldly with two companions. Later there was talk of a miracle, a vision of St Peter and St Paul with drawn swords before whom Attila recoiled. But it was late in the season and the Huns had already as much booty as they could carry. Attila was on the point of withdrawal anyway. It was a chance, not a miracle, that he died that winter (453).

The facts detract little from the courage of the Pope and nothing from the significance of his confrontation with Attila: the emperor had resigned into the hands of the Church his task of defending his subjects. Three years later Vandal pirates sailed up the Tiber and methodically plundered Rome. The emperor had as usual removed to the greater safety of Ravenna but the Pope stayed in the city to negotiate with the Vandals and give what help he could to the people.

Fugitives from some of the northern cities made settlements in the water-logged islands of the lagoons at the head of the Adriatic (452). This group of wretched fishing villages profited by its sheltered position and gradually developed a trade in saltfish. In the ninth century it became known by the name of Venice.

During this final disintegration, the imperial court kept its state with unabated luxury at Ravenna. The weak and vicious emperor, Valentinian III, was the son of Galla Placidia, who as a young princess had been carried off and married to a Goth. Later she had returned to become the wife of a respectable Roman and live out her days as empress mother. The mosaics in her tomb at Ravenna are among the loveliest in the world: the Good Shepherd guards his trusting flock under a starry dome of melting blue: tender, dignified, noble, reflecting nothing of the surrounding disasters from which the imperial court had isolated itself.

By the latter half of the fifth century effective power in Italy was exercised by barbarian generals in the Roman army. Out of respect to the imperial past they used Roman titles. The 'patrician' Ricimer (a Swabian and in no sense a patrician) set up and pulled down four puppet emperors in fifteen years. At Constantinople the emperor, powerful in his own dominions, was not strong enough to intervene in the west; he merely asserted a nominal control by recognizing these Roman puppets. Ricimer's successor, another 'patrician' of Germanic stock, Odovacar, gave up the farce, deposed the last of the puppets and ruled independently. Loth to abandon the Roman west, the emperor at Constantinople commissioned Theodoric, a chief of the Ostrogoths, to get rid of him.

Theodoric defeated Odovacar, established himself at Ravenna as ruler of an independent Ostrogothic kingdom in Italy, giving nominal allegiance to the emperor at Constantinople. He was flattered when his son was raised by imperial favour to the now meaningless rank of consul. He was, to all intents, an independent ruler, relying on the strength of his well disciplined army and conducting the civil government within the conventions of Roman law and with the help of what was left of the bureaucracy. He chose his advisers from the old administrative families, men of experience and integrity, among them the philosopher Boethius. He was the best ruler Italy had known since Theodosius died.

Meanwhile the last of the Roman troops had been withdrawn from Britain, too remote to be worth defending. The inhabitants were left to the mercy of sea-borne invaders from North Germany, the Angles, the Saxons and the Frisians who overran three-quarters of the island during the next dark century. The Britons (such as survived) fell back to the mountains of Wales and the peninsula of Cornwall, preserving their language, something of their Romano-British culture and their Christian religion. A temporary halt to the heathen conquerors, a period of respite under a successful chieftain, may have occurred somewhere in the west and may have created the dim folk memory from which the legend of King Arthur grew. More certain, though confused in outline, is the story of the British boy (well born, since his name was Patricius) carried off by pirates and sold as a slave in Ireland whence he escaped, returning later because of a dream to preach Christianity to the Irish – in fact to organize existing Christianity and to bring Ireland into touch with Rome. Fragmentary, simple, strangely moving, the 'Confession' of Saint Patrick has survived.

The traditional date for the end of the Roman empire in the west is AD 476, the year in which Odovacar deposed his last nominee. This event was little noticed at the time. The empire did not end

suddenly; it faded away over several generations. Italian landowners and their families on their country estates experienced a
steep deterioration in their standards of living as Italy ceased to be
the heart of empire, trade and agriculture declined and the population fell. Fields went out of cultivation and the term *agri in deserti*
became frequent in late Roman Gaul. This decline went on for
several generations and there was time for adjustment. Landowners
learnt to live frugally on their own produce with a few luxuries and
very few slaves but their condition, all told, was less dangerous and
dreadful than that of the rich landed class who had been involved in
the convulsive collapse of the Roman Republic.

The raids of the barbarians could be shockingly destructive, but
much of the countryside was unaffected and peacefully stagnant.
Locally, they came in large numbers but in waves and groups, the
overall number at any one time not overwhelmingly great. The
collapse of administration at the lower levels happened slowly; men
became accustomed to the worsening condition of the roads, the
inefficient servicing of water supplies, the falling value of money,
the gradual recourse to barter, the confusion and delay in every legal
or administrative transaction. Country landowners still preserved
their cultured, old-fashioned traditions, read books, wrote letters,
made music, from time to time spent a little on the beautification of
house or garden. Small peasant farmers, scraping a bare existence
from the soil, may even have gained some relief from the heavy
burden of taxation through the scarcity of tax collectors, and were
more directly troubled at any time by bad weather than by barbarians.

Town dwellers suffered most. They were the first objective of
plundering barbarians, and many of them had depended on imported corn which no longer came. Yet even in Rome, where
thousands had lived on free corn and starved when it failed, the
descendants of older families were able to live conspicuously idle
lives in the midst of disaster. They attended the now wholly
powerless senate, entertained provincial visitors with condescend-
ing hospitality and believed that Rome would survive its present
troubles as it had survived others in the past.

Rutilius Namatianus, a poet from Provence, descendant of
many civil servants, was prefect of the city in 412, two years after
the Goths sacked it. Four years later he composed a poem on his
return to Gaul; in this he lamented the 'long wars and ruined fields'

of his native land but praised the glory of Rome with its splendid buildings and busy life as though nothing terrible had happened. He returned by sea because the Via Aurelia was in the hands of the Goths and the bridges were all broken, but he punctuated his journey with pleasant visits to old friends on the coast and was joyously welcomed in Pisa where his father had been governor and the grateful citizens had recently put up a statue to him. His poem breathes a calm confidence in the survival of empire. After all, Rome had suffered many vicissitudes and had always triumphed in the end.

> Let the Goths in panic expose their necks to you;
> Let the peaceful lands pay bounties to you;
> May your lap be filled with barbarian treasures . . . . . Fortune
> Which is cruel today will be kind tomorrow,
> Let your law extend to all the known world,
> It will not die.[9]

There at least he was right. Roman law infiltrated barbarian practice as the Churchmen of the west assisted the Franks and the Goths to codify their customs. It was Rome's most lasting legacy.

What else? Latin survived as the language of the Church although much Latin literature vanished later through clerical disapproval and barbarian illiteracy. Some conception of the Pax Romana, the peace and unity which had been, however ineffectively, the guiding concept of Roman rule, was handed on by tradition. Among older people memories lingered of a time when the West had been united by a common language, a common code of law and a network of well-kept highways, when Roman armies had defended the frontiers and Roman ships had controlled the Mediterranean: all this in contrast to pirate-infested seas, and warring tribal kingdoms. The reunion of Europe, by force of arms, diplomacy or economic necessity lingered on as a political ideal.

Some roads survived, where they met the needs of the barbarian states. Most public works fell into decay. At the height of empire, it had been a matter of prestige for Roman cities to have fine buildings, often generously built by their richest citizens. Small and remote towns might well have a well-planned forum, baths, a theatre, statues of respected benefactors. Such buildings could no longer be maintained, though some public baths survived, after a fashion, into the Middle Ages. Tombs and theatres were converted into fortresses; temples served the same purpose or became granaries, while a few were taken over for Christian churches.

The Romans were notable architects and engineers, but in other spheres they made few technical advances. Their water supplies and their central heating by means of hypocausts have been justly praised. But they made no advance in lighting; flaring torches and miserable oil lamps were all they had after dark. Their success in arms was the result of good organization, rarely of tactical innovations or new weapons. The riches of Italian agriculture in the last century of the Republic came from the intelligent specialization of a few and the unlimited exploitation of slave labour.

The social disorders which resulted from the disappearance of an independent peasantry had destroyed the Republic, but the later custom of rewarding veteran soldiers with small grants of land had, over generations, recreated a peasant agriculture. When, with the decline of population Diocletian, with the best intentions, compelled the peasants to stay on their land, he created a type of hereditary tenure which foreshadowed the serfdom of the Middle Ages and made experiment and enterprise impossible. The agriculture of Italy sank to subsistence level.

The Romans speculated little on theories of government, but their tradition and training encouraged a sense of social responsibility and civic pride. The doles of grain and free amusements offered to the poor, at first in Rome and later in most of the cities, might in their immediate origin be moves in a political campaign or precautions against civil disorder, but they were also a social service. When Pliny in his will left money for the children of the poor in his native city of Como, he was actuated partly by the desire to stimulate the birth-rate and partly by civic pride, but also by genuine benevolence: some of the money was to be spent on an annual party for the children. The *alimenta* – children's allowances – available to the poor of Rome and ultimately to almost all the larger cities, failed to stimulate the falling birth-rate, but were nonetheless social services of some significance.

The better treatment of slaves in the later centuries of the empire was in part due to shortage of supply, but also to a more generous attitude. Before Rome became Christian the emperor Vespasian had regulated and improved the diet, conditions and hours of the most wretched of all groups – the slaves who worked in the mines. The Christian Church condemned inhuman usage of slaves but did not condemn slavery. Constantine, confirming an earlier edict of Hadrian, made no distinction between the murder of a slave and the murder of a free man: both were punishable by death. The atrocious combats of enslaved gladiators were finally stopped by Christian influence.

There were incurable evils in the rule of Rome but there were also ideals worth preserving. Far back, before the growth of empire, before the collapse of the Republic, the Romans had cultivated (or their descendants thought they had cultivated) the virtues of courage, endurance and loyalty. They had valued liberty above all things, sacrifice for the nation and the community, integrity in public life, a certain noble austerity in private. The 'history' which propagated this conception of Roman virtue was at best uncertain. By the fifth century it was not often remembered, nor would it have been of much interest to the barbarians if it had been.

The buried Roman virtues praised by Livy, Tacitus and Seneca came into their own again with the editing of classical texts in the Renaissance. From the sixteenth century onwards Roman history was increasingly studied; by the end of the seventeenth century it was an essential part of a gentleman's education in western Europe. Even before that, Roman precedents were cited in European politics. Admiration for the old Republican virtues of Rome was believed by erudite contemporaries to have strengthened the opposition to Charles I of England; they were freely cited in the late eighteenth century against George III in the American Revolution; they were the common stuff of political rhetoric in Europe for much of the nineteenth century. This posthumous influence has yielded alike to the processes of more accurate historical research and to the decline of classical education. But the accidents of time may not yet have exhausted the legacy of Rome.

VI

The eastern empire survived the west through many vicissitudes, for more than seven hundred years, as the greatest and most influential state in the Christian world. Even after its wanton destruction by the Crusaders in 1204, it maintained something of its prestige, civilization and learning until its final extinction by the Ottoman Turks in 1453. Its citizens regarded themselves as the custodians of

Greek culture and Roman law, and believed also that they were first among Christians, the Chosen People of the New Covenant, a conviction which gave them the confidence and sense of purpose that the Romans had lost.

The reigning emperor at the close of the fifth century had asserted only a nominal authority over Theodoric, but neither he nor his successors accepted barbarian rule in the west as anything but temporary. They were still *Roman* emperors, and when the time was ripe would reassert their authority in Italy. Theodoric had not been dead ten years when a campaign against the Goths was launched by the emperor Justinian, confident in the resources of Byzantium and the strength of his army.

Justinian came of peasant stock in the Balkans. His uncle the emperor Justin who had risen from the ranks, brought him to Constantinople to be educated as his heir. He was learned, serious, religious and deeply respectful of Roman institutions as he understood them. In spite of this, he insisted on marrying an actress who, if not a prostitute, had certainly been the mistress of other men. When he became emperor he proclaimed her co-ruler with himself. The empress Theodora was equal to the position: her conduct was dignified, her judgement good, her character stronger than her husband's.

In the east, as once in the west, the emperor was all-powerful but since the coming of Christianity he was no longer a god on earth, merely God's chosen representative. He worked with his own circle of advisers, relying much on churchmen. A senate met in Constantinople as in Rome, but had no legislative power, could not offer unsolicited advice and was, simply, a court of justice for offences against the state.

The emperor appointed provincial governors and, for a time, the division of civil and military power was maintained as Diocletian had planned it. But, under pressure of continual invasion, this had been abandoned in the frontier provinces before Justinian's time.

The imperial court was ceremoniously magnificent. The greater saints days were marked by imperial processions which pleased the people and impressed foreign ambassadors. The tradition of intellectual leadership which had flickered out in Athens and passed for a time to Alexandria was now inherited by Constantinople, where Justinian set up a university under the guidance of the Church, after closing the few remaining schools of pagen philosophy in Athens.

He began his reign by a thorough reform of government. Justice was slow and corrupt, bribery widespread in the public services, informers pullulated and taxation was intolerably heavy. Justinian abolished the sale of offices, increased salaries to obviate bribery, and issued edicts against extortioners and informers. More lasting and more memorable was his codification of the law. Previous efforts had been made to simplify the accumulation of imperial pronouncements, but confusions and contradictions still hampered the course of justice. Justinian planned a clear codex of all imperial edicts since the time of Hadrian; he followed this with a collection of commentaries by learned jurists, the *Pandects*, and a general handbook of the law, the *Institutes*; a reduction of about two thousand law books, to the manageable number of fifty. At intervals until the end of his long reign, he issued *Novellae*, short digests of new edicts and modifications of older ones. Hundreds of copies of these were distributed to magistrates throughout the empire. Not an innovator or a reformer, Justinian was a 'great simplifier and stabilizer'.[10]

Though he had neither gifts nor taste for the life of a soldier, his ambition was to reunite the empire by force of arms if no other way seemed open. But early in his reign he almost lost his life in a circus riot at Constantinople.

The city counted perhaps 300,000 inhabitants. The centre of popular life was the hippodrome, where the emperor was proclaimed, public ceremonies were performed and processions held. It was also the principal place of free entertainment. The attractions included chariot races, wrestling, contests with wild animals, acrobatics and dancing. Gladiatorial combats had been stopped by the Church and Justinian himself put an end to the execution of criminals by throwing them to the lions, though he was careful to provide more wild beast shows to satisfy the populace. The audience enhanced the excitement by dividing into two factions, the Blues and the Greens, who had their own favourites among athletes and actors. Their intemperate and often violent partisanship could be exploited for political reasons. In 532 a riot directed against an extortionate official exploded from the hippodrome into the city, with looting, burning and murder. Justinian would have fled but Theodora made him stay. Born and bred in the circus (it is thought that her father was a keeper of animals), she knew the ephemeral nature of popular fury. The rioters set fire to half the city, then collapsed, exhausted and were ruthlessly dealt with by the imperial troops.

Justinian, who had probably saved his throne by remaining in his capital, now went forward with his projected reforms. He restored or created reservoirs, aqueducts and more especially roads, the arteries of trade, with hostelries for merchants and travellers. He was particularly anxious to establish a direct connection between his dominions and the silk route from China, so as to avoid the hostile Persian empire.

He was a great builder. The burning of Constantinople gave him an opportunity for magnificent re-planning. The cathedral of Santa Sophia (Holy Wisdom) rose superbly from the ruins. Its Greek architects were perhaps the first to solve the problem of placing a dome on a rectangular building: 'perhaps' because at very much the same epoch the problem was solved in slightly different ways in Anatolia and in Persia. Technological priority apart, Santa Sophia is incomparable.

The architecture that we know as Byzantine was born at this time, remarkable for its richness of detail, for the multiplication of arches, galleries and apses, for subtle patterns of colour in polished marble on columns and pavements, and rich mosaic on walls and ceilings, all brought into harmony by an unfailing sense of dignity and form.

Justinian began the systematic re-conquest of the lost provinces. His general, Belisarius, in seven years (532–9) recovered North Africa from the Vandals, regained control of Sicily, and fought his way up Italy defeating the Goths and capturing first Rome, then Ravenna. To celebrate the restoration of empire, Justinian built the great church of San Vitale at Ravenna with its airy octagonal dome and glittering mosaics, showing emperor and empress with their councillors ranged about them. His popularity grew with the victories of his armies and the returning commercial prosperity of Constantinople, now once again in control of the eastern Mediterranean. Belisarius celebrated a Triumph, his army marching through the hippodrome with waggon loads of spoil and troops of captives, among them the king of the Vandals.

A reversal of fortune followed. The Goths rallied in Italy and recaptured Rome, the Bulgars and the Huns broke through the defences of the Danube and raided as far as Corinth, the Persians invaded Syria and occupied Antioch, the second city of the empire; worst of all, plague spread from the east. But Justinian refused to relinquish Italy. After nearly twenty years the Goths were finally defeated. A devastated Italy and the wreckage of Rome (which had changed hands five times and lost three-quarters of its inhabitants) became again part of a united empire. Ironically, Justinian's campaigns brought about the final collapse of Roman culture.

The chief advantage of the Italian conquest, followed within a few years by the conquest of the Spanish Mediterranean coast, was commercial. Whatever occurred inland, the ports of Italy, Sicily and southern Spain enabled Byzantine merchants to dominate Mediterranean trade. About the year 552 some monks (early industrial spies?) brought silk worms and the secret of making silk to Constantinople. With remarkable speed, the manufacture was established under government control; Byzantium no longer needed to import silk either direct from China or from Persia and soon captured most of the Mediterranean trade. The revenues from this imperial monopoly helped to defray the cost of the frontier wars and to bribe the Bulgars and the Huns to withdraw – though never for long.

In Constantinople Justinian, old, sad and alone – he outlived Theodora by seventeen years – watched over the publication of the *Novellae* and tried pedantically to settle obscure points of religious dogma which divided his own people and made a growing breach between eastern and western Christianity.

He died in 565. He had begun in the belief that he could restore the empire, regain the lost provinces, reform the administration and the law. He had essayed the impossible and the result was disillusion, if not disaster. He left the empire more vulnerable than he found it, its most vital frontier seriously weakened. His ambition was misconceived: the Roman empire of the west was gone beyond recall long before he was born. Yet few citizens of Constantinople would have disagreed with his conception of the Greco-Roman heritage and the duty of restoring the west.

His administrative reforms, like all reforms, were only successful for a time. His lasting monument was the codification of the law which clarified the processes of justice and brought them within reach of his subjects. The guiding ideas of this immense work would be reflected in the codification of western law from medieval times onwards. Later, 'Roman law' provided the basic structure of most European legal codes as well as those of the New World.

Within a year of Justinian's death a new barbarian horde, the Lombards, overran North Italy – burning, plundering and seizing impartially the estates of Italian, Byzantine and Gothic landowners. They settled most thickly in the north, making a capital at Pavia, but their scattered conquests reached into Tuscany and beyond. Ravenna, most of the eastern seaports and the south remained under the often feeble rule of Byzantium. Successive Popes did what they could to protect the Roman region. But in the confusion anything that still remained of Roman administration died away. Aqueducts and bridges fell into ruin, roads were abandoned, trade gave way to barter and great areas of cultivated land reverted to waste.

The partnership of Church and state initiated by Constantine and consolidated by Theodosius left the Church as the natural guardian of law and order when the state decayed. In the fourth and fifth centuries Roman officials were sometimes raised to bishoprics by popular acclaim. Ambrose, the powerful bishop of Milan, had been a provincial governor and was not ordained until after he had been elected bishop. A wealthy landowner in Gaul, Sidonius Apollinaris, had held numerous secular offices before he accepted the bishopric of Auvergne, the better to defend his people against invaders.

Clovis, the remarkable leader who consolidated the kingdom of the Franks and established himself in Paris, looked for advice to the Gallo-Roman bishops of his new dominions. Like Theodoric the Ostrogoth, who married his sister, he believed in coexistence with the Gallo-Roman population. In due course he received baptism from the bishop of Rheims, Remigius, who also codified the unwritten laws of the Franks as a first step towards a settled society. Not long after, Caesarius, bishop of Arles, codified the laws of the Visigoths.

The greatest of these statesmen-priests was Pope Gregory the Great. He came of an aristocratic Roman family, and had served as prefect of Rome before he became a monk and, at the age of about fifty, was elected Pope during an epidemic of plague. In the sixteen years of his rule (590–606) he made a treaty with the Lombards which stemmed their advance and consolidated central Italy as a virtually independent state under papal control. By restoring and encouraging agriculture in this relatively peaceful region he made it the most prosperous in Italy and thereby increased the resources of the Papacy. He expressed his sense of responsibility towards his people by styling himself *Servus servorum Dei* – 'Servant of the servants of God', a title which his successors still carry. But he is perhaps best remembered for the missionaries he despatched from Rome to convert the overrun and abandoned outposts of empire in the north, more especially Britain which the heathen Anglo-Saxons had conquered, and which was restored to Christianity by his missionaries.

Besides the administrators and statesmen, scholars and thinkers also preserved the light of civilization. The greatest figure of all was Saint Augustine, bishop of Hippo in North Africa (354–430). His *Confessions* are the most remarkable spiritual autobiography known to the West. With the Vandals invading, and the empire disintegrating round him, he expounded in 'The City of God' his conception of man's total dependence on God, a work which, far into the Middle Ages, would be one of the most influential in Christian thought.

His near contemporary, Saint Jerome (348–420), withdrew from the world to live as a hermit near Jerusalem whence he directed a number of devout Christian ladies by letter, and translated the Gospels into Latin, thus bringing direct knowledge of them to thousands of believers who had no Greek.

As early as the third century some disillusioned Christians in Egypt had become solitary hermits. The most famous was Saint Anthony, whose astonishing hallucinations later became a favourite subject in western painting. A more genial figure was Pachomius who, about the year 318 founded also in Egypt the first community of monks and later eight other small monasteries. The rules were not very harsh: each monk had his own cell and his own appointed work, but meals were in common and the monastery was supported by their joint labour. Inspired by visiting some of these settlements, an ascetic theologian from Asia Minor, Basil, founded more monasteries in his own country under rules which established the character of Byzantine monasticism. He too emphasized the importance of communal living which encouraged brotherly love and was preferable to the introspective solitude of the hermit.

A century later St Benedict laid the foundations of monasticism in Italy. He had begun as a hermit, but so many sought to join him that he founded no less than twelve small communities and in 529 the largest and most famous at Monte Cassino. He also emphasized the benefits of communal life; his monks were to have at least a year's probation before taking vows of obedience, humility and silence. All property was in common; the monastery was to be self-supporting and every monk must work four hours a day in the fields or garden, read the Scriptures for another four and spend five or six hours in prayer.

As the monasteries grew, division of labour was introduced. Some monks worked in the fields, others taught the young or copied manuscripts. The activity of the Benedictines in preserving not only the Scriptures but much of Roman literature was stimulated by Cassiodorus. Once a Roman official under Theodoric, he lived to see the disastrous wreckage wrought by the Byzantine re-conquest. In his old age he brought together a small group of scribes who devoted themselves to copying such books as survived, a task then taken up by the Benedictines. Through this, in the words of Arnoldo Momigliano, 'The cloister would replace the Court as a centre of culture'.[11]

CHAPTER VI

---•---

CIRCA 500–1000

I

IN THE EARLY YEARS of the sixth century Persia was again disrupted by a religious reformer. Mazdak preached equality, vegetarianism and community of possessions including women. He condemned war but commended robbery of the rich to relieve the poor. The troubles he provoked were enhanced by the ambivalent attitude of a weak king who encouraged the Mazdakites as a counterpoise to the overpowerful Magi, the priesthood of the now somewhat debased religion of Zoroaster.

Thirty years of disorder were brought to an end when a masterful young heir succeeded to the throne, called the leading Mazdakites to a conference and massacred them all. The grateful Magi hailed him as 'Khusrau of the Immortal Soul', under which name he ruled Persia successfully for forty-eight years (531–79). Much of his time was spent in fighting the Byzantine empire for the coveted monopoly of the silk trade. But he also made intelligent reforms in the system of taxation, introducing a regular, fixed assessment to be paid in cash. His demands though heavy, were endurable as the money was applied to essential services: roads and irrigation, hospitals, schools, the army, and the relief of famine. In this last respect he himself set an example by eating no meat in times of distress.

As a patron of learning, he gave hospitality at his court to seven fugitive philosophers from Greece when Justinian closed the Schools of Athens. (But they found Persia more barbarous than they had expected, and returned sadly to Greece.)[1] He also organized the translation of the *Panchatantra*, a Sanskrit anthology of lively animal tales illustrating human foibles. Translated later from Persian into Arabic, thence (over the centuries) by way of Hebrew into German, Dutch and Danish, and by way of Greek or Latin into

Italian, they became familiar in France in the witty verse of La Fontaine and in simpler prose reached the children's books of the West.

The great Arab historian Ibn Khaldun attributed to Khusrau a clear analysis of his duty and his interest. 'Royal authority exists through the army, the army through money, money through taxes, taxes through cultivation, cultivation through justice, justice through improvement of officials . . . the whole thing in the first place through the ruler's personal supervision of his subjects' condition and his ability to educate them, so that he may rule them, and not they him.'[2]

Khusrau I was the last great king of the Sassanid line. His ostentatious grandson Khusrau II (591–628) was said to have a harem of three hundred and to play chess with pieces of solid emerald, but his glory ended in disaster. At first, in a prolonged war against Byzantium, his forces reached the gates of Constantinople. But the empire found an able leader in the emperor Heraclius (610–641) whose fleet outflanked the Persians by sea while his army invaded Khusrau's dominions and utterly defeated him. After Khusrau's inevitable deposition and murder, Heraclius made peace with his successor, but Sassanid power was broken.

Within twenty years, the dynasty was extinguished and Persia overwhelmed by irresistible invaders who came storming out of Arabia. The power which unloosed this torrential conquest was the teaching of the prophet Muhammad.

Among the founders of the great religions Muhammad had the least propitious beginnings. The Buddha was born into the ruling class of an already ancient civilization. Confucius was a sage among people who respected learning. Jesus of Nazareth was an artisan in a politically disturbed province of the Roman empire, but his people had an accepted tradition of holy men and a deep commitment to religion.

Muhammad, who was early left an orphan, grew up among people whose chief concern was commerce. Mecca had a thriving trade in spices and slaves, and a highly favourable position on the route across Arabia from the Red Sea to the Persian Gulf. Byzantines and Persians schemed and occasionally fought for a dominating influence over its citizens, who themselves sometimes fought rival cities in Arabia, but were more usually concerned with profits and the organization of camel transport. Their religion was derived from the same pastoral origins as that of the Jews and they revered a cubical building, the Ka'abah, in the midst of their town, said to have been built by Abraham. But the Meccans had no objection to the intrusion of numerous other gods and idols even into this sacred place.

In such a community what place was there for a man who longed for the life of the spirit? Muhammad grew up to be a camel driver. He was probably illiterate; he picked up, piecemeal and by hearsay, the religions of those with whom he came into contact on his journeys: some of the Jewish prophetic writings, fragments of the Christian scriptures. He pondered these things deeply. His employer, a rich widow, Khadījah, was more than ten years his senior but when he was twenty five he married her and as long as she lived took no other wife.

He was about forty when he began to meditate in solitary places and had visions at daybreak in which the Angel Gabriel told him he was the prophet of Allāh, the one true God. He saw himself as the last of the biblical prophets, among whom he counted Jesus of Nazareth as the greatest of his forerunners, but did not believe him to be the Son of God, because Allāh could not stoop to beget a human son. He also dismissed the Crucifixion as a wicked fabrication, for Allāh 'the compassionate, the merciful' would not have condemned one of his prophets to so terrible a death.

Muhammad's wife and a small but growing band of disciples – some of them from the city of Medina, two hundred miles away – accepted his teaching. But the majority in Mecca felt that his call to repentance and his insistence on the virtues of honesty and compassion was a menace to their way of life. Rumours of a plot to kill him caused him to flee from Mecca to Medina, with his devoted son-in-law Ali and a band of followers. His flight, called the *Hejra*, occurred in the year 622 of the Christian era, which became the year one of Islam.

Muhammad hoped for recognition from the Jews of Medina, but they did not hesitate to point out errors in his knowledge of their Scriptures. The animosity between them and his followers culminated in the expulsion of the Jews – a bad beginning and an evil omen for the future. Muhammad also instituted the practice of praying towards Mecca and not, as his followers had previously done, towards Jerusalem. Meanwhile his many converts among the people of Medina, inspired by his teaching and eager to enforce the new faith, willingly followed him into battle. After some skirmishing in the desert, he entered Mecca in triumph, seven years after he had left it, rejected and in darkness. The Ka'abah, purged of idols, was recognized as the sacred spot where the God of Abraham, the one true god, had touched the earth.

Before Muhammad's death in 632 the Muslim warriors of Islam were spreading the faith in Syria. ('Islam' means submission to the will of Allāh, 'Muslim' applied to all believers, means 'those who have submitted'.) It would be some years yet before the prophet's teaching was set down in the holy book, the Koran. It emphasized the mercy of Allāh above all but 'Every man is the hostage of his own deeds' and his wrongful acts will be a millstone round his neck.[3] His life must be regulated and inspired by prayer at stated intervals every day, he must practise self-discipline, abstain from wine and give help to the sick, the destitute and the fatherless. The Five Pillars of Wisdom were faith, prayer, charity, fasting and the pilgrimage to Mecca.

Muhammad's teaching on women must be seen in the setting of seventh-century Arabia, where polygamy was the common practice and the condition of women was often worse than that of chattel slaves. He laid obligations of love and humanity on the husband, emphasized that women had a right of inheritance, and condemned the unscrupulous speculator who married a wife for her dowry and repudiated her as soon as he had possession. A woman was not to be married without her own consent, or passed from one man to another like a domestic animal. She was to be protected against malicious accusers: four witnesses were needed for a charge of adultery. A man might not expel a pregnant wife, and although no husband could be expected to love all his wives equally, he must not treat any of them unkindly. If this was hardly a charter of liberty it was at least a charter of defence and in some ways it gave women more security than they enjoyed at that time in the monogamous Christian world.

Later the number of a man's wives was limited to four. But Muhammad himself, after the death of Khadījah, took no less than nine. He seems to have lived in harmony with them all, but with one, the young 'A'ishah, he had a singularly tender and touching relationship. He left daughters, but no living son.

Within twenty years, the Faithful had overrun Syria and destroyed the Persian empire. This was the beginning of centuries of fanatical conversion at the sword's point. The Zoroastrians went underground; some fled to India and established the still surviving community of the Parsees. By and large, the Persians accepted Islam. But the Jewish colony in Babylon, the chief centre of ancient Hebrew studies, was dispersed; survivors carried their learning to their brethren in Christendom.

Controlling the Syrian seaboard, the Muslim forces infested the eastern Mediterranean and seized Cyprus. By sea and land they now threatened Byzantium. But the superior military organization of the empire, the superb fortifications of the cities, the resources of Constantinople in food and arms, and the jets of burning liquid, known as Greek fire, with which they repelled attack, proved too much for the Arabs. The fury of Islam was deflected but Egypt was lost. The highlands of Ethiopia remained independent, isolated and Christian. Christian also, since the last century, the Nubian bowmen of the Sudan repelled the fanatics.

The tide of conquest swept North Africa as far as the Atlantic seaboard of Morocco, where the Arab leader rode into the waves, and called Allāh to witness that he could carry the faith no further. Another twenty years' fighting made converts of the fierce Berbers of the Atlas mountains. Meanwhile the conquerors became aware of the desert beyond the Atlas, and heard of an undefined great kingdom on the further side, apparently called Ghana, whose dark inhabitants possessed gold. Deserts were no problem to the Arabs: they established camel routes between oases to carry merchandise (and the Faith) to the tribes beyond, and to bring back the gold.

A tempting prize lay across the narrow straits which separated Morocco from Europe. Led by the Berber chief Tariq – who left his name to Gibraltar (Gebel el Tariq – the Rock of Tariq) – they crossed the straits in 711, and fought their way into Visigothic Spain. The conquest was easy; oppressed serfs, persecuted Jews, rose against the hated Visigoths. At Toledo they opened the gates to the Muslims. Soon they had conquered all but the mountainous north west.[4] A Christian kingdom survived in Asturias. Hence in later times the king of Spain's eldest son would be called Prince of the Asturias.

Less than a century after the Hejra the followers of the prophet were pouring through the passes of the Pyrenees into the kingdom of the Franks. Here the feeble successors of Clovis still ruled in name and were regarded as, in some sort, holy. All power was exercised in their name by a sequence of soldier-administrators called Mayors of the Palace. At the time of the Arab invasion this office was held by Charles Martel, who had resolution and influence enough to unite the Frankish chieftains and defeat the Muslim invaders. The momentum of their attack was at last exhausted. They fell back beyond the Pyrenees. This was in the year 732 of the Christian era; meanwhile the forces of Islam, after attempting to outflank the Byzantine empire in the east, abandoned their attempt to cross the Caucasus.

They still dominated the Mediterranean, raided the coasts of France and Italy for booty and slaves and, in the course of the next century, took possession of Sicily, Corsica, Sardinia, and the Balearic Islands, descended periodically on the Italian coast and, on at least one occasion, sacked Rome. On the credit side, they introduced the cultivation of oranges, lemons and peaches from China, also rice, which was to become a staple food of the Italian poor. They brought with them, when more stable government succeeded conquest, a respect for learning and an interest in science unknown to the Franks and Visigoths. While Byzantium preserved its distinguished form of Greek learning and Christian scholarship, the Muslim rulers in North Africa, Spain and the Middle East disseminated their own astronomy, medicine and science, and their respect for knowledge among the peoples with whom they had settled.

Long before the first impetus of Muslim advance was spent, Islam was irrevocably divided. The quarrel was about leadership, not about doctrine although that inevitably followed. The first four leaders after Muhammad (called 'Caliph' – meaning successor) were his surviving companions. The fourth, Ali, husband of his daughter Fatima, was murdered, and his son and successor Hussein, overthrown and killed in battle by a rival caliph (680). These two deaths, especially that of Hussein, inspired the cult of the martyred leader among their followers. They formed the Shi-ite sect who held that the true caliph – the Imam, the leader – must be descended from the prophet himself. A larger group, the Sunni, held that any descendant of the prophet's tribe was eligible.

Hussein's rival caliph founded the Umayyid dynasty with a capital at Damascus. Within a century (661—750) they were overthrown by the Abbasids, descendants of Muhammad's uncle. This family married into the old nobility of Persia, founded a new city, Baghdad on the Tigris (762) near the ruins of Babylon and revived the glories of the Persian empire.

A fugitive scion of the Umayyid family reached Spain and established his capital at Cordova, where the greatest ruler of his line, Abdar Rahman III, took the title of caliph in 929. The pattern was further complicated when descendants of Ali, the Fatimids, re-emerged, conquered Egypt and set up a third caliphate at their new city of Cairo (969). All three caliphates became important centres of Muslim culture, with influence radiating out over Asia, the Middle East, the Mediterranean basin and, from Cordova, over western Europe.

The Abbasids in Persia built their power on the framework of the old empire, which was not difficult as the Persians on the whole accepted Islam, assimilated with the conquerors, and were willing to serve a strong government. A sequence of four remarkable caliphs (754—833) built up the prosperity and wealth of Persia. Al-Mansūr (754—775) repelled Byzantine invasion, restored and fortified the frontiers, quelled internal revolt, and founded the city of Baghdad. His son Al-Mahdi (775—85) stimulated trade by building new roads, restored the trans-Asiatic Silk Road, founded schools and encouraged new industries. Al Mahdi was also a patron of learning and the arts.

The third great caliph, Hārūn al Raschīd (786—809) – who figures majestically in *The Arabian Nights,* a collection of tales of a much later date – was famous for the splendour of his court, the prosperity of his rule and the awe in which his neighbours held him.

Baghdad owed its wealth to a key situation; it was a centre for the trade routes from India to the Persian Gulf and the Mediterranean, or to Samarkand and the trans-Asiatic caravan trails to China. The Arabs had long been known as adventurous traders by sea and land. Their ships dominated the maritime commerce of India; they were known to the merchants of Canton, and they penetrated into East Africa with textiles and jewelry to exchange for ivory and slaves. By the mid-tenth century they had a fringe of small settlements on the East African coast with a principal port at Kilwa in what is now Tanzania.

Baghdad, which became the capital, was the meeting place of many peoples, Arabs, Greeks, Jews, Persians and Asiatic tribesmen, a clearing-house not only for trade but for different cultures, a centre for the interchange of ideas and of practical experience. Here Arab mathematicians discovered the advantage of the numerical system, based on ten, long practised in India, and, in their turn, introduced it to the West. Here under the patronage of the most intellectual of the Abbasid caliphs, Al-Mamun (813–33), an observatory and a House of Knowledge was set up where philosophic and scientific works from Greek, Persian and Sanskrit were assiduously translated to assist Arab scholars in the study of medicine, mathematics and astronomy. The works of Aristotle, Galen, Ptolemy, Euclid and Hippocrates were also annotated and later disseminated to the Mediterranean.

Cordova was inferior to Baghdad in power and wealth, but at its height in the tenth century was the finest city in the West. It was well fortified, with paved and lighted streets, fountains and public baths; at its heart was the great mosque, a forest of open-ended colonnades illuminated in changing patterns by sunlight and moonlight. Even today when the colonnades, transformed into the aisles of a Christian church, no longer let in the sun, it remains a building of unique beauty.

Apart from the agriculture of its countryside, Cordova manufactured textiles and had the secret of silk, by now fairly widely dispersed in the West. It was equally famous for leatherwork, brocades and jewelry. The conquerors here as elsewhere in Spain, married Spanish wives; by the third generation their Moorish blood was diluted with Gothic, Latin and old Iberian strains. Only the Jewish communities remained relatively pure. The regime was tolerant; too many conversions could have been inconvenient, as Muslims were tax-exempt. Prosperous and populous, Cordova was a centre for both Islamic and Judaic studies. Its scholars were also interested in the scientific works of the Greeks, so that it became a centre for their distribution by means of a well-organized system of professional copyists, most of them women. Re-translated from the Arabic usually by Jewish intermediaries, these half-forgotten works now reached the Christian West in Latin. Their propagation was made all the easier because the Arabs introduced the use of paper which they had learnt from the Chinese. It was typical of the broad-based toleration of Umayyid rule that their greatest caliph,

Abdar Rahman III (912–961), used a famous Jewish physician as his principal adviser in diplomacy and politics.

More aggressive and less intellectual caliphs followed Abdar Rahman III, and provoked attack from rival Moorish kingdoms and Christian Spain. Cordova was temporarily captured and destructively looted early in the eleventh century. It did not lose its intellectual pre-eminence but its political primacy in Muslim Spain passed to Seville.

The third caliphate, that of the Fatimids at Cairo, rose to greatness as Cordova declined, and belongs to a later period.

II

While Europe foundered, the Chinese empire was restored. The famous T'ang dynasty (618–906), like the Han before them, inherited the conquests of a brief preceding dynasty, the Sui (581–618) who had reunited China by force of arms. It was three hundred years since the Han had fallen and eight hundred since their empire had been formed. But tradition in China prevailed against centuries of division and decay. The Han themselves had believed that they were recreating the empire of the Chou, their predecessors by more than a thousand years. So the Sui, and after them the T'ang, regarded a united imperial state as the norm, in spite of intervening centuries of confusion, which was the more usual condition of China.

Some recollection of the Han administration, and some surviving fragments, remained. Behind this there was an even dimmer tradition of the rule of the Chou. The Sui set up an administration supposedly on the model of these, which was, in effect, almost wholly new. The China they united was more than twice the size of the Chou empire, and considerably larger than that of the Han. It was divided first into ten, later into fifteen administrative regions, from each of which an annual quota of candidates was selected for the civil service, which was henceforward the career of most educated Chinese. Entry was by competitive examination in the works of Confucius. The curriculum was narrow but the principle was new and unique. Successful candidates entered the lowest of the nine ranks in the official hierarchy and were promoted (in theory at least) on merit alone.

The strength of the system lay in the dedication of its public servants. There were enough of them to be in touch with the problems of every region, the far frontiers, the northern plain, the Yellow River, the fertile region of the lower Yangtze, the mountains of Szechwuan, the cities and the coast. The weakness of the system was the remoteness of the emperor and the inevitable failings of man. There was supposed to be a channel from the subject to the ruler through which grievances could be redressed. But the oppressed were often far off and inarticulate. What use were those traditional imperial audiences, kept at dawn and dusk every day from antiquity until 1912? A wronged peasant in Kansu could not travel so far, or make an intelligible protest if he did.

The Sui emperors repaired and extended the road and canal system. Their most ambitious project was a canal over a thousand miles long linking the Yangtze to the Yellow River so that corn could be carried from the fertile south to the poorer north and to the garrisons on the Wall. The conception was sound, but the mortality among the peasants conscripted for the work (over a million were said to have died) caused a revolt which dethroned the dynasty.

The T'ang, who succeeded, lasted in splendour for well over a hundred years (618–755), and continued with diminished power for as long again before their final collapse (906). Theirs was perhaps the greatest of the recurrent grea⁺ epochs in the history of China, for political power, commercial enterprise, poetry, painting and the arts.

The T'ang dynasty was not of pure Chinese stock; the first emperor had a barbarian mother, from a Turkic people beyond the Wall. All along the border, for the last century, the races had mingled; some of the nomad hordes encamped within the empire, while adventurous Chinese peasants made settlements beyond the frontier. Nomad methods of fighting, equipment, and horses were familiar in China; the hostile relationship became fruitful.

The tribal organization of the nomads was the basis of their military strength. They were herdsmen, but they were also, all of them, soldiers. The T'ang conceived the idea of a peasant army for China. They split the land up into small units, allocated to peasant families. On the death of the father the land reverted to the state. Neither purchase nor the accumulation of land was permitted. The sole tax throughout the country was rent, payable in kind, and twenty days of service on public works when necessary. All the men were to do a period of military service, and to be mobilized in time of war.

This division into 'equitable fields' was intended to prevent the emergence of large landowners, dangerous to the state, to ensure a regular flow of revenue from rent, to encourage agriculture, and to create a reliable peasant army. It worked for about a century but from the first there were too many exceptions. Officials were allowed to buy land, and soon began to accumulate estates while adventurous peasants migrated to regions beyond the reach of imperial authority. Above all an active middle-class had emerged, as merchants and craftsmen played an ever larger part in the economy of the state. Industry and commerce were becoming more important than agriculture.

The conscript army, on the other hand, was at first successful. T'ai Tsung, the second emperor of the dynasty (627–49), a brave leader and a good general, put a stop to nomadic incursions and reopened the trans-Asiatic Silk Road by defeating and exacting obedience from the tribes as far as Turkestan. He restored the Great Wall and completed the empire's network of roads and canals, without exacting forced labour from his subjects. Prisoners of war provided all he needed. Chinese authority was re-established in Korea; diplomatic relations were maintained with Japan, Tibet, Nepal, Burma, North India and the kingdoms of South East Asia. The power and influence of China reached its widest extent.

Confucian principles formed the outlook of the Chinese ruling class: rational, conservative, respectful of age and tradition, valuing moderation, courtesy and loyalty. Ancient rituals in honour of ancestors were dutifully performed, as Confucius directed: cere-monies which were rather a respectful convention than a religious observance.

Essentially tolerant, the government, at least in times of prosper-ity, did nothing to discourage the various forms of Buddhism and Tao-ism which had grown up during the years of disorder. There was no reason why an educated man should not accept some of the beliefs and ethics of Buddhism and Tao-ism as well as the Confucian code. The great mass of the people, the illiterate peasantry, on the other hand, found little to help them in the teaching of Confucius, but they religiously observed the ancient rituals, the Spring and Autumn celebrations and the rites at their ancestral graves. Many also found comfort in a debased Buddhism picked up from begging monks, or the superstitious magic into which popular Tao-ism degenerated.

This was a very different matter from the Buddhism and Tao-ism of the educated. The emperor T'ai Tsung himself, who had restored the authority of Confucius, was attracted to Tao-ism, deeply interested in Buddhism, and friendly to other foreign cults. He permitted an emigrant Nestorian monk to preach Christianity. 'A priest of good character' – so ran the imperial description – 'has brought images and books from the Roman domain. His doctrines are pacific and have a very creditable perspicacity in respect to moral principles, being logical and without vagueness.'[5]

The emperor came out personally to welcome the Chinese philosopher, Hsüan Tsang, on his return with books and relics from a pilgrimage to India. While there he had noticed with approval the fastidious cleanliness of the Indians, and their charming habit of presenting and wearing garlands of flowers. 'Their disposition is soft and humane, and they are earnestly given to study', but some of . them spent rather too much on trinkets.[6] He had been welcomed to a religious debate with the learned sages at the court of the powerful king, Harsha of Thanesar, who attended the discussion in person riding an elephant and dressed as the god Vishnu. On his return Hsüan Tsang presided over a committee which translated into Chinese seventy-five important works in Sanskrit.

The busy beautiful cities of China, the many loaded waggons on the roads, the barges on the canals and the shipping in the ports astounded travellers. Chang-an, the capital, was a cosmopolitan city, attracting traders from India, the ubiquitous Arabs from the Red Sea, a large colony of Jews, visiting musicians and dancers from Burma, Java and Sumatra, Japanese and Turkish pilgrims, young Tibetans come to study Buddhist scripture in the Chinese libraries, traders from Sogdiana and Turkestan, fugitive Manicheans from Persia, together with their one-time persecutors, the Magian priests now also in exile: even a prince of the Sassanid dynasty.

Chang-an (the modern Sian) may have had over a million inhabitants. It was superbly planned, within a rectangular wall, eleven miles by fourteen, with the imperial palace at the north side. When the emperor looked towards the sun, he saw the whole city spread out before him. A broad avenue led direct from the palace to the Gate of Brilliant Virtue in the south wall. Main streets dissected the city into self-contained sections each with its own wall, and each further dissected by smaller alleys, practicable for riding or walking. Sections were set apart for the different professions and trades: government officials, foreign envoys, merchants, different kinds of craftsmen, and of course the houses of pleasure where beautiful girls, trained to sing, dance, make music and make love, entertained the rich Chinese. A piped water supply fed the many fountains; there were open spaces, trees, flower gardens and an artificial lake.

Canton, the principal port, was enlarged and beautified, with flowering trees and pleasure gardens. It long retained in Chinese eyes a 'barbarian' look with its many thatched roofs, but after several destructive fires these were forbidden, and coloured tiles became obligatory. Along its quays could be seen numberless ships from India, the spice islands, the Red Sea and the Persian Gulf, piled high with rare and precious things. The imports of China were luxuries — ivory, tortoiseshell, aromatic drugs, tea from Burma, even jewels and statues from the Mediterranean shores. There was also an illicit but profitable trade in skilled or beautiful domestic slaves, mostly from India and the islands. The chief and growing exports of China were pottery and silk. Such commerce with its rich rewards affected only a small minority of manufacturers, and merchants, concentrated in the larger cities. Commerce and its advantages were altogether remote from the millions who – over the vast extent of China – cultivated the land, and paid their taxes in rice and grain and coarse cloth woven by their women.

The arts were renewed by the prosperity and confidence of the new era, and by foreign contacts. In pottery above all the T'ang epoch was revolutionary. With easy mastery, the Chinese potters now took over and adapted the shapes and decorative designs of vases from the Greeks, Persians and Indians, and strong naturalistic modelling of figures and animals from their Mongol neighbours. The T'ang style was unique in the contrast of bold form with lavish and often very delicate ornament.

Their shapely bowls and vases, their vigorous figures of horses, camels and warriors were enriched with multi-coloured glazes they had recently evolved, the browns and greens were splashed on with a careless mastery which enlivened the surface and enhanced the form. Most of the figures were made for the tombs of the rich, but some must have been sold abroad, for soon they were copied in Persia and Mesopotamia with less assurance and strength but well enough to confuse western collectors of the twentieth century, when the possession of a T'ang horse became a status symbol.

For luxury use they developed a much finer body than traditional earthenware and by the eighth century they had perfected a hard translucent ware which amazed the traders from the West: 'pottery so fine that the sparkle of water can be seen through it'.[7]

Their sculpture was less adventurous than their modelling in pottery. The series of horses, in low relief, which decorated the tomb of T'ai-tsung, are strong and impressive, although the sculptor seems to have aimed at no more than a linear representation based perhaps on line drawings. T'ang paintings (landscapes, figures and, of course, horses) were, by all accounts, as free and lively as their ceramics. Crowds gathered to watch the famous painter, Wu Tao-tzu, as his 'whirlwind brush' frescoed the walls of temples in Changan with graceful figures rich in colour. But a few later copies are all that survive of the works of the T'ang painters.

Literature was encouraged by the state, especially where it could be useful. The Imperial Academy of Letters founded by the emperor Hsüan-tsung in 725 is the oldest institution of this kind in the world. The same emperor established schools in every part of China. The writing and study of history was held, as in Greece and Rome, to be an education in politics, but in politics of one sort only: faith in the unity of China and respect for the ruling dynasty. T'ang history fell far below the standard set by Ssu Ma Ch'ien at the time of the Han.

The spread of Buddhism created a demand for written amulets, charms and prayers; this led to the proliferation of block-printing in the seventh century, a process only possible because of their previous invention of paper. Chinese printing was used for religious and educational purposes. It had nothing to do with their greatest literary achievement – poetry. For poetry was closely linked to calligraphy and printing was no substitute for the calligrapher's art.

Many T'ang poems have survived, though not in the original beauty of the authors' handwriting, and most of us must be content to know them only in translation: ghosts of the original poems, but still beautiful. An anthology of T'ang poetry, compiled several centuries later, contained nearly fifty thousand poems by more than two thousand poets.

Chinese lyric poetry touched its zenith. Li Po (699–762) the genial 'bon vivant' who, according to an unreliable tradition, was drowned 'trying to embrace the moon in the Yellow River', and

Wang Wei, his friend (699—759), were supreme masters. Tu Fu (712—80) whom the Chinese regard as the greatest, was a few years younger, but the last of all, Po Chu i (772—846) has become the best known in the West through Arthur Waley's translation. Chinese poets wrote in a sophisticated tradition for a small public so that many subtleties and allusions are inevitably lost on readers of a different culture more than a thousand years later. But there is no mistaking their magical power to arrest an instant in time, to capture the mood, the sound and the colour of a single moment.

> Blue water, a clear moon . . .
> In the moonlight the white herons are flying.
> Listen? Do you hear the girls who are gathering water chestnuts?
> They are going home in the night singing.[8]

The court of the emperor Hsüan-tsung (713—56) was probably the most brilliant in Chinese history. Poets and artists flourished. The emperor took particular delight in the music of central Asia and was captivated by a troop of Sogdian girls, in red robes and red deerskin boots who danced on top of spinning balls. The courtiers, men and women alike, amused themselves with music, drama, dancing, even polo (newly introduced from Persia by way of India): on the surface a happy and civilized life.

The brilliant imperial court survived the decay of T'ang power, but not for long. Desolation came up from below. At last the conscripted peasants broke down under the burden of frontier warfare. The poet Tu Fu lamented the fate of country boys recruited at fifteen and still in service on the Wall when their hair was grey, while their women strove in vain to cultivate the land and meet the taxes:

> In thousands of villages nothing grows but weeds,
> And though strong women have bent to the ploughing,
> East and west the furrows all are broken down . . .[9]

The men deserted and mutterings of revolt grew louder. The emperor instituted a professional army and recruited friendly tribes of barbarians, as the Romans had done. He appointed a barbarian general, who seized his opportunity and led a revolt against the emperor. The irrational hatred of the rebels centred on Hsüan-tsung's favourite concubine and he was forced to give her up to them.

Thirty miles from the capital, beyond the western gate
The men of the army stopped, not one of them would stir
Till under the horses' hoofs they might trample those moth eyebrows.
Flowering hairpins fell to the ground, no one picked them up,
And a green and white jade hair tassel and a yellow-gold hair bird.
The Emperor could not save her, he could only cover his face.
And later when he turned to look, the place of blood and tears
Was hidden in a yellow dust, blown by a cold wind.[10]

Hsüan-tsung died soon after, and with him the glory of the T'ang. Their authority in Central Asia was eroded by the advance of the Muslims, who defeated a Chinese army in 751, infiltrated Turkestan and gained control of Samarkand. The Muslim conquerors captured some Chinese craftsmen who knew how to make paper, and others with knowledge of the most recent improvements in sericulture. Paper became a valuable help in spreading the message of the Koran, and the latest methods in silk manufacture were soon exploited in Persia. Meanwhile the Tibetans revolted and carried war into the heart of China, briefly capturing Chang-an itself (763).

Tax-collectors, compelled to raise a fixed sum from half deserted villages, provoked peasant revolt and banditry. Regional governors, with independent power, appointed to crush revolt and defend the frontiers, frequently became independent war-lords. Succeeding emperors called in more supposedly friendly barbarians as allies, until the frontiers broke up into independent warring states.

As the central government lost power and confidence the old tolerance towards foreign religions vanished. Tao-ists hated Buddhist intruders, and envied them for the number and wealth of their monasteries. Tao-ist fervour was the official cause, but it was greed and the desperation of a bankrupt government which led in 845 to the expulsion of Buddhist monks and the plunder of their monasteries. Thirty years later hatred of foreigners exploded at Canton in the massacre of thousands of Muslim, Christian and Jewish merchants and the looting, burning and almost total destruction of the city.

The attack on Buddhism dried up the fruitful contacts between China and the Buddhist kingdoms of south eastern Asia and India. The Japanese, who had sent no less than twelve missions to China since the early years of the T'ang, withdrew their envoys in 847, taking a number of distinguished Chinese Buddhists with them, mostly doctors and mathematicians.

The end of the T'ang was not long delayed. As general and provincial governors threw off control, a confusion of dynasts and warlords brought fifty years of anarchy (c.906—960).

Of the many peoples of Asia, the Khmer of the Menam valley had early fallen under the influence of Hindu civilization and more especially of Buddhism. Early in the eighth century a number of migrants to the Menam valley had established an independent Buddhist kingdom. By the eleventh century the more aggressive Cambodians had annexed a great part of it, but the region called Haripunjaya retained its isolated independence.

Here in the early twelfth century Khmer architects, working for their king Suryavarman II, raised the incomparable temples now known as Angkor Wat. Today they are impressive ruins, mysterious, majestic, invaded by the jungle, but still the monuments of a great past and a great achievement.

Their time of glory had been short. The growing kingdom of Siam overwhelmed and conquered the Khmer by the fourteenth century.

· III

During the great epoch of the T'ang the Japanese people emerged, through admiration and imitation of Chinese culture, to the realization of their own powers. Their mountainous islands, part of which were still inhabited by the hostile Ainu, were fertile only on the coastal plains; they had little natural riches, and their people were divided (as mountaineers so often are) into separate and frequently hostile clans. Their ancient religion, Shinto, was a form of animism, reverence for their forefathers, hence also loyalty to the family, the village community of related families, and the clan. As time went on, loyalty to the nation came to override all the rest but the development was slow.

The symbol of the nation was the emperor. He was indeed a symbol, for he wielded no real power. He was not the regent of god on earth (a conception later familiar in the West), nor a potential god, like the Roman emperors. He *was* god; lineally descended from the sun goddess, he was a god in his own right. But his divinity gave him no power to stop the clan wars of his people because that was not his function. He existed to embody the spirit of the nation, not to rule it. The clan chieftains, some of whom also claimed descent from gods, did not fight against the emperor; they fought against each other to gain control of his sacred person. Whoever won, the emperor survived.

The Yamato dynasty, claiming descent from a legendary hero who had subdued the barbarian tribes and flown to heaven in the shape of a bird, seems to have been established by the fourth century. In the fifth and sixth centuries craftsmen from Korea, and later from China taught the Japanese how to make silk, to embroider and to weave brocades, with other useful arts – lacquer, pottery, sculpture, metalwork. The craftsmen (by the seventh century most of them were Japanese) formed corporations not unlike guilds; the head of each was often ennobled. The high rank given to skill in Japanese society was, in a warrior nation, significant of unusual perspicacity.

For this period was not peaceful. The introduction of Buddhism, most unwarlike of all religions, led to fifty years of civil war. This can be interpreted as a struggle between a more forward looking party who saw Buddhism as an integral part of the culture and knowledge that could be learnt from China, and the traditionalists who disliked change. But most of the time it was simply a power struggle between different clans.

In 593 Shotoku, a young prince of the Soga clan, became regent for the emperor, and remained in power until his death nearly thirty years later. He was possibly the best and certainly the most sympathetic ruler in the history of Japan. Influenced equally by Chinese Buddhism and by the Confucian code, he encouraged all contacts with China, opened direct diplomatic relations and sent many promising young men to study Chinese administration. Thus a steady flow of Chinese books influenced the thinking and enlarged the minds of the ruling class. During his government Buddhism became fully established, but in harmony with Shinto the ancient faith. He also introduced the Chinese calendar, which was far in advance of any reckoning the Japanese had yet evolved. He attempted to maintain order and prevent quarrels about precedence by introducing 'cap ranks' – the ancient Chinese system by which a man's seniority was immediately apparent from the colour of the button on his cap. He is credited with promulgating a constitution of a markedly Confucian character in 604, but this is probably the pious invention of historians who, after his death, drafted his ideas into a plausible-sounding document. But if Shotoku gave Japan no constitution, he consolidated the foundations of the state.

After Shotoku's death his clan, the Soga, fought their most powerful rivals, the Nakatomi, for over twenty years. In 645 the Nakatomi won, and founded a dynasty that dominated Japan for five centuries. Their leader, Kamatori, changed the old clan name to Fujiwara, which means 'wistaria', because the *coup* which brought him to power was plotted in a wistaria garden. Once in power he completed the work of Shotoku, issued the edicts known as the Taika or Great Reform, which made the administration of Japan a close copy of T'ang government.

The land was to be fairly distributed between all families, so that each should have a reasonable share of rice-growing fields. For this purpose, the whole population was to be registered. Inheritance was abolished: purchase was abolished: all ancient taxes, forced labour and slavery were abolished. Taxation was to be on land alone. This of course required elaborate organization and an army of administrators. An Imperial Code was issued, regulating the number and hierarchy of these officials. The headman of each village was answerable to the regional governor, usually a local landowner. Above these were provincial governors appointed in the emperor's name. Below them were tax-collectors, clerks, registrars and the rest. Japanese officials derived their methods indirectly from China. The fortunate few who had actually been there came back to impart what they had observed, and introduce methods, ideas and books. For lighter hours the travellers brought the biwa, the Chinese four-stringed lute, and the game of chess, which was much encouraged as a pastime for young men as it taught them the elements of military strategy. But neither imports nor experience enabled the Japanese to work the Chinese administrative system which, however impressive, was quite unsuitable to Japan.

The vast expanse of China, with its problems of defence, irrigation and communication called for central planning and co-ordination. There was a tradition of guidance and supervision. No such tradition existed in Japan, where the rice plots were small, and the nature of the country, divided as it was into islands, further divided by mountains, had created small, self-reliant villages and farmsteads – people who looked to their richer neighbours, to their local nobility, to their clan chiefs for help and guidance, not to a mechanism of officials operating under remote control.

The new laws were widely evaded; much land stayed in the hands of the local chiefs. Peasants avoided taxes by 'commending' themselves to richer men who shouldered the burden (or bribed the tax-collectors) in return for services. It was better still for a peasant to 'commend' his land to a Buddhist temple or monastery for these were exempted from taxes, and asked only a small rent of their tenants. In this way large estates grew up, peasant serfdom developed and state revenues fell. Clan loyalties showed little sign of withering away. Land continued to be a source of power, and local rivalries a source of disturbance.

There was another and a stronger reason for the failure of the Chinese system in Japan. Their attitude to officials was different. The Chinese believed that ability, and the successful passing of examinations, were necessary. The Japanese, in spite of their respect for the wisdom and knowledge of China and the privileges they accorded to outstanding craftsmen, believed that in matters of government birth and descent came first. An edict of 682 listed the qualities necessary for a civil servant: birth, character and capacity, in that order. If birth was more significant to the Japanese than character or capacity, it was inevitable that the Chinese idea of government by trained officials would be adapted by the Japanese into government by the noble families of each region – with the consequent danger of endemic civil war.

The influence of Chinese thought and example first made Japan into a viable state, and brought out the latent capacities of the people for occupations other than fighting, growing rice and contemplating, in rapt religious moments, the beauties of nature. But the Japanese worked out their own fate in their own way.

Chinese Buddhism lasted longer in Japan than did Chinese administration, and was a far-reaching civilizing influence. Buddhism satisfied the Japanese need for a more ethical faith than Shinto; seriously practised, it compelled its adherents to meditate on life and death, the mystery of human suffering, and the means of escape by the power of thought. Shinto offered no such perspectives. But Buddhism had the chameleon quality of taking colour and character from the local religions with which it blended and the Shinto nature gods could well be other manifestations of the Buddha. So the rites and doctrines mingled.

Forty-six Buddhist monasteries existed before Shotoku died in 622, by the end of the century there were five hundred and forty-five. Gradually Buddhism became too closely associated with the ruling class and the court, too conventional – a matter of processions, the building of sanctuaries, the setting up of beautiful statues and the making of rich gifts to temples.

In the ninth century, hermit saints arose to reanimate belief. Saicho (Dengo Daishi) (767–822) fled to the mountains and there (like Saint Benedict or Saint Basil) founded small groups of contemplative monks. The emperor became interested and sent him to study in a Chinese monastery, whence he returned a dedicated contemplative. His following, the Tendai Lotus sect, remained a valuable influence in Japan for many centuries. His near contemporary, the monk Kukai, also went to China, but he returned with Tantric Buddhism, the Buddhism of sensual symbolism and magical amulets. The Japanese form, called Shingon (True Word), attracted both high and low. Its ritual satisfied the aesthetic needs of the court, its images and spells appealed to the people, and it gave new impetus to the visual arts, both elegant and popular, by the rich symbolism of its worship. So it was that after the expulsion of the Buddhists from China, Japan inherited and developed the high aesthetic tradition of Buddhist art.

Less fortunately, the monks of the two rival sects were hostile to each other and sometimes came to blows. The Tendai Lotus sect split into factions with strong-arm bullies attached to its monasteries – a deplorable decadence which set in about 150 years after the deaths of the founders.

The first capital of Japan was at Nara, of the 'seven sacred buildings and the eightfold cherry blossom' as a later poem very prettily described it. It was built in imitation of the Chinese capital, but much smaller, and never finished, for the court remained there for less than a century: 710–784. This brief Nara period was the spring flowering of Japanese culture. Here, in effect, Japanese written literature began, with two official histories and an immense anthology of poetry. The anthology, called *Monyoshu* or *Collection of a Myriad Leaves*, contains 4500 poems, and includes the remaining work of Hitomaro, Japan's first great poet who died just as the Nara epoch opened. But the Japanese language did not fit easily into

Chinese characters and it was over a century before they simplified Chinese writing into a syllabic script more suited to their purpose.

The greatest achievement of the Nara epoch was in the visual arts. Buddhist temples, built in ascending tiers of richly decorated, wide-eaved roofs of wood were enriched with bronze statues and wall paintings. The influence of China was paramount, and something of the lost wonder of T'ang painting was for centuries preserved in the beautiful colours and graceful figures which covered the walls of the Horyuji temple: *was* preserved, because the paintings were destroyed by fire in 1949, an irreparable loss.

Japanese artists and craftsmen were ambitious in their bronze casting; in 752 they set up with immense pomp a gilded bronze Buddha, fifty-three feet high, which had been successfully completed only after a number of costly experiments. The grand colossus is still to be seen, impressive but less beautiful than Buddhas on a more human scale in the temples and monasteries of the same epoch.

Not long after the triumphant completion of the huge Buddha, a widowed empress dedicated to it all the works of art that her husband had collected – Chinese cups, vases, bronzes, silver and lacquer, some also from Persia and Arabia; there were also examples of Japanese workmanship – furniture, musical instruments and palace toys of every kind in gold, silver, tortoiseshell, and the rarest woods. By astonishing good fortune this collection has survived almost intact to the present day.

The Nara epoch was rich in achievement, but it was still, except perhaps in literature, a period of tutelage. At the end of the eighth century, the court left Nara, because the influence of the Buddhist establishment, entrenched all round the city in temples and monasteries, had become stifling. Their riches provoked popular criticism and the councillors who controlled the throne were alive to danger. A sequence of empresses – female succession was not as yet barred – had fallen under this unpopular priestly influence. To check the muttering of revolt, male succession was proclaimed for the future, and the capital was moved to Kyoto.

That name is of a later date; it was at first called Heiankyo, the Capital of Eternal Tranquillity. The first centuries of its existence, called the Heian period, marked the emancipation of Japanese culture from the dominance of China, and the evolution of a way of living which, for a fortunate minority, was one of the most delightful known to history.

IV

The province of Britain, abandoned to its fate when the Romans recalled the legions, was soon overwhelmed by invading tribes from North Germany, Saxons, Frisians and Angles (who gave it its new name of England). Roman civilization was wiped out; comfortable villas and prosperous little towns fell into ruin. Agriculture reverted to the primitive; coinage vanished altogether – it was no longer needed. Christianity, not very deep-rooted, disappeared.

The surviving British population was absorbed by the prolific conquerors. Only in Wales and Cornwall the pre-Roman Celtic race and language survived. In Ireland and much of Scotland, kindred races and languages had not been disturbed by Roman rule. The Celts of Cornwall and southern Ireland made contact across the sea with the most westerly and largely Celtic region of Gaul, the region which became Brittany when the rest of Gaul became France.

Ireland, which was converted to Christianity by St Patrick while the heathen Saxons conquered Britain, developed with astonishing speed into a centre of Christian teaching. The schools at Aranmore and Clonard may not have been as large as tradition claims, but they were large enough to send a stream of missionaries to northern Europe and the Germanic tribes beyond the Rhine, on whom neither Rome nor Byzantium had yet shed enlightenment. Columban, a missionary of great courage and learning from Bangor, founded monasteries at Luxeuil in France, at Sankt Gall in Switzerland and in northern Italy. The more famous Saint Columba founded the monastery on Iona (*c.*560) whence his monks reached and converted a great part of Scotland. Later, a monk from Iona, Aidan, founded Lindisfarne off the Northumbrian coast for the conversion of northern England.

From the seventh century onwards the monks of Ireland and Northumbria developed a form of writing clearer and more beautiful than any at that time in use in Europe, or even in the world. They decorated their work with bold, linear figures and geometrical borders like the carvings on Celtic crosses, enlivened with representations of birds and animals, in delicate harmonies of colour. The *Lindisfarne Gospel* and the *Book of Kells* from an Irish monastery are the most famous surviving examples.

Meanwhile Pope Gregory the Great, in 997, despatched a band of monks to convert the Saxon kingdom of Kent. Their leader,

Augustine, became the first archbishop of Canterbury, but in a reign of about eight years, he was fully recognized only in the south east. His confrontation of the Celtic bishops and clergy of the south west and Wales was unsuccessful, and the partly Christianized north was altogether too far away. He proved, nonetheless, to be the founder of the English Church. Not quite a century later, his work was consolidated and extended by Theodore of Tarsus.

This remarkable man, Greek by birth, knew nothing of England and was already in his sixty-seventh year when he landed. He soon proved himself to be an organizer of outstanding skill. For over twenty years (667–690) he survived the rigours of the English climate and the barbarism of Anglo-Saxon society, while he established an episcopal system under the guidance of regular synods, which over-rode the boundaries of local kingdoms and is still the basis of the English diocesan system.

Gradually England was brought back into the mainstream of western culture. Benedict Biscop (628–690), the remarkable founder of two northern monasteries, Wearmouth and Jarrow, travelled four times to Rome, returning with precious books to form a library, relics, vestments, pictures and a teacher to instruct his monks in the Roman method of singing. He also sent for stonemasons and glaziers from France to teach his people crafts which had long been neglected.

One of the most remarkable scholars of the age grew up in Biscop's monastery of Wearmouth and never left it. The venerable Bede (673–735) devoted his life to teaching, translating and writing. One of his pupils founded a school at York which achieved European fame. Bede's outstanding achievement was his *Ecclesiastical History of England*, a work which, within the limitations of his epoch and his resources, reveals him as a great historian, humane, judicious, careful, with a consuming desire to establish the truth.

Bede's contemporary Boniface (672–754) left England to convert the German tribes. After working in Bavaria, Thuringia and the Rhineland where he was encouraged by Charles Martel (that same Frankish magnate who had defeated the Moors) to convert the pagans of the Rhineland, he founded the bishopric of Mainz and the abbey of Fulda, crowned Charles's son Pepin and still had energy to attempt the conversion of the Frisians, at whose hands the undaunted octogenarian met his death.

From Rome, successive Popes began to look with hope towards

these northern Christians whose missionaries were indefatigable and whose warrior chiefs might be useful protectors. Offa of Mercia, ruler of what he described as the 'Kingdom of all the English', issued silver coinage of great distinction based on Roman models. He was of European stature, had travelled to Rome at least once and was on good terms with Pope Adrian I, who had created the bishopric of Lichfield at his request. In later years he negotiated a treaty of trade and friendship with Charlemagne.

The relations of the West with Byzantium were increasingly difficult and the empire was in trouble. Hard-pressed by the Muslims in the Mediterranean and the Middle East (Constantinople sustained a second great siege in 717), threatened by the Slavs on the north west frontier, the empire was also divided by religious controversy. A reforming party condemned the use of images as idolatrous; the emperor Leo III, a strong man of great administrative ability, supported the iconoclasts in order to undermine the influence of the too numerous monasteries. The Pope had quite different problems: images had played a great part in the conversion of northern Europe, and missionaries had freely substituted holy relics and pictures for pagan objects of worship. The new austerity of Byzantium might well undermine the faith of the less sophisticated western converts by destroying its outward symbols. The Pope could only denounce the iconoclasts.

This rift with Byzantium was shortly followed by a new advance of the Lombards in North Italy. They captured the imperial city of Ravenna and extinguished all Byzantine power north of Rome, excepting only in the island city of Venice (751).

In these circumstances the Pope must of necessity look towards the Franks, the only effective Christian power in the West. Charles Martel had left the empty title of king to the decadent descendants of Clovis. His son, Pepin, abandoned the pretence and in 754 the Pope crossed the Alps to crown him king of the Franks; he also gave him the title of 'Patricius romanorum', a title hitherto only given by the emperor. In return the new king drove the Lombards out of Ravenna and by the 'Donation of Pepin' gave the Pope the reconquered land and most of central Italy. It was not, legally, his to give; but the emperor at Byzantium was in no position to object.

Pepin's son Charles carried his father's policy to its logical conclusion. He defeated the Lombards, absorbed their kingdom into the Frankish empire, then restored order in Rome, where faction fighting between the local nobility had produced anarchy, and confirmed his protective alliance with the Pope.

No direct challenge had yet been made to the theoretical supremacy of Byzantium, now ruled by the atrocious empress regent, Irene (who later blinded her son and took his place). A general council of the Church, called by Irene at Nicaea, was attended by the papal legate and ended in the defeat of the iconoclasts; images were allowed in moderation, a welcome outcome for the Pope. It was therefore an embarrassment to him when the king of the Franks denounced the proceedings at Nicaea and called his own council of western prelates. Charles's official objections to the proceedings at Nicaea were partly due to Frankish misunderstanding (perhaps deliberate?) of edicts promulgated in Greek. The real reason was his just resentment, and that of his prelates, that no representative of western Christendom, except the papal legate, had been invited to Nicaea.

This king of the Franks was one of the great rulers of history. Two nations, the French and the Germans, claim him for their own, but a time honoured French colloquialism moulded his personal name of Charles and the adjective *magnus* into the single word: Charlemagne. Few have better deserved such an honour.

A man of commanding presence and height, a splendid athlete, handsome, smiling, equable, he had also great tenacity of purpose, keen political insight and good judgement. He spoke Latin as well as his native dialect, and understood Greek; he tried, but did not succeed, in learning to write. In a reign of over forty years (771 –814) he extended his rule north eastward to the Elbe, southward to the head waters of the Danube and over the Alps into Italy; and he campaigned against the predatory Avar tribes in the Balkans. In almost twenty years of campaigning he brought the heathen Saxons under control and converted them to Christianity at the sword's point. (His most trusted councillor, the priest Alcuin, an English scholar from York, disapproved of forcible conversion, but the recalcitrant Saxons were hardly amenable to any other argument.) In campaigns against the Moors, he established defences south of the Pyrenees in Catalonia – the Spanish March – but his attempt to reduce Saragossa failed. This incident was perpetuated in epic verse as the rearguard action at Roncesvalles in which one of his finest commanders – Roland – was killed.

As a conqueror, Charlemagne was also a civilizer who brought administrative order to his extensive dominions. He placed churchmen in authority where possible, but in unsettled districts and especially on the frontiers he chose soldiers, to whom he granted land and the title of 'count'. (Later, under weaker rulers, these military governors would become independent as in comparable circumstances they did in the Persian empire.)

He also legislated for the reform of the clergy, to whom fell the task of educating the people in religion. Obedience to the will of God and obedience to the king were the chief essentials. But it was also an advantage for the priest to know the Lord's Prayer in Latin, if nothing else.

In the vigour of his years Charlemagne travelled constantly over his dominions. He restored as far as possible the old Roman roads and built others (primitive but passable) to the further provinces of empire. He had a system of mounted messengers – the *missi* – who carried his orders to every region and returned with reports, suggestions and complaints, gathered from local assemblies, mostly of tribal origin, which met regularly.

As a lawgiver he was greatly concerned with the administration of justice and, in the manner of Justinian, issued regular additions to the existing codes. He made a significant change in the organization of the army. A paid standing army was unknown to the Franks. The usual arrangement was for the ruler to rely on chieftains who brought in their tail of followers. Charlemagne introduced a system based on land: so many soldiers to be recruited and equipped from a specific area. This spread the burden more evenly and reduced the power of individual chiefs.

The economy of the Frankish kingdom was very primitive. Households, from the king's downwards, were almost wholly self-supporting, grew their own corn, pastured their own flocks, wove their own clothes, brewed their own beer. Markets were held occasionally for the exchange of produce. The making of arms and armour was a principal industry; smiths flourished. The other important surviving crafts were pottery and jewelry. Very little coinage was minted and none in gold. Charlemagne's control and organization of minted money indicates a certain revival of trade, the outcome of more settled conditions. He issued copper and silver coins – twelve copper coins to one silver coin, and twenty silver coins to a pound of silver. (It remains a mystery why something like this arrangement of the small cash was later adopted in England – never a part of Charlemagne's empire – where it survived until 1971.)

As he grew older, his favourite residence was at Aix la Chapelle where he enjoyed bathing in the thermal springs, and built a cathedral, in respectful imitation of Justinian's noble church of San Vitale which he had seen with wonder when he drove the Lombards out of Ravenna. Here he gathered scholars about him and, with the advice of Alcuin, set up a school to educate promising boys for the priesthood or the service of the state.

Alcuin was also concerned for the preservation of Latin literature, a work of rescue begun by Cassiodorus and the Benedictines more than two centuries earlier, and since neglected. Once again, Latin manuscripts were sought out and diligently copied by well-trained scribes in 'Carolingian minuscule', a writing of classical elegance, very small but easier to read than the elaborately decorative scripts of Ireland and the north. It was a long and expensive project. The best parchment was made of sheepskin; twelve sheep contributed to a book of two hundred pages, to say nothing of the number of man hours expended in smoothing and preparing the skins. In his later years Alcuin retired to the monastery of St Martin at Tours which became the chief centre of this work, to which we owe the preservation of much classical literature. In culture, as in adminstration, the Frankish king was – with Alcuin's help – one of the founders of modern Europe.

Early in his reign, after the conquest of Lombardy, Charlemagne had restored order in Rome. But the gangster aristocracy repeatedly defied the Pope and fought each other for control of the city. Pope Leo III, after narrowly escaping assassination, fled to the Frankish court. Charlemagne, at the head of his well-disciplined troops, occupied Rome and restored order. On Christmas Day, 800, he attended mass in St Peter's; as he knelt for the papal blessing, Leo drew a crown from under his mantle, placed it on his head and proclaimed him emperor of the West.

Charlemagne probably had some foreknowledge of Leo's intention, but the idea seems to have originated with the Pope. It was a gesture of recognition to the man who had restored order in the West but also a tacit assertion of the Pope's spiritual power. Dependent as he was on the arms of Charlemagne for physical survival, he yet claimed, as God's Vicar on earth, the right to bestow the greatest of temporal honours, the imperial crown.

Superficially it looked like an act of inspired ecclesiastical statesmanship. It proved otherwise, and has been described not unjustly as the greatest mistake the medieval Popes ever made. Yet it was an understandable error, since in the circumstances of the time the spiritual arm could not survive without the aid of the temporal arm, and the assertion of spiritual authority was rather a symbolic religious act than a bid for the realities of power. Alcuin, who had probably discussed the possibility with Charlemagne, invented the symbol of the two swords, spiritual and temporal, equal to each other, operating each in its own sphere. But Alcuin had also once written to Charlemagne, 'On you alone depends the whole safety of the churches of Christ', and had freely admitted that he was 'in power more excellent than the Pope'.[11]

There was no probability, in the year 800, that the Pope would challenge the emperor in the political sphere. When this ultimately occurred it was more damaging to the Papacy than to the empire. In any dispute for material power the Church forfeits something of its spiritual character, but the state has no spiritual character to lose.

All this lay in the future. On Christmas Day 800, with the Roman populace and the Frankish soldiers cheering the Holy Father and the eagle-eyed, grey-haired warrior who towered over him, the coronation seemed an omen of peace, order and unity. ·

In Constantinople the news was received with anger and contempt. The 'Roman' empire could only be divided into east and west by the legitimate 'Roman' emperor – or in this case empress. Irene, shortly to be deposed, had made no such division. Her successor, struggling with a new Muslim onslaught by land and sea, compromised by recognizing Charlemagne as 'Basileus' – king – and exchanging ambassadors.

Whatever he was called in Constantinople, Charlemagne had the reality of power and used it until his death with justice and judgement. Respected throughout the West he was in diplomatic contact with Christian and Muslim Spain, with Ireland, England, Denmark, the Byzantine empire and the Abbasid caliphate. The caliph, Harun al Raschid, conceded to him the right of guarding the Holy Sepulchre in Jerusalem, and guaranteed that pilgrims would not be molested. In token of his esteem, he sent Charlemagne a present of an elephant.

Charlemagne died at Aachen in 814 mourned by the warriors he had led, the ministers who had served him, the scholars he had protected and fully deserving the praise bestowed on him by his friend and biographer Einhard – 'by far the most able and noble spirited of all those who ruled over the nations in his Time'.

V

The Byzantine empire is one of the miracles of history. During the millennium of its existence it rarely enjoyed more than twenty years of peace at a stretch. Its frontiers continually expanded or contracted with the shifting pressure of invaders. At its fullest extent it controlled the Danube valley, the Balkans, a great part of Italy, southern Spain, Greece, most of the Mediterranean islands, North Africa, Asia Minor, Syria, Palestine and the old Persian empire as far as the Tigris. Under attack from Arabs, Slavs, Magyars, Bulgars, Avars, Serbs and others it lost whole provinces, regained them, lost them again . . . It was sometimes dominant in the Mediterranean, sometimes powerless. But the Byzantines had reserves of confidence and tenacity, skill and experience. They also had their secret weapon – Greek fire, jets of flame inextinguishable by water, with which (in 673) they shattered the Arab fleet then blockading Constantinople. Thereafter they used it sparingly but with devastating effect.

Always revival came and the resurgence of power. Like some indomitable ship, the empire battled on through heavy seas, through elemental storms, through brief intervals of calm, driven almost on to the reefs, surviving, still bearing onward its precious cargo of Romano-Christian-Hellenic culture, rich with the spoils of time, creatively renewed almost to the end . . .

At the time of Charlemagne, when the empress Irene schemed her way to the throne (797) the Byzantine empire was in deep distress, the court rotten with intrigue, the Arabs exacting tribute, the Bulgars poised to attack. Irene's hapless successor, Nicephorus, who exchanged ambassadors with Charlemagne, was first defeated by the Arabs, then killed fighting the Bulgars (811). The misfortunes of the empire did not end there; Crete was lost to freebooting Moors from Spain, and Sicily to Muslim invaders from Africa. The Mediterranean became an Arab lake.

Still, the centre held. The same was not true of the newly formed

Frankish empire of the West. In the century after Charlemagne's death it looked as though all he had gained would be lost again to barbarism. After the undistinguished reign of his son, discouragingly called Louis the Pious, Charlemagne's three grandsons divided the empire and sowed the seeds of war. The eldest, the feeble Lothair, had to have Charlemagne's capital of Aachen and the imperial capital of Rome; he was given a narrow serpentine strip up the Rhine, over the Alps and down into Italy; his name is perpetuated in Lorraine, Lothringen. When he died, the two more resolute survivors, Louis and Charles, left only the Italian provinces to his son, and themselves divided everything north of the Alps. Louis, the stronger, took the eastern half but retained also a substantial strip of land west of the Rhine, thus creating a highly debatable frontier between the regions which later became Germany and France. At one point in these dynastic arguments Louis and Charles with their followers, made an agreement at Strasbourg. The two groups of Franks by this time (842) spoke markedly different dialects: Charles's men had acquired Latin inflections from their Gallo-Roman subjects while the followers of Louis spoke a Germanic dialect. The Strasbourg oaths had to be taken in both languages. This was felt to be ominous of trouble to come.

While dispute and division weakened the dynasty of Charlemagne a new menace appeared. Sea-rovers from Scandinavia had raided the northern coasts of Europe before the death of Charlemagne. With his habitual energy he organized look-out points and maritime patrols. But the Franks – and for that matter the Germanic tribes in general – were essentially land-fighters, inexperienced against the skill, ferocity and increasing number of these raiders from the sea.

By the middle of the ninth century the long, dark boats of the Vikings, like evil sea-serpents, were nosing their way up every navigable river. They raided the English and Irish coasts, Scotland and the Hebrides, Germany, France and Spain. They infested the Mediterranean from Cadiz to the Gulf of Genoa, attacked the Balearic Islands, landed in North Africa and briefly threatened Constantinople.

At first they came for plunder, not for conquest, took what they wanted, destroyed what they did not, killed all who resisted and carried off boys and girls into slavery. They sacked Hamburg and Utrecht, Nantes, Bordeaux and Seville; twice they besieged Paris;

they plundered the island sanctuaries of Lindisfarne and Iona, and the great church and library of St Martin of Tours; they slaughtered monks and nuns indiscriminately and, in a drunken orgy pelted poor old Archbishop Alphage to death with meat bones. By the time of this outrage they had changed from raiders to conquerors and settlers, had established their chieftaincies in Scotland and Ireland, in the north and east of England and in a wide swathe across the midlands. Only in the south, after long fighting, King Alfred had stemmed their advance.

This English king (870–899) was, in his lesser sphere, as remarkable as Charlemagne. At first defeated, he held doggedly on, reorganized the Anglo-Saxon army, built ships to patrol the coast and stubbornly re-established a position of strength from which he was able to make terms. He used the years of peace to lay the foundations of a stable society; he set up courts of justice open to all his people, simplified the laws and planned a system of primary education whereby 'all the free-born youth of England' should be able to read their own language. He even provided them with books to read, and himself translated into Anglo-Saxon the philosophy of Boethius, the universal history of Orosius, and the historical works of Bede. He set on foot the compilation of the *Anglo-Saxon Chronicle*, a factual history of England up to his own time, which was faithfully continued over the years, for more than two centuries after his death. In a very dark age Alfred stands out as a ruler of exceptional humanity and wisdom – the only English king to be called 'the Great'.

The Vikings, like the peoples who had infiltrated the Roman empire, were driven by necessity and the need for land. Scandinavia could not support its growing population. The raids satisfied immediate needs and the lust for adventure, but settlement soon became the real objective. In their sea-roving they were indomitably enterprising, enduring and courageous. They braved the Atlantic, made settlements in Iceland and some in Greenland, reached and for a time settled the northern tip of Newfoundland. From these remote shores they sent home walrus ivory for sale to the princes and nobles of northern Europe. (It was the only ivory available, since the Arabs had cut them off from trade with Africa.) Learning to combine commerce with plunder, they penetrated up the rivers of northern Europe and Poland into the heart of Russia, founding settlements from Lake Ladoga to the Black Sea, a route on which Novgorod and

Kiev were the chief cities, for trading furs, wax, amber, honey and slaves to the Black Sea and Byzantium.

They disputed possession of the Orkneys and northern Scotland for nearly three centuries and dominated Ireland until Brian Boru built ships to drive them out of the Shannon, united the quarrelling Irish chiefs and, as High King, defeated the Northmen utterly at Clontarf. By then over seventy, Brian was murdered in his tent after the battle by some of the fleeing Northmen (1014). Their influence on Irish history outlasted their defeat: they were the first to build towns in pastoral Ireland – Dublin, Waterford and Limerick.

One of the ablest chieftains Canute (Knut) by a mixture of warfare and diplomacy established briefly a Scandinavian empire which included Denmark, England and Norway (1018–35). He was a ruler of European significance who attended an imperial coronation in Rome and won praise from the Church for his piety. (He became, with the increase of his power, a better man than in his earlier years when he had freely used murder and torture as instruments of policy.)

More lasting than the ephemeral empire of Canute was the Viking influence which stemmed from the Duchy of Normandy. In 912 a band of a few thousand was granted land on the north coast of France. Though more Scandinavian settlers joined them, the men far outnumbered the women so that intermarriage and assimilation with the original inhabitants followed naturally. Within three generations the Normans – as they were usually called – spoke a predominantly French dialect. Hardy, energetic and with the adaptability which is often the characteristic of mixed races they later extended their power to England, southern Italy, Sicily and Asia Minor and became a major force in moulding the character of the West.

There were other predators as well as the Vikings. Overland migrations into Europe were not yet at an end. Franks, Alemanni and Burgundians had become respectable settled peoples. Charlemagne had forcibly incorporated the Saxons into his empire. But more tribes appeared on the Elbe frontier, the Wends in the north, the Slavs further south. Charlemagne had only temporarily checked the Avars, an Asiatic tribe akin to the Huns, who were active on the Danube. So also were their ethnic cousins, the Magyars, who overran the fertile Danubian plain and set the enslaved inhabitants to till the soil on their behalf while they raided the settled subjects of Byzantium on the one side and Charlemagne's empire on the other. Meanwhile the Arabs, equally formidable by sea and land, descended on South Italy, plundered Rome, established bases on the coast of Provence whence they plundered southern France, reached the Alpine passes and, in 972, captured and held to ransom the abbot of Cluny. Within fifty years of Charlemagne's death central authority in the West had disintegrated. Defence was in the hands of anyone with enterprise and courage enough to attempt it.

In these conditions the feudal system took shape. (The name is of a later date; it appears first in the work of the English John Selden, in the seventeenth century.) Basically a system of agreed mutual obligations, its origins are to be found in the bonds of loyalty inherent in a tribal society between the chief and his followers. Frankish kings had granted land to their warriors in return for services, a system regulated and rationalized by Charlemagne into the basis of a reliable army. As the central power faltered, this could no longer be enforced. Landowners looked to themselves: the greater men granted land to tenants of their own on the same terms, these in turn to lesser men, a whole hierarchy of military tenure and mutual obligation. The 'counts', whom Charlemagne had placed on the borders with authority to organize against invasion, were among the first to become independent rulers with tenants who owed them allegiance and service in war. Germany was thus sub-divided into rival duchies – Bavaria, Franconia, Lorraine, Saxony – while the great fiefs of France, long before the end of the ninth century, were self-governing in the same way. The system proliferated everywhere; in spite of its inherent defects it was the means of survival.

Below the different grades of tenant by military service, lowest of all, were the serfs, the peasants who paid for the protection of the warrior landowners by working their lord's land as well as their own. This agricultural element had scarcely existed in primitive Frankish society. The serfs, the essential foundation, derived from the *coloni* of the Roman empire, those smallholders who had paid for their tenancies on the great Roman and Gallo-Roman estates by labour or in kind and had, in the last centuries of the empire, been legally bound to the soil.

There were many local variations of the basic pattern, but the principle was the same. With the exception of the Church and the monasteries, landowners were of necessity warriors. Fighting, which was at first their legitimate business, became their business altogether. When they were not fighting the Northmen, the Magyars, the Moors or the Slavs, they took to fighting their neighbours. In such minor warfare successful warriors might increase their power until they could defy king or emperor.

Yet the feudal system was not disorderly in itself: very much the reverse. The obligations which bound the knight to his lord, the lord to his knights and the knights to their humbler tenants were closely defined. Even the serf had a clear right to his share of land, to communal facilities for grinding corn and drawing water, to protection against enemies, and to rations in time of famine. Alongside a duty to protect the weak, the knight had a more complex obligation of honour which might be (and often was) an excuse for the resentment of affronts and for local quarrels which could last for generations. But it was also some guarantee of loyalty to the oaths he had sworn of duty to God and fellow Christians which he took before he received (from the hand of a proved knight) the accolade which elevated him to the same rank. It was a rough system designed for a rough world but it served its purpose in preserving western Christendom. Later, when it had outlived its use, it became a cause of incessant local fighting in which the great usually destroyed themselves. Where feudalism survived it became a monstrous travesty of itself by which a landowning aristocracy enjoyed all the privileges and an oppressed peasantry carried all the burdens.

Imperial authority in the West vanished within a generation of Charlemagne, but the idea survived and a dim sequence of princes carried the empty title. The reality was revived in the tenth century by a dynasty from Saxony, a region outside the frontier of the Roman empire which Charlemagne had conquered and forcibly converted. The dukes of Saxony, descendants of a border count appointed by the son of Charlemagne, were indefatigable and often successful in defending their people against invading hordes, Wends, Slavs, Magyars. Henry the Fowler (919–36) set up border garrisons permanently manned by contingents of cavalry who were regularly relieved. He built key fortresses on the Elbe and Weser, occupied Schleswig in despite of the Danes and compelled their king to pay tribute. Gradually he asserted his authority westward as far as the Rhine, controlled Lorraine and built up diplomatic contacts with England, marrying his son and successor to a granddaughter of

Alfred the Great. Although formally offered the imperial crown, he could not spare time for a coronation.

The revival of the empire was left to his son Otto (936–73) who completed his work, reduced the rebellious dukes in Germany to obedience, compelled the marauding Czechs, fiercest of the Slav invaders, to settle in Bohemia, and inflicted a decisive defeat on the Magyars at Lechfeld, near Augsburg (955) after which they fell back to the Danubian plain which became their permanent home.

In all this Otto made full use of the Church as an instrument of government and civilization. He created new bishoprics on the northern and eastern frontiers, Magdeburg, Havelberg, Schleswig and others; and he was instrumental in establishing the archbishopric of Prague. He encouraged the foundation of monasteries which spread a knowledge of agriculture and brought the means of education to the newly settled frontier peoples.

His position as the greatest ruler in the West was unassailable after his resounding victory at Lechfeld. He had already been crowned in Charlemagne's cathedral at Aachen, but not in Rome. The holiest city of the Christian West had sunk during the last fifty years to its lowest depth of degradation. The most powerful of the brigands (so-called 'noble' families) who fought for dominance in Rome, had gained absolute control over the chair of St Peter to which they or their mistresses elevated their protégés and their bastards. The clergy, who were restoring order and spreading civilization in northern Europe, owned the traditional authority of the Pope but no longer looked to Rome for help or direction. Otto responded to an appeal for help from a disreputable Pope who had fallen out with his even more disreputable patrons. After his coronation in St Peter's, Otto called a synod of the Church which with his full approval deposed the Pope who had crowned him. After a tough trial of arms with the Roman factions he established imperial control over papal elections, a power which his son confirmed. Under imperial control the Papacy climbed slowly out of the pit of corruption but did not regain for the best part of a century the spiritual prestige to defy imperial power.

As emperor of the West, Otto sent messengers to Byzantium suggesting an alliance for his son with a princess of the imperial house. The idea did not at first commend itself in Constantinople, but when Otto had reformed the Papacy and had his son crowned as emperor-elect, a Byzantine princess was duly despatched. Historians are not agreed as to whether she was *porphyrogenita* – 'born in the purple', that is the daughter of an emperor, or whether she was merely a niece. In either case Theophano was an active, intelligent woman and a civilizing influence on the taste and manners of the Germanic court.

A year after this triumphant marriage of his son, Otto died (973). He had created a different kind of empire from that of Charlemagne – based on central Europe, on lands most of which had been outside the direct control of ancient Rome. But it upheld the Roman conception of an overall power maintaining peace and order in the West, a conception doomed to be an ideal rather than a reality.

The reign of Charlemagne was marked by a cultural revival which is sometimes called the Carolingian Renaissance. The epoch of Otto the Great and his immediate successors is associated with an Ottonian Renaissance. In spite of the destructive invasions and the collapse of law and order over whole regions of the West, during the dismal end of the ninth century and the earlier years of the tenth, a continuous development can be traced between the Carolingian and Ottonian civilizations. At the darkest times of the Viking raids, when monasteries were laid waste, libraries destroyed, reliquaries torn apart for their gold and jewels, portable things could be saved and often were. Some descendants of Charlemagne, who appear as defeated figures in political history, had the time and taste to commission fine copies of books, mostly devotional, and such minor works of art as crucifixes or book bindings of delicately carved ivory or beaten gold set with precious stones. The arts of calligraphy and illumination showed no decline, rather an enrichment. But with Otto the major development was in architecture. Charlemagne's attempt in Aachen cathedral to reproduce the spacious elegance he had admired at Ravenna in San Vitale is a stumbling aspiration towards the unattainable. By the tenth century, and especially after the coming of the empress Theophano, building in Germany shows a new confidence, and not in Germany alone. The Romanesque architecture of the Ottonian revival is impressive in solidity and strength, noble in proportion, enhanced by sculpture of high imaginative power.

The Byzantine empire experienced its worst disasters, and was again restored as western Europe went down. Battered by the Bulgars, driven out of Sicily by the Arabs, threatened even by the Viking colonies in Russia, Byzantium reached its nadir in the middle of the ninth century, then steadily rose again. Before the end of the century the south Italian provinces were recovered and the Arab pirates defeated in the Mediterranean. The most dangerous enemies were now the Bulgars – a Turkic people who had come into Europe from the Eurasian steppes, and were now occupying the land between the Danube and the Balkan mountains. Their principal chief, Boris, was a Christian convert and converted his people, but they copied or adapted what they liked of Byzantine culture and rejected the rest. Attempts were made to tame them by Christian missions and by educating the son of their chief and other young nobles at Constantinople but the young man who became Tsar Simeon (893–927) used his superior education to fight, usually with success, against those who had educated him. In 913 he threatened Constantinople itself hoping to be recognized as an equal Bulgarian emperor. The Byzantine empire admitted no equal, but the Bulgarian menace was not brought under control for another hundred years.

Meantime the empire maintained its superiority by a system of bribes and alliances with its half-barbarian neighbours. During the troubles with the Bulgars the emperor Leo VI made an alliance with the Russo-Scandinavian prince, Oleg of Kiev, ceding him privileges in trade in return for a tribute of fighting men. The Vikings may have been numerous enough to take over Kiev, but more probably it was a small but dominating minority who inter-married with the Slavs and created a mixed race, as significant as the mixed race of Normans in France. This was in 911, the first authentic date in the history of Russia. By the middle of the century, the widowed princess of Kiev, regent for her son, visited Constantinople, was received into the Orthodox Church and dined in state with the empress. But Christianity was not for some time acceptable to the Russo-Vikings, and it was not until 988 that the formidable Vladimir, Prince of Kiev, who united under his rule all the Russo-Viking communities from Poland to the Black Sea, accepted Christianity for himself and his people, gave substantial help to the emperor against the Bulgars and was rewarded by marriage to his sister. His morals were hardly an example to fellow-Christians, but his vigorous conversion of all his subjects and the encouragement he gave to the Church won him his canonization by the Orthodox Church and his posthumous fame as the founder of Holy Russia. Vladimir's territory commanded the north–south trade route across Europe, and Kiev, its commercial centre reached the height of its prosperity at this time, boasting four hundred churches and eight markets.

The disruptive Iconoclastic Controversy being at last settled, the revival of intellectual life began at Constantinople, with renewed studies of mathematics and astronomy. In the latter part of the ninth century a new code of laws, the *Basilica*, eliminated the obsolete and clarified the confused overgrowth which had come to obscure the code of Justinian. In the tenth century succeeding emperors (copying the ancient practice of Diocletian and Constantine) encouraged the growth of a peasant economy of smallholders from whom they recruited hardy soldiers with a stake in the land.

Before the end of the tenth century Byzantium had recovered military strength. Syria and most of Asia Minor were regained for the empire. The Moorish hold on the eastern Mediterranean was weakened by the recapture of Crete and Cyprus. The final defeat of the Bulgars by Basil II (surnamed 'Bulgaroctonus', slayer of the Bulgarians) left Byzantium at the beginning of the eleventh century not only the most civilized but also, once again undeniably, the most powerful state in the West.

An inevitable victim was the small state of Armenia, a Christian people settled between the Black Sea and the Caspian, which Basil II absorbed into the Byzantine empire after a brief period of independence. Their greatest century (*c*.862–970) had followed the recognition of their king, Ashot the Great, of the Bagratid dynasty, both by the neighbouring Arab states and the Byzantine empire. But it was under Ashot III, the Merciful, in the later tenth century that they built the cathedral of Ani and other stately churches, among the most beautiful in the Christian world, which now stand, as monuments to a great past, in the Armenian Soviet Republic.

The process of Christianization in Europe was completed by the eleventh century. All Scandinavia was brought into the fold, largely by missions from Germany; bishoprics were established in Iceland and even Greenland (though the bishops did not always get there). Before the end of the tenth century the ruling chief of the Magyars, now calling himself king of Hungary, was approached from both

Rome and Constantinople but drew back from conversion when the Pope insisted that he must have no Christian slaves. 'As the agriculture of Hungary depended almost entirely on the labour of the enslaved Christian inhabitants, the papal ruling presented difficulties. The problem was surmounted, or perhaps overlooked, by the next king, Stephen, who was baptized on Christmas Day in the year 1000. He, like Vladimir of Kiev, earned canonization by the forcible conversion of his subjects; he substituted for slavery the serfdom of the West, which may have been a marginal improvement.

The year 1000 of the Christian era, the millennium, was marked by no striking phenomena in Europe. Freedom from invasion and the relative orderliness of feudal society had created a modest prosperity and improvements in agriculture. The horse-shoe appears before the year 900, also the horse-collar (originating in China) making ploughing easier and more effective – small advances by modern standards but bringing relief to the tenth century peasant. More land under cultivation meant more food, more possibilities of exchange, a steady increase in population, and a steady extension of agriculture as new settlements pushed out into the wasteland.

Relations between the Pope at Rome and the patriarch at Constantinople, were for the moment friendly. The emperor in the east was the experienced and victorious Basil II; the emperor in the west was Otto the Great's grandson, Otto III, Greek on his mother's side, young, scholarly, something of a visionary. He placed his own tutor in the chair of Saint Peter – Sylvester II, from Auvergne, the first Pope of Frankish blood, and a scholar of distinction whose pastoral correspondence reached almost every region and many of the rulers of Christendom. This partnership of Pope and emperor was dissolved soon after the turn of the century. The outlook, nonetheless, seemed propitious, and the fighting of rival tribesmen on the fringes of the now decaying Persian empire suggested no particular threat to the unity of Christendom. The Seljuk Turks were not yet even a name in the West. It was a time of hope.

VI

Divided from the Eurasian land mass by two great oceans, far to the west of Europe, far to the east of Asia, lay an unknown continent.

Viking adventurers had made landfall on the northern coast of Newfoundland and briefly settled there, but their stay had not been long. America was peopled from the east by nomadic wanderers who from Palaeolithic times had crossed from the northern wastes of Asia, over ice and islands, to the coast of Alaska. The gradual flow of immigrants, which had sparsely peopled the whole continent, still continued.

In the north, tribal cultures were based on hunting in the forests and fishing in the lakes and rivers. More settled groups learnt to grow one crop, maize. This woodland culture, as the anthropologists have called it, persisted almost unchanged for centuries until the Europeans came.

In the extreme south, cold and infertile, little emerged that could be dignified by the name of culture. But in central America, in what is now Mexico, and in the high uplands and the river valleys of Peru, impressive civilizations developed. Without draft animals, they performed almost all labour by hand or with the sulky help of llamas who could carry light packs though they could not draw wagons. Without iron, they inserted sharpened slivers of obsidian into their arrows, tipped their spears in the same way, and made daggers with obsidian blades. They cultivated maize, beans and manioc, made pottery, wove textiles, carved and modelled images of their gods, and eventually built temples and cities.

From about the ninth to the third century before the Christian era, a people inhabiting the northern highlands of Peru built a ceremonial centre or place of pilgrimage; the principal building is faced with dressed stone, three storeys high, equipped with ventilation shafts and adorned with grotesque carved heads. Other carvings show a feline deity – jaguar or puma – formalized and powerful. Remains of fine woven cloth have been found, gold ornaments and a dark coloured pottery with incised patterns. From the position of the ruins, near the modern village of Chavin de Huantar, this is called the Chavin culture.

No less remarkable was the Olmec culture, which may have begun on or near the Pacific coast but left its richest remains in Mexico, at La Venta. Here are the ruins of a city of about 1000 BC centred on a sacred enclosure with an immense pyramid of beaten earth, more than a hundred feet high. An adjoining arena was apparently used for a ball game, possibly of a ritual kind. Their pottery, glazed a lustrous black, often represented animals, especially fish and duck, and has realism and charm; they also made masks of fine earthenware representing jaguars and other beasts, and numerous unexplained small mannikins of jade. They appear to have performed human sacrifices.

The largest of the South American pyramids, the Huaca del Sol, near Trujillo in Peru, dates from a later time, probably about AD 300 and forms part of another ceremonial complex. It is built entirely of adobe bricks. The builders, whom archaeologists call the Mochica, were an advanced people. They dug irrigation canals for their crops as much as seventy miles long. They were powerful sculptors and inventive potters and jewellers, who worked in gold and other precious metals under moderate heat by the method of annealing. They cast in bronze and knew the techniques of making wire and filigree. They painted their pottery with vigorous and rather unpleasing scenes, such as executions. They appear to have been well-organized, active, able and aggressive. But they have so far no decipherable history.

Thirteen thousand feet up in the uplands of Bolivia, near the village of Tiahuanaco are what seems to be the remains of another religious centre – a stone terraced pyramid and a monolithic portal surmounted by the figure of a god. Not far off are red sandstone monoliths carved to represent human figures with heads and hands. The people who built it are unknown.

The most advanced and stable culture in these unrecorded times is associated with the Maya in what is now Guatemala and Yucatan. They were a history-conscious people and had a singularly elaborate method of calculating dates over many years. They used also a hieroglyphic script, the secret of which has not yet been broken. Their greatest epoch of temple and city building seems to have coincided – more or less – with the fourth to the ninth centuries of our era: with the fall of Rome, the rise of Byzantium, the Moslem conquests and the greatness of the T'ang in China. Their architecture was the finest in pre-Columbian America. They did not discover the arch, but could make a corbelled vault. They constructed pyramids, comparable to those of Egypt and raised monoliths of considerable height. Their pyramids were stepped platforms on which they built their temples, so that ceremonies performed by the priests in front of the sacred building would be clearly visible to large crowds gathered below. They often thatched their buildings with reeds and decorated façades and lintels with sculpture in low relief. The tall monoliths with which they adorned their ceremonial centres were also enriched with carving, human and animal motifs powerfully formalized.

Inside, their buildings were covered with stucco and painted with scenes of battle and religious rites. From these we know that their priests and rulers wore gorgeous robes and head-dresses of bright feathers. We know also that they appeased their gods by offerings of blood drawn from their ears and tongues, and on occasion, by human sacrifice. Their economy was based on the cultivation of maize, and their chief gods were those who controlled rain and sun, with a moon goddess for fertility, and a god who specially protected the maize crop.

There is evidence from excavated artefacts that they traded with Teotihuacan in the highlands of Mexico. This last city covered about eight square miles and was probably the largest in America. Its inhabitants seem to have made and exported pottery as well as obsidian knives, blades and other tools. The houses of the rich were spacious with rooms plastered and brightly painted, the poorer quarters cramped and crowded. There is no evidence of literacy. Teotihuacan had fine temples set up on pyramidal bases to a sun god, a rain god, and Quetzalcoatl, the Plumed Serpent, terrifyingly represented with eyes of polished obsidian. This name came later; Quetzalcoatl was a god of the Toltec people who overran Teotihuacan and conquered the Maya at much the same time as the Vikings descended on the coasts of Europe.

The people of the Americas were divided by great distances, deserts, forests, raging rivers and mountain barriers. Their varied cultures developed, for the most part, in isolation. They were unaware that their ancestors had once crossed from unknown lands in the north, and trekked southwards for upwards of 30,000 years; nor, except in the remote north, did anyone know that the immigration still continued. It would be several centuries yet before the last sturdy slant-eyed, fur-clad traveller crossed the Bering Straits and joined the Eskimos.

Meanwhile we are in the eleventh century AD, with western Europe slowly recovering strength, with China entering into a new phase of creative civilization under the Sung, with Japan rising to an early zenith, with the Muslims in North Africa, Persia, Spain and the Middle East creating a strong, varied, mercantile culture; with the

Byzantine empire holding aloft the twin standards of Hellenism and the Christian Church; with India, much divided, but unshaken in its ancient civilization, at the crossroads between East and West.

The most active centres of civilization were still in the Asiatic–Indian–European group in the regions that had access to the Indian Ocean, the Red Sea, the Persian Gulf and the Mediterranean. The Atlantic and the Pacific were more impassable than the deserts of central Asia or Africa.

Africa? North Africa on the Mediterranean, and East Africa with the Red Sea littoral – these were in touch, trading with the ports of India, or the Byzantine empire, Italy and the Syrian coasts. But only the fringe of the great continent south of the Sahara was known to Moorish and Arab merchants who trafficked for gold and ivory with secretive tribesmen whom they never saw face to face. The Phoenicians long ago had sailed some way up the Senegal, menaced by crocodiles, hippopotami and angry natives, but had not discovered its source. The source of the Nile was also a mystery. The vast extent of the continent, the tropical forests, the great lakes and waterways, the grasslands, the formidable mountains were all unknown. Yet Africa was populated by peoples organized into families, tribes and kingdoms, with their own beliefs, laws, customs and means of existence; people with powerful traditions and ancestral pride, with poetry and history that came down by word of mouth and – in Nigeria – with remarkable skill for portrait sculpture in bronze or terracotta; an alert and able people of great ingenuity and resource, but without written records.

At least the existence of Africa was known, unlike the Americas, or that great southern continent the Greeks had guessed at, Terra Australis so-called and only half believed in, where primitive peoples remained undisturbed for many centuries more.

CHAPTER VII

———————•••———————

CIRCA 900—1200

I

NORTHERN INDIA, united for two centuries under the Gupta dynasty, fell apart in the sixth century; the south had not been united since Asoka's time. Division was natural in a country so large and various, fertile in some regions, arid in others or subject to devastating floods; there were hilly regions rich in timber, there were rocky ravines and towering gorges, stupendous mountains and impassable jungles. India was peopled by different races, the ancient Dravidians dominant in the south, the Aryan invaders in the north, mountaineers, pastoralists, farmers and seafarers, a multitude of different traditions and different languages. With so many diverse elements, division was inevitable and the recurrent attempts at union all the more remarkable. Hinduism, with its all-embracing conception of unity in variety, was the binding force, strengthened in the end, rather than weakened by its offshoot, and sometime rival, Buddhism.

The political history of India is that of conflicting kingdoms from time to time pacified by amalgamation under a conqueror. In the north one powerful king, Harsha of Thanesar, in a reign of over forty years (606—647) extended his authority from the Ganges plain over all the Punjab and as far north as Nepal and Kashmir. A devout Buddhist, he was also a great warrior. Unlike Asoka, he never conquered *all* his enemies and could not afford to renounce war. Yet he was remarkable for the benevolence of his government and his devotion to Buddhism, both of which won the approval of the Chinese philosopher Hsüan Tsang when he visited his court (see p. 214).

Before Harsha's death, Muslim conquerors overwhelmed Persia. Twenty years later, they were in possession of Afghanistan, whence they crossed the mountains, overran the Indus valley and conquered the province of Sind. After a period of quiescence, they launched a series of raids against Gujarat. By that time, Harsha's kingdom had broken up and three dynasties had emerged – the Pala in the north east, the Pratihara in the northern Deccan and the Rashtrakuta in the south. A Pratihara king put a stop to the Muslim incursions by one decisive victory (c.760), but in the end the wars of the Rashtrakuta and Pratihara were fatal to both. The Pala survived longest but their power was undermined by the attacks (not unprovoked) of the Chola kings from the south. The north, meanwhile, was splintered into a score of quarrelsome states so that, when another Muslim invader fell upon them, early in the eleventh century, no prince was strong enough to hold him back.

The Muslim hordes who devastated the Punjab in hurricane raids for a quarter of a century (1001–1026) were led by Mahmud of Ghazni, the first in a series of Turkish conquerors of 'slave' origin. Their slavery was of a special kind. The 'Abbāsid caliphs and their tributary rulers in the Middle East, regularly strengthened their armies by buying from the Turkish nomads on their north eastern frontier the prisoners taken in their tribal wars. These slave-soldiers were only slaves during their training. Later, when they had accepted the faith of Islam they became free: no Muslim could remain a slave. Many rose to high command and some carved out independent states for themselves. Mahmud of Ghazni was the son of a Mamluk or slave-soldier who had extended his power from Afghanistan to the Indus. His own ambition was to build a yet greater kingdom controlling the trade routes of south central Asia. Early in his reign he became master of Khorasan and thereafter financed the consolidation of his Asian conquests by plundering India. The great Hindu temples were his objective; here he showed his devotion to the Prophet by shattering idols while collecting a maximum of movable wealth in a minimum of time. Thousands of devout Hindus were killed vainly defending their shrines, thousands more carried off as slaves.

Yet Mahmud saw himself as a patron of learning and the arts. Immensely rich, possessing the fertile region of Khorasan, controlling the passes through the Pamirs and the trade routes to China (and imposing tribute on every caravan) he collected a superb library and attracted to his court scholars, artists and writers. He took with him to India the polymath Al Biruni, the greatest scholar and observer of his time, who recorded the culture which Mahmud was doing so much to destroy. Also at his court was the Persian poet Firdausi (*c*.940–1020) who delved in the riches of his library for the legends of ancient Persian kings which he wove together into his epic *Book of Kings* – *Shāhnāmeh*: a work which established the classical tradition of Persian poetry, while giving delight to thousands who, to this day, listen spellbound to stories of adventure, love and glory – often embodying deeper spiritual meaning – taken from its pages.

The death of Mahmud of Ghazni and the almost immediate fall of his dynasty, saved North India from Muslim devastation for over a century. They were left to fight among themselves until once again Muslim hordes poured through the passes of Afghanistan. This time their leader was Muhammad of Ghur, who overran Sind, took Lahore and sent his underlings to conquer Bihar and Bengal. The North Indian princes, briefly united, defeated him once, and then were themselves defeated. Muhammad captured and plundered Delhi, but in 1206 he was assassinated. One of his generals, Qutb ud Din, another Mamluk, established a dynasty – the so-called 'Slave Kings'. They never won the loyalty of their Hindu subjects, whose temples they destroyed to make way for mosques. In the heart of Delhi the famous Qutb Minar, a minaret of exquisite grace, soaring upwards two hundred and forty feet into the dazzling sky, recalls the rule of the Slave Kings.

South India was more prosperous, although by no means peaceful, during these centuries. In the extreme south the Pandya dynasty was the dominating power from the sixth to the fourteenth century – something of a record.

The Venetian traveller Marco Polo, the earliest European to describe the wonders of the East, was received by a king of Pandya about the year 1292. The monarch was an impressive figure, clothed, in the burning heat, only in a glittering golden loin-cloth and wearing bracelets and anklets studded with gems. The nobility imported horses at great expense from Persia, a traffic in the hands of Arab merchants, but the principal trade of the country, Marco Polo surmised, was in ginger, pepper and precious stones, though the peasants lived on rice and had not always enough of that.

Marco Polo described with admiration the devoted sacrifice of Indian widows on the funeral pyres of their husbands; the practice was said to be voluntary and not subject to the abuses which in later centuries made it abhorrent. Later he watched pearl fishers diving for oysters, from which they extracted pearls 'in quantities beyond computation'. They dived only by daylight, when holy men protected them from predatory fish by chanting incantations. The merchants who employed the divers paid a tenth of their profits to the king and one pearl in every twenty to the holy men. What they paid the divers Marco Polo does not say.

In the fertile plain south of Madras, the Pallava dynasty flourished until overthrown in the eighth century by the Chalukya who controlled much of the southern Deccan. Though divided, the south was not fragmented like the north, nor was it subject to recurrent Muslim invasion. The damage wrought by inter-dynastic wars was limited.

Later in the tenth century, the Chola, a Tamil dynasty, emerged as the strongest rulers. After consolidating their position in the south, they extended their power over the Deccan, built a fleet and competed successfully with the Arabs in trade with eastern Africa, the Persian gulf and the Red Sea. They had a naval base in the Maldive Islands, exacted tribute from the kingdoms of the Malayan peninsula, Sumatra and Pegu and dominated the sea-route to China. Twice they invaded and over fifty years occupied most of Ceylon. At its height their maritime power was the greatest in the known world.

The ancient religion of India had for centuries fallen behind Buddhism both in intellectual and spiritual influence. Hinduism, with its comprehensive tolerance of innumerable local gods and magic rites had never lost its popularity with the ignorant, poor and hungry. But the great scriptural writings, the Vedic hymns, the Upanishads, and the Mahabharata were in Sanskrit which had disappeared from general use and was known only to the learned.

About the sixth century, translations began to be made of the Hindu scriptures, first into Tamil, the principal language of the south, then into the vernacular languages of the north. All over India the literate population once again began to know the pre-Buddhist scriptures and the diverse and comprehensive nature of the religion from which Buddhism had sprung. The revival was slow but sure.

The two most popular gods were Vishnu and Shiva, who emerged as equally inspiring figures, each with his own following, the Vaishnavas mainly in the north, the Shaivas dominant in the south.

Vishnu, the all-pervading preserver of the world, was said to have lived among men in many different forms. He was incarnate again in the Buddha, making possible the coexistence of Buddhists and Hindus. Temples in his honour, richly decorated with sculpture, multiplied in the northern provinces, culminating in the amazing series of erotically decorated temples – originally eighty of which twenty-three are still standing – built over seventy years (930–1002) at Khajuraho by the Chandella kings, an otherwise obscure dynasty.

Shiva, an older god than Vishnu, probably of Dravidian origin, was the destroyer of the world. This too could be seen as a creative act, leading to rebirth.

Mahendravarman I, of the Pallava dynasty (600–630) gave the initial impetus to Shaivism in South India. A poet and seeker after truth, he had at first been converted to Jainism; when he turned to the worship of Shiva he destroyed the Jain temples and dedicated to Shiva the famous monolithic shrines at Mamallapuram, huge boulders carved all over with the acts and miracles of the god. His successor continued the work and crowned it with a great stone-built, free-standing temple on the seashore. This was the beginning and early maturity of Hindu sculpture in the south.

Shaivism spread northwards, was adopted by the Chalukyas, then the Rashtrakutas. A Rashtracuta king made the grandiose cave temple at Elephanta; at Ellora in the northern Deccan, it was again the Rashtrakuta who had a temple as large as the Parthenon cut out of a solid cliff, with columns, arcades, staircases, deep-cut reliefs and a myriad statues. At Ellora, as also at Ajanta (where the famous painted caves cover a span of nearly a thousand years), sanctuaries in honour of Vishnu, of Shiva and of the Buddha, survive together. With few exceptions Hindu worshippers of whatever group did not feel impelled to destroy shrines set up at other times and to other gods.

The revival of Hinduism increased the power of the priestly caste, the Brahmans. They now took over education, which for generations had been a principal activity of the Buddhists. A new kind of school grew up: the *matha*. By origin rest houses for pilgrims situated on the main roads of India, the *mathas* became centres of education and religious debate.

About the year 800, the reformer Shankara appeared among the Brahmans of the south. He further refined and idealized the ancient Vedic tradition; the material world, he taught, was an illusion; reality was not perceptible to the senses, only to the spirit. Shankara travelled widely, preaching his doctrine, and founding *mathas* in North India and in the foothills of the Himalayas. His ascetic form of Hinduism, which had absorbed much from Buddhist thought, made many converts in the north, where Buddhism itself had been debased by superstitious accretions and too much ritual. Revitalized and purified, Hinduism now made the stronger appeal.

The Muslim invasions of the tenth and eleventh centuries hastened the decline of Buddhism; in North India monasteries were sacked and their libraries scattered. Hindu temples were of course also destroyed, but the ancient faith now had a new resilience and was strengthened by suffering and martyrdom. Buddhism gradually withdrew from India. It survived in Nepal, in the Tantric form which reached back to deep-rooted fertility cults and emphasized the mystical significance of sexual union. It took fast hold in Tibet, where the philosophic Buddhism of China mingled with the Tantric symbolism of Nepal. It survived also in Ceylon, perhaps in part as a gesture of defiant independence directed at the aggressive Indian kings, the Chola, who tried (and failed) to conquer them.

In India itself Buddhism was absorbed into the older religion from which it had sprung, still a living influence but never again (as in the days of Asoka) a dominant faith.

II

In China, Buddhism which flourished at the height of the T'ang civilization almost disappeared during the ferocious persecutions of the dynasty's declining years. One sect survived: the Ch'an Buddhists (better known under their Japanese name of Zen). Their teaching exercised a strong appeal in the period of disorder after the fall of the T'ang when North China was overrun by invaders from Central Asia, and South China broke up into half a dozen rival kingdoms. The Ch'an Buddhists taught indifference to all material affairs, a doctrine which besides giving great comfort in hard times had close affinities with Chinese Tao-ism. In Szechwan, a school of Chinese painters even applied the calculated indifference of Ch'an

Buddhism to their art, abandoned all the established rules and tried instead to capture the elusive flash of revelation by complete spontaneity – in fact 'doing their own thing'.

Chinese historians, who like clear definitions, call the period of anarchy which followed the fall of the T'ang, *The Five Dynasties*. There were, in fact, more than five. One 'emperor', Li Hon-Chu, who ruled at Nanking (961–975) sustained the literary traditions of the T'ang, himself wrote poetry, and gathered painters, writers and musicians at his court. But already a resolute warlord had conquered most of South China and initiated the Sung dynasty taking the imperial name T'ai Tsu. It was only a matter of time until he took over Nanking and carried off the poet-emperor to lament his fate in captivity:

> When will the last flower fall, the last moon fade?
> So many sorrows lie behind.
> Again last night the east wind filled my room –
> O gaze not on the lost kingdom under the bright moon.[1]

The Sung were never as powerful as the T'ang. The Great Wall had been abandoned and much of the north was already occupied by nomad tribes who had settled down into independent kingdoms which had, in some degree, adopted Chinese ways. They were unreliable and often hostile neighbours. The Sung were too weak to regain what had been lost, but they managed to resist further encroachment for a hundred and sixty years.

In spite of their inevitable misfortunes the Sung stand high in the history of Chinese culture and world civilization. Their founder T'ai Tsu was a convinced Confucian, who built his government on principles of honesty and responsibility. Foreign conquest and military glory were out of the question, but it was possible to create first a stable government and then a prosperous economy. Power could not be won on land, but trade could be extended by sea. The coastal Chinese had always been good seamen and under the Sung their skill and knowledge rapidly advanced. Their ships were capable of long voyages and by the twelfth century they were already navigating by a primitive compass. Succeeding the Chola dynasty of South India as masters of the southern seas they traded not only to Korea, Japan, the coasts of south east Asia, Sumatra and Java, but also to India, Ceylon and even across the Indian Ocean to the Persian Gulf and the Red Sea. By AD 960 Chinese immigration into the Yangtse valley, Fukien and Kwantung and assimilation with the natives had made China the 'world's largest body of culturally unified people'. Soon after this, the introduction of a new strain of drought-resistant rice made it possible to reap two crops in a year.

The fine, hard, translucent pottery which had amazed an Indian traveller as early as the ninth century, became under the Sung a principal luxury export manufactured on an increasing scale by factories under imperial control. It was popular in Japan, as was also another – this time invisible – export, Zen Buddhism.

Shortly before the advent of the Sung, printing developed. The earliest printing, from characters incised on a wooden block, seems to have appeared in the eighth century, and was used chiefly for making copies of Buddhist prayers. By the early tenth century, at Cheng-tu in Szechwan, movable type was in use but this had relatively few advantages in China, with its multitude of different characters. The wood block was usually preferred. Either way the immense advantages of printing for spreading knowledge were made manifest by a hundred and thirty volumes of the Chinese classics issued from the presses of Chengtu between 932 and 953. Works designed to give general information: handbooks on botany, medicine, agriculture, painting, literature and history were also published.

The Chinese were not the first to have the encyclopaedic idea. The Greeks had had it; Aristotle had systematized natural history, ethics, politics and poetry. Ptolemy had aimed at the same goal for astronomy and geography. More than one Roman had provided some kind of Enquire-Within-About-Everything; the work of Varro in the first century BC is almost wholly lost, but a century later Celsus on the Arts and Pliny on Natural History compiled handbooks of general information. The late Roman Cassiodorus, in the time of Theodoric the Ostrogoth, laid down a groundwork of general knowledge, which was imitated a century later, in Visigothic Spain, by Isidore of Seville. Very primitive handbooks, these last two, and often misleading, but they embodied some useful knowledge and some wisdom, and at least a conception that knowledge was something to be respected and preserved.

The Sung explosion of knowledge caused the examination system for the civil service to be revised and broadened. Meanwhile a remarkable administrator, Wang An-Shih (1021–86), introduced reforms which were intended to strengthen Imperial China against her invaders by promoting general prosperity and to put Confucian ideals of government into practice. These ideals were described by the contemporary poet and administrator Su Shih: 'a state depends for its survival not upon the measure of its power but upon the loftiness of its ethical standards and for length of life not upon the degree of its prosperity but upon the soundness of its national character'. Wang An-Shih introduced a system by which the annual produce of each province was divided into three parts: the first for the payment of taxes, the second to meet local needs and the surplus to be bought at a fair price by the government for re-sale or re-distribution. The farmer thus had an assured market and was able to build up a reserve of money. A system of state loans at low interest was also organized to protect peasants from corrupt moneylenders.

Tax assessments were revised annually, conscripted labour on public works was abolished and taxes were graded, so that the rich paid something to alleviate the hardships of the poor. The system did not do all that its creator expected, because, Confucian principles notwithstanding, officials were often corrupt and the rich were good at tax evasion. Nonetheless, these paternalist schemes, together with the introduction of new crops, and in some cases of greater knowledge acquired from printed handbooks, made for a modest prosperity among the peasants.

The economic achievement of the Sung was admirable in view of the pressure under which they laboured. It never equalled the glory of the T'ang at its highest. Their two greatest cities – Kai Feng in the north, and later Hangchow in the south, though busy, comfortable and prosperous, were less splendid by far than the T'ang cities of Chang-an and Canton.

The arts which flourished under the Sung were not architecture, sculpture and wall paintings but the less expensive arts of pottery, more intimate painting, calligraphy and literature. Screen paintings were popular, and scroll paintings began under the Sung. The scrolls were light and portable; some were for hanging on walls, others, of much greater length, were for unrolling on a flat surface to be enjoyed a foot or two at a time so that the connoisseur might imagine, as he looked at the painted landscape, that he was himself climbing the pass into the mountains or walking along the river bank, with all its passing incidents. They are often in monochrome or very slight colour – rivers, waterfalls, mountains, trees and rocky gorges, which miraculously convey the atmosphere of mist and sunshine, autumn or spring, as in the landscape of the tenth century Tung Yüan, one of the greatest of Chinese painters.

The Chinese aimed at accurate observation of detail, but were not bound by the realistic treatment of perspective which for many years dominated European art. They did not limit their pictures to what could be seen from one fixed point of view but included all that they knew to be there; in their vase paintings, they subtly indicated distance by using paler colours for things further off.

In the second century of the Sung and more especially under the emperor Hui Tsung (1101–25) art became more mannered; landscape was less favoured than detailed paintings of flowers and birds. Hui Tsung, himself a painter of elegant pictures, encouraged artists to come to his court but controlled their subjects and their manner in a way which must have stifled originality. He cultivated the Tao-ist philosophy of indifference to material matters – or at least he cared only for his beautiful garden and the works of art which he assiduously collected. Corruption undermined the administration and the disaster of 1126 followed. A massive invasion of nomad tribes from Manchuria overwhelmed the north. The Sung capital was captured, the imperial palace was burnt with all its treasures, and the emperor carried off to die a prisoner in Mongolia.

The dynasty survived the disaster, with half its territory gone. The Southern Sung, as they came to be called, rebuilt their empire in the south, with its capital at Hangchow (then called Lin-an), and maintained as far as they could, for another century and a half the administrative traditions and economic policies of their forebears. In this latter period Confucianism absorbed elements of a different kind from Tao-ism and Buddhism. The philosopher chiefly associated with this neo-Confucianism, was Chu-Hsi, whose teaching and career illumined the last century of the Sung, and remained a vital influence in the Far East long after the Sung had perished.

It was also in the time of the Sung that the cult of Kwanyin, giver of children, goddess of mercy, took hold in China. She is one of the loveliest figures in Chinese art from the time of the Sung until the eighteenth century: tender and serene. Yet she came into being through an error; the original of Kwanyin was a male Buddhist saint, or Bodhisattva, from whom the goddess of mercy evolved by a sequence of popular misunderstandings.

During the last century of the Southern Sung the civilized arts still flourished. Chinese vases had never been more beautiful in shape, nor the colour of their glazes more subtle. The glazes, from Lung-chüan which Europeans later called Celadon, are among the loveliest in the world.

Painting also flourished, encouraged by a newly-founded imperial academy. A new subject was added to the bird and flower paintings and landscapes – dragon paintings of splendid imaginative power. The dragon, in Chinese folklore a friendly monster who controlled the rain, was a mystical symbol to the Tao-ists and Zen Buddhists. The dragon breaking through clouds was the sudden illumination, the moment of truth. The greatest of the dragon painters, Ch'en Jung, had a peculiar technique: when drunk, it is said, he would 'give a great shout, seize his cap, soak it with ink and smear on his design with it, afterwards finishing the details with a brush'.[2] Ch'en Jung was a responsible civil servant who can, when sober, have had no illusions about the future. But imaginary dragons might at least temporarily divert the mind from the Mongol hordes massing in the north to make an end of the Sung.

III

Although Chinese influence in Japan had waned during the T'ang decline and the quieter rule of the Sung, the Japanese still deeply respected Chinese philosophy, literature and the arts. But from the time of Prince Shotoku they had worked out their own forms of government. They had copied printing gratefully from the Chinese but had gradually worked out a method of writing better suited to their language than Chinese ideographs.

The first of the Fujiwara dynasty, who had gained control over the imperial government in the seventh century, issued the so-called Taika Reforms (the *Great Change*) by which judicial and fiscal administration was centralized, and the accumulation of land by inheritance was forbidden (645). But such comprehensive legislation could not be effective in a land where the geographical divisions imposed by mountains and the sea lent themselves to the growth of regional power. The edicts of government had little force against the interests of the clan chieftains. The power of the Fujiwara, exercised in theory because they controlled the sacred person of the emperor, was in fact based on their great estates and the manpower they could command. It was in the nature of things that the laws concerning inheritance should be evaded and rival families combine against the Fujiwara. The wonder was that their dominion lasted for over four centuries.

By relieving the god-emperor and his court of all duties except the performance of ceremonial rites, the Fujiwara regime made possible the development of a rarefied and exquisite court culture. This epoch, known as the Heian period in Japanese history, reached its height during the long predominance of Fujiwara Michinaga (995–1027). Father-in-law of four emperors and grandfather of three, he compared himself to a flawless full moon riding the skies.

Nothing could have been further removed from the crude life of the regions, the brawls and feuds of lesser chieftains or the hard lives of peasant farmers and fisherfolk, than life at the imperial court. Formal occasions and imperial audiences took place with grace and precision varied, when the weather was suitable, by processions and pilgrimages to favourite shrines. Otherwise life at court was given over to hunting, love-making and the cultivation of elegance in life and the arts.

Courtiers and court ladies flirted, exchanged presents and wrote poems to each other. They made delightful expeditions into the surrounding country, the women in palanquins or light carriages of wickerwork and woven leaves, the men on horseback. They devoted much time and thought to the style and arrangement of their clothes, the dressing of their hair and the correctness of their manners. There was intrigue and jealousy, of course, and a fashionable melancholy was cultivated, an acute awareness of the ephemeral nature of things. Nonetheless, it was a lively court, with good conversation and much music-making, with pet dogs, birds, cats and many pretty children.

Women played as large a part as men in the intellectual life of the time. Two stand out above all. Lady Murasaki, at one time beloved of Michinaga himself, was Japan's first novelist; her *Tale of Genji* reflects the tastes, preoccupations and character of the court and has enchanted the West in twentieth-century translations for its subtle delineation of mood and character. Another court lady, Sei Shōnagon, left a discursive personal record in her *Pillow Book*, full of anecdotes and gossip, laughter, music and casual love affairs – 'when the moon is shining I love to receive a visitor ... .' Here and there we catch a glimpse of imperial relaxation: 'I love to hear His Majesty playing the flute in the middle of the night'.[3] Her pages gleam with her delight in natural beauty, fresh-fallen snow, dew on flowers – but there was no love lost between her and Lady Murasaki.

At this educated and leisured court, most of the men (though not the women) could speak Chinese and quote Chinese poetry, but they composed their own poetry in Japanese and had their own style, marked by a more directly sensual response to beauty and great ingenuity in playing with words – acrostics, puns and double-meanings. They had evolved a style of life entirely their own, enclosed, self-sufficient and isolated from the world outside.

The court was largely inhabited by favoured protégés of the Fujiwara, far removed from the coarser life of the regional land-owners, and indifferent to all that went on outside the palace walls. Sei Shōnagon observed the doings of ordinary people as though they were a different species. 'They looked like so many basket-worms as they crowded together in their hideous clothes', she wrote of the crowd in a Buddhist temple; and she was disgusted by the eating habits of some carpenters at work in the palace grounds, yet she took delight in the rhythmic movements of peasants reaping the rice crop.[4]

What indeed was the life of the common people of Japan? It was in the interest of each chieftain to protect the peasantry on his land so that neither the manpower nor the crops on which he depended for essential work and essential stores should fail him. The more powerful the landowner, the more likely were his tenants to be able to sustain themselves and their families from their small plots of soil, without fear of alien devastation.

Beyond this, they had Shinto, the deep-rooted nature worship, which inspired loyalty to the emperor as the divine descendant of the sun goddess, who had created the land of Japan and decreed its superiority to all other nations. By the tenth century it had a supporting pantheon of over three thousand deities of trees and mountains, waterfalls, winds, stars and rivers. It gave to many a religious devotion to their land and a sense of wonder and delight in the beauties of nature, which has persisted with the Japanese people to this day.

Shinto had been enriched by Buddhism and the growth of

Buddhist monasticism. Japanese Buddhists sought peace for contemplation in the mountains, the traditional holy places of Japan.
Such solitary hermits often gave spiritual comfort to the troubled
men and women who sought them out, whether noble or peasant.
Later, monasteries became centres of pilgrimage for all.

There was no inherent contradiction between Shinto-ism and
Buddhism. As in India, so in Japan, local gods, familiar rites and
legends could be absorbed into popular Buddhism. The common
people of Japan found comfort in ceremonies and might be inspired
by glimpses of holiness and visions outside their own harsh experience. But Buddhism as a rule of life, demanded a concentration of
thought and a disregard of material necessity which was unaccept-
able to the peasant who knew that his family would starve if he did
not work. Contemplative Buddhism attracted those who could
afford to be idle; a few gave up all to enter the monasteries but, on
the whole, appreciated the ceremonies more than the ideas behind
them. Many, from princes downwards, gave gifts of land and
money to the monks so that communities vowed to contemplation
and poverty became rich in land and goods. They remained places
of pilgrimage where (in theory at least) all were welcome; but they
also became centres of comfortable retirement for the rich. Fujiwara
Michinaga himself retired to a monastery, and several emperors did
likewise. Inevitably the monasteries became wealthy and worldly
and, when civil war broke out, joined in on the side of their
powerful patrons. Some even had their own armies, with which they
intimidated the countryside and sometimes even the government.

The position of a god-emperor who exercised no power was
irksome to an intelligent man. Towards the close of the eleventh
century the god-emperor found a way out; he abdicated while still
young, usually in favour of a minor, and retired to a monastery.
Here, as the 'cloistered emperor' free from the ritual demands of
god-head but revered for his holiness, he could build up a considerable influence on affairs of state. This extraordinary system undermined the Fujiwara, weakened the central government, and increased the resentment of the warrior chieftains to the point of
revolt. The character of the court had already made a division
between the court nobility and the much larger number of provincial landowners who envied and despised them. When, in the
middle of the twelfth century the last Fujiwara was killed, Japan
was engulfed in a struggle to the death between the two most

powerful warrior clans, the Taira and the Minamoto. Earthquakes of exceptional violence, plague, famine and private banditry on the part of 'Buddhist' soldier-monks aggravated the horrors of a civil war, which ended only in 1185 with the annihilation of the Taira in a sea-battle of appalling ferocity. They left their mark on the literature of Japan in an heroic poem *Heike Monogatori* which tells the tale of their glory and their fall.

Yoritomo Minamoto became the effective ruler of Japan, with a docile god-emperor, who performed his religious functions from the old capital Kyoto, now sadly burnt and devastated. The Fujiwara shōguns had been essentially aristocrats, loftily despising the lesser nobility and conducting affairs from the inner circle of the court. Yoritomo was wholly different. He directed the government from Kamakura, chosen because it enabled him to overlook and control the more dangerous of the eastern warlords. (Hence the epoch − 1185−1333 − is known as the Kamakura Age.) He was unscrupulous, cunning and consumed with ambition, but also bold, clear-headed and a good organizer who shaped the development of Japanese society for several generations. His political organization realistically reflected the needs and interests of the warrior land-owners without whose co-operation no government could work. His title of Shōgun meant commander-in-chief; his council was called Bakufu, or headquarters. Discipline and loyalty became the essential virtues and a new aristocracy of his own henchmen replaced the dispossessed chieftains who had supported his rivals.

Yoritomo's arrangements were effective though his family never truly succeeded to his authority. His weak successor allowed power to slip into the hands of a chief minister Hojo, whose descendants ruled through puppet shōguns for over a century.

The strength of the Japanese system lay in the *Samurai*: chosen warriors who followed their personal chiefs with absolute devotion. Trained from early youth in military discipline and impregnated with a rigid conception of loyalty, their code was more exacting and more binding than that of feudal Europe. There was no mitigating compassion for the weak or respect for the honourably defeated. In war there was no system of surrender and ransom, as in the West; the defeated *Samurai* must either die on the battlefield or commit suicide. (No man of honour surrendered: this unrelenting belief survived into the twentieth century and was one cause of the ill-treatment of western prisoners, who had followed the milder and more rational codes of their own people.) Further, the chief could command a self-inflicted death for any failure of duty. Strangely enough the *Samurai* were often also adherents of Zen Buddhism; the cult of indifference to material things could be reconciled with their way of life, and those who survived beyond the fighting age often became monks. The code of honour, unwritten, all powerful, the famous Bushido, or 'way of the warrior', was not fully formed in Yoritomo's time. But the foundations were laid. It grew over the centuries, heightened by legend and literature. Yoritomo's brother, Yoshitsume, for instance, was driven to suicide by his brother's jealousy, though by far the ablest of Yoritomo's generals. He became a national hero, the type of the loyal knight.

The Bushido code was followed only by the military class. A code of law for the guidance of the shōgun's courts of justice – the Jōei Formulary – applied only to warriors, who were thus set apart from peasants, craftsmen and traders as rigidly as by the caste system of India.

This military rule ensured law and order, most welcome to the Japanese after the disorders of the last years of the Fujiwara. The peasants were not necessarily worse off because they had to look for justice to local courts, not unlike the manorial courts of the West, and were excluded from the judicial privileges and obligations of the *Samurai*. Japanese peasants were at least free men, small proprietors, yeomen in the western sense, rather than serfs.

Court culture declined but the Minamoto Shōgunate brought an increase of general prosperity. Relations with China were on the whole friendly, based on commerce which owed much to the enterprise of the defeated Taira clan, who had, in their time of power, built good harbours and developed overseas trade.

Having learnt the art of lacquer from the Chinese, the Japanese by the thirteenth century were themselves exporting lacquer cabinets to China. They exploited also the mineral wealth of their mountains for gold and mercury.

But the greatest demand of all was for Japanese swords. The long, curved blades were a marvel of strength and sharpness. The hilts and sheaths were designed and decorated with superb craftsmanship. For the Japanese, the making of a sword, the long process of repeated tempering, was a religious rite, preceded by ceremonies of purification. Over all the East, Japanese swords were renowned and sought after.

The old imperial court still survived, delicate and inbred, treated with formal respect but wholly powerless. The sword was now the symbol of Japanese culture, and had assumed, in the workshops of their craftsmen and the hands of the *Samurai* a terrible and dangerous beauty.

IV

After the death of their greatest ruler, Al-Mamun, in 833, the Abbasid caliphate in Persia fell into decline. The Mamluks, those Turkish slave-soldiers — like the Pretorian Guard in the Roman empire — ceased to be the guardians and became the masters of the caliphs, whom they elected, deposed or murdered. As caliphs became mere puppets, provincial governors who were mostly of the old Persian nobility, began to exercise independent power and found hereditary states. This was often as much to the advantage of their subjects as to their own although the predominance of military over civil government was, in the long run, to prove disastrous.

The authority of the Samanids reached from their capital at Bokhara almost to the Tigris. The Buyids by the tenth century controlled Baghdad and most of modern Iraq. Both were discriminating patrons of arts, letters and science and between them they brought about a revival of Persian culture.

The astronomer, Abd-al-Rahman-al-Sufi (903—36) watched the sky from the observatory built in the previous century by Al Mamun and, in his *Book of Fixed Stars*, revised Ptolemy's *Almagest*, which had been the seaman's handbook for over seven hundred years. Abd-al-Rahman's revision became the accepted authority for very nearly as long — until Tycho Brahe's catalogue of the stars in 1572 and Galileo's use of the telescope about 1600. Another Arab scientist, an authority on optics known as Al-Hazen to the Christian world, believed that the stars could be made to look very much nearer by the use of parabolic mirrors and magnifying lenses. (The pre-telescopic observatories were no more than high buildings with well-placed windows and access to a flat roof equipped with a few simple geometrical instruments.)

In another sphere the physician and polymath Ibn Sina (980

–1037) studied and taught under Samanid patronage. His medical and philosophic writings, transmitted by way of Moorish Spain, greatly influenced the scholars of western Europe – who mispronounced his name as 'Avicenna'. His *Book of Healing* was still in use in some European medical schools as late as the eighteenth century, which indicates the snail's pace at which knowledge advanced rather than the soundness of its contents.

The pattern of power in the Middle East was violently altered when the restless Turkish tribes from the Elburz mountains, under the leadership of the Seljuks, came down on the Persian kingdom and in 1055 captured Baghdad. In the next twenty years they overran Asia Minor – where they set up a separate kingdom, the Sultanate of Rum – defeated and captured the Byzantine emperor, Romanus IV, at the disastrous battle of Manzikert (1071), conquered Syria and Palestine and occupied Jerusalem.

In Persia, where the Seljuks had two capitals, Baghdad and Isfahan, they changed little in the method of government, allowing one powerless puppet after another to carry the title of caliph, and drawing on the talent and experience of their Persian subjects as councillors and administrators. They were seriously concerned to maintain a just government, and to encourage commerce, learning and the arts, but their nomadic origin insensibly affected their priorities. Roads were restored and maintained and caravanserais set up for merchants, but the irrigation so essential for agriculture, which had been neglected since the fall of the Sassanids, continued to decay.

Seljuk Persia was rich above all in ceramics and architecture. The clay available to Persian potters was coarse so that no very delicate texture could be evolved, but they developed a technique of modelled decoration in low relief (something they had originally imitated from T'ang China) and raised their ceramic art to unique beauty by the range and intensity of their blue glazes and the invention of lustre.

Their outstanding achievement was in architecture. Devout Muslims, they built mosques, tombs and minarets, schools and hospitals. The plan of their mosques went back to the classic Persian palace plan at Persepolis: a wide open courtyard with domed rooms symmetrically opening off it. (Many of their mosques were to be altered in the affluent sixteenth century, the domes covered with dazzling blue mosaic and the walls with coloured tiles, exciting and beautiful in themselves, but reflecting an age very different from that of the Seljuks whose conceptions were spacious, grand and austere.)

Persian buildings of the Seljuk age excel in the imaginative use of brick. In the century before their arrival Persian builders were already making experimental patterns in this way; under the Seljuks this art reached its height. By laying small narrow bricks in geometrical designs and by slightly varying their projection, they created wall surfaces, which from dawn to dusk, offered to the beholder subtle and ever-changing patterns according to the quality of the light and the angle of the sun. The internal walls, especially the domes, caught the filtered daylight or the glow of lamps with the same magical effect. This was enough, without the addition of colour or other decoration. Of all the masterpieces of this style the north and south chambers in the Friday Mosque at Isfahan are the most beautiful. Both were built at the close of the eleventh century in the time of the Seljuk's greatest ruler Malik Shah (1072–1117). The north chamber has long been famous, but a recent restoration has revealed the dome of the south chamber as a masterpiece beyond all comparison. It was built by Malik Shah's Persian chief minister, Nizam-al-Mulk, who wrote a famous treatise on government, founded a university in Baghdad and initiated the *madrasehs*, for students of the Koran, which spread over all Persia. Malik Shah, also a patron of learning, commissioned Omar Khayyam to write a textbook on algebra and to make some necessary adjustments to the Muslim calendar. Omar (d. 1123), the best known of all Persian poets in the West through the famous adaptation of his work by Edward Fitzgerald, was the leading astronomer-mathematician of his own time.

The Seljuks were devout believers, but tolerant of other religions. Jews and Christians lived unmolested. The Nestorians and other Christian sects which had been persecuted as heretics under Byzantine rule much preferred the tolerant Seljuks.

Like the majority of Muslims, the Seljuks belonged to the Sunni persuasion (see p. 208). The followers of the Prophet's son-in-law, the caliph Ali (murdered in 661), had adopted a more rigid form of the faith, Shi-ism, and some of them believed also in the return of the Prophet, reincarnated as the Mahdi, to lead them to victory. For many generations the Shi-ites seemed almost to have disappeared, but early in the tenth century they gained converts among the Berbers, emerged as a militant force and attacked indiscriminately the Byzantines and the Arab rulers of North Africa and Syria. By 969, when their caliph Al-Muizz set up his government in the newly founded city of Cairo (the name means 'victory') they held all of North Africa, Syria, Sicily and part of Calabria. Cairo, under the rule of this Fatimid dynasty, became a prosperous and well-planned city, tolerant of Jews and Copts, with noble mosques, schools, and a House of Science where men of learning could pursue their studies in peace.

Early in the eleventh century the fanatic caliph Al-Hakim destroyed all monuments in Jerusalem held sacred by Christians. (The situation was relieved only when the more tolerant Seljuks captured the city later in the century.) But Al-Hakim lost the support of his own people by asserting that he was himself divine; to orthodox Shi-ites he became the 'Mad Caliph', though he is a holy figure to this day among that small secretive people, the Druses.

A dispute over the succession of the caliph caused a division in the Shi-ite ranks. Irreconcilable splinter groups took refuge in Syria and Persia and occupied (or built) fortresses in mountainous regions, whence they sent out emissaries of death to murder their enemies – among them the greatest of the Seljuk rulers, Malik Shah and his minister Nizam al Mulk. These murders were committed in a state of religious ecstasy apparently induced by hashish, so that they became known as the *Hashishi*, transliterated in the West to Assassins. They persisted in their religious terrorism for over a century until wiped out by the Mongols.

Meanwhile in Africa a tribe of fanatic Berbers, the Almoravids, overran Morocco. Their leader, Yusuf ibn Tashfin, built the walled town of Marrakesh (*c.*1066). Born in the desert, his ideal city was an oasis, and Marrakesh became the largest oasis in the world, surrounded on all sides by a vast palm grove of his own planting, beautified with green gardens and huge reservoirs fed by streams channelled across the intervening plain from the snows of the Atlas mountains. Until twentieth-century tourism upset all previous calculations, Marrakesh needed no other water supply. His yearning for the perfect oasis was one of the few endearing characteristics of this fanatic conqueror.

Another group of Berber warriors carried the Muslim faith across the Sahara into the black kingdom of Ghana, between the

Niger and the Senegal. They recklessly destroyed its capital at Kumbi but achieved no lasting conquest, merely broke up a once prosperous and united kingdom into a dozen tribal chieftaincies. Yet they served the Prophet well, for they converted the people.

Yusuf ibn Tashfin and his Almoravids, now masters of Morocco, looked across the straits towards Spain and disapproved of what they saw. The original Moorish conquerors of Spain had brought few women with them: three centuries of inter-marriage with the natives had diluted their blood and gone far towards creating a mixed Christian-Islamic culture.

The north – Asturias, Leon and Navarre – had remained Christian. Their king, Sancho III, had fostered Santiago de Compostela as a place of pilgrimage and invited Cluniac monks to keep watch over the holy place. It was rapidly becoming one of the most popular pilgrimages in western Europe.

The more southerly Christian kingdom of Castile, profiting by divisions among the Moors and the decline of their fighting qualities, grew steadily in power. But Christians and Moors in war and peace found much to admire and imitate in each other's ways. Hostilities were intermittent with occasional violent explosions. An aggressive caliph of Cordova provoked a Christian counter-attack, which ended in the sack of the city in 1010. But the rulers of Seville, after Cordova's fall the principal Moorish state, were more conciliatory. By the time of Ibn Tashfin, an amiable caliph who wrote poetry was willing to give a daughter in marriage to the Christian Alphonso of Castile.

Alfonso VI (1065–1109) in his earlier years admired the agricultural and commercial methods of the Moors, encouraged them to bring new crafts into his kingdom and to introduce systems of irrigation. He noticed also how much Moorish economy profited by the Jewish communities in their midst. Fruitful co-operation might have led to a joint culture of great fertility but there was opposition on both sides. Muslim holy men reproached the ruler of Seville for compromising with unbelievers and Cluniac monks preached the Christian duty of fighting the infidels until Alphonso launched a campaign of conquest, pushed the Christian frontier forward to the Tagus and in 1085 took Toledo. Yusuf ibn Tashfin waited no longer. Invading with his fierce Berbers, who advanced to the menacing sound of drums (Africa's gift to the warfare of Europe) he deposed the feeble ruler of Seville and turned all his forces against

Christian Spain. The ensuing war, in which the Christians with difficulty held their own, changed the direction of Spanish history and linked their civilization irrevocably to Catholic Europe, repudiating the Muslim world.

Historians have done justice to Alfonso VI as a stubborn fighter and a wary diplomat. But popular opinion gave credit for the defence of Christian Spain to a man of very different character. The Spanish national hero, Rodrigo Diaz de Vivar, called El Cid Campeador ('Cid', the title given him by the Moors, means 'Lord' and 'Campeador' is the Spanish for 'Warrior'). Historically speaking, this tough fighter from Castile was more concerned to carve out an independent position for himself than to defeat the Moors though he did at least block their advance by establishing his sphere of influence at Valencia. But his reputation rests on popular ballads and the epic *Cantar de Mio Cid*, written about fifty years after his death. The man behind the myth was a brave and cunning adventurer; of the many in Europe at his time he alone became the symbol and the hero of a people.

V

The most successful of these adventurers were the Normans, descendants of that Viking group which, in 912, had been granted land in France. The duke of Normandy, as their leader came to call himself, owed allegiance, theoretically at least, to the French king. His people took wives among their Frankish-Celtic subjects, producing a mixed race, the Normans, who combined the unbridled adventurousness and energy of the Vikings with an extraordinary adaptability. Soon these descendants of sea-rovers became famous for their skill in horsemanship and evolved a method of maintaining and increasing their power based on cavalry and the castle.

Their castles, built where possible on a hill but otherwise on an artificial mound, consisted of a central watch tower which served as store-house, guard-room and magazine, and was surrounded by an outer stockade and ditch. This was the basic plan, which they found in northern France, but enlarged and adapted to their purposes. The watch tower might be a formidable building of stone, the stockade a solid wall broad enough to be manned by armed men, the ditch an embanked moat twenty feet broad, spanned by a drawbridge. A second or third encircling wall might be added, with further build-ings for stables, stores and arms. Growing ever larger, stronger and more complex, the 'motte and bailey' castle dominated the military architecture of western Europe. The 'motte' was the mound, the 'bailey' the ground enclosed between the encircling walls – ground in some cases large enough to pasture cattle and increase essential food supplies. The largest of such castles were self-contained units with resources to stand long sieges, and from them bands of cavalry patrolled the surrounding country, kept the peasantry in awe and repelled hostile intruders.

The Normans had accepted Christianity on settling in France, and, as they learnt to speak their own peculiar dialect of French, they abandoned the legends of their ancestors and took over those of their new home. Roland, Charlemagne's paladin, who had died fighting the Saracens in the pass of Roncevalles, was the hero of their favourite 'Chanson de Geste', composed in the eleventh century. They also took over from the French the practice, essential for a largely illiterate ruling class, of using the clergy as administra-tors and advisers. Very soon they were putting their younger sons and their bastards into the Church regardless of vocation, so that many of the clergy were bound to the duke and his barons by family ties. Yet they also employed, and even revered, learned, wise and devout men. Their religion was superstitious and superficial, but it was sincere.

During the later tenth and eleventh centuries the calmer condi-tions of Europe allowed the population to rise. In Normandy, depopulated by a century of Viking raids, then revitalized by the vigorous newcomers, the increase gave additional impetus to the zest for adventure. Moreover, their duke ruled them with a firm hand; no castles were built without his licence, and the *vicecomes* (viscounts), his ubiquitous officials, controlled taxation and justice. Younger sons of Norman knights, chafing for opportunity, took a few followers with them, and offered themselves as mercenaries abroad: a custom also practised by their kinsfolk of Norway, who could be found as far from home as the imperial armies of Byzan-tium.

The Normans wanted more than pay and plunder; like the Turkish slave-soldiers of the Abbasid caliphs, the ablest and most ambitious wanted to rule as independent princes. By infiltration, diplomacy or conquest, a handful of these adventurers gradually made themselves masters of half Italy, all Sicily, Corfu, Rhodes, Cyprus, parts of Syria, and Asia Minor. Among them one remarkable family stands out – the sons of a petty knight whose castle at Hauteville was too small to contain their ambitions. Three brothers in turn set off for Italy with a band of followers to make their fortunes as mercenaries. They had gained control of Apulia before they were joined by a fourth brother, Robert, later surnamed Guiscard (or the Guileful), who mastered all southern Italy. His elder brothers having conveniently died, the Pope recognized Robert as duke of Apulia, holding his lands from the Vatican, but he soon became the master rather than the vassal of the Pope. Championing the Roman against the Byzantine Church he seized the port of Bari, the last Byzantine outpost in South Italy, built a fleet, occupied Corfu, established a foothold on the Dalmatian coast and even landed an invading force in Epirus. Meanwhile as a true Christian knight, he set out to 'liberate' Sicily from the Moors; after capturing Messina, he left his self-willed younger brother Roger to complete the conquest. Roger fought and schemed his way to the mastery of the whole island, and of Malta and Gozo for good measure.

All this the brothers achieved in less than fifty years (1042 –1091) by a remarkable gift for leadership, and the intelligent opportunism with which they exploited the quarrels of Italian rulers, Byzantine officials and, in Sicily, rival Muslim emirs. Their success attracted many Normans to join them but they raised the bulk of their armies locally, absorbed into their ranks prisoners and runaway serfs, and in Sicily recruited hundreds of Muslim slaves. They secured their possessions by strategically placed castles and took especial care to hold and fortify the seaports. As rulers they claimed to own all the land, but they dispossessed only their irreconcilable enemies. The rest, whether natives or Norman followers of their own, recognized them as their feudal overlords. Once their rule was established, they were tolerant of their non-Christian subjects, allowed the large Muslim population of Sicily and the numerous Jewish communities to live, trade and thrive in peace. But they replaced bishops appointed from Constantinople with bishops appointed from Rome – and thus perpetuated the schism between the Latin and the Greek Churches.

In administration they behaved as most wise conquerors do. Finding an administrative system already established, they took it

over and injected it with their own energy. In southern Italy
Byzantine methods, and in Sicily those of the Muslims, were far in
advance of anything they had seen before. Here was a cadre of
experienced officials, with well-trained clerks, operating a highly
developed judicial and fiscal system, of which the Normans took
full advantage.

The most famous of these rulers of Sicily was Roger II who
succeeded as a minor in 1105 but ruled effectively from 1130 to
1154. He developed Sicily as the wealthy nucleus of a Mediterranean empire, greatly strengthening his position by gaining control
of part of the North African coast and of southern Italy, in spite of
opposition by the Pope, who was ultimately compelled to recognize
him as king of Sicily and southern Italy. He proved to be an able and
tolerant ruler, treating his Arab, Jewish and Christian subjects as
equals. At his brilliant court in Palermo he encouraged, among
other scholars, the geographer Al Idrisi, who compiled a world map
for him and made a silver planisphere, since lost.

Meanwhile in 1066 the duke of Normandy conquered England. A
cousin of the childless English king, Edward the Confessor, he
asserted that he was the rightful heir. But he was himself illegitimate
and his right to succeed had been contested even in Normandy.
William the Bastard was a child when his father died and the first
twelve years of his Norman reign were spent fighting to secure his
position. At twenty he was an experienced soldier, respected for his
ability, feared for his vindictive ruthlessness. Master in his own
duchy, he soon enlarged it by annexing the province of Maine.

On the death of Edward the Confessor, Harold, the ablest and
most powerful of the Anglo-Saxon earls, was crowned king in
England. Ten months later William the Bastard crossed the Channel
with his invading force. Harold, who had just defeated and killed
another invader, the king of Norway, in the north, marched south at
breakneck speed. William had already landed not far from Hast-
ings. On 14 October 1066 after a long-fought battle, William's
cavalry defeated the Saxon infantry who lost heart when Harold
was killed. William the Bastard became William the Conqueror and
England, ruthlessly welded into his dominions, became henceforward a part of western Europe. The Scandinavian connection, so
strong for the last century, was no longer of importance.

Organized fighting ended with the death of Harold, although

sporadic revolts and stubborn resistance in the wilder regions went on for years. William quelled the north with obliterating ferocity. He had his own warriors to reward; to do so he dispossessed all who rebelled or resisted, which came in the end to include nearly all the Anglo-Saxon ruling class. His grants to his followers always involved feudal obligations, especially the provision of a quota of armed knights, which were very clearly set down and sworn to by the beneficiary before he entered into his estates. In this way, the Normans, strangers in a conquered land, were strongly bound to their formidable duke, now their king, by bonds of personal loyalty and self-interest.

For the rest he took over Anglo-Saxon institutions as they stood, with some ingenious improvements. He altered little in the judicial system, and retained the administrative division of the country into shires, sub-divided into 'hundreds' with their local courts, but he increased the authority of the sheriff, the official appointed by the king as overseer of the shire. In Normandy he had brought his barons under control through the *vicecomes* who were responsible directly to him. He now gave the same kind of authority to the English sheriffs. He also combined the old Anglo-Saxon *Witan* – a general council of 'wise men', nobles, clergy and judges – with the European feudal council, the meeting of the king's principal nobility. The great councils, which met regularly in his reign, were designed to keep him in touch, not indeed with the people, but with all the people who counted.

He also retained the Anglo-Saxon system of taxation based on land, but with Norman thoroughness ordered a full and accurate survey of England south of the Humber to facilitate its collection. The astounding work was completed within a year (1086/7) and became generally known as Doomsday Book, because there was no more appeal from its findings than from the Last Judgement. Teams of commissioners, with their scribes and clerks, travelled indefatigably over the abominable roads, set up their courts of enquiry, summoned six villagers, with their priest and reeve, from every place visited, and by dint of questioning on oath, extracted the names of the tenants and sub-tenants, the number of families, and of ploughs, the area of ploughland and of pasture, the number of mills and fishponds, and any other relevant information. (Anglo-Saxon peasants operated a co-operative system, sharing ploughs and oxen and dividing the land into three fields, two sown and one fallow in rotation.) The reports were then collected together into orderly and manageable shape for the assessment of taxes. The result is the most valuable and illuminating document in English history and a monument to Norman administration. Nothing comparable to it in scope and detail had been achieved before in the West.

William the Conqueror, like Guiscard in Italy, was in alliance with the Pope. The English Church, in spite of the piety of Edward the Confessor who founded Westminster Abbey, had seriously declined in the last century. The Pope had therefore blessed William's enterprise as a means of restoring order. The new archbishop, a learned and sympathetic Benedictine monk, Lanfranc, was an Italian who had been long resident in Normandy, and was on terms of mutual respect with the Conqueror. Though he supported William's policy of appointing Normans to the English bishoprics, the monastic reforms which he introduced, his interest in education and his care for charitable works were civilizing influences. While he believed in the partnership of Church and state, he saw their ultimate responsibilities as quite separate, and persuaded the king to divide the ecclesiastical from the secular courts – a division good at the time but later a cause of friction and a source of abuses.

The Norman Conquest restored law and order which had almost vanished during the last years of the Anglo-Saxon kingdom. Old institutions given new life by Norman administration, were the foundation on which a valuable structure of government and justice would arise. But at the time the English suffered in sullen resentment the Conqueror's savage repression of revolt and the brutalities inflicted by Norman landowners on their tenants. Furthermore, villages were destroyed in large areas of the country to create the hunting forests on which the king and his barons depended to fill their larders. It would be long before the downtrodden Saxons, ruled by armed strangers who did not speak their language, began to feel any community of purpose, respect or loyalty to their Norman overlords. It came, in the end, with the mingling of the races through interbreeding, and, more surprisingly, through the steady upward penetration of the English language until, in the fourteenth century, it displaced Norman French throughout society and even at court – everywhere except in the jargon of lawyers.

The century before the Conquest, in spite of Danish invasions, social disorder and political vicissitudes, had seen a final flowering of Anglo-Saxon culture. Builders had begun to use stone, and to ornament their churches with strong and simple sculpture in low-relief; monastic scribes had not lost the art of illumination once practised by the Northumbrian and Irish monks. More important for the future of English literature, they wrote down Anglo-Saxon poetry. They naturally preferred hymns and religious verse, but they also preserved the ancient epic of Beowulf, and other secular pieces. On the eve of the Norman Conquest a varied and imaginative Anglo-Saxon literature existed not in oral tradition alone, but in writing. It is to this perhaps that we owe the survival and ultimate triumph of English over the Norman-French of the Conquerors.

VI

With the rising population of Europe came gradual improvement in agriculture and a revival of economic life. Watermills, known but little used by the Romans, now proliferated: Doomsday Book recorded 6000 in England. They could be used, too, for stone-cutting and wood-cutting after some anonymous benefactor invented the geared wheel. Mining which had almost disappeared since Roman times, began again on a small scale, chiefly copper, iron and a little silver. Ploughing with horses was well-established by Norman times; in the eleventh century the use of a transverse bar, joining the two harnesses, the whipple-tree, made it possible to equalize the load between two horses, and carts were again built with a pivoted front-axle (a device the Romans had used). By the twelfth century, the big four-wheeled wagon, drawn by several teams of horses, came into use and caused something like a revolution in road transport. (Coaches and the earliest design for railway carriages stem from this lumbering old monster.)

As early as the seventh century the Church encouraged markets and fairs, at favourite places of pilgrimage or under the protection of abbeys. The fair at St Denis outside Paris is one of the oldest in Europe. The goods sold were few and simple: grain, wine, sheepskin, salt, butter, dried fish, honey and madder – the source of a popular red dye. Travelling merchants might bring such luxuries as spices, silk, silver trinkets and ornaments or chessmen of walrus ivory.

Another sign of stability was the gradual adoption throughout the West, from the eleventh century onwards, of the dating system promulgated by the Vatican in the sixth century which, though probably inaccurate as to the birth of Christ, ultimately prevailed throughout the Christian world.

The habit of pilgrimage, which had almost vanished during the Viking raids, revived again. Successful warriors with their bands of followers, felt the need for absolution when their days of conquest were over. Sweyn Godwineson, with several murders and the rape of an abbess on his conscience, vowed to walk barefoot to Jerusalem. William the Conqueror's father, justifiably surnamed Robert the Devil, had made the same journey in more comfortable style, but died on his way home. The journey was long and dangerous but thousands undertook it: once even a huge conducted tour (7000 it is said) set out from Germany: 2000 of them survived the hazards of accident and disease to return home again. Multitudes of pilgrims, rich and poor, made the shorter pilgrimages to Rome, or to Santiago de Compostela.

The devastation of monasteries by the Vikings had discouraged monasticism. In the tenth century a new spirit of enthusiasm and reform spread from the famous abbey of Cluny, founded near Macon in 909. The Black Monks, as these reformed Benedictines came to be called, strictly performed the fasts, prayers and labours enjoined on them by the order but believed in glorifying God by study as well as devotion and by the beauty and splendour of their churches. Cluniac abbeys and priories grew up over all the West, enriched by sculpture, painted in bright colours, and furnished with elaborately wrought candlesticks and ornaments of gold whenever possible. The mother house for long controlled the appointment of abbots to the many related foundations and thus maintained unity of organization and spirit. Cluniac influence dominated the Church throughout the eleventh century.

At the close of the eleventh century another reformed Benedictine order, the Cistercians, the White Monks, came into being at Cîteaux. In little more than fifty years there were over 300 monasteries of this order, thanks largely to the single-minded energy of St Bernard of Clairvaux. The Cistercians reacted against Cluniac exuberance, repudiated delight in man-made beauty, and spent their time in prayer, study, self-discipline and devotion, above all, to the Virgin Mary. For choice they built their priories in remote and barren places; the number of monks was small, but they introduced increasing numbers of lay brothers to work the land and so became great redeemers of the waste, pioneers and experts in agriculture, wine-growing and the breeding of sheep. In course of generations the austere Cistercians became successful farmers and wool-merchants whose influence on the economy of western Europe was, in the end, more enduring than their spiritual effect.

The influence of the Cluniacs had social and political repercussions. Their teaching modified the ferocity of the ruling warrior class by creating the ideal of the true Christian knight who fought only in a just cause, honoured women, protected the weak and was true to his word. Few knights kept the rules but their existence was at least a brake on violence. The Cluniacs taught the doctrine of the 'just war' – a concept derived from Saint Augustine. The most just of all wars was the war on unbelievers. In Spain they put a stop to the peaceful co-operation of Christians and Moors. (In fairness it should be added that Muslim fanatics were doing the same.) Above all else the Cluniacs preached the liberation of Jerusalem as the great objective of Christian chivalry.

In politics the first fruit of Cluniac reform was the breach between Pope and emperor, known as the Investiture Conflict, which divided western Europe for well over a century. The partnership of Church and state had long been the foundation of stable government. Kings and emperors naturally took counsel with feudal magnates whose arms were indispensable, but in matters of civil government they depended on the advice of their bishops, men with education, administrative experience, and knowledge of the law. This co-operation inevitably corrupted the Church. Astute rulers arranged for their brothers and bastards to become priests so that they could be sure of subservient churchmen, while ambitious young men, who had no taste for fighting, regarded the Church as a road to power.

The Cluniac monks and their pupils introduced a new and uncorrupted element into the Church. They captured the Papacy in 1049 with the election of Pope Leo IX. In his brief five years rule he took his stand on the supremacy of the spiritual authority. After a short interval he was followed by another Cluniac monk, Hildebrand, one of his chief assistants, who was elected Pope as Gregory VII in 1073.

The worst abuse, as Gregory saw it, was the dominance of the layer ruler. These crude, powerful men had gradually come to exercise, and then to claim as their due, the right to appoint their own bishops. But the bishop's office was holy; he could only hold it by apostolic succession and the laying on of hands by another bishop; ultimately only by the consent of the bishop of Rome, the Pope. But what lay ruler would willingly tolerate the appointment of his ministers by an alien power?

This was a serious matter for both parties. Once the secular power gained control, the way was open for intriguers, for the licentious relations and the servile dependants of the ruler. The Papacy, under Cluniac influence, made a stand. Gregory's predecessor prohibited lay investiture and Gregory took up the sacred quarrel.

His opponent was the young emperor Henry IV. Since the time of Otto the Great the imperial title had been held by a series of German kings, at least one of whom had been canonized. Their power, bounded approximately by the Rhine in the west, the Elbe in the east, the Danube in the south and the Baltic in the north, was the greatest in western Christendom, though it was continually menaced by over-powerful nobility. It was, self-evidently, important for the ruler of Germany to appoint the bishops whose support was vital to him as a counterweight to that of the secular magnates.

The Pope was morally right. The emperor was politically right. No compromise was possible. Gregory excommunicated Henry, then, in fear of powerful enemies, took refuge in the castle of Canossa in the foothills of the Alps. Henry was too clever for him. Suddenly, at Christmas, with snow thick on the ground, he appeared at the gates of Canossa in humble garb as a penitent, some say barefoot. In Christian charity Gregory could not refuse to absolve him (1077). Henry, no longer excommunicate, waited for a suitable opportunity, then set up an anti-Pope of his own and made war on Gregory. Gregory turned to his most formidable vassal, Robert Guiscard, duke of Apulia. Henry reached Rome first, battered his way in and was crowned in St Peter's by his puppet Pope while Gregory barricaded himself in the Castle of Sant'Angelo. Then Guiscard appeared leading a mixed army of Normans and Arabs from Sicily. The emperor fled. Guiscard allowed his troops to sack Rome with appalling ferocity and carried Gregory off to die, in safety but in despair, at Salerno (1085). 'I have loved righteousness and hated iniquity', he said, 'therefore I die in exile.'

He *had* loved righteousness. He had striven to save the Church from political subservience and material corruption. As a result Rome had been devastated and Christendom was divided. But the Investiture Conflict is only a part of the story; in other ways he had served the Church well, had put down simony – the purchase of ecclesiastical preferment – with a firm hand and done much to elevate the character of the priesthood. He had also tried to heal the widening breach between Rome and the eastern Church, which had arisen twenty years earlier over papal jurisdiction in southern Italy. Since that time the Seljuk Turks had overrun Asia Minor, seized Antioch, the second city of the empire, and wiped out the Christian kingdom of Armenia.

On the lower Danube Turkish tribes plagued the enfeebled Byzantine empire, while the Normans captured their last outposts in South Italy. The eastern empire was tottering and the safety of the West was threatened by its fall. Gregory VII understood this. It was his dearest desire that all good Christian knights should join in that just war for which the Cluniacs hoped, to help their hard-pressed eastern brethren, to break the power of the infidel and liberate the Holy Land. After so great a service, the eastern Church would surely yield to the supremacy of Rome.

The Crusade that Gregory had dreamed of became reality thirteen years after his death. By then the case was altered; the Byzantine empire had already saved itself.

VII

Ten years after the overwhelming defeat of the Byzantine forces by the Seljuk Turks at Manzikert in 1071 Alexius Comnenus, an experienced general with great political ability, seized the throne. He reigned for thirty-seven years (1081–1118) and was by far the ablest emperor in the last four centuries of Byzantium. He was fortunate also in his chronicler, his daughter Anna, whose *Alexiad* is a work of exceptional value, though sometimes coloured by filial piety.

Alexius tackled his enemies systematically. He defeated the nomadic tribes in the Danube basin, made the best terms he could with the Seljuks in Asia Minor, then enlisted Venetian help to oust the Normans from the Adriatic coast, a service for which the Venetians exacted a substantial reward.

Those once pitiful settlements of fugitives in the lagoons had early joined together in a communal government under an elected head, the doge. By the ninth century the island of the Rialto (Rivo alto) became their accepted centre and the whole group was known as Venice. By the tenth century they had a navy powerful enough to clear the Adriatic of Arab pirates and command the sea route to the Holy Land. The Venetians knew their strength: as a reward for their help against the Normans they exacted from the emperor Alexius rights of free trade throughout the empire and a grant of land at the port of Durazzo. The now flourishing maritime republic was still technically subject to him, but Alexius must have known how little control he could exert, and how injurious Venetian enterprise might be to the commerce of his own people.

Since the Seljuk conquests Byzantium was a beleaguered outpost to which no permanent relief would ever come again. Alexius and his successors had to buy immediate help where they could and leave the consequences to the future. Thus Alexius paid for the strengthening of the frontier defences and the army by raiding the accumulated riches of the Church, a policy which he defended on the grounds that King David had done the same. It was bound, in the long run, to weaken the clerical support on which the imperial government depended, but for nearly a century he and his successors John (1118–43) and Manuel (1143–80) restored order, prosperity and even glory to the most civilized nation of the West.

At one time Alexius considered employing Norman mercenaries against the Seljuks, and sent messages which were interpreted in the West as an appeal for help. This gave new momentum to the plan for a war on the Muslims, adumbrated by Pope Gregory VII and encouraged by the Cluniacs. If only those innumerable younger sons, landless, footloose knights who lived by fighting, could be drawn off to the East on a gigantic military pilgrimage to liberate Jerusalem they might achieve much. At the very least, their absence would remove inflammable material from Europe. At Clermont-Ferrand in 1095, Pope Urban II, a French Cluniac, proclaimed the Holy War.

The response was overwhelming, reaching far beyond the barons and knights to whom Urban's appeal was principally directed. Popular preachers raised bands of labourers and peasants, demoralized by a series of bad harvests and elated by the hope of plunder in this world and salvation hereafter; possibly even confused as to the nature of Jerusalem – were they marching towards no earthly city but to the heavenly Jerusalem of which they had heard so much?

The ragged multitudes set off without equipment, supplies or discipline, led by men as ignorant as themselves. They lived on charity or robbery when charity was refused. They fell upon and massacred the Jews of the Rhineland cities to the horror of other citizens and the dismay of the Pope. But as they straggled, fought and plundered their way down the Danube valley the Hungarian peasantry fell upon them and killed almost all. Meanwhile barons and knights (mostly from France and Norman Italy) gathered under their more experienced leaders and the long sequence of the Crusades began in earnest. The familiar term 'Crusade' was not used before the thirteenth century and became general only when historians adopted it in the later eighteenth century. The Crusaders called their undertaking a *Peregrinatio*: simply a pilgrimage, but in arms.

They were impelled by the powerful forces of fear and faith and hope. The Last Judgement was a vivid reality to them; crude paintings of it adorned their churches; their priests constantly reminded them of it. They believed that eternal torment was the certain fate of the wicked, of unbelievers and of all who had the misfortune to die in mortal sin. Confession and penance in this world assured the soul's salvation after a necessary period of suffering in Purgatory. The penances imposed were often heavy but could be bought off by 'indulgences', in return for offerings to the Church. (There was no way of avoiding Purgatory; not until the sixteenth century did the Church offer 'indulgences' alleged to reduce the penitential period *after* death.)

God's mercy could also be bought by going on pilgrimage, or by devotion to some powerful saint. Robert Guiscard hopefully bribed Saint Matthew with ostentatious devotion. A death-bed repentance (like the death-bed baptisms so common in the age of Constantine) was a certain way to salvation, but when sudden death was so common it was unwise to rely on that. Confused traditions inherited from Babylon, from Persia, from the Jews, peopled the world with unseen presences, angels and devils fighting for the soul of man. Almost everyone believed in miracles, in direct judgements of God, in demonic possession, and everyone believed in Hell. They believed, but their belief made little difference to their daily conduct. This was hardly surprising since, for the majority, the unrelenting struggle for existence in this world left little time for consideration of the next. The Crusade was at the same time an escape from immediate duties, a pilgrimage, an adventure and a means of avoiding Hell.

The emperor Alexius had no illusions about the western barons and their armed followers now inexorably approaching Constantinople on their way to Jerusalem. 'He dreaded their arrival', wrote his daughter Anna Comnena, 'knowing as he did their uncontrollable passions, their erratic character . . . and their greed for money . . . which always led them to break their agreements without scruple.'[5] The western 'barbarians' had little in common with the Byzantine Greeks, neither language nor culture, scarcely even religion. The Byzantine churches, with their Greek liturgy, were alien to them and the rift with Rome, though temporarily plastered over, was already in effect final. Besides, the leader of the Norman contingent, Bohemund, son of Robert Guiscard, had recently been at open war with the emperor.

Alexius provided camping ground and provisions for the troops, graciously received the leaders, exacted an oath of allegiance which he knew they would break, and hurried them across into Asia Minor. Here they recaptured Edessa and Antioch from the Turks, but made them into principalities of their own instead of returning them to Byzantine rule. In July 1099 they stormed, took and murderously sacked Jerusalem, before inaugurating their Christian rule in a ruined and almost deserted city. The Latin Kingdom, as it came to be called, guarded by strong castles at strategic points, and patrolled by mounted knights, was for a time a bulwark, though sometimes also an irritant, to the Byzantine empire.

In the course of the next century the three military orders came into being. Their members were knights living under monastic discipline, dedicated to the defence of the Holy Land – the Templars (1128), the Hospitallers (1137), and the Teutonic Knights (1196). Although largely independent of state authority and sometimes on bad terms with each other, they formed in effect the standing army of the Latin Kingdom.

The Pope had intended that the holy places when conquered should become a fief of the Church. Instead, the Crusaders created a secular kingdom. True, its first ruler, Godfrey of Bouillon, was chosen on account of his virtues and with pious humility refused to bear the title of king in the city where his Saviour had been crucified. His successors had no such scruples. Beside the kingdom of Jerusalem, three other secular states, theoretically dependent on it, came into being – at Antioch and Tripoli, and further to the north east, the bastion state of Edessa on the head waters of the Euphrates.

These crusaders' states were ruled by a small western military caste divided from the native population by language, customs, race and usually also religion. The native Christians, most numerous in the principality of Antioch but present everywhere, belonged to the Greek or even the Nestorian Church. As peasants and cultivators the Syrian Christians shared the land with the Arabs, but their villages were separate and segregation was total. The Crusaders can hardly be blamed for following this established pattern. They at least allowed for marriage to native women provided they were Christians – 'a Syrian or an Armenian woman perhaps, or even a Saracen who has received the grace of baptism'.[6] But married or single, there was still the segregation of the rulers from the ruled.

The army which captured Jerusalem numbered perhaps 30,000 men, many of whom went home again. Those who stayed acquired a share in the conquered land, large estates for the barons, small for the knights. In either case the land was cultivated by the peasants already on the soil, whether Muslims or Syrian Christians, or both. (The only difference to them was that the poll-tax imposed on Christians under Muslim rule was transferred to the Muslims by the new masters.) Crusading landowners needed the peasants to till the soil and took no further steps to convert unbelievers.

A half-hearted attempt was made to encourage immigrants from the West, but the greater number went to the towns, Jerusalem itself or the sea ports, to swell the ranks of craftsmen, tradesmen and merchants. Italian cities, especially Pisa, Genoa and Venice, encouraged their citizens to form colonies in the ports, alert to capture trade. A sustained effort was made to re-populate Jerusalem – said to have had only two hundred inhabitants left after the victorious Crusaders had done their worst.

Some attempts were made to start new villages with western Christian immigrants. The Church encouraged such plans and a few villages grew up under the protection of monasteries. Others were founded in the shadow of the great fortresses built by the military orders. Such villages were themselves fortified, strictly segregated and very few in number.

Noble or simple, the newcomers were always alien to the East, but they did not feel so. The land of 'Outremer' became their home. Only thirty years after the conquest the French chronicler Fulcher of Chartres wrote:

> We who had been Occidentals became Orientals: the man who had been a Roman or a Frank has here become a Galilean or a Palestinian . . . we have already forgotten the places where we were born . . . He who was once a stranger here is now a native.[7]

But in less than fifty years the Latin kingdoms began to crumble. In 1144, the outlying state of Edessa was recaptured by the Turks, and the Christians in the West and in Outremer rallied again to the Cross. In France, Bernard of Clairvaux, the most powerful figure in the austere Cistercian order, preached a new Crusade, which was joined this time by the rulers of France and Germany. These hopeful beginnings came to little. The leaders travelled by different routes to avoid quarrelling. A contingent of knights, voyaging by sea from England and Flanders, sailed up the Tagus and captured Lisbon from the Moors; this was the only Christian gain from the Crusade. The Norman ruler of Sicily, the unscrupulous Roger II, waged a personal war on Byzantium under cover of the Crusade, ravaged Corfu and sacked Corinth and Thebes. This purposeful operation, designed to benefit the Sicilian silk industry by eliminating Byzantine manufacture, succeeded in its aim. Meanwhile the Byzantine emperor made an alliance with the Turks. The rulers of France and Germany after vainly besieging Damascus went home separately and in dudgeon. The Venetians, the Genoese and the Pisans, who had supplied the Crusaders with transport, were rewarded with trading privileges in Syria. Edessa was not regained.

Yet in face of desperate danger, the Christians could still unite. The danger was from Egypt. The Fatimid caliphs of Cairo had several times attempted to recapture Jerusalem and had been defeated. But in the latter years of the twelfth century a great leader again appeared in Islam. Saladin, as he is known in the West, was the nephew of a Kurdish general who had overrun Egypt and appointed himself vizier to the Fatimid caliph. Saladin succeeded to his uncle's power in 1169. He became, in Crusading legends, the pattern of the noble enemy: honourable, magnanimous, courteous, a brave soldier, a skilful performer at polo, and a man who was always true to his word.

Saladin's ambition was to reunite the divided forces of Islam. He began by replacing the army of the Fatimids with a newly organized and hand-picked army of his own. His political ability was, however, an asset of equal importance By a subtle mixture of diplomacy and force he extended his power from Egypt into Arabia, then over northern Syria and Mesopotamia, and completed the encirclement of the Crusading states by defeating the Byzantine emperor at Myriocephalon in Asia Minor (1176). The reunion of Islam spelt disaster for the kingdom of Jerusalem. In 1187 Saladin annihilated the Christian forces at Hattin and took Jerusalem. The Crusaders were now confined to a few inland castles and the cities of Antioch, Tripoli and Tyre.

The catastrophe inspired a Third Crusade, led by the Holy Roman emperor, the venerable Frederick Barbarossa, Philip-Augustus, the king of France, and Richard Coeur-de-Lion, king of England. Barbarossa was drowned, trying with characteristic impatience to swim a river in Asia Minor. Philip-Augustus and Richard Coeur-de-Lion came by sea quarrelling most of the way; their conduct was reflected in the bad relations of their followers. In spite of this they successfully besieged the port of Acre thus regaining a strategic advantage on the coast. Philip then went home while Richard remained, until even he realized that he could not take Jerusalem. He did at least successfully negotiate with Saladin a truce by which the Christians held the coast from Jaffa to Tyre and were guaranteed free access to Jerusalem (1190).

Fourteen years later came the disastrous Fourth Crusade which never reached the Holy Land. The Crusaders, led by a powerful French contingent but dominated by the Venetians (who supplied transport and provisions) found a scene of political and social chaos in Constantinople. The dynasty of Alexius Comnenus had ended in confusion: the minority of one emperor had been followed by a succession of usurpations, depositions and murders. The French took up the cause of a youthful fugitive 'emperor', entered the city by force and set him on the throne along with his deposed and blinded father. At this, Byzantine hatred of the 'Latins', the intrusive Crusaders, exploded in a furious popular insurrection. The Byzantines murdered both emperors and raised a tough soldier, Alexius Dukas, to the throne. The Venetians, led by their equally tough (though blind and aged) doge, Enrico Dandolo, joined with the French in a new attack on the city. In April 1204 they carried Constantinople by storm (Alexius Dukas was killed fighting) and sacked it for three days. The soldiers seized everything of material value that they did not wantonly destroy. French priests filled their sleeves and pouches with holy relics in which the city abounded – pieces of the True Cross, arms, legs, teeth and other fragments of saints, which found their way to the abbeys and churches of France. (Most of these were ultimately destroyed by the iconoclasts of the French Revolution.) The Venetians carried off among other treasures the greatest prize: four horses of gilt bronze, probably Greek work of the sixth century BC. They had survived the glory and ruin of Greece, the grandeur and decay of Byzantium; set up anew on the facade of St Mark's they saw the culminating splendour of Venice and have long survived its fall.

The Byzantine empire fell apart. A succession of minor western princes ruled at Constantinople, western adventurers divided Greece, the Bulgars invaded, and Byzantine nobles set up rival empires. In 1261 a capable Byzantine general (Michael Palaeologus) expelled the last Latin emperor from Constantinople and restored Greek rule; the greatness of Byzantium he could not restore. This small central fragment of empire would stagger bravely on for two centuries, with interludes of deceptive revival, before it finally fell to the Turks in 1453. But the mortal blow had been struck by the Crusade in 1204.

The gainers were the Venetians. During the past century they had exacted concessions on the Syrian coast from the Crusaders and trading privileges from Byzantine emperors; they had defeated Manuel Comnenus in war and taken Ragusa and Chios as the price of peace. After the fall of Constantinople they took three-eighths of the city itself including St Sophia, the best harbours on the Hellespont and the Sea of Marmora, the Adriatic coast, the ports on the west coast of the Peloponnese, the Ionian Islands, the Cyclades and Crete. They had now outmanoeuvred all their rivals and controlled the eastern Mediterranean and the commerce of the East. They had not only destroyed the Byzantine empire; they had absorbed almost all its sources of wealth. The long-resistant bulwark against Turkish inroads into Europe had gone. In time the Venetians would pay a heavy price for this crime.

The fall of Byzantium was the fatal outcome of the Crusades. Associated with it was the now irreparable breach between eastern and western Christendom. Any advantages were slight in comparison. The contact between Christian and Muslim civilization was limited and superficial. The Crusaders imitated a few comforts and luxuries from the East but there was no such fruitful exchange of ideas as had existed between Christians and Muslims in Spain or Sicily. Few of the Christian settlers learnt Arabic; no Arab scholars received their patronage.

In technology they learnt a little about the virtues of sanitation by running water for which primitive arrangements began to appear in European castles by the thirteenth century. The introduction of the windmill also seems to date from then. The idea needed some elaboration from the simpler forms of the Middle East: the winds of northern Europe are more capricious and variable. The great Crusading castles are basically European in structure, remarkable for the thickness of their walls and the strategic judgement with which they were sited. The Crusaders also built a few round churches, imitated from the Dome of the Rock, the great mosque in Jerusalem which they believed to be the temple. The old tradition that they introduced the pointed Gothic arch has no foundation. The shape grew naturally from the interlacement of round-headed Romanesque arches.

Of the three military orders, the Templars disappeared, callously destroyed to gain possession of their wealth by the king of France. The Hospitallers continued to hold outposts in the Mediterranean islands and valiantly defended Rhodes against the Turks until 1522; survivors continued thereafter in Malta. The Teutonic Knights transferred their crusading energies in the thirteenth century to North Germany and the heathen Wends of the Baltic coast.

Elsewhere missionary zeal engendered by the Crusades stimulated the forcible suppression of heresies. The most atrocious example was the destruction of a Manichaean sect, the Albigenses, in the South of France. More insidious and more lasting was hostility to the Jews which, quiescent in the earlier Middle Ages, became explosive and frequent. In vain the Vatican denounced as falsehood the accusation of ritual murder which took hold in northern Europe during the twelfth century. In 1179 the Church prohibited intercourse between Christians and Jews in the hope that separation of the communities would reduce friction. But ten years later the departure of Richard Coeur-de-Lion on Crusade led to extortionate taxation of the Jews in England and riots in York during which the greater part of the Jewish community took refuge in a fortified tower and committed mass suicide.

In the commercial sphere the Crusades increased and diversified the trade of western Europe with the East. This commerce, going back to Roman times, had never altogether dried up and had increased rather than diminished with the Muslim conquest of Spain and dominance in the Mediterranean. Under the Fatimid caliphate Egypt, and more especially Alexandria, had been the central link in the trade of Arabia and India with the West. The Crusades brought into existence an increasing volume of trade from Persia, Mesopotamia and Syria channelled through their ports of Acre and Tyre. (Tyre had not enjoyed such prosperity since classical times.) The imports which increased the amenities of life in Europe consisted of spices and medicaments, senna and camphor, aloes, myrrh, pepper, cinnamon and cloves, silk, damask and muslin for the wealthy, ivory, sandalwood, and the finely tempered steel of Damascus. The kingdom of Jerusalem itself exported glass, largely a Jewish monopoly, and Galilean wine. It was not entirely a one-way traffic from the East; European exports to the Middle East included woollen cloth from England, France and Flanders and such necessities as copper, iron, lead and saddles.

The First Crusade – the only successful Crusade – gave new confidence to the Christian West. In spite of the divisive quarrel between Church and state, Pope and emperor, the great mass of the people, rich and poor, peasant and merchant, noble and serf were united in the desire to glorify God and celebrate their redemption (somewhat confused with the redemption of the earthly Jerusalem). The building of the great cathedrals of the West was the first astounding expression of their common faith. The building was directed by master-masons of great skill and growing experience, using primitive means: hoists of rope and wood, horse-drawn sledges or river barges to move the stone. Patient years were needed to complete the work; sculptors chiselled out great single figures, or complex, populous groups of saints and prophets; anonymous glassworkers, lead workers and artists put together jewel-rich windows telling the Bible story; painters, mosaic-workers, coppersmiths and goldsmiths – all united to make for the glory of God and the honour of their city the most beautiful building in the world.

In the remote north at Trondjhem, Kirkwall, Lund, they did not achieve quite that, but what they did achieve was miraculous for the time and place. At Durham, the cathedral rose like a holy fortress from the sheer rock; at Salamanca, stately and spacious, in the harsh landscape of Spain; gorgeous in warm and fertile Sicily, at Monreale, at Cefalu, where massive forms derived from the north glittered with mosaics of Byzantine craftsmanship. On the Rhine at Mainz, at Worms, the gentle texture of red sandstone softened the forbidding majesty of the great Romanesque arches. In Italy the builders dug out layers of the ruined past and elevated the fallen columns of heathen temples to support architraves inlaid with mosaic pictures of the Christian story. In France above all, abbeys, churches and cathedrals proclaimed a new confidence. Their architects built with ambition, for future generations as much as for themselves. They represented and delighted in the human form and human activities, or allowed imagination full play in creating strange beasts, devils, angels and grotesques. Their new-found mastery in architectural design culminated in the incomparable cathedral of Chartres.

The creative power of faith was manifest in the great cathedrals. The creative power of thought and speculation revived more slowly. Scholars did indeed begin to debate and argue, and to apply logic to the elucidation of theology which was still central to all study. Guilds of scholars came into being, the forerunners of universities. Salerno was already famous for medicine in the eleventh century, Bologna for law. By the twelfth century Paris was renowned for dialectic – dialectic being the prescribed method of argument for the establishment of truth. English scholars who fled from Paris in a plague year originated the University of Oxford.

The greatest thinker of the twelfth century, Peter Abelard (1070–1142), taught in the School of Paris, but was too far in advance of his time for his own good. With a questioning mind and a powerful intellect, his reputation stood high, but his pride and his intellectual integrity made him enemies. Inevitably he found himself contesting charges of heresy and was in the end to withdraw into silence.

By the irony of fate he is best known to popular fame for his irrelevant seduction of his pupil Heloise. A victim of his age, and at the end a defeated and disillusioned man, he shared in its faith and in its commitment to the beauty of religion. He left, among other lasting memorials, some of the most beautiful of the Easter hymns:

> Nox ista flebilis praeseusque triduum
> Quod demorabitur fletus sit vesperum,
> Donec laetitiae mane gratissimum
> Surgente Domino sit maestis redditum . . .

or, in Helen Waddell's translation:

> This is that night of tears, the three days' space,
> Sorrow abiding of the eventide,
> Until the day break with the risen Christ,
> And hearts that sorrowed shall be satisfied.[8]

CHAPTER VIII

CIRCA 1200–1450

I

IN 1206 THE TRIBES OF CENTRAL ASIA, after a long period of weakness and division, were forcibly united by a Mongol warrior of genius, Temujin, better known under his title Genghis Khan: King of all between the Oceans. In the next fifty years the Mongols extended their power from the Pacific coast to the Volga and the Mediterranean, with tidal waves into Poland, Silesia and Hungary.

The Mongols, like the Huns, the Khasars, and other Asiatic nomads were expert horsemen who won their victories by a technique of feigned retreat and surprise attack. Their discipline and organization made them more dangerous than any of their predecessors. They were deadly bowmen and could execute any manoeuvre on their strong, swift horses while keeping their hands free for shooting. Their armies were divided into units of a thousand, subdivided into hundreds and tens and directed in battle by an efficient system of signalling with small black flags. Their tactics were to provoke attack, disperse as the enemy charged, harass their flanks until they were exhausted, and close in for the kill.

Genghis Khan aimed at world conquest. His armies overran North China, captured Peking, made an obliterating descent on Korea, conquered from Lake Balkash to the frontiers of Tibet, and sacked the cities of Samarkand, Bokhara and Balkh. His son and successor, Ogdai, reconquered Persia, overran Korea, South China, Georgia and Armenia, also Vladimir and Kiev in Russia and Buda in Hungary.

The Mongol chiefs hated and feared the civilization of farmers and town-dwellers, deliberately wrecking their agriculture by destroying canals and cutting down orchards. The stories of systematic massacre and pyramids of skulls are no exaggeration. They turned

Khorasan into a desert and destroyed the age-old cultivation and most of the inhabitants of the North China plain.

A remnant of the amiable Sung empire survived for a time in the south. (It was here that the mathematician Ch'in Chiu-Shao did his pioneer work in mathematics and corrected the Chinese calendar.) Fortunately, Genghis Khan's grandson Kublai Khan, who in due course conquered the south, had more civilized habits. To do him justice, Genghis Khan himself had taken advice from one of his prisoners. Ye-lü Ch'u-ts'ai belonged to a Tartar tribe which had established a kingdom in North China and so far imitated Chinese ways as to call themselves the Chin dynasty. 'The Mongol empire', Ch'u-ts'ai told Genghis Khan, 'was conquered from the saddle, but it cannot be ruled from the saddle.' Peasants must survive if the land was to be cultivated. Besides, the Chinese had a well-established system of tax-collecting which Genghis Khan would do well to take over. Later Ye-lü Ch'u-ts'ai saved many scholars from death, by pointing out the need for literate administrators. His teaching took full effect when, on the extinction of the Sung, the grandson of Genghis Khan, Kublai Khan (1260–94), founded a new dynasty, the Yuan. Kublai lived with Chinese ceremony (although he could not read or speak Chinese) and relied on Chinese officials in the lower and middle ranks of the hierarchy. But he elevated Mongols, Turks, Arabs and even Europeans to the highest positions.[1]

After visiting Tibet, which recognized his suzerainty, Kublai was converted to Buddhism; this caused him to build orphanages, rest homes for aged scholars and hospitals for the sick poor, to provide against famine by storing surplus grain and to remit taxes in regions where the harvest had failed. His intentions were often benevolent but he could not restore what his father and grandfather had destroyed, so that a much reduced population now had to support the enormous Mongol army. For the rest he had the Great Canal extended as far as Peking and restored the major roads. Posting stations with horses always ready were set up at intervals of 25 miles along the main roads; in emergencies runners in the imperial service, relieving each other every three miles, could reduce to 36 hours a journey which normally took ten days.

One invention, due originally to the Sung was increasingly exploited in war. Gunpowder was first used to intimidate the enemy with foul-smelling smoke. Later explosive gunpowder and the fire bomb appeared; by the fourteenth century the Mongols had invented the metal-barrelled gun.

Paper money, a convenient invention first suggested during the T'ang dynasty, was widely introduced and seemed at first beneficial. Later in the reign inadequate control and increasing corruption undermined government credit, and Kublai's minister of finance, an Arab, who was hated as a foreign extortioner, was assassinated by a Chinese patriot. But the luxury commerce of China recovered; fine silk tapestries were sent overland to Europe, some of which came to be used as vestments in the cathedrals of the West. Cargoes of silk and porcelain went to Java, Malaya, Ceylon, India and the Persian Gulf to be exchanged for spices, gems and pearls. This benefited the few: the mass of the people remained poor and hungry.

Kublai's palace at Khanbalik (as Peking was called) glittered with mosaics of dragons, birds, warriors and horses. The roof blazed with green, blue and red tiles. Six thousand guests – it was said – could be entertained in the great hall. It was surrounded by a park with fine trees, mysterious glades, fishponds and herds of deer; on its outer wall Kublai built an observatory for his astronomers.

He kept some nomad characteristics. On journeys he and his court camped in tents, hung with lion and tiger skins outside and inside with sable and ermine. On the march, if he saw cranes in the sky, he cast loose his falcon and watched the chase, comfortably reclining on his couch on an elephant's back. Our vivid knowledge of him comes from the memoirs dictated in old age by the Venetian traveller, Marco Polo.

As the eldest surviving grandson of Genghis Khan, Kublai's suzerainty was recognized by his family and a considerable trade grew up between China and Persia, ruled by his brother Hulagu. Communications were restored by way of the neglected Silk Road so that soon Chinese porcelain and textiles influenced Persian design while the Chinese admired and adapted the lustres and blue glazes of Persian pottery. But the introduction of paper money was no more successful in Persia than in China.

Kublai Khan exacted recognition and tribute from Tibet, Burma, and Siam but was unsuccessful in Cambodia, Annam and Java. Twice he sent a formidable fleet and landed troops in Japan, only to be decisively repelled. On the second occasion (1281) the Japanese owed their deliverance to a storm which dispersed the ships. They called it *Kamikaze*, the Divine Wind – a term which evoked heroic responses in Japan even into the present century, when the term was used for the suicide planes of the Second World War.

The Japanese victory over Kublai Khan had unfortunate consequences for the victors. Landowners, who had armed their followers and fortified the vulnerable coast, were left with a burden of debt and resentment. A weak government cancelled some of the debts, which aroused the wrath of those not so favoured. The resultant local rivalries and private wars led to intermittent anarchy in Japan for the next century and a half.

While Kublai Khan ruled in China his ruthless brother Hulagu consolidated Mongol power in Mesopotamia. This conquest seems to have had some confused ideological content. Islam was seen as the enemy; this meant not only the fanatic Assassins in the Elburz mountains (see p. 266) but also the caliph at Baghdad, who had long ceased to exercise any power. Hulagu's forces exterminated the Assassins, then captured Baghdad with great slaughter, smothered the caliph in a carpet, and went on to overrun Syria. Here they were, for the first time, decisively defeated at Ain Jalut in Galilee (1260).

The victory which destroyed the legend of Mongol invincibility was gained by the Mamluks. These descendants of Turkish slave-soldiers, the finest troops in the Egyptian army, had recently seized power in Cairo. After their victory they invited a kinsman of the murdered caliph to Egypt, set him up as the new caliph under their protection, and became the acknowledged leaders of Islam. Cairo, enriched by scholars, astronomers and physicians who had escaped from the wreckage of Baghdad, became the new intellectual capital of the Muhammedan world. Ibn Khaldun, the greatest of Arab historians, hailed the Turks as a civilizing power.

The victory of the Mamluks was the doom of the Crusaders in Palestine. They still held part of the Mediterranean coast – Acre, Tyre, Sidon and Tripoli – but they were hampered by fatal rivalries. When the Genosese occupied Tripoli, the Venetians appealed to the Mamluks who ousted the Genoese and themselves took possession of all that remained to the Christians on the coast of Palestine.

After their defeat by the Mamluks the Mongols withdrew from Syria while Hulagu and his warriors settled in Persia and Mesopotamia where his descendants, known as the Ilkhanids, ruled for over a century as the leading power in the Middle East. At some time in his career Hulagu, like Kublai Khan, seems to have embraced Buddhism. His wife, and some of his principal ministers were Christians converted by Nestorian monks whose settlements reached far into Asia. But the initial hostility to Islam (which may have given rise to these conversions) did not long outlast his reign. Most of the Mongol invaders had been absorbed into the Muslim faith by the second or third generation.

The Ilkhanids after the destructive violence of their conquest were not unduly oppressive. Like Kublai Khan, Hulagu encouraged learning and built an observatory where an Arab scientist compiled the astronomical data known as the 'Ilkhanid Tables'. The old Persian administration, adapted by the Seljuks, still continued to function, with decreasing efficiency, but in Persia as in China, taxation to support the Mongol army was an intolerable burden on a sinking population. Furthermore, the Mongols had no understanding of agriculture. Essential irrigation, neglected by the Seljuks, continued to decay; salination destroyed the fertility of the soil, villages dwindled and disappeared.

Literature, on the other hand, flourished. During the last century of Seljuk rule and throughout the Ilkhanid period, Persian poetry was largely inspired by Sufism, a mystical sect of Islam. The Sufis believed that all material things were illusory and served only to obscure the absolute: God. Sana'i (1070–1140) was the first Persian poet whose work, *The Garden of Truth*, was inspired by Sufism.

A long sequence of mystical poets followed, chief among them Jalal ad Din ar Rumi (1207–73), contemporary with the Mongol conquest and probably Persia's greatest mystical poet; his *Mathnavi* is regarded by many as second only to the Koran in its spiritual significance.

Shiraz became at this time an intellectual centre, a city of civilized pleasures, with its gardens, fountains and lively *vie de café*. Here lived the greatest of Persian lyric poets Hafiz (1320–81). The surface charm of his verses, with their themes of love and wine and flowers, conceals other meanings in the language of mysticism, and he is to this day quoted, consulted, expounded and loved for wisdom and subtleties which are beyond translation. He needed the deeper strength which was within him, for the sweetness of life in

Shiraz was overshadowed by dread; he lived to see the entry into his beloved city of Timur (Marlowe's atrocious *Tamburlaine*), a conquerer as ruthless as Genghis Khan.

The Mongol empire of Genghis Khan was in theory still united under his grandsons with Kublai Khan the sovereign. In fact it was already three separate states: the brothers Kublai and Hulagu in China and Persia, their cousin, Batu, in Europe. Batu led his hordes westward, south of the Caspian, north of the Black Sea. He overran southern and central Russia, wrecking Kiev and Moscow. He then divided his forces. One army went west, crossed the Vistula and defeated the massed cavalry of Polish and German knights at Liegnitz (1241); their armoured horsemen had not the speed or accuracy of the Mongol archers. A second army, with Batu at its head, went south, devastated Moravia and Hungary, then struck across to the Adriatic coast and sacked the port of Kotor. Dynastic troubles caused Batu to withdraw, ravaging Bulgaria as he went. Soon after he set up a vast permanent camp in the estuary of the Volga. He called it Sarai Batu, but it became known in the West by the mysterious name of the Golden Horde, for the glittering splendour of its tents.

The Rus, or Russians – as the mixed Slav-Viking people of Kiev came to be called – were divided under many chieftains but united by a common language and the Christianity they had learnt from Byzantium. They faced enemies on two fronts: the Mongols already on the Volga and the countless nomads of central Asia in the south and east: the Swedes and Germans in the north west.

With the collapse of the Crusading states, one of the military orders, the Teutonic Knights, led by Hermann von Salza, undertook to preach Christianity and extend German influence across the north east frontier of the empire. This was an extension of the policy initiated by Charlemagne when he conquered the Saxons. It had been carried further eastward by Otto the Great and, in the latter half of the twelfth century, by Henry of Saxony, surnamed the Lion. By 1200 the furthest point of the Germano-Christian advance was at the newly founded seaport of Riga at the mouth of the Duina. Cistercian monks introduced agriculture and settled peasants from western Germany on the land. (This – the *Drang nach Osten*, as German historians have called it – was the inevitable expansion of a growing agricultural population into under-populated land.) About thirty years after the foundation of Riga, the Teutonic Knights were empowered by the emperor to take over this northern Crusade.

In the course of the next century, acting in conjunction with a group of earlier missionaries, the Livonian Brothers, the knights tamed the recalcitrant Prussians, built churches, schools and hospitals, greatly extended the area of cultivation, and founded a line of cities on the Baltic coast – Narva, Dorpat, Dantzig. They attempted also to extend their influence into Russia and impose Roman Christianity on a people who belonged to the Byzantine fold. Their objective was the city of Novgorod which already had a flourishing settlement of German merchants, but the majority of whose citizens had no intention of changing their faith.

Novgorod was under the protection of Alexander, a prince who came of the royal lineage of Kiev, and had gained the surname of Nevski when he defeated the invading Swedes on the banks of the Neva. Supported by the priests and people of Novgorod he broke the army of the Teutonic Knights in a winter battle on the ice of Lake Peipus (1242). Nevski combined military prowess with diplomacy and cautious calculation. He took no risks with the Mongols of the Golden Horde whom he knew he could not overcome. Instead he negotiated with them, accepted them as overlords and held from them large grants of land including Kiev. These actions enhanced his personal power but also preserved his territories and their people from Mongol invasion. The Russian Church proclaimed him a saint in 1547 and Stalin pronounced him a national hero in 1942: surely a unique apotheosis?

The course of Russian history was deflected by these events. For three centuries, since the Vikings had settled on the Volga, the emergent Russian people had looked both to Europe and to Byzantium. Two Germanic emperors and one French king had married Russian princesses. But the Teutonic Knights, entrenched on the Baltic, now blocked their outlet to the West, while the Swedes had built the fortified port of Viborg on the Gulf of Finland. Alexander Nevski had driven the Teutonic Knights from Russian soil but not from the Baltic. The threat from the Asiatic nomads of the interior continually on the move, and the need to strengthen and protect the growing city of Moscow, soon to be the acknowledged capital, compelled the Russians to concentrate on their own defence and to withdraw from further political commitments in the West.

II

In Europe the great cathedrals of the twelfth century symbolized the unifying force of the fragmented continent – the Catholic Church. Cathedrals, abbeys and churches in all their splendour of carved stone, painted and gilded wood, pictures in mosaic and glass, were the manifestations of a popular culture, not the taste only of an educated few but a visual expression of faith in which the illiterate majority and the literate minority joined as one. The greatest masterpieces of early medieval art, the stained glass that told the Gospel story in the glowing windows of Chartres, or the bold and vital sculpture at Autun, Adam and Eve on the bronze doors of Hildesheim and the tragic head of Christ at Cologne – these were created by a people united in faith. From the baron in his castle with his armed retainers, grooms, falconers and servants, to the serf in his hovel – they joined in doing honour to their God by gifts, labour or special skills, and were proud of the achievement and of their part in it.

Politically what had once been the Roman empire of the West was splintered among a score of quarrelsome rulers, whose relationships were further complicated by feudal law. Henry II of England (1154–89) achieved an 'empire' that extended from the Scottish border to the Pyrenees; he held Normandy by inheritance and the rich province of Aquitaine (the south west quarter of France) through his wife. He owed allegiance to the French king for these provinces, but was in effect independent. The unfortunate king of France had direct control of less than half his country because Provence was also independent under powerful vassals. The Iberian peninsula had four Christian kingdoms in the north (later amalgamated into two, Castile and Aragon), Portugal on the Atlantic coast, and a number of Moorish emirates in the south. The elected kings of Germany, not all of whom managed to be crowned emperor, exercised very little power outside their personal hereditary lands, and were often at the mercy of their once powerful vassals in Saxony, Bavaria, or Austria. The Normans had united Sicily and southern Italy under their rule but, from the papal states northward, Italy was divided among conflicting independent states – the cities of Tuscany and the Lombard plain, the growing maritime powers of Genoa, Pisa and Venice.

Beyond the boundaries of what had been the Roman empire lay

other active kingdoms, linked into western Europe by a common religion but divided by conflicting interests: Scotland, Ireland, Norway, Sweden, Denmark, Poland, Bohemia. Leagues and alliances formed and dissolved; the rivalries, the aggressions, the petty wars were unceasing.

The Greco-Roman culture of the Mediterranean had been a unifying influence for six hundred years, from the Roman defeat of the Carthaginians until the conquest of Africa by the Vandals. The Mediterranean in the Middle Ages probably carried a greater volume of trade than in Roman times, but its shores were divided between different peoples and rival cultures; the Byzantine empire, the Islamic states of Egypt, Morocco, southern Spain, and the Middle East; the Aragonese, the Catalans, the Normans, the French, the independent kingdom of Majorca, the maritime cities of Italy, the Genoese, the Venetians . . . most of them competing for control of strategic ports and islands and a greater share of commerce.

The knowledge of Roman law and administration which the Church had transmitted to the barbarian conquerors had been gradually submerged under laws and customs which more adequately answered the needs of their very different society. Never at any time had the Church managed to replace the Pax Romana by a Christian peace.

By the time of the Crusades the unity of the Church applied only to the western part of Europe. The culture of the West bore less and less resemblance to that of Byzantium; mutual distrust and the relatively backward civilization of the West, far more than the doctrinal differences which were the immediate cause of quarrel, made the separation inevitable and irreconcilable.

Yet in spite of disunion and endemic warfare Europe moved towards greater material prosperity. The tin and copper mines of Spain, fallen into neglect since Roman times, were redeveloped by the Moors as early as the tenth century, then taken over by the Christians as they advanced into Moorish territory. The Germans developed the mines of the Harz mountains, rich in veins of silver-bearing lead. Later, German miners were brought in by rulers interested in revenue, to open up the mineral wealth of the Slav borderlands, Poland, Silesia, Bohemia; they often formed lasting colonies and did their work well but were naturally unwelcome to the peasants whose land they disturbed.

Copper was mined in Sweden and Saxony, iron in Styria and Carinthia where craftsmen had the secret of producing the best steel in Europe. The Cornish tin mines flourished. In the thirteenth century the discovery of lead mines in Bohemia, immensely rich in veins of silver, made her king, Ottakar the Great, the richest in Europe.

Coal had long been quarried in many parts of Europe in small quantities from surface workings, but in the thirteenth century pit workings began, near Liege and Mons, also in southern Scotland, South Wales and in the north and midland regions of England.

The development of mining led to experiment and improvement in the working of metal. Late in the thirteenth century a process of iron casting was evolved which made plate armour possible; used at first to reinforce chain mail, it gradually superseded it.

Stonemasons learnt by experience and experiment as more cathedrals and castles were built. Stone quarries multiplied, wooden castles and stockades were replaced by stone; townsfolk and even villagers built new churches of stone. Stone bridges spanned the rivers on the main highways.

In the north, wool and linen cloth formed the basis of a growing textile industry. Sicilian and Italian towns (Lucca was foremost) specialized in silk and had learnt to breed silk worms and make their own raw material. Cotton textiles were first introduced into Europe by the Moors of Spain who imported the raw material from Egypt. The manufacture spread rapidly over the continent. A cheap mixed cloth, fustian – cotton with a linen warp – was particularly popular, and intensively produced in England for export. Water power was used to drive fulling mills and the bellows of blast furnaces. The spinning wheel, that early example of belt power transmission, came into general use.

The coloured glass which filled the windows of cathedrals was an art which began in the south and spread rapidly northwards. It required patient experiment in the addition of different minerals to the molten glass, and exact control of heat. The Venetians alone had the secret of making clear glass, and were consequently the first to make spectacles, about 1300. The inventor is unknown. Two small circles of convex glass were joined together and perched on the bridge of the nose: not very efficient but presumably helpful in the earlier stages of presbyopia.

The growth of trade stimulated improvement in roads and

waterways, sailing and navigation. The canal known as the *Naviglio Grande* between the towns of the Lombard plain was completed early in the thirteenth century. The Low Countries developed a network of waterways which carried nearly all their transport; as early as 1180 they had invented a primitive forerunner of the modern pound lock. The lateen sail, an Arab invention, spread from the Mediterranean to most European coasts. The sternpost rudder appeared in the Netherlands about 1200 and came into general use in the course of the next century, as did the magnetic compass. All this increased the accuracy of navigation and the speed and safety of voyages. Mediterranean seamen (the Genoese in particular) had by the fourteenth century established sea-routes to Scandinavia and the growing German ports of the Baltic.

Among the comforts of life, public baths should be recorded. Most of the Roman baths had fallen into ruin, but by the thirteenth century, even in northern Europe, public baths were reappearing, with mixed bathing – disapproved of by the Church.

The happy invention of soap should have improved health and hygiene, but this was counteracted by a change of fashion in dress. Loose drafty tunics belted together at the waist gave way to closer fitting garments – among the rich and fashionable almost indecently so. The use of buttons was common by the later fourteenth century: neither Greeks nor Romans had used them. These made clothes snugger and warmer so that in the northern winter a comfortable body heat could easily be maintained by not undressing at all. The number of deaths from cold must have been reduced, but the vermin population multiplied and probably also the incidence of related diseases.

The conflict between Church and state, between the spiritual claims of the Pope and the secular claims of the princes had not ceased since the initial clash between Gregory VII and the emperor Henry IV (see Chapter VII.VI). In Germany Frederick Barbarossa (1152–90), the ablest emperor since Otto the Great, combined a splendid presence and strong character with shrewd judgement. He conciliated and controlled the recalcitrant German nobility, then reformed the administration by the introduction of *ministeriales*, officers directly responsible to him. He appointed bishops for their loyalty and ability, and built up anew within the German realm the old interdependence of Church and state. Seeing himself as the restorer of a

God-directed empire, an idea which his legal advisers derived from Justinian, he introduced the official term 'Holy Empire'. He also adopted the late Roman practice of associating his eldest son in the government under the title of 'Caesar'. The effect of these antiquarian antics was to be unfortunate, but his achievement in restoring peace and order to Germany earned him the name of *Pacificus*.

It was different in Italy where his ecclesiastical policy was unpopular with the Vatican, and when he asserted his power south of the Alps he met with formidable opposition from the cities of the Lombard plain, in which they had papal support. Six times in thirty years he invaded Italy and at the end of it all gained an empty shell: his suzerainty was recognized, but Italian cities remained independent in all but name and the Vatican was always hostile.

In England a dramatic conflict broke out between Church and state when the strong-willed Henry II (1154–1189), as part of his policy of judicial reform, attempted to bring clergy guilty of criminal offences within the jurisdiction of the civil courts. Supported by the Pope, the archbishop of Canterbury, Thomas Becket, defied the king. Henry, in a fit of rage uttered a threat which led to the archbishop's murder on the altar steps of Canterbury Cathedral (1170). After that sacrilege Henry could only redeem his position by doing public penance and giving in to the Church. Thomas Becket became England's favourite saint, pilgrimages to his shrine made the fortune of Canterbury, and the shocking scandal by which 'clerks in holy orders' could not be tried by the secular courts went unreformed for another three centuries.

Soon after this, Pope Innocent III (1198–1216) made so many princes yield to him that the victory of Church over State seemed assured. Trained in the canon law, with exceptional administrative gifts, Innocent was a man of strong character, great diplomatic skill, keen judgement and absolute certainty of his objectives. From the first he made his position clear: 'We are the successor of the Prince of the Apostles, but we are not his vicar, nor the vicar of any man or Apostle, but the vicar of Jesus Christ himself'.[2] No earlier Pope had claimed so much.

His success was remarkable. He compelled John of England to make his kingdom a fief of the Papacy. Philip of France bowed to his will. He became regent of Sicily and southern Italy by taking Frederick II, who was a minor, under his protection. He intervened as arbitrator in the dynastic affairs of Sweden, Denmark and

Hungary. He persuaded the Christian kings of Spain to unite against the Moors, whom they then overwhelmingly defeated at the famous battle of Las Navas de Tolosa (1212). He nominated an emperor who swore obedience to him, deposed him when he rebelled, and set up another nominee, his ward, the king of Sicily, who was sixteen years old. He brought the Churches of Bulgaria, Armenia and Serbia (for a time) into the Roman communion. At the fourth Lateran council in 1215 – the climax of his pontificate – he reformed the laxities of the religious orders and authorized two new ones: the Franciscans and the Dominicans; proclaimed the doctrine of transubstantiation, forbade trial by battle or ordeal and condemned the heresies of the Cathars. Finally he pronounced the Church One and Universal.[3]

This most glorious epoch of the medieval Papacy was the origin of its decline. The Vicar of Christ had triumphed only by using his unique spiritual authority in the struggle for political power. The corrupting consequences of this involvement became apparent by the end of the century. But Innocent's error in placing his ward, the young king of Sicily, on the imperial throne was evident very soon after the Pope's death. A grandson of Barbarossa and, through his mother, heir to the Norman rulers of Sicily and southern Italy, Frederick II was a brilliant egotist of extraordinary gifts: poet, polymath, experimentalist, with a subtle mind and keen judgement, untroubled by scruples.

He had the Norman capacity for government, was sympathetic (through his Sicilian upbringing) to Arabs and Greeks, but was ruthless to those who opposed him. Gorgeous mosaics on the walls of the cathedral at Monreale and in the chapel of his palace at Palermo showed his grandfather Roger II and his immediate predecessor William II receiving a mandate direct from the Almighty.[4] Frederick in so far as he believed in God at all, believed that he had inherited this authority.

It was as the protégé and nominee of Innocent III that he was called from the south at the age of sixteen to make himself king in Germany as the first step to the imperial title. He achieved this surprisingly fast (his dynasty still had strong support and the king of France saw him as a useful counterweight to Anglo-Norman power). He then bought the loyalty of the nobles, bishops and abbots of Germany by increasing their privileges. This gained him a short-term advantage, enabling him to return to Italy where his authority had been undermined by his long minority. Crowned at Rome by the Pope, he pledged himself to go on Crusade (1220). But first he set his Italian kingdom in order, crushing revolt, centralizing the government and restoring an efficient administration. Showing a characteristic care for learning, he revived the medical school at Salerno and founded the University of Naples, the first university in Europe to be a royal foundation. Following the example of his predecessors, especially his grandfather Roger II, he filled his court with scholars, philosophers, men of learning and poets. Among others he was the patron of Walter von der Vogelweide, probably the greatest lyric poet of the German Middle Ages. Frederick himself composed verses in the vernacular, creating by example and patronage the earliest school of Italian poetry. He was also one of the first to seek for and preserve Greek and Roman statues.

Order being restored in Sicily and southern Italy, he renewed his Crusader's vow and set sail for Palestine, only to be compelled to return by a serious illness. The Pope (Gregory IX) – a kinsman of Innocent III – by now thoroughly alarmed at the extent of Frederick's power, excommunicated him. Disregarding this, Frederick again set out, landed his small force in Palestine, entered into diplomatic relations with the Muslims, regained Jerusalem by treaty, and crowned himself king (1229). This bloodless conquest by an excommunicate, unique in the history of the Crusades, further exasperated the Pope, and Frederick had to leave hurriedly to defend his Italian kingdom from invasion. He spent the rest of his reign fighting the Pope, or the Italian cities in alliance with the Pope, and putting down rebellions in Germany mostly inspired by the Vatican.

In spite of this his court remained the most intellectually re-markable in Europe. His own interest in the arts, philosophy, astronomy, natural history speculation and enquiry into many branches of knowledge, persisted almost to the end of his stormy life and earned him the name *Stupor Mundi*, the wonder of the world. After the manner of his time he also investigated astrology, magic and the occult: so that when he died many believed that he yet lived on, in some secret cavern, ready to rise again when his time should come.

The conflict between Church and state, which had arisen from two respectable but incompatible theories of government, gradually degenerated into a series of vendettas between the supporters of the

Pope and the emperor. (The usual names for the two parties in Italy, Guelfs and Ghibellines, arose from the rallying cry of two German factions: the Ghibelines [originally 'Waiblingen'] being the imperial party, the Guelfs the papal supporters.)

After the death of Frederick II in 1250 successive Popes hunted his dynasty down. It was extinguished eighteen years later with the defeat, capture and execution of his grandson Conradin, a boy of fifteen. This cold-blooded judicial murder gravely damaged the reputation of the Papacy, especially in Germany.

The commitment of the Vatican to such ruthless politics brought no lasting increase of power. It needed a Pope of exceptional stature to dominate the secular princes. Soon the reverse process began: unscrupulous rulers found means to manipulate the decisions of the Pope.

Celestine V, a pious hermit, was dragged from his cell by popular acclaim as one whose indifference to worldly interests would change everything. His unworldliness was easily exploited by the French king's faction who got him to create eight new French cardinals in as many weeks, whereat the opposing faction persuaded, deceived, or compelled him into resigning: the only Pope ever to have done so (1294).

He was succeeded by Boniface VIII who came of a Roman family much involved in the bitter feuds of the city. He was a brilliant lawyer, confident, worldly, hot-tempered and a good hater. But he was a true patron of the arts (he brought Giotto to Rome) and he had a flair for public relations: he proclaimed the first Jubilee, in the year 1300. Pilgrims poured into Rome and money into the papal coffers: he needed it to increase his family's possessions and to pay soldiers to defend the papal states.

He had already enraged the kings of France and England by forbidding their clergy to pay taxes imposed by lay rulers. Elated by the success of the Jubilee he issued the bull *Unam Sanctam* which proclaimed the power of the Pope over all Christian kings but was aimed more particularly at his chief opponent, Philip IV of France. Philip unhesitatingly arranged to have him kidnapped. The kidnappers, set upon by an angry mob of papal supporters, lost their nerve and their victim, but Boniface died of the shock (1303).

Two years later a French Pope, Clement V, vainly tried to evade the royal bully by taking refuge in Avignon, which was legally in papal territory and independent of the king. This was a haven of peace after the gang warfare of Rome but no safe retreat from political pressure. The will of the king of France could not be flouted; in anguish of mind Clement was compelled to excommunicate the Knights Templars so that they perished as heretics and Philip of France seized their wealth.

Six Avignon Popes in succession reigned in dignified splendour; they revised the canon law, straightened out the administration, set their finances in order, and organized missions to the Far East. Much useful work was done at Avignon, but this well-run central office of western Christendom was as far removed from the spiritual fervour which had, from time to time, illuminated the Papacy from Gregory the Great to Innocent III as it was from the material corruption which, at other times, had plunged it in darkness.

The spiritual influence of Christianity came from other sources. Two new religious orders, the Franciscans and the Dominicans, vowed themselves to lives of poverty and self-denial, preaching and ministering to the common people.

Francesco Bernardone (c.1182–1226) was a merchant's son of Assisi, a prosperous town in central Italy. He was a sociable young man with many friends, lively, attractive, and a little wild, until he suddenly awoke to the sufferings of the poor and the indifference of the rich. To his father's dismay, he renounced all possessions, vowed himself to poverty and went out of Assisi a beggar.

Ascetic, mystic, poet, inspired by love for all God's creation (not men only, but beasts, flowers, trees and stars) he carried into his new life the courtesy and joy which had distinguished his worldly youth. (He still sang songs and wrote poems: his *Canticle of Created Things* has placed him – incongruously alongside the emperor Frederick II – among the founders of Italian vernacular poetry.) His many followers foreswore all worldly comfort, lived among the poor, caring for the sick and outcast, preaching in simple language the Gospel of Christ and imitating his wandering life. It was probably Francis who initiated the *presepio* – the crib – that artless and popular representation of the Nativity in churches at Christmas time. His followers carried the custom over all western Europe. The Franciscans multiplied and spread because they fulfilled a need for direct teaching and contact with ordinary people which the Church had neglected. They also, in their early years, did much by their poverty and dedication to counteract the worldly image of the Vatican.

Domingo de Guzman – Saint Dominic–(1170–1221) a Spanish priest was troubled like Saint Francis by the poverty and ignorance of the urban poor. But as an intellectual and a theologian he thought first of the danger to their souls. Neglected by the Church, they easily fell victims to false prophets. On a journey through southern France he noticed that heresy was widespread and that heretics were more devout and had stronger feelings of mutual love and care among themselves than Catholics. His remedy was to create an order of preaching brethren who would instruct the people truly, and set an example of charity and self-denial in their own lives.

Heretics at this time were credibly stated to outnumber the Catholics in southern France. Chief among them were the *Cathari*, 'the pure', popularly called the Albigenses from their principal centre, the town of Albi. They believed, like the Manichaeans (see page 187) in the dual powers of Good and Evil continually at war. They rejected all matter as evil. In their opinion Christ could not have been a man (since all matter is evil). He must have been an angel, and the Crucifixion a lie or an illusion.

Special clothing was worn by an élite among them – those who had been 'consoled', their form of baptism. These ate no meat, rejected all human attachments and were known as the 'perfecti'; as the only full members of the Church they alone were empowered to 'console' others. The great majority postponed 'consolation' indefinitely, and in the meantime behaved neither better nor worse than other people, cheerfully having children and thus (according to the tenets of their faith) propagating yet more evil in the world.

Innocent III launched a crusade against them which Philip Augustus, king of France, turned to political advantage. The greater part of southern France was virtually independent under powerful vassals, especially Count Raymond of Toulouse. By allowing his northern vassals to attack the Albigenses, Philip calculated that the whole province would be brought under the crown. Dominic, who was charged to accompany the Crusaders and preach to the heretics, was bitterly disillusioned; the military leaders had no interest in saving souls, but only in burning, killing and getting possession of the land. They destroyed the unique culture of Provence, although later some of its poetic and musical traditions fertilized the French court and the Minnesänger of Germany.

Undeterred by this painful experience, Dominic went on to recruit a great following and to found training centres for his preaching friars all over Europe. From their earliest beginnings the Dominicans emphasized the teaching of true doctrine and sent their most gifted men to the universities – Paris, Oxford and Cologne – where some became famous teachers. The Franciscans, though not at first committed to the intellectual life, began, after the founder's death, to compete in scholarship, a rivalry which stimulated discussion and broadened the scope of study and speculation. The great Dominican scholar Albertus Magnus (c.1200–1280) studied the scientific works of Aristotle, and taught that knowledge could be obtained by observation and reason, could go hand in hand with faith and revelation. Through his influence the natural world was recognized as a legitimate object of Christian study. His more famous pupil Thomas Aquinas (c.1225–74) in his *Summa Theologica* enlarged the scope of Christian learning so as to include much of the Greek inheritance and to adapt Aristotle in particular to the mainstream of Christian thought. After some obscurantist protests, the work of Aquinas was officially recognized by the Church and formed the framework of legitimate speculation until the scientific explosion of the seventeenth century. (As religious philosophy it enjoyed a significant revival in the present century.)

In contrast to these intellectuals the German Dominican, known as Meister Eckhart (c.1260–1327) ranks among the greatest of European mystics. His doctrines were condemned in his own time, but later influenced the Protestant sects, the Romantics, and in more recent times the idealist and existentialist schools of philosophy. It was the misfortune of the Dominicans that their emphasis on doctrine and their theological knowledge made them the principal officers of the Inquisition, set up by the Vatican not long after Dominic's death to check the growth of heresy.

The Franciscan intellectual tradition developed – as might be expected – on different lines. Aquinas, who had insisted that truth could be established by reason operating within faith, found his chief opponent in the Franciscan Bonaventure, who conceived of the quest for truth as a part of divine worship but was in other spheres a reconciler of differences. He worked hard (though in vain) for the reunion of the Byzantine Church with Rome. On a higher intellectual plane were Duns Scotus and the remarkable William of Ockham.

Robert Grosseteste, bishop of London, another Franciscan scholar, lavishly encouraged the study of astronomy and mathematics, possessed Greek books and was the patron of the eccentric monk Roger Bacon who studied alchemy and linguistics, astronomy, mathematics and optics: he *may* have been the unidentified inventor of spectacles and at one time was thought – along with the German monk, Berthold Schwartz – to have a claim to be the western inventor of gunpowder. Aggressive, over-credulous, teeming with ideas, he was sure that mechanically propelled vehicles on land, sea and in the air could be constructed but he never quite managed to set about it.

III

The continent of Europe is not geographically designed for unity. Roman conquest had imposed an artificial unity on its western half, but had not touched Scandinavia, northern Scotland and Ireland, or anywhere beyond the Elbe. As Roman authority declined and the barbarians came in, the continent split into tribal kingdoms with shifting boundaries according to the military success or dynastic alliances of their chiefs. Later Arab, Viking and Magyar invasions forged bonds of unity between their victims, while, in northern Europe, the feudal system created regional loyalties.

Thus, through a variety of circumstances, the nation states of Europe came into being. The character of their rulers was only one element among many in shaping their destinies, but it was sometimes significant.

France's canonized king, Louis IX (1226–1270) was a model of Christian knighthood, just, compassionate, brave: he was also impressive on public occasions 'having the face of an angel and a mien full of grace', and possessing considerable diplomatic skill. A firm ruler, he prohibited private warfare, and the carrying of arms in peacetime, and established the right of appeal from the feudal to the royal courts. At set times, he heard the complaints of his people in person, speaking freely to all who came 'without disturbance of ushers'. A generous almsgiver he fed the poor at his table every day. In that much smaller world it was possible to have such easy and frequent contact with 'all sorts and conditions of men', though few rulers availed themselves of the opportunity as often as Saint Louis.

His reign saw the completion of the cathedrals of Chartres, Amiens and Rheims, and the building of his own particular jewel, the Sainte Chapelle in Paris as a setting for the Crown of Thorns, a relic which he had bought from the bankrupt emperor of Byzantium.

Inevitably he went on Crusade (1248). Defeated and captured in Egypt, he refused to buy his release till he had ransomed his men. He then went on to Palestine where the remnants of the Christian states were quarrelling among themselves, while the threat of Mongol invasion overhung them. By his quiet authority he imposed peace, restored the fortifications and prolonged the life of the Christian states for a few more years.

On his return to France he became the accepted arbiter of European quarrels small and great – between Pope and emperor, between the king of England and his barons, between the Venetians and the Genoese. The two missions which he sent to the Mongols, hoping to instruct them in the Christian faith, were coldly received but one of his envoys, William of Rubruc, wrote a full account of the journey – an early and valuable record of central Asia.

After sixteen more years of harmonious government Louis again embarked for the Holy Land. This time he got no further than Tunis where he died of fever. 'A pitiful thing and one worthy to be wept over, is the passing of this saintly prince, that kept his kingdom in such righteous fashion, and made such fair alms-giving therein, and instituted therein so many fair ordinances . . .', wrote his seneschal, biographer and friend, Jean de Joinville.[5]

Charles of Anjou, the aggressive younger brother of Louis IX, was meanwhile trying to replace Manfred, the illegitimate son of the emperor Frederick II, as king of Sicily and southern Italy. Manfred, the better man, and the better soldier, was unfortunately killed in battle. Charles of Anjou reigned in Sicily until 1282, when the bloody rising known as the Sicilian Vespers put an end to his rule in favour of Pedro III of Aragon.

In Spain Moorish power declined after the Christian victory at Las Navas de Tolosa (1212). The Moors lost Cordova and Seville by the mid-century. Only Granada in the extreme south east remained to them, not through their strength but because the Christian king-doms were disunited.

The peninsula was divided between Portugal on the Atlantic

sea-board, Castile in the central plain and the north, and Aragon with Catalonia, the greatest maritime power in the western Mediterranean. The principal seaport, Barcelona was also famous for its scholars, philosophers and poets, among whom Ramon Lull was the best known.

A substantial Moorish population, and many Jewish minorities, invaluable as administrators, survived in the reconquered cities till late in the fourteenth century. This sometimes produced social friction, but also created a rich and varied culture.

Alfonso X of Castile, called El Sabio (the Learned), in a reign of over thirty years (1252–84) substituted Spanish for Latin in all official documents and codified the laws in his *Siete Partidas*, which remained the basis of Spanish law until the nineteenth century.

An astronomer and poet himself, he collected medieval lyrics and composed in his *Cronica General* a history of Spain which encouraged national patriotism and established Castilian as the literary language of Spain. He also founded the University of Salamanca. His services to Spanish culture were more effective than his politics. He wasted his country's resources in a frontier quarrel with Portugal, in bribing the German princes (unsuccessfully) to elect him emperor, and in civil war with his son. It was left for his great-grandson, Alfonso XI, to end all possibility of a Moorish revival by defeating an invasion from Morocco. After the battle of Rio Salado (1340) nothing remained to the Moors in Spain except Granada.

The liberation of Portugal, overrun by the Moors in the ninth century, began about two hundred years later with the successful campaigns of Ferdinand of Leon and Castile, called 'the Great'. In 1093 a knight adventurer from France, Henry of Burgundy, who claimed descent from the French royal house, was empowered by the king of Castile to complete the re-conquest. His son Alfonso Henriquez established the dynasty and his own fame by defeating the Moors at the battle of Ourique (1139). The Portuguese Cortes proclaimed him king, and the Pope arranged a treaty by which Castile recognized the independence of Portugal. By 1147 Alfonso was in possession of Lisbon.

Among his successors was Diniz (1279–1325), one of the

greatest of medieval kings. Poet and patron of learning, he founded a university at Lisbon (later moved to Coimbra where it still flourishes). But his people called him *El Rei Lavrador*, the Farmer King, because of his special care for agriculture. He stabilized the sandy soil round Leiria by planting pine trees, encouraged the holding of markets by improving the roads, stimulated trade at home and abroad by minting money of an agreed standard, and called in Genoese and Venetian experts to advise him in building a navy. In effect he laid the foundations of Portugal's economic and maritime future. He was generous, too; when Philip IV of France launched his attack on the Templars, those who managed to escape found refuge and safety in Portugal.

In England the conflict between royal authority, clerical privilege and baronial power had long-lasting effects on the nature of law and government. Henry II (1154–89), great-grandson of William the Conqueror, was territorially one of the greatest princes in Europe, since he owned more than half of France, inheriting Normandy, Maine and Anjou from his father Geoffrey and acquiring Gascony, Poitou and Aquitaine by marriage. A man of iron will, impetuous temper and – except in his quarrel with Becket – sound political judgement, he reduced the power of his barons by pulling down all castles built without royal permission, and by increasing the power of the sheriffs, those country officials instituted by the Conqueror, who were appointed by the crown from outside the baronial class. He further weakened the barons by making each county responsible for raising its quota of men for the army in time of need. (Henceforward he was no longer dependent, like so many European kings, on his barons and their retainers.) He reorganized the exchequer and made the counties answerable for money as well as men by assigning the assessment of taxes to locally appointed juries. He extended the transfer of judicial cases from local to royal courts, set up a permanent central court of justice and appointed itinerant judges to travel the country at regular intervals.

His headstrong son, John (1199–1216) lost almost all his father's French possessions except Bordeaux and provoked the joint opposition of the barons, the Church and the citizens of London. Led by the archbishop of Canterbury, Stephen Langton, the barons were brought together and compelled the king to accept the curtailment of his power imposed by Magna Carta (1215). This famous charter of English liberties was in fact a feudal document which confirmed the privileges of the barons and of London citizens; it also prohibited the seizure of property by the king, made provision for the calling (from time to time) of a great council to advise him, and guaranteed every free man (a rather limited category at that time) against arrest, imprisonment or banishment except by the judgement of his equals and the law of the land. A generous, fortunate and mistaken interpretation of its clauses by lawyers in the seventeenth century, turned it into a charter of common rights and government by consent of parliament: ideas which never crossed the minds of its medieval authors. A rather similar charter (the General Privilege) was to be extracted later in the century from Pedro III of Aragon.

King John's long-reigning son Henry III (1216–72) provoked the barons and the Londoners, a dangerous combination, by feckless generosity to his wife's poor relations. (One of them, Peter of Savoy, built a palace on the site now occupied by the Savoy hotel.) Led by Simon de Montfort, the barons defeated Henry in battle, confirmed their rights, and – more fruitfully – developed the idea of the great council (which was already being called by the name of 'Parliament'); it was in future to include knights as well as barons and representatives of the principal towns. The first parliament so constituted met in 1265.

Henry III had little gift for politics but, like the even less politically gifted Charles I, he was sensitive to the arts. A great collector of curiosities, he owned the first elephant in England, a present from Saint Louis. He was a friend of Matthew Paris, the historian, whose Abbey of St Albans was at that time one of the great artistic centres of Europe. His court attracted the best French and English craftsmen, and the Painted Chamber in his palace of Westminster was justly famous. (This masterpiece of medieval wall-painting, damaged, neglected and covered by tapestry in Tudor and Stuart times, perished in the great fire of 1834.)

Henry's son, the formidable Edward I (1272–1307) continued to reform the law, by dividing Henry II's central court at Westminster into three sections for swifter operation, and making his own council the final court of appeal. In his reign began the careful recording of cases in the Year Books, a development much influenced by the work of Ranulf Glanvil, chief justiciar to Henry II. Written in excruciating Norman-Anglo-French, these detailed records of cases built up over the centuries a treasury of legal experience which formed the Common Law of England. The development of legal tradition was made easier by the establishment of the 'Inns of Court' on the fringe of London, where young men came to study.

Edward, the 'English Justinian' to his admirers, appeared in a harsher light to the other nations of the British Isles. In his father's time Wales had been dominated by Llewellyn the Great, a generous patron of bards but otherwise a ruthless barbarian who created no real unity. His grandson, another Llewellyn, lost control of South Wales, mistakenly sided with rebel barons in England, defied Edward and, after a fruitless resistance, fell victim to a brother's treachery. Wales was subdued, strong castles were built at all strategic points, Anglo-Norman settlers were introduced, and administration on the English pattern imposed on a resentful people.

Ireland had been intermittently colonized by Anglo-Norman adventurers for the last century. At first they settled on the eastern sea-board and brought a modest prosperity to Dublin through trade with the growing port of Bristol. Intent on extending good administration (as he saw it) Edward imposed his legal reforms on Ireland, where (outside the Anglo-Norman enclave) they were incomprehensible and irrelevant. There was here a clash of cultures – ancient Irish society, tribal and pastoral, covering most of the country: Anglo-Norman society, feudal and agricultural, slowly impinging. This conflict, scarcely yet begun, was to escalate, in the shattering crisis of the seventeenth century, to a disaster the consequences of which are still with us.

Scotland was divided between two cultures, the mountainous north where the pastoral clans lived on the milk, meat and hides of their herds, and the feudal, Normanized south, with its richer agriculture and trading seaports. This division had not come by invasion but through the expansion of Scottish power southward. Malcolm Canmore (son of Shakespeare's murdered King Duncan), first overthrew the highlander, Macbeth, later defeated the English and annexed the lowlands between Forth and Tweed, fixing his capital on the rock of Edinburgh (1057–93). He also married an English princess, the canonized St Margaret.

Scotland thus came to be dominated by the richer lowlands and ruled after the Anglo-Norman fashion. Norman and Anglo-Norman knights at the court of Malcolm and his sons, including the ancestors of the Bruce and Stewart dynasties, settled on the land. Malcolm's youngest son David I, who reigned from 1124–1153, completed what has been called the 'bloodless Norman Conquest'. A hard-working, pious and gifted administrator, he established law, order and a great measure of prosperity in the lowlands. Following the approved European method of spreading civilization and agriculture, he planted abbeys in the wilder parts of the kingdom, a form of inoculation which never quite 'took' in the highlands and islands.

The direct line of descent having failed early in the fourteenth century, Edward I was called in to mediate in a disputed succession. He appointed John Balliol whom he subsequently deposed, assuming the crown himself. This provoked a revolt led by the lowland knight William Wallace, who was defeated – after one spectacular victory – tracked down and executed in London (1305). Within a year Robert Bruce, a Scottish nobleman of Norman origin, was crowned king at Scone and became the leader of a revolt which Edward did not live to quell. After many vicissitudes, Bruce won an overwhelming victory against the English, at Bannockburn, near the strategic centre of Stirling (1314).

King Robert combined the virtues of patience and military judgement with the skill to unite a headstrong people. He kept his barons loyal by frequently summoning councils, and before he died a Scottish parliament was well-established. When, in 1320, the 'barons and freeholders and whole community of the Kingdom of Scotland', assembled in parliament at Arbroath, appealed to the Pope they described their king as 'another Joshua' who had led them through 'toil, fatigue, hardship and hazard'. But, they continued, if he should 'leave those principles he has so nobly pursued . . . we will immediately endeavour to expel him as our enemy and as the subverter both of his own and our rights . . . For it is not glory, it is not riches, neither is it honour, but it is liberty alone that we fight and contend for'.[6] This statement of the obligation between the king and his subjects, more especially his baronial subjects, clearly expresses the limitations which, in western Europe, hedged the power of the feudal monarch.

Not long after, in England, the incompetent Edward II was formally deposed. His robust son Edward III occupied his barons by making war in France, an undertaking which proved in the end equally destructive to both nations.

The Germans, though united by a common language, were deeply divided politically. The greater magnates, the cities and the Teutonic Order (the greatest landowner in the north east based on the prosperous city of Marienburg), did much for trade, for education and for the organized cultivation of the land. The emperor Rudolf of Habsburg (1273–91) – the founder of what proved to be the longest ruling line in Germany – had made himself the greatest power in the south west and in alliance with Hungary had defeated and killed Ottakar the Great of Bohemia in 1278. But advances in Germany were always liable to be checked by disputes about the imperial succession often ending in civil war.

Even the greatest emperor of the fourteenth century, Charles IV (1347–78) was much less effective as emperor than he was in his hereditary kingdom of Bohemia. Serious, conscientious, intellectual, descended from the native dynasty of Bohemia through his mother, he belonged on his father's side to the Rhineland nobility, the house of Luxembourg, and had been educated at the French court.

Charles succeeded to many problems, but also to advantages. The Czechs bitterly resented the German immigrants who had come into their country from the thirteenth century onwards to work in the mines. A privileged group, they lived under their own laws. But the country was the richer for them and the silver mines brought general profit.

The Bohemians took a pride in the European position achieved by Ottakar the Great in the previous century. Ottakar had extended Bohemia by conquest across Carinthia and Carniola to Istria – thus briefly giving Bohemia access to the sea.

The Bohemian nobility were notoriously unamenable to authority but Charles had the patience and tact to win their confidence. He based his government on the joint support of nobility and clergy, while studying to create an administrative order which would as far as possible insure general prosperity. He codified Bohemian law, built the Charles bridge over the Moldau, encouraged the commerce of Prague, while giving it also the dignity of an imperial capital and persuading the Pope to make it the seat of an archbishopric. For many years he would be remembered as the 'father of his country'.

In his other role, as Holy Roman Emperor, he was less successful. He did what he could to check private warfare and to guard against the danger of disputed imperial elections. In 1356 he issued the Golden Bull which regulated the procedure and fixed the number of electors at seven – three archbishops and four secular princes. This document continued in force until the dissolution of the empire in 1806 and was moderately effective in preventing contested elections, but it did nothing to restore the authority of the emperor. It lay with him to summon the diet, or general meeting of the princes, but his power depended wholly on his own political abilities and the resources of his dominions. Charles IV 'legalized anarchy and called it a constitution' was the verdict of a distinguished nineteenth-century historian; but legalized anarchy may sometimes be an improvement on uncontrolled anarchy.

The reign of Casimir III of Poland (1333–70) partly coincided with that of the emperor Charles IV, but he successfully resisted the emperor's plan to link Poland with Bohemia. Although the geographical advantages of Poland had been seriously limited when the Teutonic Knights established themselves on the Baltic coast, Casimir had his own ideas for the strength and prosperity of his country.

Ever since the devastating passage of the Crusaders across Central Europe, the once prosperous Jewish colonies in Germany had lived in fear. Casimir now invited all who wished to settle in Poland under his protection. The response was immediate. The newcomers made their own settlements, while their privileges were agreed and guaranteed by the crown.

Casimir, meanwhile, strengthened his frontiers against attack, especially from the Czechs whose incursions he successfully repelled. He also founded a school at Cracow which in the following century became a major university. All his policies tended to the defence, peace and enrichment of Poland.

Unhappily he had no male heir. The inheritance continued through the female line, causing both the Teutonic Knights and the Polish magnates to defy the crown. It was not until the accession of Casimir IV in 1447 that Poland again had a king strong enough to bring the Polish nobility under control and to defy the Teutonic

Knights, with whom war had become endemic. Defeated at last, the knights became vassals of the Polish crown, and gave Poland the long needed access to the Baltic. Casimir IV proved in fact to be Poland's greatest ruler in what would later be called a Golden Age.

In the West, Spain was still divided between Castile, Aragon, Portugal and the remaining Moslem outpost of Granada. Penned between the Sierra Nevada and the sea, Granada survived only because the Spanish kingdoms were fighting each other. This gave the Muslims over a hundred years of borrowed time.

In the fourteenth century therefore France and England were the two greatest kingdoms of the West. Edward III of England owned a great part of France by inheritance. Nominally the French king was his feudal overlord in these territories, but the position was nonetheless galling to France. Philip VI of France (1328–50) inherited a prosperous kingdom, had also dynastic connections with Naples, Hungary, Navarre and the county of Flanders, and influence in the Rhineland. He was rich enough to round off his dominions in the south by purchasing the province of Dauphiné from the emperor. He also had considerable power over the Pope in voluntary exile at Avignon – a 'free' city entirely under French control.

But it was a cause of annoyance to him that the wealthy cities of Flanders were largely dependent for the manufacture of the cloth, on which their prosperity depended, on wool imported from England. Rightly suspecting the danger of English influence, he decided to put his power to the test and impetuously invaded Flanders. At this the king of England prohibited further export of wool, whereupon the burghers of Ghent rose in arms against Philip and made a commercial treaty with England. Edward III, whose mother was a French princess, now claimed the French crown by right of descent, a claim which the Flemings immediately recognized (1340). So began the Hundred Years' War between England and France.

Philip VI, like some later European leaders, failed to realize the vital importance of the Channel. The English gained control in a sea battle off Sluys at the outset of the war, and had the north coast of France at their mercy. Twenty years of fighting followed, initiated by Edward's invasion of Normandy and resounding victory at Crecy (1346). Here the French mounted knights were thrown into disorder by the deadly accuracy of the English bowmen supported by their own dismounted knights – a form of attack which the English had developed during their wars in Scotland and Wales, and which created a solidarity between different ranks unique for the period.

The key town of Calais fell to the English in the following year. King Philip died, his successor was taken prisoner, but not until 1360, when both sides were exhausted, was a truce concluded.

A disaster, not made by man, now reached the West from Asia – bubonic plague, the Black Death. In the words of the traveller Ibn Battuta, 'it devastated nations and caused populations to vanish . . . laid cities waste . . . obliterated roads, changed the entire inhabited world'.[7]

Boccaccio has left a grim account of its effect in Florence, where civil order broke down because no one was left to enforce it. In terror of infection 'brother was forsaken by brother and oftentimes husband by wife . . . fathers and mothers abandoned their children, untended, unvisited . . .' The dead were thrown into pits 'piled up like merchandise in the hold of a ship'. Peasants shut themselves into their houses and feasted on all the food and drink they had, convinced they would be dead before harvest. The same feverish desire to enjoy the present, moved the elegant young people in Boccaccio's *Decameron* to isolate themselves in a country villa, making love and telling each other stories.

There had been no such plague in Europe since the epidemic which almost overwhelmed the Byzantine empire in the sixth century. The Black Death reached the West about 1347, ravaged Italy first and longest, then France, then England, then Germany. It was dying down by 1350 though sporadic outbreaks occurred to the end of the century.

The population over all Europe was reduced by a third, a loss which was not made good for a hundred and fifty years. All classes suffered but the peasants worst, because starvation and neglect killed many whom the plague spared. The immediate result was a shortage of labour. Serfs deserted unpopular landlords and went in search of better conditions and pay. In England the Peasants' Revolt of 1381 was inspired by a fanatic priest – John Ball – who preached that all things should be held in common and that all men were equal: a belief summed up in the distich: 'When Adam delved and Eve span, Who was then the gentleman?' He and the ringleader of the revolt, Wat Tyler, encouraged their followers to burn the houses of lawyers and kill all nobles and prelates. After they had caught and hanged the archbishop of Canterbury, it is not surprising that Ball was himself hanged by outraged authority after the death of Tyler and the collapse of the revolt.

In France the ravages of the long war added to the horrors of plague. Over all the north east the peasants rose, made desperate by famine, plunder, taxation and the indifference of their masters. More mobility of labour was possible for craftsmen and town dwellers, although the rigidly hierarchic nature of European society was unfavourable to the wandering journeyman, and towns often offered the privileges of citizenship and the membership of a guild only to those already well rooted there.

Italy suffered as badly as other parts of Europe and was reduced to extreme disorder by the rival aggression of cities and princes.

In Rome, in the wake of the plague, Cola de Rienzo, half visionary, half demagogue, set himself up to restore the Roman Republic. He had imbibed classical knowledge from Petrarch, but put it to his own use, overthrew the nobility with popular support, summoned representatives from all the Italian cities to meet in Rome and himself assumed the ancient name of tribune. But the fickle Roman populace deserted him and he fled after less than a year. Wandering over Europe, he tried to enlist the emperor to set up a triumvirate – Emperor, Pope and Rienzo – to govern the world. The emperor, Charles IV, would have none of it. Returning to Rome, Rienzo was carried again to power by a popular revolt – and lynched nine weeks later (1354).

Neither John Ball nor Rienzo can be fairly seen as liberating or civilizing influences. The Black Death brought forth no great movement towards better government, only the ill-organized revolts of the oppressed and the temporary triumphs of demagogues. In spite of the deep suffering and the heavy loss of population, Europe at the close of the fourteenth century was still a mass of quarrelling political units.

IV

During the twelfth and thirteenth centuries, the cities of western Europe grew in number and size, but townsfolk were still a minority. The great mass of the population were peasants working the land and providing the essential food for all. Illiterate, bound down by tradition and custom as much as by their low position in the feudal scheme, their muttered grievances exploded from time to time in violent revolt. The minority, the vocal and active townsfolk, had an influence out of all proportion to their numbers. The shortage of skilled craftsmen which followed the Black Death raised the status of those surviving and a new and confident artisan class grew up; the ideas and inventions which changed society came from them. *Stadt luft macht frei*, said the Germans. 'City air makes a man free.'

The extent of their freedom varied. Some cities had their own courts of law and their own fiscal system, could mint their own money, make leagues and alliances with other towns, even make war. Such privileges were granted where the power of the king or feudal magnate was weak, and he would give much in return for money or political support. Other towns had a limited right of self-government in their internal affairs only, and were under the jurisdiction of their feudal overlord. The kings of England and France encouraged commerce and gave local privileges, but never parted with their fiscal or judicial authority. Philip Augustus of France (1180–1223) exacted payment in services or in kind for the charters he granted but held the people of Paris on a tight rein, with no charter at all, buying their goodwill instead by paving their streets, improving the drainage and building them a new city wall. Over the border, the cities of the Low Countries usually had jurisdiction in their own affairs and control of their own taxes but the counts of Flanders retained ultimate sovereignty.

The Swiss cantons were the exception to all rules as their control of vital passes over the Alps gave them a unique advantage. In 1291 the three Forest Cantons of Uri, Schwyz and Unterwalden had formed a defensive alliance but did not claim independence, as such a gesture could have provoked a challenge.

The German towns had most freedom because the emperor himself and his greatest nobles vied for the support of the cities in their own repeated conflicts, and bought it by granting unusual privileges. The free cities of the empire were almost wholly independent of higher authority, minted their own coinage, made their own alliances, legislated for themselves and had their own jurisdiction.

The North German cities flourished on the Baltic trade in

timber, copper, pitch and iron, and luxuries such as amber and furs, but above all on the export of barrelled herring, the staple diet of Catholic Europe on Fridays and in Lent. The towns of North Germany on the coast and on navigable rivers, specially the Rhine, joined together to protect their common interests. The first surviving reference to the famous Hanseatic League does not occur until 1344, but representatives of the cities were meeting in conference at the Baltic city of Lübeck almost a century earlier. The Lübeckers organized and co-ordinated the fishing fleets of the Baltic, assembled the catch and financed the preparation of salt fish for distribution throughout Europe and dominated the league.

The league acquired trading privileges and had merchant colonies in other cities – London, Novgorod, and lesser places. Profiting by a dynastic war in Denmark, the Hanseatic merchants encroached on Danish trade; King Waldemar IV fought back but in the end capitulated to their superior sea-power at the Peace of Stralsund (1370). While the Scandinavian kingdoms were disunited, the league controlled the Baltic, but in 1387 the Union of Kalmar brought all three kingdoms together under Queen Margaret, heiress of Denmark, widow of the king of Norway and queen of Sweden by election. This strong-minded woman exercised effective control over the three kingdoms but failed to create a constitutional union. On her death rivalry and revolt, encouraged by the Hanseatic League, gradually undermined Scandinavian unity and gave the league once again control of the Baltic.

The usual form of government in cities was by elected representatives of the citizens. These *communes*, as they were called, had at first the elements of popular government but, as time went on, they often became self-perpetuating oligarchies of the richer citizens, varied in time of stress by the short-lived dictatorship of some popular demagogue.

Rome, with a tradition of social unrest going back over a thousand years, had its own insoluble problems. The bulk of the people lived on the pilgrim traffic, which brought great riches into Rome and made it a breeding ground for every parasitic vice. Very few Popes managed to control the rival groups of nobility who fought for mastery of the city, and not infrequently arranged the election of the Pope and the choice of cardinals to suit themselves. In the twelfth century a visionary priest, Arnold of Brescia, had excited a popular rising and established a *commune* which collapsed when the emperor, Frederick Barbarossa, entered Rome and hanged Arnold (1155). A period of relative stability in the later thirteenth century ended with the rise of the Orsini and Colonna families which caused the Pope to remove to Avignon and plunged Rome into renewed disorders which were later exacerbated by the Black Death and the posturings of Cola di Rienzo (see p. 319).

In Italy the cities were more closely related to the country than elsewhere in Europe – a heritage from Roman times. The nobility had their town houses as well as their country estates while rich merchants built country villas and bought land. (This transformation of merchants into landed gentry only became the custom in France and England at a later date.)

North Italian communities had first learnt to look after themselves as the Roman empire declined. Later, growing stronger they made leagues against trans-alpine emperors, oppressive Popes, or rival cities. The allied towns of Lombardy had defeated Frederick Barbarossa in battle at Legnano (1176) where their disciplined infantry outmanoeuvred his feudal cavalry: a portent of things to come.

The greatest city in North Italy, Milan, commanding the passes of the western Alps, and self-sufficient in food from the irrigated plain of Lombardy, had profitable industries in textiles and the manufacture of arms. Late in the thirteenth century a family of tough adventurers, the Visconti, made Milan the centre of a widespread military dominion, which at various times included Verona, Vicenza, Padua, Siena, Assisi, Perugia and Pisa and even the powerful seaport of Genoa. The threat to Florence was only averted by their family quarrels. Their rule in Milan lasted for nearly two hundred years.

The incessant wars of Venice and Genoa, rival maritime powers, were mostly fought at sea. The Genoese had the harder struggle because they simultaneously competed with the Venetians for the Levant trade and with the ports of Spain and Sicily for control of the western Mediterranean. By the thirteenth century the Venetians had the largest share in eastern trade, were paramount on the Dalmatian coast and had possession of Crete and Thessalonica. They also extended their power to the Italian mainland, gaining control first of Treviso and Belluno, then of Padua, Vicenza and Verona. Wisely, as it turned out, they did not trust to sea-power alone.

Florence, in a position to command the north—south route through Italy, became by the thirteenth century a financial centre of European importance. The gold florin, first minted in 1252, fixed an international standard for purity. Florentine banking houses managed the revenues of the Vatican and advanced loans to kings and princes, though two great firms, the Bardi and the Peruzzi, went bankrupt, dragging down hundreds of lesser men in their fall, when Edward III of England repudiated his debt in 1343. Unemployment, hunger and riots followed in Florence, aggravated by the plague, the Black Death, which devastated the city.

But the Florentines were resilient. Their merchants rebuilt their shaken fortunes. Early in the next century the greatest of all Florentine families the Medici, their fortunes based on the wool trade, rose to power. Giovanni de' Medici, probably the richest man in Italy, found the money which enabled Florence to buy the submission of Pisa and Leghorn, thus gaining an invaluable outlet to the sea. Giovanni was a man of peace as were many of his family.

In most European towns the various crafts were organized into guilds, by no means always friendly to each other. In Florence there had at first been only the *grandi* – the nobles, the landed families, and the *arti* – the craft guilds. Then the guilds divided against each other, while a growing number of labourers and journeymen formed the largest group of all, the *popolo*. The tendency was for the *grandi* to ally with the lesser guilds against the greater, and for all parties to court the *popolo* when it suited them to stir up riot.

The political history of Florence in the thirteenth and fourteenth centuries was one of recurrent social disorder, violent changes of government, expulsion of leading citizens, internal and external warfare. Yet in this stormy epoch there began a creative achievement which spread to all Italy and later, stimulated from Byzantium, revolutionized the art and thinking of the West – the Renaissance.

In the latter half of the thirteenth century a new humanity, possibly associated with Franciscan influence, appeared in the visual arts of Italy which had been dominated for centuries by traditional Byzantine models. In Florence Cimabue (1240–1302), painting still within the tradition of Byzantine design, introduced natural light and shade, painted architecture to indicate space and distance, and humanized the expression and pose of his Madonna and Child. In Rome Pietro Cavallini painted draperies to suggest the modelling of the figure and made his prophets and patriarchs into human beings. He was probably influenced by frescoes dating from the later Roman empire which he had been commissioned to restore. The Pisani brothers and their pupil Arnolfo di Cambio, the architect of the Duomo at Florence, brought a new vision to architecture and sculpture.

The Florentine Giotto may have been Cimabue's pupil; he certainly worked with Cavallini in Rome. He broke away altogether from the static images of Byzantium and created living beings, with human feelings and natural gestures. His Christ and Virgin are no longer remote figures of religious cult, but sharers in the emotions and sufferings of humanity. The cathedral tower, in Ruskin's words, 'that serene height of mountain alabaster, coloured like a moving cloud and chased like a sea-shell', was his architectural masterpiece. Giotto swept all before him during his life and was acclaimed after his death as the man who had brought back to life the classical art of painting, lost for six hundred years. This opinion, uttered by Ghiberti who designed the bronze doors of the Baptistery during the most fruitful century of the Florentine genius, gave rise to the term *Rinascita* – rebirth – used by Vasari a century later in his famous lives of Italian painters. Hence, ultimately, the current term 'Renaissance' for that extraordinary revival of human imagination, inspired by the rediscovery of the past, but in itself essentially modern: a renewed excitement and interest in life's possibilities and in art as the mirror of life.

Dante, Giotto's contemporary, holds a unique position in the literature of the West: the last and greatest poet of the medieval world, the first of the moderns. He began his *Divine Comedy* by tradition in the Jubilee Year 1300, when he found himself *nel mezzo del cammin di nostra vita in selvaggio oscura* . . . 'in the midway of life in a dark forest'. He was indeed in a dark forest, this lawyer and scholar, a political exile from Florence, with no home and no future. In his vision of a pilgrimage through the circles of Hell, up the steep mountain of Purgatory, into the joys of Paradise, he saw the life and politics of his time, the friendships, rivalries and hatreds of his own life, the whole of human activity and experience encompassed by a vision of eternity and encircled by *l'amor che muove il sole e l'altri stelle* – 'the love which moves the sun and the other stars'. The setting and indeed the geography of the poem is medieval; the thought is timeless. He used the Tuscan dialect of Italian, which through his poem became the literary language of Italy: a vivid and economical language of great precision and flexibility. The poem with its dramatic characters, ever-changing incidents, its moments of terror and joy, and its unrolling panorama of human life is as close to us today as when it was written.

Dante had for his guide in Hell and Purgatory the poet Virgil, until in Paradise, where the pagan Virgil could not enter, his lady, Beatrice, took him by the hand. Virgil occupied a special position in medieval Christendom because he was thought (owing to a mis-understanding of a text) to have prophesied the birth of Christ. Few other classical poets were known. For centuries western scholars had studied the Christian writers, the late Roman Boethius, the historian Orosius. They knew as much of the Greeks as had reached them from the Moors of Spain – this meant almost exclusively scientific works. It was not that all classical manuscripts were lost, though many were. Transcriptions of Latin works made in the Carolingian age still existed. There were Greek manuscripts at Constantinople, but very few in the West, where Greek was rarely taught. But the increased contact with Constantinople, owing to the otherwise disastrous capture of the city by the Crusaders in 1204, had brought some additional knowledge to scholars in the West.

Petrarch, the greatest figure in the classical revival, was born during the lifetime of Dante and Giotto in 1304. Florentine by descent, he grew up (and lived much of his life) in the papal court at Avignon. Scholar and diplomatist as well as poet, he travelled widely, using the intervals of his business journeys to seek out manuscripts. His ambition was to reconcile the creative thought of the classical past with the Christian tradition. Meanwhile he achieved contemporary fame as a poet, both in Latin and in the vernacular, and was crowned with laurels in Rome on the Capitoline Hill. His younger friend Boccaccio joined him in the quest for lost classical texts (Martial, Ovid, Seneca and Tacitus were among those recovered); and a Greek scholar was found to translate Homer into Latin. In spite of Boccaccio's learning and his efforts on behalf of classical knowledge, it is perhaps not unjust that he is best known for his *Decameron*, a collection of tales covering human life in its earthiest as well as its most exalted moments which became a mine of treasure for poets and playwrights of many nations, Chaucer and Shakespeare included.

Petrarch remained always on a more exalted plane. His best known poems – the *Rime* – which introduced the sonnet to Europe, were addressed to Laura, the object of his chaste love, who died of plague in 1348. Outliving her by twenty-six years, he was found dead one morning in his study, his head peacefully resting on a manuscript of Virgil. The continuous, persuasive influence of his writings, his discovery of manuscripts, his talk to other scholars, and to a whole younger generation made the way clear for the new outlook, at once Christian and classical, which came to be called Humanism.

When France and England called a truce in 1360 the English had been left in possession of Calais, Ponthieu and south western France, which they governed from Bordeaux, and controlled from strong castles in the Dordogne and elsewhere but the claim to the French crown had been dropped. Both sides had supplemented their feudal armies by employing mercenaries, the so-called 'Free Companies'. These men, never easy to control, could not be disbanded and continued, after the truce, to live on the country establishing private areas for plunder, terrorism and blackmail. Few nobility even attempted to fulfil the feudal obligation to defend their tenants, though they continued to enforce their right to free labour and a share of the peasants' crops. The immediate cause of a revolt in the Ile de France – called the Jacquerie – was a government decree that peasants must assist in restoring the castles of their overlords. This measure came as a culminating insult to the oppressed who were thus forced to increase the power of their persecutors with the labour of their own hands.

Paris had revolted in 1356 and set up a commune under a rich burgher, Etienne Marcel who soon lost the support of the citizens by appealing for help to foreign powers, including even the English. He was assassinated and the revolt collapsed.

But there was, at last, a stronger hand on the reins of government. Charles, the eighteen-year-old son of John II, became regent while his father was a prisoner, and succeeded to the throne eight years later. He was cool, realistic and hard-working. In French history his soubriquet is *Charles le Sage*. He rebuilt the walls of Paris, brought the most strategically important castles under the control of the crown, organized a professional army, and established a hierarchy of command – a necessary move to prevent the rivalries of the nobility.

By 1370 he was strong enough to challenge the English. The best soldier in France – and probably in Europe – was a knight from Brittany, Bertrand du Guesclin, who had made his reputation fighting in Spain. Boldly disregarding precedent, Charles made him Constable of France, a post usually reserved for the highest nobility. Du Guesclin avoided pitched battles, used harassing tactics and soon had the English on the run. The French and Castilian fleets meanwhile patrolled the Channel. Within a decade English possessions in France were reduced to a few fortified towns – among them Bordeaux, Bayonne, Cherbourg and, of course, Calais. For the time being the war was over.

In civil government Charles V reorganized the royal finances and, by getting the Estates General – the French equivalent of parliament – to vote fixed taxes for an indefinite period, freed himself from the necessity of consulting them for several years. This greatly increased the authority of the crown which, under the English threat, had become closely identified with the nation.

But unity and peace were both threatened by the growing power of the duchy of Burgundy. It had been granted to Philip, the younger brother of Charles; his subsequent marriage to the heiress of Flanders made him the master of a powerful border state, theoretically subject to the crown of France. By an unlucky chance Charles V was succeeded by the mentally unstable Charles VI. Quarrels broke out over the regency, leading to civil war and the alienation of the duke of Burgundy from the crown.

In England a young and ambitious king, Henry V, had succeeded to the throne. He invaded France, re-conquered Normandy and annihilated a French force three times the size of his own at Agincourt (1415). Almost all the leading nobles of France were captured or killed; heavily armed knights on heavily armed horses, they were still obstinately fighting in the old manner. The firing of the English archers broke the force of their charge and reduced them to stumbling chaos.

Henry V now revived the English claim to the throne of France. The poor half-mad Charles VI ceded all France north of the Loire to Henry and – disregarding the claims of his own son – accepted Henry as his successor and gave him his daughter Katharine in marriage. This arrangement was inevitably repudiated by the legitimate heir, the Dauphin, and his supporters. The war continued. Henry was on campaign when his wife gave birth to a son. Riding with all haste to see the child he contracted a fever and died. The infant Henry VI was acclaimed king of England and France.

The sense of religious mission can take many forms. A peasant girl of unfaltering faith and courage who grew up in Lorraine during the disorders of the Hundred Years' War might have felt a call of quite a different kind if she had been born at another time. As it was, the voices that she heard and the visions she saw directed her to save France.

The story of Joan of Arc has become so familiar that it no longer astounds us. But it would be incredible if it had not happened. She was about seventeen, illiterate, but practical, intelligent, with a quick wit and an unusual command of words. She had no money and no powerful backers; but a few believed in the visions she had seen and the mission with which she believed she had been entrusted. They set her on the way to Chinon to see the rightful king, the uncrowned Dauphin who had very little of France left to call his own.

Very brave, totally inexperienced, with a rooted objection to fighting on Sunday, Joan obtained the royal permission to relieve Orleans where – amazingly – her small force dispersed the English besiegers. Less than a year later she stood in the cathedral at Rheims and saw the Dauphin consecrated king of France as Charles VII. Captured soon after and abandoned by her thankless king, she was condemned as a witch and burnt at Rouen. But the English never regained the confidence that she had shaken; their expulsion from France was now only a matter of time.

The condemnation was formally reversed within twenty years of her death – chiefly because the king's position might have been weakened if he had owed his coronation to a witch. Further recognition followed slowly. The movement for her canonization began only in the nineteenth century and succeeded in 1920 in the aftermath of the First World War. The political significance of her career and her position as a martial figure and a national heroine tend to obscure the religious fervour which made her mission possible. The significance of her brief career lay not so much in the victories she won as in the single-minded faith which enabled her to rouse a king, inspire an army and renew the hope of a people.

The latter part of the fifteenth century in England was consumed by a dynastic feud due in part to the incapacity of the gentle and pious Henry VI and the ambition of his wife Margaret of Anjou. The Wars of the Roses, so-called from the red and white roses chosen by the combatants, lasted for some thirty years. Henry VI was deposed and murdered, making way for the reasonably competent rule of Edward IV, who brought Caxton and his printing press to England.

In spite of recurrent war, France in the late fourteenth and early fifteenth century witnessed a revival in literature and the arts. Charles V commissioned his chaplain, Nicolas Orèsmes, to translate Aristotle into French, a work which became a basic influence on the language. A late Gothic style, lovely and delicate as spring, flowered in the visual arts, in architecture, in the graceful literary conventions of *amour courtois*. Events of the early years of the Hundred Years' War were recorded (and embellished) in the imaginative prose of Jean Froissart, but there is no shadow of war on the delicate love poetry of Christine de Pisan. A generation later, François Villon, no respecter of persons, defiantly aware of his sins and the greatest lyric poet of France, reflected a harsher world.

Jean, Duc de Berry, the pleasure-loving brother of Charles the Wise, built exotic castles, cultivated the arts, and commissioned richly illuminated books while France foundered in civil war. He brought the Limburg brothers from Flanders, who with unerring eyes for colour and detail, illuminated his missal with the varying beauties of the seasons. There would be no miniaturists equal to them after printing was invented.

The English, in spite of their French commitments, were beginning to write literature in their own language, and even to speak it at court. Geoffrey Chaucer (*c*.1340–1400) was a vintner's son who enjoyed court patronage and, in a minor capacity, accompanied diplomatic missions to France, Lombardy, Genoa and Florence, where he may have met his older contemporaries Boccaccio and Petrarch. He wrote in English a version of the French *Romance of the Rose*; his courtly *Troylus and Cryseyde* owed much to Italian influence, but his most famous *The Canterbury Tales* shows him as the master of an individual idiom drawing on the variety and texture of his own language. The prologue, describing the pilgrims as they set out for Canterbury, is an anthology of typical English characters – priests, lawyers, tradesmen, craftsmen, country folk and townsfolk – an incomparable piece of social observation.

The authority of the Church had been more seriously undermined by the Black Death and the consequent disturbances than that of the state. Two Popes, who returned to Rome from Avignon, were so shocked by the state of the city that one left at once; and the other was only prevented from doing so by his sudden death. This led to a papal election in Rome, the first for over seventy years. The elected Pope unfortunately alienated a number of cardinals who set up a rival Pope once again at Avignon. For fifty years the scandal of a double Papacy continued. The Popes at Avignon were mostly able, and some were conscientious men. A thorough reform of papal administration and finance took place during the exile. Some of the financial measures were questionable: for instance, the increasing sale of indulgences (a system inaugurated in the Crusades). Indulgences for sins were not technically sold, but the recipient contributed to papal funds (for Church and hospital building, or financing a Holy War) and received the pardon in return.

Avignon lies in a rich peaceful region, abounding in vineyards and washed by the waters of the Rhone. The climate bred an atmosphere of luxury and comfort, and once removed from Rome, the accepted capital of Christendom, Popes and cardinals began to imitate the growing splendour of medieval kings and barons. It seemed almost a necessity that the papal court at Avignon should outshine all secular courts.

The luxury of Pope, cardinals and many of the higher clergy contrasted with the teaching of Christ. The secular clergy were increasingly worldly (if not corrupt) in the higher ranges of the hierarchy; parish priests, after the plague, were too few to meet the needs of the people, and though there were noble exceptions, most were given to the simpler and more squalid vices – greed, drink, fornication, worst of all, apathy. The Franciscans, falling away from their original ideals, were ready salesmen of pardons and indulgences rather than active teachers of the Gospel among the people. The great monastic orders had changed character: the once-austere Cistercians had become successful dealers in wool and other produce of the lands their predecessors had redeemed for cultivation with fasting, prayer and heavy manual labour: hired servants now did much of the hard work. The Cluniacs, who had once reformed and purified the Benedictine order, ran their monasteries as comfortable retreats for retired nobility, and lived well on the rich legacies they received for singing masses for the redemption of knights and nobles too busy to have time to look after their own souls.

Yet in rich city-states no less than in villages wrecked by famine, plague or plunder, the poor, the sick, the helpless, the hopeless and the lost were a daily reproach to the Church.

The muttering undercurrent of criticism and revolt grew louder. Some devout Franciscans tried to restore the ideals of the founder. The Fraticelli (as they were called) went back to the old austerity; most were simple and sincere, others sincere but not so simple, given to more aggressive political attitudes which antagonized both Church and state and led to their brutal suppression on heresy charges – which freely exploited instruments of social and political control.

More long-lived and successful was the group which came into being in the Netherlands under the influence of Gerard Groote (1340–84), the Brethren of the Common Life. They were not all monks, though some of them were; they were certainly not heretics. They were obedient members of the Church who sought to live according to the teaching of Christ, without necessarily leaving the world. They believed in prayer and contemplation, but also in charity. Their influence spread in northern Europe and their example stirred the consciences of less dedicated men and women to greater effort on behalf of the suffering and the poor. The most famous of the brethren Thomas à Kempis, 1379–1471, wrote the best known of all guides to the Christian life – *The Imitation of Christ*.

The brethren were practising Christians, not deep thinkers. Others, no less devout, saw the accretion of wealth, the political commitments and the top-heavy theological superstructure of the Church as fatal to the Christian ideal, and tried to restore simplicity of doctrine. Soon after the Black Death had swept the country, an English priest, John Wyclif, an Oxford theologian with connections at court, advocated a more direct and simple faith, condemned the sale of indulgences and the holding of property by the Church, translated the Gospels into the vernacular and insisted that a believer could make direct approach to God without the intermediacy of a priest. He made converts and inspired young priests to go out (as the early Franciscans had done) to teach the people. Wyclif enjoyed powerful protection but the social effects of his teaching and especially some apparent similarity to that of John Ball at the time of the Peasants' Revolt of 1381 (see p. 318) alienated his patrons and he was fortunate to die peacefully in his country parish (1384). Not long after his death his followers – the Lollards – protested in parliament against clerical abuse and found themselves too weak to challenge the establishment. Legislation exposed them to charges of heresy; some were burnt, and the movement went underground for the next century.

A similar movement in Bohemia, led by a theologian of the University of Prague, John Hus (1369–1415) an eloquent preacher in the vernacular, became deeply involved with the antagonism of the Czechs towards the infiltration of Germans. Like Wyclif he attacked the sale of indulgences and advocated a return to the Scriptures, obscured by centuries of theological argument.

By the beginning of the fifteenth century the scandal of the divided Papacy shocked all Christendom. Owing to further disputed elections there were now three Popes: one at Rome, one at Avignon, and one hopefully elected by a council at Pisa after it had deposed the other two, neither of whom took the least notice. (The third Pope was a soldier of fortune of notoriously evil life; he took the name of John, and so blackened it by his conduct that no Pope had the courage to use it again until 1958.)

The council at Pisa was a fiasco, but the time-honoured idea of a general council seemed to offer the only hope of clerical reform. Councils had stabilized and unified the Church in the early days of Christianity. Why not now? In 1415, after careful preparation, a council met at Constance, under the aegis of the emperor Sigismund (son of Charles IV) who had a fine presence, a weak will and an empty head. The purpose of the council was to combat heresy and end the papal schism. In this latter task it succeeded. Pope John was deposed, the Pope at Rome resigned, the Pope at Avignon did not, but was disregarded and forgotten. Western Christendom was reunited under a newly elected Pope, Martin V, an aristocratic Roman whose first act was to dissolve the council. It had not improved the spiritual quality of the Church but seemed, superficially, to have defeated heresy. John Hus and his strongest supporter, Jerome of Prague, were summoned to appear before it and given safe conduct by the emperor. Hus, who did not see himself as a heretic, came willingly and was asked to abjure the false doctrines he had taught. Fatally obstinate, he pointed out that he had never taught the doctrines attributed to him and so could not abjure them.

The emperor withdrew the safe-conduct and Hus went to the stake. But he was a national hero as well as a reformer and within five years of his death his followers, led by the formidable soldier John Ziska, initiated in Bohemia the first of the bloody religious wars which plagued Europe, on and off for the next two centuries.

The century after the Black Death in Europe was essentially an age of faith, and for that reason critical of the shortcomings of the Church. It was also an age of growing national consciousness, stimulated by conflict. The Spaniards were increasingly aware of a national mission to drive out the Moors. The French, in conflict with the English, developed a sense of unity belied by the quarrels of their nobility. The Bohemians came together against German in-filtration. In almost all countries of western Europe the spoken language of the people became the language of literature, though Latin long remained the language of learning and international communication. This attitude to nation and language played its part in criticism of the Church. The very merit and strength of the Church – that it was supra-national and spoke an international language – became cause for suspicion. The Pope for over a century had been the tool of the French king, or the prey of Roman factions; the Latin language which had once held the Roman empire together, had become a stumbling-block to all but the educated. Hence the emphasis laid by Wyclif, Hus and others on the transla-tion of the Scriptures for the people.

V

The Mongol empire of Genghis Khan formed a link between East and West. While his descendants controlled the trans-Asiatic routes from China to the Black Sea, the Middle East and North India, trade increased and Europeans, stimulated by the reports of travellers, began to enquire and speculate about the East. (The compliment was not returned: the East was incurious about the West.)

As early as the thirteenth century Roger Bacon had been enthral-led by William of Rubruc's report of his mission to the great Khan (see p. 309). Soon after, Franciscan missionaries reached Persia, India and China. John of Montecorvino lived first in Persia, then in India, finally for thirty years in Peking, of which the Pope made him archbishop. Here he translated the Gospels into Chinese, built a cathedral, claimed six thousand converts in six years, and taught his choir to sing so tunefully in the European manner as to delight the emperor. Another Franciscan made converts so easily that he feared they did not all 'walk rightly in the path of Christianity'.[8] Few of these missionaries spoke Chinese; they spoke Tartar dialects and their converts were among the Mongol population.

In spite of their great distance from Europe, they sent home reports of their travels some of which reached their destination. They described the noble cities of China, much larger than Paris or Florence, the plentiful rice, the sugar plantations, the high price of meat, the great rivers and lakes, where numbers of people lived all the year round in boats like houses, and the quantities of luxurious merchandise, spices, gems and silk. Others, reporting on their journey through South India, noted the growing trade in cinnamon from Ceylon, the innumerable islands of the ocean, the fertility of Java, where the king's palace was paved with gold, and the power of some of the island princes who possessed 'many elephants and many wives'.

This information can have filtered through only to a few. Returning merchants must have spread more essential and detailed knowledge by word of mouth, though few of them had the leisure or the skill to record their impressions; even Marco Polo dictated his recollections, while temporarily in prison, to a professional author, a Frenchman. Polo, the most famous of all medieval travellers, left Venice as a boy of seventeen with his father and uncle, in 1271. They reached China by way of Persia and Afghanistan and, after a terrible crossing of the Pamirs, reached Kashgar, the Silk Road and – eventually – China.

Marco spent fifteen years in the service of Kublai Khan. In that time he travelled over a great part of China, Cambodia, Annam and Burma before returning to Europe by way of Sumatra, South India and Persia. His recollections became the most popular of all travel books in fourteenth-century Europe and spread ever more widely the belief in the fabulous riches and commercial prospects offered by the East. By 1350 another useful handbook of trans-Asiatic travel was available; compiled by a Florentine, Francesco Pergalotti, it described the routes and the best manner of travel, estimated the costs, and explained the paper money of China, its use and appearance.

Trade between India and the Mediterranean went back into antiquity. It began with the Egyptians, flourished under the Roman empire and survived the disturbances of the Islamic conquest. The clearing-house was the Middle East, dominated by the Arabs, while the Byzantines, and the rival maritime powers, the Genoese and Venetians, competed for their custom. The Venetians gained in the end practically a monopoly of the trade so that the Genoese began to consider an alternative route to India, possibly by circumnavigating Africa; the Vivaldi brothers, who set sail in 1291, were never seen again, and Genoa ultimately diverted her interest to the corn trade of the Black Sea ports in which Venice did not compete.

Among the greatest travellers of the fourteenth century was a learned Muslim of insatiable curiosity and great diplomatic gifts, Ibn Battuta. A native of Morocco, his travels (c.1325—54) covered Egypt, Arabia, Byzantium, the Crimea, central Asia, India and China. He had been amazed at Alexandria, glorious alike in commerce and learning; he enjoyed the elegance of Shiraz and deplored the decay of Baghdad. Once he crossed the Sahara to visit the empire of Mandingo (Mali), which included the Gambia and Senegal rivers and the upper waters of the Niger (then still believed to be a part of the Nile) and did a brisk trans-Saharan trade in copper, ivory and gold. Mandingo was a group of small tribal kingdoms owing obedience to a single overlord strong enough to maintain peace, good communications, trade and prosperity. The sultan of Mandingo, and most of his advisers, were Muslims, for the conversion imposed on the black Africans by the Almoravids in the eleventh century had persisted among the governing elite.

Ibn Battuta found much to admire. 'The negroes,' he wrote, 'are seldom unjust and have a greater abhorrence of injustice than any other people . . . there is complete security in their country. Neither traveller nor inhabitant has anything to fear from robbers or men of violence.'

But he was critical in other respects. Their women, so far from being veiled, went about naked, even to the king's daughters. He was deeply shocked when the sultan gave a slave-girl to some visiting tribesmen who killed and ate her. This he was told, was what they expected when they visited the court.[9] The cannibals were from Wangara, the source of the gold on which the riches of the kingdom depended, a secretive people who cut off the gold supply if their way of life was not respected.

Though largely pastoral country, Mandingo had a number of towns. Kumbi, the capital, Gao and Jenne were principal centres of trade, but were surpassed by Timbuktu, on the northern-most stretch of the Niger, the meeting place between trans-Saharan caravans from Morocco, nomads of the desert and river-borne traffic from the interior. Its mosque and college of Islamic learning were famous throughout West Africa.

Ibn Battuta arrived, however, when Mandingo's greatness was already in decline. One of the greatest of its rulers, Mansa Musa, had established diplomatic relations with the Egyptian caliphate, the ruler of Fez, and the sheikhs of Arabia. His entourage had included an Andalusian poet and architect, who introduced burnt brick, a building material new to West Africa, for the mosque which he designed at Gao. On pilgrimage to Mecca he had travelled with five hundred slaves marching before him each with a staff of gold, and a hundred camels following after laden with sacks of gold dust. In the holy cities he distributed all the gold he had with him in largesse to the poor, borrowed more for the same purpose and repaid every debt with interest and in gold as soon as he returned home. Truly did Ibn Battuta praise the justice and honesty of the Africans. He was more critical of the Arab merchants at Mogadishu, the people were all too fat; it was different at Mombasa where pious Muslims lived frugally on fish and bananas.

Earlier in his travels Ibn Battuta had spent thirteen years in India attached to the court of the formidable Muhammad Tughlak, sultan of Delhi. Muhammad (1325–51) came of one of the Muslim dynasties which had ruled at Delhi since the Afghans had begun their periodic conquests of North India with the terrible Muhammad of Ghur in 1203 (see p. 249). Some of the Afghan conquerors cherished visions of reuniting all India, which invariably ended in bloodshed and destruction. Muhammad Tughluk, great warrior, obsessive builder of fortresses (including the stupendous Daulatabad), pursued this ideal of unity with relentless ferocity.

Ibn Battuta describes the formal splendour of his audiences, his lavish generosity and religious devotion: also the executioners always at the palace gate with the bodies of their latest victims exposed as a warning. 'This King', wrote Ibn Battuta, 'is of all men the most addicted to the making of gifts and the shedding of blood.'[10] He distributed food in famine, and flung largesse to the multitude, but instantly executed any who dared to criticize him. Peasants who could not pay their taxes, and revenue officials who failed to reach their quota were alike executed. In one of his rages he planned to destroy Delhi and forcibly move the whole population to Daulatabad. Ibn Battuta had at least one very narrow escape from Tughluk's insensate rage, but regained favour and was entrusted with a mission to China. Meanwhile Tughluk planned to conquer Tibet and lost an army in the Himalayas. Bengal rose against him, rebellion flared up everywhere. He died with almost all North India in revolt.

By the time that Ibn Battuta reached China, about 1345, the dynasty of Genghis Khan was in decline. The educated Chinese had long been restive under a system which reserved all the best appointments in government service for Mongols or foreigners, confining the Chinese to lesser posts, regardless of their abilities. Chinese merchants resented the numerous privileges accorded to foreign traders at the principal ports and Chinese peasants were crushed by the burden of taxes to support the Mongol army. When Ibn Battuta arrived, the plague – which Europe would know as the Black Death – was sweeping the land. Earthquakes and famine were followed by distress and social demoralization. Banditry, the last recourse of the starving peasant, was rife in the mountain districts. (It was in this unhappy time that Sung Chiang, a brigand of an earlier epoch who, like Robin Hood, repeatedly outwitted the authorities, became a folk hero and the central figure of a lively sequence of stories called *The Men of the Marshes*, which are a permanent part of Chinese popular literature.)

Meanwhile the many Buddhist monasteries became at first places of retreat from the troubled times, then centres of resistance to Mongol rule, or nests of bandits.

Out of the ranks of the bandits came the founder of the Ming dynasty. Chu Yuan-chang was of humble origin, orphaned by plague and famine, sheltered by monks and employed as a shepherd until he ran away. He became first a successful bandit leader, then a warlord. An able soldier, he was also diplomatic and added to his territory by alliance as well as conquest. Naturally the peasants joined him, but he sought and gained also the confidence of the educated. By the time he captured Nanking (1356) – which he made his capital – he had among his following scholars and administrators to establish a settled government, as well as his loyal peasant army. He was still under thirty. It took him fourteen more years to drive the last Mongol emperor out of Peking, to reunite China and restore the boundaries of the empire as they had been in the great days of the T'ang, with Manchuria added for good measure and Korea a submissive ally.

Chu Yuan-chang took the reign title of Hung Wu and called his dynasty 'Ming' – Bright: which symbolized his hopes. In a reign of thirty years, counting from the defeat of the last Mongol emperor (1368), he broke up the bandit gangs, rebuilt roads, dykes, canals and bridges with conscripted labour, and, by a mixture of bribery and force, compelled the peasants once more to cultivate the land. He maintained an efficient army to guard the frontiers, after first destroying the old Mongol capital at Kara Korum, and built a fleet which proved to be the foundation of Chinese sea-power in the following century.

He and his successors shared that hostility to foreigners which had grown up among the Chinese during Mongol rule. Christian missionaries were no longer welcome and colonies of foreign merchants dwindled away.

Seeing that Hung Wu had himself known the sufferings of the poor, he has been criticized for exploiting their labour and doing too little to improve their condition. But the re-establishment of law and order with the restoration of roads, waterways and agriculture brought back a certain prosperity in which they shared. These calmer conditions were shaken when Hung Wu died, leaving a grandson, still a child, as his heir. The inevitable civil war followed, but order was restored when the child conveniently died and his uncle Yung Lo, an able ruler, succeeded to the throne.

The Ming prospered for well over a century (and the dynasty outlasted its prosperity until 1644). Their epoch was marked by great activity in learning and the arts, but little that was imaginatively new except in ceramics and the theatre.

Under Mongol rule Chinese painters had found escape and inspiration in the study of landscape. Chao-Meng-fu (1257–1322) was favoured by the conquerors for his skill as a painter of horses, but his compatriots revered him as a calligrapher, and in landscape painting he revived the calm and concentrated vision of the great eleventh-century masters, enlivened by his own accurate and often witty observation. His famous pupil Huang Kung-wang. (1269

–1354) led the retired life of a scholar and over many long years perfected one of the greatest of Chinese landscapes, 'Living in the Fu-ch'un Mountains'.

The Ming encouraged painters, but only within the limits of the re-established academic convention. Correctness and fine crafts-manship were the characteristics of their epoch, which was more productive in porcelain than in literature or painting. An improved white translucent ware was created; subtle glazes were developed, and vases were painted with great brilliance and precision in over-glaze enamels. The famous blue and white ware appeared very early in the Ming period – white porcelain decorated in blue under a transparent glaze. It became the most popular of all Chinese exports, sought after in the luxurious East, but also sold by astute Arab traders to merchants on the east coast of Africa who created a demand for it among the black chiefs of the interior to whom the possession of such plates was a status symbol. Later this porcelain reached Europe through the Dutch East India Company, to set a European fashion and to be assiduously copied in coarser forms in the Netherlands, especially at Delft.

In learning, the early Ming was a period of recapitulation and preservation. The ancient Han Lin Academy of Letters, founded under the T'ang, entered on a new phase of activity; a committee of over two thousand scholars undertook an encyclopaedic collection of all existing works on science, philosophy and literature, planned to fill eleven thousand volumes. Chinese classics were reissued in critical editions, and a digest of the philosophy of the neo-Confucian school of Chu Hsi was published by imperial order.

The drama also enjoyed a great revival. The Yuan had been the Golden Age of Chinese theatre. Under the Ming a new Golden Age began, possibly because of the great number of educated young men who entered the civil service and occupied their excessive leisure writing plays. These were in verse; the principal part being sung, the other parts spoken. Enthusiasm for the drama, once renewed, lasted for the best part of a century.

CHAPTER IX

—•—

CIRCA 1350–1550

I

AFTER THE CONQUEST of Constantinople by the Crusaders in 1204, the Byzantine empire had fallen into fragments. A 'Latin' emperor reigned in the city itself, but two rival Greek emperors maintained the Byzantine tradition, one at Trebizond, the other at Nicea. Mainland Greece was a prey to any bold adventurers who could carve themselves out independent states. The Morea, bristling with defensive castles, was divided into Frankish baronies based on the French feudal system, with Greek vassal landowners whom the Franks were anxious to appease and whose religion they tolerated, although the Greek Orthodox priests were ejected. Of the three 'empires', Trebizond was the richest and most stable and Nicea was reasonably prosperous; they both had access to the Black Sea and the eastern trade-routes from which Constantinople was now cut off. The Latin emperors, isolated in a ruined and depopulated city could barely pay their way: one of them was reduced to selling relics from the churches.

In 1261 the Nicean emperor, Michael Palaeologus, who had already deposed and blinded his predecessor, founded the last Christian dynasty of Byzantium. Ambitious, cunning and a good soldier, Michael made an ally of the Venetians to secure some control of the eastern Mediterranean for himself, re-conquered parts of Greece and drove the Bulgarians out of Macedonia. But the dwindling resources of the empire were exhausted by these continual wars. His successors hired mercenaries whom they could not pay; naturally some of them revolted. A ferocious band of Catalans took possession of Athens, and noticed, as others did before and since, the strategic uses of the Parthenon, but their spiritual guide, the Catalan bishop John Boyl, sent to Spain for a special guard to protect it as 'the richest jewel in the world'.[1]

Constantinople remained commercially prosperous. When the observant traveller Ibn Battuta visited it about 1326 he was impressed by the busy port and foreign quarter and admired the superb Santa Sophia and many convents, but found the Christian population and their churches extremely dirty.

The Turks were still advancing. By 1340 they had reached the Bosphorus. Meanwhile the tottering empire was torn by civil war between rival emperors and a revolt of religious fanatics, the Hezychasts, who preached egalitarian anarchy and set up an independent republic in Thessalonica. During these confusions, Stephen Dushan, king of the Serbs, made himself supreme from the Adriatic to the Black Sea, occupied Macedonia and Epirus and had himself crowned emperor of the Serbs, Bulgars, Albanians and Greeks in 1346. When he introduced Byzantine ceremonial at his court and codified the laws of his people in the manner of Justinian, it was clear that he aimed to take over Byzantium. The reigning emperor, John Cantacuzene, himself a usurper, called on the Turks for help. They came readily, checked the Serbian advance and rewarded themselves by occupying Gallipoli – their first foothold in Europe.

Stephen withdrew only to strike again. First he seized Belgrade and thereby checked the king of Hungary who was friendly to Byzantium; he was almost before the walls of Constantinople when he died suddenly of a fever (1355). His empire fell apart, and the 'sickly days' of Byzantium were prolonged a little longer. Had Stephen Dushan lived another ten years (he was only 46) he might conceivably have built a Balkan empire strong enough to hold back the Ottoman advance.

The king of Hungary, Louis I (1342–82), now emerged as the strong man of eastern Europe, the only king of Hungary to be called 'the Great'. He came of that junior branch of the French royal house, descended from Charles of Anjou the unsaintly brother of Saint Louis, who had ruled in Sicily and Naples. He was a good soldier, chivalrous and magnanimous in all his dealings, an imaginative and capable ruler, a great patron of learning and the arts, and immensely rich. During his reign, and that of his father Charles before him, the mines of Transylvania, the richest source of gold and silver in Europe, were fully exploited. More than a third of the bullion came direct to the crown. Louis was thus able to sustain a glittering court at Buda and an effective army, and to mint the most reliable coinage in Europe. His father had brought to Hungary the French conception of chivalry which was quickly adopted by the Hungarian magnates. Louis's wealth, however, made him almost independent of his nobility so that he was able to curtail their privileges, reduce the burden of taxes on their peasants, and encourage the growth of independent self-governing towns. In 1370 he inherited the crown of Poland from Casimir III (see p. 316) who had enriched and improved the administration and culture of his difficult country.

In spite of his despotic power and his exaggerated expenditure on foreign wars, Louis remained a popular king. The Hungarian nobles had the glory of following him to victory when he regained Belgrade, established his domination over the Serbian chieftains, drove the Turks out of Bulgaria and finally compelled the Venetians to recognize his authority in Dalmatia. He secured his most vulnerable frontier by creating a sequence of strongly fortified border districts, the *banats*, south of the Danube and the Sava.

These defences proved their worth when some years after his death, the Turks overwhelmed the Serbs at Kossovo (1389) and directly menaced Hungary. Sigismund, the son-in-law and successor of Louis, tried to redeem the situation by calling on the chivalry of Europe to unite in a new Crusade. Nobles and knights responded to the call in great numbers but proved a disunited and inefficient army and were totally defeated at Nicopolis (1396).

The disaster left Constantinople devoid of help against the victorious sultan Bayezid. Poor and ruinous with only a few thousand citizens left, the city was still encircled by formidable defences. As long as these could be manned, it was impregnable. Bayezid besieged it, intermittently, for six years, until he was forced to abandon the project when the armies of a new and terrible Asiatic conqueror surged into Asia Minor.

Timur Lenk, Timur the Lame, or Tamerlane as he became known in the West, claimed to be of the race of Genghis Khan whom he resembled in his powers of leadership but exceeded in cruelty and lust for destruction. Before he confronted Bayezid he had laid waste Khorasan, Afghanistan and Persia, then made a detour into Russia to destroy the Golden Horde; then back to the Middle East to massacre the citizens of Baghdad. Next he descended on India leaving a trail of destruction as far as Delhi, where he is said to have killed 100,000 Hindu prisoners; and so back to Asia Minor to confront Bayezid whom he destroyed at the battle of Ankara (1402). After making a meal of Bayezid and all his glory, the ogre licked his lips and set off on the long march to China, his next objective. But death caught up with him before he reached his goal.

Timur had few, if any, mitigating virtues; he was evidently clever, a good mathematician, a good chess player, interested in astronomy and architecture. He was also fond of debating theological questions with Muslim sages, a taste which gratified his belief that he was a devout Muslim. He built several fine monuments in Samarkand which he regarded as his capital, but as he destroyed the agriculture and commerce on which it depended, he condemned it to years of famine. His insane butcheries did less damage, in the end, than his disruption and destruction of the Asiatic trade routes. But his victory at Ankara relieved the pressure on Constantinople.

The respite lasted only twenty years. By 1422 the Turks were attacking again, in force. The emperor, unable to defend Thessalonica, sold it to the Venetians, who lost it to the Turks eight years later. The situation was desperate if the Christian kingdoms of the West would not help, but their price was nothing less than the submission of the Greek Church to Rome. The emperor, John VIII Palaeologus, led a mission to Italy. His sad and noble bearing (depicted by Benozzo Gozzoli in the fresco at the Riccardi palace in Florence) made a deep impression, and the theologians who came with him worked earnestly for reconciliation. But the agreement they made was angrily repudiated by the clergy and people of Constantinople who thus destroyed their last hope of rescue (1439). This suicidal fanaticism was – perhaps – justified; previous rescue operations from the West had not been conspicuously successful and the Greek Church was allowed to maintain its rites and its identity under Turkish rule.

The king of Hungary, encouraged by the successes against the Turks of a brilliant border chieftain, John Hunyadi, attempted a final rescue with Venetian help in 1444, only to be defeated at Varna. Hunyadi survived to relieve Belgrade and to rebuild the strength of Hungary so that it became a bulwark against the Ottoman advance after Constantinople fell.

There was much heroic resistance in the Balkans, scattered and ill-recorded, over many generations. Most memorable was that of the Albanian chief, George Kastriota, better known as Scanderbeg, a superb guerrilla leader who baffled the Turks for twenty years

(1443–63), and Stephen the Great Voivode of Moldavia who thrice defeated them in the last quarter of the century.

The Byzantine empire survived the disaster at Varna for nine years. John VIII died and was succeeded by his brother, Constantine XI; he was the last, and knew it. In April 1453 the energetic young sultan Mehmet II (whose portrait was later painted by Gentile Bellini) began the final siege of Constantinople. His seventy powerful bronze cannon battered the strong walls; he had a fleet of small ships dragged overland to bypass the chain which guarded the Golden Horn. On 29 May the Turks broke through the defences at the Romanos gate and fought their way in. Constantine the Last died fighting.

More than eleven centuries had passed since Constantine I made the city his capital. It had survived the fall of Rome by a thousand years; the civilization, of which it was the heart, had preserved, transformed and re-animinated the classical heritage of antiquity while barbarism submerged the West. It had repelled Goths and Moors, Bulgars, Seljuks and Serbs. The Christian city conquered by Mehmet II rose to new splendour as the Muslim city of Istanbul, capital of the Turkish empire. Byzantium and its achievement was within a few generations covered over, neglected and misunderstood by its western heirs, derided by Gibbon, and restored to honour only in the last century by the pioneer research and perceptive scholarship of a few.

One of the great civilizations of the world, it had repeatedly renewed its creative power. The penultimate century of empire had seen a revival of art and architecture, even in impoverished Constantinople; the splendid frescoes in the church of Saint Saviour in Chora reveal no sign of decadence. But it was in the small principalities of the Morea, especially at Mistra, that the renewed Byzantine energy lasted longest. Here, far into the fifteenth century, anonymous painters filled the churches with scenes from the Gospel, humane in conception, full of lively detail, controlled by an unerring sense of form and softened by dreamlike harmonies of colour. Mistra, too, was a centre for scholars drawn to the academy directed by George Plethon, one of the most original thinkers in Byzantine history and the teacher of many who later carried his influence to the West.

Those repeated appeals for help, those vain efforts at reconciliation with the western Church had at least created a mutual respect and understanding between the scholars of both parties. The learned Chrysoloras, who first came to Italy on a political mission, settled in Florence, translated Homer and Plato into Latin and re-introduced the study of classical Greek into the West. Basil Bessarion, one of the theologians who accompanied John VIII to Italy, subsequently settled there, became a cardinal and helped to found the Academy of History in Rome and the Platonic Academy in Florence. Direct knowledge of Greek thought and the Greek classics thus came again to western Europe, gradually during the last century of Byzantium, then in a swelling flood as scholars fled the fallen empire carrying what books they could.

Florence, an independent republic, came in the course of the fifteenth century to be dominated by the great banking family of the Medici. Cosimo, called Pater Patriae, the father of his people ruled for thirty years from 1453; his two grandsons, Cosimo and Lorenzo who came to power in 1467 faced the opposition of jealous factions. Cosimo was murdered in church. Lorenzo narrowly escaped but was confirmed in power by a resurgence of popular support. In a reign of twenty-three years he filled his court with scholars, scientists, painters and architects and was known to contemporaries as 'the Magnificent'.

This century in Florence saw pictorial and plastic art flower into a new amazing achievement, influenced by the study of classical designs and Greek and Roman monuments. The masons who created the great medieval cathedrals had worked for the glory of God; their names are rarely known. But the artists of the Renaissance consciously identified themselves with their work and were often ambitious of personal fame.

Masaccio who died in 1428 at the age of twenty-seven, treated the human nude with powerful realism but achieved also a monumental grandeur – as in the Trinity in Santa Maria Novella. His posthumous influence was out of all proportion to the brevity of his life. In sculpture the development was even more striking. A generation after the Pisano brothers, Donatello learnt from Greco-Roman statuary to represent the youthful human body in all its natural grace – though he could also depict an emaciated saint with pitiless truth. His masterpiece is undoubtedly the superb equestrian statue of Gattamelata, a leader of *condottieri*, in front of the cathedral at Padua. This was probably the first equestrian statue to be cast in Italy since Roman times. It would be quickly followed by Verrocchio's statue of Colleoni in Venice (another successful general of mercenaries). The greatest work of Brunelleschi, contemporary and friend of Masaccio and Donatello, was the incomparable cupola of the Florentine Duomo.

Later in the century, painting became imbued with a new poetry, as in the charm of Pinturicchio's landscapes or the falling flowers and dancing graces of Botticelli's *Primavera*, ultimately in the mysterious classicism of Leonardo. Among smaller cities which achieved a style of their own was Urbino under Federigo Montefeltro. An outstanding soldier, he ensured the peace of his state and made his court a centre of learning. His son brought into his circle Baldassare Castiglione, author of *Il Cortegiano*, a manual of polite behaviour which civilized the once haughty and violent manners of Italian courtiers, and gradually spread its influence over western Europe.

A new interest in classical learning had begun in Italy a century before Constantinople fell. Dante, though great enough to transcend the limitations of his age and speak to all men, yet thought within a medieval framework. Petrarch, forty years younger, contemplated the world with the ease and freedom which had characterized the Greco-Roman world. (See pp. 324–5).

Already scholars and their patrons, were seeking out classical manuscripts, Greek as well as Latin. Cosimo de' Medici, gathered many such manuscripts in Florence and on the advice of the future Pope Nicolas V, built the library of San Marco, where scholars could study them. It was here that Ficino translated Plato. Nicolas V (1447–55), himself a collector, built the splendid Vatican library and opened it to scholars. Such noble endowment of libraries was not confined to Italy. In Hungary the son of John Hunyadi, who reigned as King Matthias Corvinus (a successful ruler in peace and war), collected over ten thousand manuscripts, and welcomed scholars to his great Bibliotheca Corvina. He also founded a university at Buda. In England, Humphrey duke of Gloucester, uncle of Henry VI, gave two hundred and seventy-nine precious classical manuscripts to the University of Oxford.

In Germany and the Low Countries inventive craftsmen studied ways to multiply the production of books. About 1456 John Gutenberg printed the first Bible; but Lawrence de Coster of

Haarlem had developed the technique some years earlier. These earliest printed books were struck off in the manner of an engraving – a new art which soon followed printing. A whole page was carved out at a time. Very soon this cumbrous process (well-known for centuries in China) was replaced by movable type, a simple matter in the West where writing, unlike Chinese, is alphabetic.

Printing spread fast; it reached England with Caxton in 1476. Not a classical scholar, Caxton began with a book about chess, and went on to print the latest (and to English ears the most beautiful) of all the works in the Arthurian cycle: Malory's *Morte d'Arthur*. The purist may find it derivative and decadent, but to the less critical reader this great prose epic is surely one of the peaks of English literature.

The Venetians had set up their printing presses in 1469 (only thirteen years after Gutenberg) and became for the next century the most influential and the best printers in Europe.

The implications of the invention were not immediately realized. It seemed at first a welcome means of multiplying the number of those rare manuscripts which before had had to be laboriously copied by hand, and an excellent way of providing priests with Bibles, the laity with missals and breviaries. Only gradually did it become apparent that it could also spread false doctrine – or necessary reform according to the point of view – faster than had ever been possible before. Within a century rulers and rebels alike realized its boundless potential as a weapon of political propaganda.

II

The Chinese emperors in the fifteenth century extended their suzerainty across Tibet to the mountain frontiers of India, south to Cambodia, Siam and Burma, the Indies and Ceylon. Their ships not only protected their long coastline but established their control of the sea. Chinese shipping at its height is said to have comprised 2700 coastguard vessels, 400 armed transports and at least as many ships specially designed for long exploratory voyages, not to mention thousands of small craft for the coastal traffic. These Chinese ships were the ultimate development of the Chinese junk. More solid and seaworthy than western ships of the same period, their structural rigidity made them especially useful in shallow, coastal waters, while their rigging enabled them to take every advantage of the wind and even to sail into it if necessary.

The emperor Yung Lo (1403–24) initiated a series of expeditions to establish Chinese naval pre-eminence. The measures taken by Hung Wu to protect the Silk Road from disturbance by nomadic raiders had been nullified by the conquests of Timur (see p. 342), and this may have been the reason why Yung Lo, and his admiral Cheng Ho, though it wise to make known the greatness of China on sea-routes hitherto dominated by Arabs and Indians.

The great, nine-masted 'treasure-ships' were said to be over four hundred feet long and a hundred and eighty-five feet wide, each carried a year's supply of grain and had tubs for growing vegetables on the lower decks. Sixty-two of them sailed on the first expedition (1405) accompanied by over two hundred smaller vessels. Admiral Cheng Ho, who in course of time led seven such voyages, was of mixed Arab–Mongol origin and had begun his career as a palace eunuch. Ambassador as well as admiral, representing the most powerful empire in the world, he opened the way for Chinese trade to Malaya, the East Indies and Ceylon, India and the Persian Gulf, the East African coast and the Red Sea. He expected the rulers on whose coasts he touched to acknowledge the supremacy of China. Some who refused – notably the king of Ceylon – were carried off as prisoners. But many states (once even Mecca) sent tribute of gold and jewels or strange beasts for the imperial menagerie – a rhinoceros, a zebra and a giraffe. The expeditions were also accompanied by astronomers, cartographers and geographers to record and chart them.

Whatever their ultimate purpose the voyages came to an end after 1432. The emperor Yung Lo's successor was involved with wars in Mongolia where the tribes were on the move. The capital was shifted back to Peking; frontier forces were increased and the Wall fully manned. These measures held back the barbarians for the next two centuries, while the naval power of China was confined to patrolling the coast. Arab traders, relieved of serious competition, made their base in Malacca, monopolized the trade of the whole region and converted the islanders to Islam.

While Cheng Ho and his great ships explored the Indian Ocean, the Persian gulf and the Red Sea, the small and far inferior vessels of the seafaring Italian and Portuguese ventured far out into the Atlantic or sailed southwards down the west coast of Africa into those regions whence few had ever returned. Already in the fourteenth century the Genoese had touched on the Canary Islands, known to ancient geographers but long-forgotten. The Portuguese, who landed there in 1340, saw at once that they were an excellent base for their further exploration of the African coast, but the Pope awarded them to Castile.

In 1419 the Portuguese found and immediately colonized the thickly-forested islands which they called Madeira (the Portuguese for 'wood'); here they planted vineyards, set up sawmills driven by the water power of the plentiful streams, and were soon exporting timber and wine. Encouraged, they ventured further into the ocean and reached the Azores where they introduced another profitable crop, the sugar-cane. More important, and more dangerous, were their recurrent expeditions down the west coast of Africa in search of gold.

These expeditions began in 1420,[2] but it was not until 1434 that Gil Eannes rounded Cape Bojador – beyond which, according to legend, all ships would be lost in fog or boiled at the equator. Nuño Tristao reached Senegal in 1443 and thereafter the Portuguese traded with the African kingdoms of the coast whence they returned with cargoes of gold dust and slaves. At about this time too they surmounted the dangers of the homeward voyage on which earlier explorers had been lost, battling against the prevalent contrary winds. They had, by this time, developed the ships known as caravels, small, solidly-built, manoeuvrable which, with two or three masts and lateen, sail could haul close to the wind. Besides, their sea captains discovered a better route: they sailed westwards across the Atlantic until they encountered southerly and easterly currents which carried them quickly home.

The man behind these ventures was the Infante of Portugal, the king's brother, known to the English-speaking world as Prince Henry the Navigator. (His mother was an English princess.) He was not, himself, a navigator, but he saw to it that his captains were equipped with the best instruments and knowledge available. His principal seat at Sagres, near Cape St Vincent, was admirably placed for collecting, from the many ships that came and went, information about winds and currents. He had been credited with setting up something like a college for the study of mathematics and astronomy; it was more like an information centre, with charts regularly revised, and data recorded and made available.

Prince Henry's interest in exploration was enhanced by a fervent desire to spread the Catholic faith. He was not himself much interested in gold and was opposed to slave-raiding and unnecessary violence. 'My Lord Infante will not permit further hurt to be done to any [natives], because he hopes that, mixing with Christians they may without difficulty be converted to our faith.' So wrote the Venetian sea captain Cadamosto who in 1455/6 led a Portuguese expedition to explore the Gambia and Senegal. Cadamosto was impressed by the power and authority of the native chiefs, observed with interest the many villages of grass huts, the hippopotami and the elephants. He walked freely among the friendly people and was amused when they rubbed his hands with moistened fingers to see if his white skin was paint.[3]

Shortly before Cadamosto's voyage Constantinople had fallen to the Ottoman Turks. The effect on the commerce of the Mediterranean was not at first disastrous: the Turks were anxious to keep open the trade routes from which they gathered considerable revenues. The Venetians preserved much of their trade by treaties and tribute. The Portuguese were not involved; even Barcelona, the richest port in Spain, mistress of the western Mediterranean, was not seriously affected until the Ottomans conquered North Africa and cut off trade with Egypt.

Some years after Prince Henry's death in 1460, the Portugese established a trading post on the Gold Coast (Ghana) for collecting bullion and slaves. In 1489 Diego Cao explored the Congo estuary. Three years later Bartolomeu Dias rounded the Cape of Good Hope but was driven back by storms. At last, in 1497, Vasco da Gama circumnavigated Africa, touched on Mozambique and put into Mombasa in the hope of getting advice from Arab traders about crossing the Indian Ocean. Jealous, they gave him none; he sailed in spite of them, reached Calicut on the coast of Malabar, and returned to Lisbon in triumph. He had found a feasible route to India which bypassed alike the Arab middlemen and the Venetians. The Pope accordingly bestowed on the king of Portugal, Manoel the Fortunate, the title 'Lord of the conquest, navigation and commerce of India, Ethiopia, Arabia and Persia'. (In the following century, Luis de Camões was to celebrate Vasco da Gama's voyage in his poem, the Lusiads, one of the greatest of European epics.)

Five years earlier, the discovery of a more direct route to Asia had been claimed on behalf of Spain by Christopher Columbus. Columbus may have been born in Genoa but nothing certain is known of his origins and he seems deliberately to have made a mystery of them. He was a man of genius of the most difficult kind – a visionary, at once tenacious and quarrelsome. But he was an experienced seaman and outstanding navigator[4] who had sailed on several of the Portuguese African voyages, and was convinced that the shortest way to Asia lay westward across the Atlantic.

The spherical shape of the earth was well-known in classical antiquity; knowledge of it, supported by the experience of seamen and the authority of Ptolemy had never been wholly lost, and was not questioned by any geographers in the time of Columbus. Ptolemy, however, who had greatly overestimated the extent of China, was the source of much error as to the size of the Atlantic which was generally assumed to be the only great ocean in the world. At least two geographers at the time of Columbus had suggested that the distance between Europe and China by sea was not much above 5000 miles. Columbus deceived himself into the even shorter estimate of 3500 miles. When he sought authority and financial help for his venture he could not get it: the king of Portugal, the king of Aragon and his wife the queen of Castile, the kings of England and France all took expert advice and all refused. Indomitably persistent, he again approached Queen Isabella. Her marriage to Ferdinand of Aragon had united Spain, and when Columbus appealed to her for the second time she was encamped with her husband before the walls of Granada, the last Moorish stronghold, awaiting its inevitable surrender. After nearly eight hundred years, Spanish soil would be free from the infidel. In the euphoria of the moment the queen gave Columbus his chance.

He set sail on 3 August 1492 and landed on 12 October on what he took to be an island off the coast of Asia (in fact one of the Bahamas). A fortnight later, further exploration brought him, as he thought, to a peninsula of mainland China. In April he was back in Spain bringing with him some of the natives, samples of many plants which he believed to be oriental spices, together with gold ornaments and other curiosities. The grateful monarchs who received him at Barcelona bestowed on him the title of 'Admiral of the Ocean Sea and Governor of the Islands that he has discovered in the Indies'.

The Portuguese who for the last half century had disputed with the Spaniards for possession of the nearer Atlantic islands, now hastily agreed to a division of the potential spoils. The Pope fixed a line of demarcation about 1175 miles west of the Azores; discoveries to the east of it belonged to Portugal; to the west of it to Spain (Treaty of Tordesillas, 1494). Through this agreement, when Pedro Cabral discovered the mainland of Brazil in 1500 it fell to the share of Portugal.

Columbus made three further voyages to confirm his discovery. On the second he found and named the Virgin Islands, touched on Puerto Rico and Jamaica and explored the southern coast of Cuba. On the third (1498–1500) he reached the mainland of South America, in the extreme west of Venezuela, the Paria peninsula. On the fourth he explored the coasts of Costa Rica, Nicaragua, Honduras and Panama. He recognized by this time that he had found a 'new world', a great region hitherto unknown to geographers, but he stubbornly believed it to be a part of the immense continent of Asia.

As he grew older he became convinced that the prophecies in the book of Esdras concerned him and his God-given mission. In his last sad years he was distressed by his dismissal from his governorship and by criticism and disputes. With the death of Queen Isabella he lost his most active supporter although Ferdinand treated him generously. He was disillusioned by the growing certainty of the geographers that his discoveries had nothing to do with India or Asia. He died in 1506, still convinced that he had found what he set out to find, yet before his death the Florentine, Amerigo Vespucci, had explored the coast of Brazil as far south as the river La Plata and established beyond doubt the existence of the new continent. Only a year after Columbus died, in 1507, a German geographer, Martin Waldseemuller, in a new map of the world, named the new continent 'America' in honour of Vespucci.

The stature of Columbus is not diminished by his error. He pioneered the Atlantic crossing, proved that it could be done, showed the way to others and made (while rejecting it) the discovery which doubled the size and changed the balance of the known world.

In 1519 Ferdinand Magellan, a Portuguese in the service of the Spanish monarchy, sailed down the coast of South America, through the straits which bear his name, into the unknown vast ocean he called the Pacific. After fearful sufferings from lack of food and water, he reached the island of Cebu in the Philippines, where he offered to help the king in a tribal war and was killed. His most experienced pilot, Juan Sebastian del Cano, took command of the reduced and battered fleet, completed the circumnavigation and brought back the *Vitoria*, the one surviving ship, with a cargo of spices and sandalwood to Seville in September 1527. This was the first circumnavigation of the globe; great credit must go to del Cano for bringing the *Vitoria* safely home, but he could hardly have done so without the example and the master plans of Magellan. On his return he was not unnaturally apt to emphasize his own achievement, but the glory of the first great circumnavigation belongs rightly to Magellan.

The survivors were given a royal welcome by the young king of Spain, Charles, grandson and heir of Ferdinand and Isabella and sovereign of territories scattered over half the globe.

The lives of Europeans, princes and peasants, capitalists and craftsmen, in every profession, in every country, would be changed: their agriculture, their diet, their trade, their hopes, their opportunities – all in course of time would be altered by the great unknown continent with its myriad islands, the New World which now lay open to them.

III

Before Columbus died, before Magellan sailed, Spanish adventurers had already descended on the West Indies – young men who in previous generations had found an outlet in the civil wars of the peninsula or in fighting the Moors. With the union of Spain under Ferdinand and Isabella, and the fall of Granada, land-hungry Spaniards now looked to the New World.

The *Casa de Contratacion* (the Board of Trade) in Seville and the *Consejo de las Indias* (the Council for the Indies) limited the amount of land they could acquire and in theory protected the natives from expropriation and enslavement. But adventurers in the Indies scoffed at distant denunciations, seized the land they wanted, kidnapped and tyrannized over the natives. Courageous priests sometimes protested. A Dominican in Hispaniola, Antonio de Montesinos, asked by what right his countrymen conquered and enslaved the natives – 'You are in mortal sin for the cruelty and tyranny you use with these innocent people'.[5] The more influential Bartolomé de las Casas vehemently complained to the government that the native population was despoiled and destroyed. But the government, though willing was too far off, and powerless to prevent it. Las Casas in angry despair recorded the horrors that he had seen in his *Historia de las Indias*. Only one of his suggestions was adopted and that the most questionable – the importation of Negro slaves to share the work. Soon these living cargoes were regularly shipped from Africa, not to save but to replace the native population destroyed by overwork and European diseases.

In the century before the discovery of America two great empires had grown up on the mainland: the Aztecs in Mexico and the Incas in Peru.

The Aztecs were a tribe of the Nahua people who, in the eleventh and twelfth centuries had created the Toltec culture, which was itself in part derived from the Maya whom they had conquered (see p. 245). The Maya, remarkable as architects, astronomers and mathematicians, fertilized almost all the subsequent cultures of central America though their own power was ultimately confined to Yucatan.

Aztec power grew throughout the twelfth and thirteenth century rather by imposing tribute on defeated neighbours than by welding them into a united empire. About 1325 they began to build their impressive capital city, Tenochtitlan in the shallows of lake Tezcuco. They used rubble and mortar and faced the greater buildings with white stucco, gleaming in the sun. Fresh water was piped across the lake from the mainland, and crops, cultivated in the shallows and marshes, supplied the basic food. During the next century the Aztecs subjected all neighbouring tribes except the mountain city of Tlaxcala. They had to have one enemy, for human sacrifice was a feature of their religion and their most powerful god, Huizilopochtuli, the war god, had a gluttonous appetite. A constant supply of prisoners of war was essential to keep him happy.

The Aztecs were an intelligent, highly disciplined people skilful in weaving, embroidery and the making of gold and silver jewelry. Their ballads and legends were handed down by word of mouth although they had pictographic writing for ordinary communication. Priests dominated the state but an elected king was its secular head. Civic and religious obligations were firmly laid down and children were strictly trained for the parts allotted to them in society.

The Aztec had no contact with the Inca: the distance between them was as great as that between the Chinese frontiers and the Mediterranean, over even more difficult country and with no incentive to cross it. The Inca empire, unlike that of the Aztec had been forcibly welded together, in little more than a century, by a dynasty of god-kings, who controlled every aspect of their subjects' lives through a well-organized bureaucracy and an invincible army. Rebellion was punished by the razing of whole villages, and conquest was sometimes made secure by transporting the native population elsewhere and replacing them by docile settlers. Fear of these methods caused some neighbouring states, notably the highly civilized Chimu people of the Peruvian coastal plain, to surrender without fighting.

The last of the conquering Inca, Huayna Capac, had ruled over all of what is now modern Peru, a good part of Chile, Ecuador and northern Argentine. His capital, Cuzco, over ten thousand feet up in the Andes, was a splendid city built of stone blocks so accurately fitted that no mortar was needed. The empire was held together by an astonishing system of roads; a coastal road over 2000 miles long, an approximately parallel road following the Andes for about 1600 miles, the two linked together by connecting roads at intervals. Ravines were built up with solid masonry to carry it, galleries were cut into the rock; but for crossing rivers suspension bridges of toughly plaited grass were strong enough. The roads were serviced by peasants in relays; all taxation was in the form of public services. Runners stationed at three mile intervals carried messages, either by word of mouth or in a code of knots on a string: the Inca had no writing.

The men were liable for military service or work on public buildings: palaces, temples, fortifications, reservoirs and vast granaries, an insurance against drought and famine. Land was the property of the state and was farmed in common by each village according to regular seasonal rules. At stated intervals officials of the Inca inspected the villages to carry off the most intelligent and beautiful children for training at court – the boys to be pages or secretaries, and to rise perhaps to administrative office, the girls to serve in the temples, to weave vestments and hangings, and some of them to become the concubines of Inca princes.

They worshipped nature gods, sun, moon, stars and earth, but none of these were so greedy for blood as the Aztec god. Even the great sun god was content with a relatively small ration on special occasions. Ancient legend told of a creator god who, when his work was done, walked away over the sea, and would one day return.

The authority of the Inca should have established peace throughout their empire which they thought was the whole world. Unhappily the last of the conquerors, Huayna Capac, divided the inheritance between Huascar, his eldest son by his principal wife, and Atahualpa, his favourite son by a concubine. Civil war immediately ensued. This, in European reckoning, was about the year 1525.

Five years before, unknown to the Inca, the Aztec empire had been destroyed by Hernan Cortés. The ungovernable son of an impoverished gentleman in the barren province of Estremadura, Cortés was shipped off to Hispaniola to make his way in the world. After a variety of adventures worthy of a picaresque romance he was given command of an expedition to the mainland. Landing in Yucatan in February 1519, he first trained his army of about five hundred men (and sixteen horses), then defiantly burnt his boats and marched into the interior sending a messenger in advance to inform the Aztec ruler Montezuma that he represented the king of Spain.

Baffled by this strange visitation, Montezuma came out to meet him in state under a feather canopy hung with pearls, while the Spaniards stared in amazement at the tall white buildings of Tenochtitlan and the hundreds of crowded canoes on the lake. With reckless daring Cortés seized Montezuma as a hostage, a *coup* which was made possible by the fear of Spanish horses, guns and swords – in a country where horses, iron and gunpowder were all unknown.

Meanwhile a Spanish force came in pursuit of the rebel Cortés. While he was parleying with them, the people of Tenochtitlan rose against him. Montezuma, his valuable hostage, was killed in a riot and Cortés with great difficulty and heavy loss escaped from the city by a narrow causeway over the lake. He now enlisted the help of the people of Tlaxcala, bitter enemies of the Aztec, recaptured Tenochtitlan, killed its priestly leaders, sacked the shining palaces, and founded Mexico City on the ruins. In due course a bewildered government in Spain appointed him governor and captain general over all his conquests.

Other Spanish adventurers were exploring the Pacific coast and settling in the isthmus of Panama. Here they heard rumours of a great empire, fabulously rich in gold and silver. In 1530, Francisco Pizarro, a grizzled adventurer well over fifty, set out to conquer the Incas with a hundred and two foot soldiers, sixty-two horsemen and a charter from the king of Spain enjoining on him the duty of Christian conduct towards the natives.

With this small force, he scaled the formidable mountain barrier between the coast and the highland heart of the Inca empire. Pizarro's arrival coincided with Atahualpa's victory over his elder brother; he had spared his brother's life but immured him in prison, after slaughtering his chief supporters. When he heard of Pizarro's approach he may have assumed that the intruder was the creator god Viracocha, returning in accordance with the prophecies. More probably he felt contempt for so small a force and curiosity about the horses which had been described to him. He came to meet the intruders borne in a litter gay with parrots' feathers, richly encrusted with silver and supported by a guard of three or four thousand men. Pizarro sent a priest to urge him to accept Christianity, but Atahualpa looked disparagingly at the Bible – doubtless the first printed book he had seen – and threw it on the ground. At once Pizarro's men charged. The astonished Incas fled and Atahualpa was taken prisoner.

Pizarro now demanded a gigantic ransom in gold. Atahualpa sent for the required sum but, in spite of his humiliation at Spanish hands, he still feared a rising in his brother's favour more than he feared his captors. He therefore privately ordered his brother's murder – an action which revolted the otherwise hardened consciences of Pizarro's men. Even so, Atahualpa might have been safe enough in captivity if it had not been for false rumours of a large rescue force marching to attack the Spaniards. Pizarro, who seems to have doubted this rumour, was compelled by the fears of his men to have Atahualpa executed – an action which would be strongly condemned by the king of Spain when he came to hear of it (1533).

With Atahualpa dead, the state machine collapsed. The Spaniards entered Cuzco and set up his younger brother as a puppet king. With a flash of spirit the new Inca took advantage of Pizarro's absence on the coast – where he was founding the future city of Lima – to rise in revolt. But his position was hopeless; his people had no firearms, their swords were made of wood, their 'armour' was padded cotton. The guns, the horses, even the mastiff dogs of the Spaniards appalled them, and besides they were now ravaged by a new illness – probably smallpox. The revolt was easily crushed. Inca rule came to an end.

The Spaniards pushed their conquest southwards into Chile, facing terrible hardships, leaving men and horses frozen to death in the high Andes, fighting the Aracaunian Indians (who had checked the Inca conquest and for years held off the Spaniards) and still fighting among themselves. Pizarro, by now a bitter, jealous, avaricious and indomitable septuagenarian, was struck down by assassins. His last gesture was to trace the sign of the cross on the ground and kiss it as he died.

The *Conquistadors*, many of whom were younger sons of old decayed families, poor and proud, could now make their choice among the most beautiful women of the conquered peoples. Many of them would later regularize their relationship by Christian marriage. A mixed race grew up, the best of them inheriting the finest qualities of both races – a proud, strong, aristocratic people.

During the epoch of conquest and long afterwards the authorities in Spain strove to restrain the greed of the settlers and to protect the native population. Church and state alike required that the conquered people be respected as men and brothers. Spanish jurists and Spanish priests at Salamanca denounced the behaviour of their compatriots in the New World as contrary to the laws of nature and of nations. The most outspoken of them, Francisco de Vitoria, gained the ear of the king. The Laws of Burgos (1515) were an attempt in the right direction, but their purpose was strengthened by the New Laws for the Indies, issued in 1542. These reduced the amount of land that could be held by any one person, forbade slavery, laid down rules for the protection of the natives and brought administration under the direct rule of the crown. But the difficulties of enforcement and the gradual failure of energy in Spain made these provisions largely ineffective. Among the minority of colonial administrators who tried conscientiously to realize the ideal of paternal government, Vasco de Quiroga stands high: a missionary and governor who used More's *Utopia* as his guide for the establishment of a co-operative commonwealth among the Tarascoan Indians of Michoacan, whom he educated in useful crafts which survive to this day, as does his memory.

The American possessions brought little profit to Spain. Much of the gold and silver (predominantly silver after the opening of the inexhaustible Potosi mine in Peru) annually carried home by the treasure fleet, went in financing Spanish wars in other parts of Europe or paying the interest on royal borrowings from German and Genoese bankers. Although Seville, the port of entry for American cargoes, profited considerably and grew in splendour, the bulk of the spices brought back from the East, by for instance the survivors of Magellan's voyage, were bought and marketed by the Welser of Augsburg. Foreign control of Spanish trade was the inevitable result of the religious and racial policy of Ferdinand and Isabella after the conquest of Granada. The expulsion of the Jews removed almost all experienced bankers and merchants from Spain at the time when they were most urgently needed.

The greatness of Spain was never securely established, although its vulnerability was at first concealed by superficial splendour, by the achievements and influence of Spanish culture, and (not least) by the rule of a powerful dynasty, the Habsburg, who dominated the politics of Europe for well over a century. Ferdinand and Isabella, *los reyes Catolicos* – the Catholic kings, as the Pope had called them – left no surviving male heir. The son of their eldest daughter, Charles, duke of Burgundy, a prince of the Habsburg family, born and brought up in the Low Countries, became in 1516 king of Spain.

This family already counted six Holy Roman Emperors. Although they came to be called the House of Austria, their original lands were in Switzerland – and had been lost. This did not greatly matter as they had acquired Austria, Styria, Carinthia, Tyrol, Artois, Luxembourg, the Netherlands, and Burgundy east of the Saone, as well as claims to the crowns of Hungary and Bohemia, and – on the accession of Charles – the Spanish kingdoms together with their dependencies Sicily, Naples and Sardinia, and the New World conquests. The Habsburg were well known for accumulating their lands more often by marriage and inheritance than by conquest. *Bella gerant alii, tu, felix Austria, nube*: so ran the contemporary saying: 'let others wage war, you, fortunate Austria, marry'. They had not yet done with marrying. Charles married the Infanta of Portugal which accordingly fell into the Habsburg net in the next generation. Charles's son, Philip II, married Mary Tudor, queen of England, but the son who was to unite England and Spain was never born.

Charles was conscientious, intelligent and capable of learning by experience. At seventeen, when he first came to Spain, he freely distributed the greatest positions in the country among his friends from the Netherlands. He levied taxes without consent of the *Cortes* (the Spanish regional parliaments) and thereby provoked a revolt of the smaller gentry and independent townsfolk of Castile – the *Comuneros* (1520–21). Led by Juan de Padilla, a man of vision and courage, they were supported by some of the nobility and clergy and at least one bishop. But they were defeated by faction within, and Juan de Padilla was executed.

The young Charles learnt wisdom: he proclaimed an amnesty and promoted no more foreigners to high office. In the meantime, through the death of his grandfather the emperor Maximilian in 1519, he had inherited the German possessions of his family. These foreign connections were never popular in Spain, though Charles himself came to love Spain best of all his dominions. His Flemish followers, so much disliked, brought with them artists and crafts-men who greatly enriched Spanish culture. They taught their highly developed methods of weaving tapestry. More significantly they brought Spanish music into the main stream of the Renaissance: the Flemish master Josquin Desprez was probably the greatest musician in Europe. His influence made possible the flowering of Spanish counterpoint, Tomas Luis de Victoria ranking with Palestrina among the outstanding masters of the sixteenth century. Above all they brought the influence of their unique school of painting: their technique in oils, their sensitivity to the colour and detail of everyday things, their direct portraiture and their un-idealized human treatment of the great religious themes – the qualities associated with Van Eyck, Memlinc and Rogier van den Weyden. These contributed, through time and assimilation, to the very different vision of Zurbaran and Velasquez.

Charles regarded his great power in the Old World and the New as divinely-ordained for bringing peace and unity to mankind. As king of Spain he welcomed at Seville the survivors of Magellan's circumnavigation, and confirmed Hernan Cortés as governor of

Mexico. As emperor and duke of Burgundy he wished all his subjects to profit by the great discoveries. He ordered the treasures of the Aztecs to be exhibited in Bruges where thousands of eager visitors gazed at them, among whom was Albrecht Dürer, the most famous artist in the north. The banking house of the Welser received the king's authority to finance projects in the New World. They recruited German miners to work in San Domingo, and their agents established a colony in Venezuela although their commission was revoked subsequently owing to the ill treatment of the natives. From this colony, Nicholas Federmann led an expedition into the Andes which, after great feats of endurance, reached Bogota, only to find that Spanish competitors were there before them. The distant emperor-king could not control the rivalry of his subjects; the beginnings of German enterprise in the New World shrivelled away partly through the hostility of the Spaniards, partly because Germany became the centre of a crisis which absorbed the resources and deflected the politics of western Europe for the next century – the Reformation.

IV

A kind of stability had been restored to the Roman Church in 1447 when the multiplicity of Popes ended with the election of Nicolas V, a respected scholar who founded the Vatican library and made his court a centre of learning. His successors for the next sixty years were chiefly concerned with increasing their worldly power and advancing the careers of their relations. Pius II (1458–1464) was an exception: although he sometimes bestowed favours on his poor relations, he was also a humane scholar who did not hesitate to reprove Cardinal Borgia for his immoral conduct, strove heroically to unite Christendom against the Turks, and died worn out by the impossible task.

At the other end of the scale was the outrageous Alexander VI (1492–1503), the Borgia Pope. But his scandalous way of life interfered neither with his encouragement of the arts nor his constructive planning. At the time of the great maritime discoveries, he was prompt to send Christian missionaries to the New World, and even to the Eskimos. He also settled the rivalry of Spain and Portugal by his famous division of the new discoveries into separate spheres of influence. After his death his bastard, the adventurer Cesare Borgia was used by Nicolo Machiavelli as the model for his book *Il Principe* – a work which analyses political power with extraordinary penetration and has been applauded and condemned with almost equal vehemence.

Alexander's successor, the forceful Julius II (1503–1513) consolidated the territorial power of the Papacy in Italy by diplomacy and war, while his discriminating patronage established Rome as the artistic capital of Italy. Leo X, an amiable and cultured scion of the Medici family who followed him, sustained the artistic heritage but had no head for politics.

This was the culminating epoch of the Renaissance when papal Rome was the magnet for architects, painters and sculptors – the cultural capital of the West as it had been under Augustus and the Antonines. Michelangelo painted the Sistine ceiling for Julius II and Raphael began for him, and completed for Leo X, the *Stanze* of the Vatican – surely the most beautiful state apartments in the world. For these things posterity owes an incalculable debt to the Popes of the High Renaissance. But they did not improve the spiritual image of the Vicar of Christ on earth. The massive rebuilding of St Peter's, to make it a worthy monument to the Prince of the Apostles and the centre of Catholic Christendom, cost fabulous sums, largely paid for by the sale of indulgences.

The glory of Renaissance Rome brought inspiration and delight to lovers of beauty and to the Italian populace with their natural response to colour and splendour. Although among the thousands of pilgrims who came from beyond the Alps some were impressed, others were shocked by the worldly wealth, the pagan works of art and the multitude of whores in a city sanctified by the blood of the martyrs. Most of all they resented the hypocrisy and rapacity of those involved in the pilgrimage business, including the officials of the Vatican. Among the disgusted was the German monk, Martin Luther.

The connection between Renaissance and Reformation has been variously interpreted and was perhaps accidental rather than organic. The Reformation was not the sole outcome of greater learning or of that spirit of enquiry nourished by the re-discovery of Greek science and philosophy; most prominent scholars remained true to the Catholic Church. Rather it was the outcome of generations of disquiet among thinking Christians at the barriers which tradition, theology and the hierarchies of the Church had inter-posed between them and the direct message of the Gospel. Reform-ing movements had existed for the past thousand years, but they were strengthened in the sixteenth century by the growing self-consciousness of European peoples.

The Renaissance belonged essentially to Italy, and to Latin Europe where humanism was nourished by contact with Byzantium in the last century of its existence, and by the study of the classical past when Rome had learnt from Greece and created a common culture. The Reformation came from outside Italy, from peoples who had little part in the inheritance of Greece and Rome. It came from England, Bohemia, North Germany, Scandinavia, Switzer-land and northern France. The religious and moral protest was long overdue as most serious-minded Catholics were aware; but it was the sense of individual and national outrage at the flouting of morals and the assumption of superiority by a Vicar of Christ who was also a foreign potentate, that animated the forces of revolt. A century later the English philosopher, Thomas Hobbes, would describe the Catholic Church as 'nothing but the ghost of the old Roman Empire sitting crowned on the grave thereof'. He expressed an idea which pervaded the northern Reformation.

The movement for reform *within* the Church was largely intel-lectual, expressed by exponents of classical learning – such as Pico della Mirandola, who wrote a discourse on the Dignity of Man; the Spanish educationalist Juan Luis Vives; the German Hebraist Johann Reuchlin who defended the study of the Jewish Scriptures against ignorant attack; the outstanding Greek scholar Lefebvre d'Etaples and greatest among them Erasmus of Rotterdam. He was famous among the learned for his critical edition of the Gospels in Greek, and popular with a wider public for that high-spirited satirical pamphlet, *In Praise of Folly*, in which he mocked the vices of Church and society. This he dedicated to another critical thinker, his English friend Thomas More who later wrote *Utopia* and later still became Lord Chancellor of England. These were men of study and moderation, critical of the Church but opposed to violent change and faithful to Catholic doctrine – a fidelity which Thomas More later sealed with his blood.

The most dynamic reformer in Italy, Girolamo Savonarola, a Dominican monk from Ferrara, was destroyed by a charge of heresy. This austere fanatic denounced the corruption of the Florentines, exhorted them to abandon luxury for the sake of their immortal souls, and to alleviate the wants of their fellow citizens. In the distresses which engulfed the city after the death of Lorenzo the Magnificent and the invasion of the French king Charles VIII, Savonarola was carried to power on a surge of popular feeling (1495). He was an eloquent visionary with no gift at all for policy or government, but for a time his fervent preaching inspired a kind of Christian democracy. Even the judicious historian Guicciardini was impressed: 'There never was in Florence such goodness and religion as in his time'.[6] The poor were fed and clothed, gambling and excess in food and drink forbidden, brothels closed. Pornographic books, false hair, cosmetics, useless adornments and profane pictures were publicly burnt; even that most sensitive painter Botticelli appears to have sacrificed some of his work on the bonfire but the tradition which credits Savonarola with destroying innumerable master-pieces is much exaggerated.

Savonarola could not create employment or sustain the hungry for long in a city crowded with peasant refugees from a war-stricken countryside. His enemies (chief among them the Borgia Pope whom he had denounced) overthrew his Christian republic and Savonar-ola went to the stake (1498).

Only in Spain was the Church reformed *from within* and secured against the coming storm by the ascetic Franciscan monk who in 1495 became archbishop of Toledo. Cardinal Ximenes attacked corruption at the root by absolutely prohibiting the sale of benefices and compelling the clergy to live in their parishes and instruct the people in the meaning of the Gospel at every celebration of the mass. He fought clerical and popular ignorance through the printing press by authorizing cheap and simple devotional works – possibly the earliest popular and propagandist use of the press. He encouraged higher studies by founding the University of Alcala and issuing the first polyglot Bible in Greek, Latin, Hebrew and Ara-maic.

His reforms had a dark side. The Spanish Church was indissolu-bly linked with the fight against the Moors, a crusade which had given it a privileged independence of Rome. Thus that great engine against heresy, the Inquisition, was in Spain under direct royal control, with officers appointed by the king. It was, strangely enough, the only truly *national* institution in Spain, because the various independent states which had been united by Ferdinand and Isabella retained their individual *Cortes* or Parliaments and often their own law. Only the Inquisition was the same everywhere. It had been introduced in 1478 to deal with the essentially Spanish problem of false converts – the hundreds of Muslims and Jews who, as the Christian re-conquest neared completion, had accepted baptism while still secretly practising their own faith. These were to be systematically detected and eliminated by means of informers, torture and the stake. The number of these *conversos* was immensely increased by Ferdinand and Isabella, who compelled all remaining Jews to choose between conversion and exile. About 170,000 chose exile and were wise to do so: those who remained were never free from fear of denunciation as false converts. A considerable number of the Moors of Granada also left the country, but far more stayed in the land they knew. Most of the so-called Moors in Spain were in truth almost wholly Spanish through centuries of intermarriage. These *Moriscoes* were, like the Jews, first forcibly converted, and then for generations exposed to persecution. The Spanish ideal was purity of faith and purity of blood. The first was, possibly, attainable: the second – *limpieza* – was an early and tragic example of racialist nonsense, since long periods of tolerant coexistence in the past had left a very mixed population in all ranks of society.

After the accession of Charles, the progress of the Inquisition was briefly checked. The young king brought with him friends and scholars from the Netherlands who had felt the humanizing influence of Erasmus, and were now appointed to chairs at Spanish universities. The thaw lasted barely a decade; the spread of the Reformation in Germany was the signal for the Inquisitors in Spain to tighten their pressure into a stranglehold on the intellectual life of the nation. One thing was gained – and much boasted of – Spain was spared the wars of religion which ravaged other countries for the next hundred years, but the price was too high.

In October 1517 Martin Luther, an Augustinian monk and professor of theology at the newly founded University of Wittenberg in Saxony, attacked the sale of indulgences, those paper certificates which deceived the ignorant into believing they could shorten their time in Purgatory without doing penance on earth. The controversy spread: Luther defended his position in writing and in debate with fervent sincerity and increasing confidence. He denounced corruption and hypocrisy, the common vices of priests and monks, and defended his opinions from the Scriptures. Like John Hus, he claimed that the Bible was a higher authority than the Church, and stood by this opinion though Hus had been burnt for it.

Luther was thirty-four, the son of a master-miner, with a restless, questioning intellect and a thirst for truth. As a monk he had wrestled with the demons of the flesh and the spirit and had been brought back from the brink of despair by the conviction that man is saved by faith alone: faith in the saving grace of Christ. For him the worldly Church, with its dishonest indulgences and hypocrite priests was a barrier between God and man. He was a powerful preacher, forthright and persuasive, with a coarse pungent humour and an impetuous earnestness that often exploded into invective. He wrote as strongly as he spoke, with the same fast-flowing vehemence; his printed pamphlets, his sermons and the reports of his debates with other theologians soon made him known far beyond Wittenberg.

The Pope, Leo X – far off and probably contemptuous of a provincial monk in Germany – was very slow to act. When at last he issued a bull (*Exsurge Domine*) condemning Luther's opinions, the fearless heretic burnt it in public before an applauding crowd (December 1520).

King Charles of Spain had by now returned to Germany to claim the imperial title left vacant by his grandfather's death. After the usual bribes and promises to the prince-electors, he was duly chosen and crowned in Charlemagne's cathedral at Aachen. Henceforward he became the emperor Charles V. Luther hailed him with joy in a pamphlet addressed *To the Christian Nobility of Germany*. In this he denounced the Church for failing to reform itself and called on the state to take the reformation on itself since 'God has given us a young and noble ruler . . . and has awakened our hearts once more to hope'.

Disillusion followed. Charles called the general assembly of the German states, the diet, to Worms and summoned Luther to defend his opinions before it. He spoke out courageously concluding with his famous words which have been simplified but not falsified by tradition: 'Here I stand. I can do no other; God help me, amen'. But Charles was no less committed than Luther to his duty as he saw it: he too could do no other. 'Ye know,' he said to the assembled delegates, 'that I am born of the most Christian Emperors of the noble German nation, who were all to the death defenders of the Catholic faith . . . It is certain that a single monk must err if he stands against the opinion of all Christendom . . . therefore I am determined to set my Kingdoms, my friends, my body, my blood, my life, my soul upon it . . .'

So the diet condemned the opinions of Luther, who disappeared on his way home from Worms and was widely rumoured to have been murdered. Albrecht Dürer passionately appealed to Erasmus to speak out and lead the reform himself if Luther was indeed dead. But Erasmus shrank from conflict and remained silent. Meantime Luther was safe and secret, protected by his most powerful patron, the elector of Saxony, in the fortress of the Wartburg, working day and night on his translation of the Bible.

The western Church had weathered many storms which had seemed more dangerous than this. But conditions were no longer favourable to its authority. Medieval society based on accepted degrees of rank and held together by mutual obligations, by rights and duties, had changed gradually with the expansion of opportunities and the growth of commerce, into a society based on the exchange of labour, services and goods for money. Enterprising landowners, from the nobility and the Church downwards, aimed to raise more from their land than a reasonable subsistence; they increased their revenues by the sale of wine, wool, grain, meat, timber, or the more specialized and profitable enterprises of the quarry and the mine. Traditional methods vanished, customary privileges were modified. The serf became the paid labourer; the successful landowner invested his surplus in more profitable enterprises, in manufacture or trade, so that his wealth was no longer based on the acres which gave him his feudal title and his position in society. The poor landowner, the knight, with his small castle, large family and high opinion of his honour, grew poorer, angrier, more desperate. The feudal levies in which they had once been essential were no longer needed. As early as the fourteenth century, kings and independent cities had strengthened such forces by hiring professional soldiers. Gradually mercenaries took over: Swiss, Genoese, Germans, Catalan, even – for a time – the famous Albanian light cavalry.

Political power was increasingly dependent on money (or credit) for the hiring of troops. The Medici who became rulers of Florence were bankers to the Vatican. In France, Jacques Coeur, a merchant-prince of Bourges, his fortune based on trade with the Middle East, sustained and later re-organized the finances of the French crown. Genoese bankers financed the Spanish government, for a large return in American silver; the Fugger and the Welser (both Augsburg firms) financed the Habsburg in Germany in return for mining concessions in Bohemia, tax-exemption and other privileges.

As kings increased their debts (and the rates of interest were very high), taxation grew heavier. The burden fell on those least able to pay, because the higher nobility, who could be dangerous, were usually exempt. Poor knights took to banditry: the *Raubritter*, the robber knights of Germany, had their equivalents in many parts of Europe; Spanish knights – more fortunate – robbed and looted the New World. In other countries they became mercenaries, or failing that, lived by their wits: Shakespeare's Falstaff was just such a victim of social change, so was Götz von Berlichingen whose confused career inspired Goethe.

Peasants, small craftsmen, artisans, day labourers were worse off, having even less resources when faced by new poll taxes, rising demands for tolls on road and river transport, market dues and all the different ways in which payment in cash had replaced the old system of payment in service (which in some cases was also exacted). Peasant revolts were frequent, and were often joined by oppressed craftsmen from the towns and led by impoverished knights. Germany saw two serious revolts within twenty years. In Hungary an army recruited for defence against the Turks faced about under its knightly commander, George Dozsa, to lead a massive rising of peasants. These revolts invariably ended in defeat and mass executions. In bad times the poor, in both town and country, often nourished a festering venom against the rich, against fat monks and priests, lawyers, tax-collectors, merchants and moneylenders.

The Swiss Confederation – its three original members now grown to thirteen – was almost destroyed by the tension between the mercantile rulers of Zurich, Berne and Basle, and the free peasants of the rural cantons, whence came the best soldiers in Europe. Swiss mercenaries made a living, but the profits of their trade went to the city entrepreneurs who recruited them and organized contracts with foreign governments. Yet in spite of much ill-feeling, the poor cantons united with the rich in face of a common threat to their independence, and when the overweening duke of Burgundy attacked them, they destroyed him utterly (1477–8). Swiss mercenaries being even more in demand after their victories, the most unscrupulous of the entrepreneurs, Hans Waldmann, became rich enough to establish a dictatorship in Zurich for several years until overthrown and executed in a popular revolt (1489). It was in Zurich too, a restless, active centre, that a generation later a popular preacher, Zwingli, began independently of Luther to preach reform.

Social, intellectual, economic and moral forces stimulated religious revolt; but the force which enabled the Reformers to split Europe into opposing camps within a single generation, was a technical invention: the printing press. Once established, the new technique spread rapidly; no less than 40,000 editions of books are recorded before the end of the century.

Printing made the wisdom, learning and wit of Erasmus well-known in all the universities and to all educated men. Printing made Luther's writings famous outside Wittenberg, famous or infamous over all Germany, over all Europe. Printing made the outrageous humour of Rabelais – a renegade monk – a part of French literature. The printing press was the powerful, new and far from secret weapon which ensured the success of the Reformation.

Yet it looked at first as though the reforming movement would be destroyed by its own excesses. Sects began to multiply: many were sincere and sober reformers but there were also fanatic visionaries and iconoclasts. The numerous groups who rejected infant baptism were lumped together under the name of Anabaptists, but there were many different kinds of these small reformed congregations; some were quietists given only to vision and prayer, most believed in a close communal life, some opposed war or killing in all forms, others again, mingling an apocalyptic belief in the end of the world with a passionate anger against injustice, became a revolutionary force. When the poor knights of the Rhineland rose in revolt and appealed to Luther to support them they seized the lands of the Church with some idea of making all land common, but their ill-managed revolt collapsed within weeks. Far more serious was the Peasants' War which gathered momentum in South and West Germany. Huge bands of peasants, craftsmen and artisans, strengthened by footloose mercenaries and the fugitive knights, led sometimes by renegade priests and monks, swarmed across the country some in reasonably good order, but most looting and burning and inflicting atrocities. Two great artists may briefly have joined them: Tilman Riemenschneider of Würzburg, the greatest sculptor in Germany, and Matthias Grünewald, whose *Crucifixion* (the Isenheim altarpiece) is the most intensely realized representation of physical suffering in European art before Goya. One of the leaders, Thomas Münzer, a man of powerful eloquence, and a heartfelt concern for the peasants, preached death to all lawyers and churchmen.

When the insurgents invoked the name of Luther and called for his support, Luther was appalled. In all spheres save that of religion, he was deeply conservative and respectful of authority. Shaken by atrocity stories, all of which he believed, and especially embarrassed by the alleged excesses of Münzer who had once been his disciple, he condemned the insurgents in the most violent terms. No single note of compassion or understanding softened the fury of his attack. In the changing perspective of time, and especially in the present century, nothing has done more harm to his reputation than the bitterness of his attack on the peasants. The revolt, like all its predecessors, ended in defeat, and would have done so, whatever side Luther had taken, but this does not exonerate him from a failure in humanity.

Luther's break with Rome was by now absolute. He married one of his congregation, his Katie – 'mein Kätchen' – a runaway nun, imperturbable and wholly admirable as wife, mother and housekeeper, the prototype of the Protestant pastor's wife, as Luther in his later and calmer years became the prototype of the Protestant pastor. He worked out, with the help of a brilliant theologian Philip Melancthon, a new liturgy in the vernacular, and continued to pour out a stream of letters, pamphlets and sermons as well as hymns which, set to familiar tunes of the day, achieved great popularity. His church spread and prospered under the protection of the elector John Frederick of Saxony. John Frederick's religious sincerity is not in doubt, though of course it was convenient for a prince to have a domestic church under his own control without interference from a foreign Pope. Other German princes and German cities moved in the same direction, the rulers of Hesse and Brunswick, the towns of Nuremberg, Ulm, Augsburg, Strassbourg, Magdeburg. Only when Albert of Hohenzollern, the Grand Master of the Teutonic Knights, declared his conversion, took over the lands of the order and made himself duke of Prussia, was there considerable doubt as to the purity of his motives.

At an imperial diet in 1529 the Lutheran states formally protested against the enforcement of an edict against religious innovations, and were henceforward commonly called 'Protestants'. A year later, at a diet over which Charles V presided in Augsburg, Philip Melancthon presented the authoritative statement of the Lutheran position, which is known as the Confession of Augsburg. Charles rejected it; the Protestant states responded by forming a defensive league, a move which was soon answered by an opposing Catholic group. The emperor was, however, prevented from making war on the Lutheran princes because, among his many other troubles, was a recurrent war with the king of France. The unscrupulous Francis I already had an alliance with the Turks and would undoubtedly support the Protestants if it suited him. Charles therefore worked to break up the Lutherans by diplomacy and in due course won over Maurice of Saxony, head of a junior branch of the Saxon dynasty and deeply jealous of the elector, the protector of Luther. This, and the death of the king of France, enabled Charles to collect his forces and overthrow the Protestants at the battle of Mühlberg in 1547.

But Lutheranism was too deeply rooted to wilt after a single defeat, and Maurice (now raised to the rank of elector) cynically abandoned the emperor and exercised his Machiavellian talent in rebuilding the Protestant front. Charles, deeply in debt through the expenses of the war, could extract no further loan from the Fuggers, but was narrowly saved from disaster by the death of Maurice in battle. Further warfare was financially impossible, and the emperor authorized his brother Ferdinand to make a compromise peace, German rulers should have the right to decide the religion of their subjects, and subjects be free to move elsewhere if they did not agree. This settlement (the Peace of Augsburg, 1555) prevented a civil war for over sixty years, which was more than anyone expected.

Meanwhile the Reformation advanced in northern Europe. In Sweden, a strong-willed young nobleman, Gustavus Vasa threw off the incompetent tyranny of Denmark, and re-established the independence of Sweden. Finding useful allies in the Swedish reformers, Olaf and Laurence Petri, he repudiated Rome, created a national

Lutheran Church with Olaf as his archbishop (Laurence was busy translating the Bible), and persuaded the clergy to resign their property 'voluntarily' to the crown. Thus enriched, Gustavus overcame the Hanseatic cities and made Sweden the greatest power in the Baltic. A more complex sequence of events in Denmark also led to the establishment of a Lutheran Church subservient to the crown.

In England King Henry VIII had succeeded to the throne secured by his father Henry VII, the first of the Tudor dynasty. His claim was slight but after the deaths and murders of the various claimants during the Wars of the Roses there was no better candidate, and he proved a wise ruler.

His son and successor was a bolder, but not a wiser, man. He rejected the authority of the Pope and sent his Spanish wife away because he needed a male heir but could not gain from the Vatican the annulment of his marriage. The Reform movement in England had long been underground and the Anglican Church, thus removed from papal jurisdiction, was not Lutheran: under the gentle guidance of Archbishop Cranmer its liturgy, ceremonies and ecclesiastical hierarchy changed but little. This would lead in time to serious trouble from more radical reformers, but in the meantime Henry dissolved the monasteries and used their large estates to bribe the powerful and create a new rich ruling class.

In Switzerland the division of religion followed the division of the cantons: the rural cantons remained Catholic; reform flourished in the cities. The first dominant reformer was Huldrych Zwingli of Zurich. Like Luther he came of tough hard-working people, the son of a peasant; he had also served for a time as a chaplain of mercenaries and was used to the sounds and dangers of war. Preaching in the cathedral of Zurich he denounced the corruption of the Church. For him, as for Luther, what mattered was study of the Bible and the direct relationship of man and God, but he went beyond Luther in denouncing all ceremonies, images and outward symbols. Within a few years he had abolished the mass and introduced his own liturgy in Zurich. Basle followed the example under reformers of its own. Zwingli, as a soldier of Christ, was resolved to compel the stubbornly Catholic forest cantons to abandon their faith; he led his people into battle but was defeated and killed. His successor in Zurich, Heinrich Bullinger, was a man of peace who sensibly left the Catholic cantons alone.

The most influential reformer in Switzerland was John Calvin, by origin the son of a lawyer in a provincial town of northern France. His was a clearer intellect than Luther's, a colder nature, little subject to ordinary human temptations. His intellectual passion for truth and his study of the Scriptures convinced him that God's omnipotence was the essential article of faith. Hence he emphasized the helplessness of man who cannot be saved by any action of his own but only by the grace of God. This relentlessly logical doctrine embodied in his *Institutes of the Christian Religion* (1536) was the most influential single work of the Reformation. He created at Geneva a theocratic state, which became a centre of Calvinist theology and a model for other Calvinist societies. Unlike the Lutherans, the Calvinists were not content to depend on the state; their ministers claimed powers of admonition and advice which put them above the secular rulers. Hence Calvinism was a disruptive force in France, Scotland and the Netherlands. In Poland, Hungary and Bohemia it acquired a nationalist and anti-German character. In Germany itself the most important prince to be converted, the elector Frederick III of the Palatinate, seems to have worked out a fairly successful partnership with his pastors; Heidelberg, his capital and the seat of an ancient university, was second only to Geneva as a centre of Calvinist theology.

Over all Germany, over all Europe (except Spain and southern Italy) fringe movements sprang up. Almost irretrievable harm was done to the Anabaptist reputation by the excesses of the monomaniac John of Leiden who made himself dictator of the town of Munster, decreed community of property and women, burnt all books except the Bible and executed everyone who opposed him. When this burst of madness was crushed the movement went underground, to emerge later in close-knit, puritanical, highly respectable communities in the Netherlands, England and ultimately America, the forefathers of the Baptists of today.

Meanwhile the Scriptures, once locked away from all but the learned, in Greek, Latin and Hebrew, were translated into the languages of common speech. Luther's German translation was completed in 1534 and reprinted 377 times before his death twelve years later. English and French texts appeared soon after, a Danish version as early as 1529, Swedish, Polish, Finnish and Hungarian versions in the 1540s, Icelandic, Welsh and Czech in the 1580s.

In Germany and the Scandinavian countries these translations laid the foundation of the modern language by creating an accepted common usage, above local dialects; the language of the Bible thus became a unifying force in the nation. The contents of the Bible, on the other hand, were not a unifying force. As it was now open to anyone who could read to interpret the Scriptures in his own way, the age became fertile in sects and heresies. In ensuing centuries, even men of judgement and goodwill deplored the effects of giving the Bible to the people. What lunatic enthusiasms, what fatuous misinterpretations would henceforward flourish . . . The risk had to be taken, as it still has to be taken in other spheres, if freedom of thought is to survive.

V

All this time the Ottoman Turks under a series of able sultans were still advancing. Since the fall of Constantinople they had conquered Greece, most of the Balkans and the shores of the Black Sea, driven the Venetians from their outposts in Dalmatia and Albania, successfully raided the Venetian mainland, for a time occupied Otranto and threatened to close the Adriatic. They defeated the Persians, taking Baghdad and Tabriz, and established their suzerainty over Syria and Arabia. Sultan Selim the Grim conquered the North African coast as far as Tunis, dethroned the last Mamluk sultan of Egypt in 1517 and hanged him before the principal gate of Cairo. The Venetians, after two long wars, held on to Cyprus and Crete with difficulty and made a treaty with the Turks to safeguard their trading rights. The eastern trade through the Mediterranean was already declining, not on account of the Turks – they were too astute to sacrifice commercial profit – but because the Portuguese had opened a direct sea-route to India.

Sultan Suleiman the Magnificent, son and successor of Selim the Grim, renewed the war in Europe, captured Belgrade, wiped out the Hungarian army at the catastrophic battle of Mohacs (1526) and threatened Vienna. When the wave receded, only the extreme west of Hungary was left under Christian rule. Charles V recognized his younger brother Ferdinand as king over this remnant, but he had to buy exemption from further Turkish attack by paying tribute for it.

The Ottoman sultans at the height of their power had good advisers, many of them from their conquered subjects: Suleiman's admirable vizier Ibrahim Pasha was a converted Greek. It was one of the advantages of Nomadic conquerors that they had few or no administrators of their own and consequently used the abilities of the conquered. The Hungarian nobles kept their estates but had to pay an annual tribute which in turn they exacted from their peasants. Jews and Christians (of whatever persuasion) were tolerated, but taxed. As Muslims were exempt from taxation it was not in the interest of the government to convert their tax-paying subjects.

The army was recruited indiscriminately from Slavs and Greeks, Albanians, Armenians and Latins. But there was one regiment, the Janissaries, for which promising Christian boys were selected at regular intervals and removed from their homes for training. These were the finest soldiers of the Ottoman army, chosen for their strength and fitness, and carefully educated for their profession. Yet, like the Pretorian Guard in Rome, or the Mamlukes in Egypt, the Janissaries too could become a danger to the state under a weak ruler.

Suleiman was equally successful at sea. Rhodes fell in 1522 after a heroic defence by the Knights of St John (the Hospitallers who then moved to Malta). A Greek pirate from Mitylene, Chaireddin Barbarossa, made himself ruler of Tunis and, in alliance with the sultan, preyed on Christian shipping. Charles V, as king of Spain, Naples and Sicily had a direct interest in checking Barbarossa and, in 1535, with the support of Portugal and the Genoese, he successfully captured Tunis. It was not a lasting victory, for the defence of the seas against the Turk could never be effective while the rivalry of the Genoese and the Venetians persisted. (Even the alliance between them, which was achieved in 1570 and resulted in the destruction of a gigantic Turkish fleet at Lepanto, lasted for only a year. Nor did this much celebrated battle have any lasting effect; the Turks rebuilt their fleet within months.) But while Spain, Portugal and Genoa were prepared to act in unison, the western Mediterranean could not be dominated by the Turks, even from their strongholds in North Africa.

The Turks and the Protestants were only two of the major problems which troubled Charles V. The third serious problem was the king of France with whom he was almost continuously at war. The rivalry between the major powers of France and Spain was a permanent factor of European politics from the end of the fifteenth to the end of the seventeenth century. The immediate causes of war were questions of dynastic inheritance: the basic cause was jealousy and fear.

The kingdom of Sicily and Naples ('the two Sicilies') which had long been ruled by a junior branch of the French royal house, had passed to Spain through a disputed succession at the end of the fifteenth century. Two kings of France, Charles VIII and Louis XII, invaded Italy: Charles briefly occupied Florence and Naples, Louis – no less briefly – occupied Naples and some years later seized and again lost Milan. Both caused devastation in Italy, and both in the end had to withdraw.

Francis I, who married Louis's daughter – heiress of Britanny – and succeeded to the throne in 1515, was young, vain and irresponsible. But much can be forgiven him for his generous patronage of the arts. He invited Leonardo to Paris (where he died) and employed as his librarian the Greek scholar Guillaume Budé, who founded the Collège de France and built up what was to become the Bibliothèque Nationale. Francis and his sister Marguerite de Navarre were the centre of a lively and cultured court.

Undeterred by the unsuccessful Italian ventures of his predecessors, he launched a new invasion in the first year of his reign, was victorious at Marignano and occupied Milan. Charles V inherited the quarrel when he became king of Spain. In 1525 he defeated Francis at Pavia and took him prisoner. *Tout est perdu, fors l'honneur* – 'All is lost, save honour' – wrote Francis, in typically dramatic vein. The peace which was subsequently agreed involved his withdrawal from Italy and other concessions, all of which he repudiated as soon as he was free in spite of the fact that his two young sons were hostages for his good faith. Five more wars followed, four with Francis, and one with his successor, before a lasting peace was made.

This incessant strife between Europe's two greatest rulers was an added incentive to Turkish attack. Their advance into Hungary which culminated in their victory at Mohacs coincided with Charles's success at Pavia. A disaster of a different kind, the Sack of Rome, was another by-product of the same war. In 1527 the emperor's troops in Italy (many of them mercenaries) under the command of a renegade French nobleman, Charles de Bourbon, mutinied for lack of pay, and compelled their leaders to march on

Rome. Being northerners, though Catholics, most of them equated the city with luxury and vice: they took it by storm on 5 May 1527 and stayed to plunder it during a whole long, dreadful summer.

The shattered city recovered slowly but it would never again be the centre of so glorious a culture as that which reached its fullest expression on the eve of the catastrophe. Great painters and great architects were rarely born in Rome but Rome was the goal of the greatest. It was in Rome that Raphael, born in provincial Urbino, so magnificently fulfilled his youthful promise. It was in Rome that Michelangelo created some of his greatest works. It was for the Sistine Chapel that Perugino, Pinturicchio, Botticelli, Ghirlandaio, Signorelli put forth their greatest efforts.

The Sack of Rome ended an epoch, as no previous sack had done. The barbarian conquests had been only incidents in a long decline. This was something different: a shock which destroyed the illusions of patrons, poets and painters and gave the strongest impetus to Catholic reform. Paul III (1534–49) the first Pope to be elected after the sack was like many of his predecessors, a worldly man of a princely family, the Farnese, but he recognized the need for change. He set up a commission to study Church reform, and in 1540 authorized a new order, the Society of Jesus. Founded by a Basque soldier, Ignatius Loyola, and organized on military lines, the Jesuits became the spiritual shock troops of the Catholic counter-attack in Europe. Five years later Paul III opened the Council of Trent which, over a long period and after many interruptions, reformed and restored the Catholic Church.

Worn out by unremitting anxiety and hard work, Charles V abdicated in 1555 in Brussels, in his native land, in the great hall where he had been declared of age forty years before. Speaking for the last time before a public assembly he told them very simply of his hopes, his efforts and his failures. He had striven to bring peace and unity to Christendom; he had failed and could do no more; God only could give or withhold success. He had made mistakes out of weakness or self-will, but he had never intentionally wronged any man . . . At his words the huge audience wept; the emperor wept.[7] He was perhaps the only prince in Europe who could sincerely claim that he had never intentionally wronged any man. He was the most honourable, the least devious of contemporary rulers, and the most persistently hard-working. He was a conscientious ruler, not a great one; he had failed to solve – indeed failed to understand – the religious quarrels that divided Europe. His best services, in the end, had been given to Spain, the land of his adoption which he had come to love more than the land of his birth and to which he was now returning to die.

He left the Netherlands, Spain and his Italian lands to his only legitimate son, Philip II. He had already bestowed Austria and the Habsburg lands in the empire on his brother Ferdinand, in whose family they remained together with the imperial title. Charles himself withdrew to Spain to live quietly, in a villa built for the purpose adjoining the monastery of San Jeronimo de Yuste. He continued to receive information and offer advice on public affairs, and must have drawn satisfaction from the successful conclusion of the last war with France a few months before he died in September 1558.

He had found time in his burdened life to enjoy more subtle pleasures than the hunting and jousting of his youth. Music was his chief delight, but he had been a generous patron of art. As a young man, he had invited Albrecht Dürer to dine at the imperial table, and in his later years made Titian his court painter. It was Titian who painted the great altar-piece which Charles took with him to San Jeronimo and which now hangs in the Prado in Madrid – *La Gloria*. Here the emperor with his wife and son, kneel on clouds among the blessed in eternal adoration of the Trinity. Titian thus celebrated the belief which Charles held in common with other devout rulers, both Catholic and Protestant: that the king is God's chosen instrument for the sacred trust of government. Should he prove unworthy of the trust, God would punish him; if worthy, he would be high in heaven as he had been on earth. *La Gloria* is the Divine Right of kings made visible.

So the planet went on its course through space, revolving towards the sun, away from the sun, day and night, night and day, year in, year out, with perhaps a few hundred million people on board, most of them concerned only with the struggle for existence. It was a long way from one world.

NOTES

Chapter I

1. Thomas Hobbes, *Leviathan*, Part ‚I, Chapter XIII.
2. Ibn Khaldun, *The Muqaddamah*, translated by Franz Rosenthal, Routledge, 1958, II, p. 271.
3. Jacquetta Hawkes, *The Atlas of Early Man*, Macmillan, London, 1976, pp. 42–45.
4. *The Epic of Gilgamesh*, translated by N. Sandars, London, Penguin Books, 1965, p. 91.
5. James Baikie, *The Amarna Age*, A. & C. Black, London, 1926, pp. 324–5.

Chapter II

1. A. L. Bashan, *The Wonder that was India*, London, 1954, p. 162.
2. Ibid., p. 248.
3. *The Baghavadgita*, II, 20–21; XVI, 21, translated by R. C. Zaehner, Oxford, 1969.
4. F. L. Lucas, *Greek Poetry for Everyman*, London, 1951, pp. 202–3.
5. Ibid., p. 246.
6. E. O. James, *Comparative Religion*, revised ed. London, 1961, ppbk p. 32.
7. Maurice Collis, *The First Holy One*, London, 1948, p. 15.

Chapter III

1. Herodotus, *The Histories*, translated by Aubrey de Selincourt, Penguin Classics, 1954, p. 531.
2. Ibid., p. 401.
3. Thucydides, *The Peloponnesian War*, translated by Rex Warner, Penguin Classics, 1954, p. 135.
4. Plutarch, *The Rise and Fall of Athens, Nine Greek Lives*, translated by Ian Scott-Kilvert, Penguin Classics, London, 1960, p. 179.
5. *Ancient India as described by Megasthenes and Arrian*, translated by J. W. McCrindle, Calcutta, 1877.
6. *Anthology of Chinese Literature*, Penguin Classics, pp. 74–5.
7. Ibid., p. 139.

Chapter IV

1. C. H. Dodd, *The Founder of Christianity*, London, 1973, p. 5.
2. Martin Hengel, *Judaism and Hellenism*, SCM, 1974, especially Vol. I, pp. 153ff.
3. Pliny, *A Self-portrait in letters*, Folio Society, 1978, p. 242.

Chapter V

1. Homer H. Dubs, *A Roman City in Ancient China*, China Society Sinological Series, No. 5, London, 1957.
2. Cyril Birch and Donald Keene, ed. *Anthology of Chinese Literature*, Penguin Classics, 1967, p. 209.
3. Ibid., pp. 231, 225.
4. Ibid., p. 203.
5. Ibid., p. 208.
6. W. Scott Morton, *Japan its History and Culture*, Newton Abbot, 1973, p. 19.
7. L. Boubois, *The Silk Road*, translated by Dennis Chamberlin, Allen & Unwin, 1966, p. 62.
8. *Minor Latin Poets*, ed. Duff, Loeb

Classics, London, 1934, p. 445.

9. *The Last Poets of Imperial Rome*, translated by Harold Isbell, Penguin Books, 1971, pp. 224–5.

10. Gerhart B. Ladner, *Justinian's Theme of Law and the Renewal Ideology of the Leges Barbarum*, Proceedings of the Amer. Phil. Soc. Vol. 119, p. 193. Philadelphia, 1975.

11. A. Momigliano, *Cassiodorus and the Italian Culture of his Time*, Proceedings of the British Academy, 41. London, 1956, p. 225.

Chapter VI

1. Gibbon, *Decline and Fall*, Everyman Edition, Vol. IV, Chapter XL, p. 206.

2. Ibn Khaldun, *The Muquaddimah*, translated by F. Rosenthal, Routledge, 1958, I, pp. 80–1.

3. *The Koran*, translated by N. J. Dawood, Penguin Classics, revised edition, London, 1971, pp. 313–4.

4. Bernard Lewis, *The Arabs in History*, Hutchinson's University Library, London, 3rd edition, 1956.

5. Maurice Collis, *The First Holy One*, London, 1948, pp. 202–3.

6. *Buddhist Records of the Western World*, translated by Samuel Beal, London, 1884, Volume I, pp. 75–8.

7. Michael Sullivan, *A Short History of Chinese Art*, 1st edition, Faber, London, 1967, p. 166.

8. *Anthology of Chinese Literature*, ed. Cyril Birch, Penguin Classics, 1965.

9. Ibid., Tu Fu translated by Witter Bynner, pp. 257–8.

10. Ibid., Po Chü Yi, *A Song of Unending Sorrow*, translated by Witter Bynner, p. 282.

11. R. W. Southern, *Western Society and the Church in the Middle Ages*, Pelican History of the Church, Volume II, pp. 99, 32.

Chapter VII

1. *Anthology of Chinese Literature*, ed. Cyril Birch, Penguin Classics, 1965, p. 357.

2. Michael Sullivan, *A Short History of Chinese Art*, 1st edition, Faber, p. 195.

3. *The Pillow Book of Sei Shonagon*, translated and edited by Ivan Morris, Oxford University Press, 1967, section 151.

4. Ibid., sections 173, 174.

5. *The Alexiad of Anna Comnena*, translated by E. R. A. Sewter, Penguin Books, 1969, p. 308.

6. Fulcher of Chartres quoted in Hans Eberhard Mayer, *The Crusades*, translated by John Gillingham, Oxford University Press, ppbk, 1972, p. 85.

7. loc. cit.

8. Helen Waddell, *Mediaeval Latin Lyrics*, Constable, 1929, p. 166.

Chapter VIII

1. *The Mongol Mission. Letters of Franciscan Missionaries in Mongolia and China*, translated by a nun of Stanbrook Abbey, ed. Christopher Dawson, Sheed and Ward, London, 1955. See especially the Introduction by Christopher Dawson for an illuminating account of the Mongols.

2. R. W. Southern, *Western Society and the Church in the Middle Ages*, Pelican History of the Church, II, Penguin Books, 1970, p. 105.

3. Ibid., p. 146.

4. Evelyn Jamison, *The Norman Administration of Apulia and Papua 1127–1166*. Papers of the British School at Rome, Vol. VI, Macmillan, London, 1913.

5. *The History of St Louis* by Jean, Sire de Joinville, translated from the French text edited by Natalie de Wailly, by Joan Evans, Oxford University Press, 1938, p. 227.

6. *Scottish Historical Documents*, ed. Gordon Donaldson, Scottish Academic Press, Edinburgh and London, 1970, pp. 55–8.
7. *Travels of Ibn Battuta*, ed. H. A. R. Gibb, Hakluyt Society, 2nd Series, Vol. 117, Cambridge, 1962, p. 506.
8. Christopher Dawson, op. cit., pp. 225–7.
9. *Travels of Ibn Battuta*, ed. H. A. R. Gibb, Hakluyt Society, 2nd Series, Vol. 1, Cambridge, 1958, p. 18.
10. Ibid., Vol. 141, 1971, pp. 657–8, 694–6, 700, 707.

Chapter IX

1. J. B. Trend, *The Civilisation of Spain*, 2nd edition, Oxford, 1967, p. 46.
2. An English translation of one contemporary account, *The Overall Survey of the Ocean's Shores* (1433) edited by J. V. G. Mills is available in the publications of the Hakluyt Society, extra series XLII, Cambridge, 1970.
3. *Voyages of Cadamosto*, Hakluyt Society, 2nd Series, Vol. 80, Cambridge, 1937, p. 49.
4. Samuel Eliot Morison, *The European Discovery of America: The Southern Voyages, 1492–1616*, New York, Oxford University Press, 1974, pp. 175–8.
5. *History of Latin American Civilisation*, Vol. 1, *The Colonial Experience*, ed. Lewis Hanke, Methuen, London, 1969, pp. 12–20.
6. Ridolfi, *Life of Girolamo Savonarola*, translated by Cecil Grayson, London, 1959, pp. 138, 184; see also notes to Ridolfi, *Vita di Girolamo Savonarola*, II, Rome, 1952, p. 180.
7. Karl Brandi, *The Emperor Charles V*, translated by C. V. Wedgwood, London, 1939, pp. 131–2.

INDEX